Improvised Europeans

IMPROVISED EUROPEANS

*American
Literary Expatriates
and the
Siege of London*

by

ALEX ZWERDLING

BASIC
BOOKS

A MEMBER OF THE PERSEUS BOOKS GROUP

Designed by Jenny Dossin

LIBRARY OF CONGRESS CATALOGING-IN-PUBLICATION DATA

Zwerdling, Alex.
  Improvised Europeans : American literary expatriates and the siege of London / by Alex
Zwerdling.
    p.   cm.
  Includes bibliographical references and index.
  ISBN 0-465-03275-3 (hc) — 0-465-03276-1 (pbk)
    1. American literature—England—London—History and criticism.   2. Eliot, T. S. (Thomas
Stearns), 1888-1965—Homes and haunts—England—London.   3. Adams, Henry, 1838-1918—
Homes and haunts—England—London.   4. James, Henry, 1843-1916—Homes and haunts—
England—London.   5. Pound, Ezra, 1885-1972—Homes and haunts—England—London.   6.
Americans—England—London—Intellectual life.   7. Authors, American—England—London—
Biography.   8. American literature—English influences.   I. Title.
PS159.E5Z94   1998
810.9'9421—dc21   98-10835
                                                                                                          CIP

99   00   01   02   03   1   2   3   4   5   6   7   8   9   10

For Martha and Martin Meisel

"Our house is your house — any place, any time."

Contents

Preface

A sense of bewilderment was my starting point in writing a book on the American writers who fled to Europe, and more particularly to London at the end of the nineteenth century and the beginning of the twentieth. This was a moment when there was no longer any doubt that the United States would produce—*had* produced—great writers. The period now called the American Renaissance was an accomplished fact. The pantheon that included Emerson, Thoreau, Hawthorne, Whitman, and others—though not yet Melville and Dickinson—was recognized both in America and abroad. The wealth and geopolitical importance of the United States was growing at a phenomenal rate. There was little doubt in anyone's mind that the country would soon overtake its European rivals.

Why would any serious writer choose not to be associated with this vital time? How could someone with the hyperattentive eyes and ears a literary vocation demands give up the chance to be part of such momentous changes and choose instead to go "back" to what was still called the Old World—one that was already known, and in which the American would inevitably remain a petitioner and an outsider? It seemed a perverse decision, particularly because in choosing London an American writer apparently reconfirmed the pattern of cultural dependence and deference more than a century after the political ties were cut. What the United States needed was a long overdue Declaration of Cultural Independence, not a reaffirmation of her colonial links to the mother country. American writers at least since the time of James Fenimore Cooper had protested the continuing power of English reviewers and other cultural arbiters to evaluate literary works from the former colonies. They resented the need to secure a London seal of approval before even their own countrymen would take them seriously. The growing consensus was that this dispensation must finally end.

All the more puzzling, then, that a number of exceptionally gifted American writers decided to ignore these imperatives and apparently work to strengthen the older legacy. To try and make sense of their choice, I focus on four careers that strike me as closely related, even though they stretch over more than two generations: those of Henry Adams, Henry James, Ezra Pound, and T. S. Eliot. Taken as a group, they may be said to interrupt and complicate the standard teleological account of America's gradual cultural emancipation. All either settled in London or lived significant stretches of their adult lives there. Each was intensely uneasy about the forces transforming his native land and felt an urgent need to distance himself from it. There were important links: Adams and James were lifelong friends and moved in the same circles; James became the career model for Pound and Eliot; Pound confirmed Eliot's poetic vocation at a turning point in his life, and the two collaborated on the creation and institutionalization of the Anglo-American modernist movement. All four writers were highly educated men; they could trace their roots back to prerevolutionary settlers and were proud of it; they seemed headed for distinguished careers in an American Establishment—whether academic, political, or literary. What could have made such potentially important figures in their own culture lose faith in it? What was happening in the United States that repelled rather than attracted them? What tempted even the "returnee" Henry Adams to spend more time out of his country than in it during the last three decades of his life? What made them all members of a group Adams himself sarcastically called "improvised Europeans"?

In order to answer these questions I needed to examine two historical changes occurring between 1870 and 1920, even though they had no immediate bearing on literature: the transformation of America from an open society able to assimilate its mostly western European immigrants into one seen to be invaded by alien others who threatened the older settlers; and the shift in Anglo-American power relations—economic, military, geopolitical—that offered the United States a new supremacy on the world stage. All four of the writers I focus on were acutely conscious of these changes, even though only Adams could be called an important political actor. Their life choices, their careers, their individual works were all shaped by the internal and external transformation of their country. On the one hand, as America became less the Anglo-Saxon nation in which their backgrounds offered them pride of place, they felt more marginal and ready to leave. On the other, as Europeans became increasingly willing to accommodate what would be called "the American century," new opportunities opened up for these disaffected Americans as potential global players. Their losses at home might be recouped abroad.

Their estrangement at home was a response to what struck them as a changing of the guard, as the patricians of the eastern seaboard were supplanted both by the plutocrats newly in control and by the swelling waves of immigrants, first the Irish, then the southern and eastern Europeans who arrived in unprecedented numbers around the turn of the century. Though one threatening group was newly rich and the other still poor, each seemed to have a drive and hunger that the more established Americans could not match. Rather than competing for place in a greatly expanded arena, an increasingly attractive option for those who could do so was to withdraw—into their own privileged enclaves or to Europe, where they might safely ignore what was happening and live on their literal or figurative capital. To stay put was to be reminded constantly of loss—of vitality, cultural primacy, power, hope for the future. Many of them made for the exit, often with a bitter sense of being forced out or of becoming strangers in their own home.

By contrast London offered surprisingly easy entry to writers of their background. Their country's new importance made them welcome as ambassadors and informants, useful for the insights they might provide on the puzzling identity of their compatriots, who it seemed could no longer be treated as rusticated colonials exiled from the cultural center of the English-speaking world. As Britain took stock of the shift in power that threatened to relegate her to the status of a planet in America's orbit, the need to renegotiate the order of precedence and at least keep a semblance of parity encouraged a rapprochement between the two nations. American writers with Anglophile sympathies might act as go-betweens to reopen the dialogue and make it clear on both sides that these countries ought to be natural allies—at worst lately estranged members of one family, at best loyal confederates in what later came to be called the Special Relationship. The accidental conflation of the alienated Americans' revulsion from their own country with the British curiosity about a burgeoning United States demanding respectful attention created an unprecedented opportunity for writers like Adams, James, Pound, and Eliot. They made the most of it, as their particular transatlantic connections and cosmopolitan experience gave them an interpretive authority denied to their American precursors and contemporaries.

Henry James called one of his stories "The Siege of London." A volume of Leon Edel's life of James is entitled "The Conquest of London." These martial metaphors pervade the accounts of American writers in London, both as they themselves tell the story and as cultural historians have written this chapter of the transatlantic dialogue. The impact of the Americans on what was once English Literature and is now Literature in English was certainly prodigious. There is a nice irony in the fact that the volume of the Pelican History of English Literature dedicated to the modernist period is called *From James to Eliot*. To many British writers what was taking place looked like a hostile takeover: A venerable, magisterial culture was forced to cede authority to intruders from abroad promulgating a new and unpalatable set of guidelines, which one ignored at one's peril. Power breeds confidence, even if it is reflected power, and a new cultural commissar like Ezra Pound, disaffected as he was from America, was not reluctant to draw on his country's new international clout. Such intruders seemed to be establishing the literary equivalent of a London-based multinational corporation, organizing and promoting the local talent, conceding a good deal by offering to work for Anglo-American unity, but nevertheless retaining firm control.

Yet this triumphalist American version of the story is misleading. It ignores the resistances, concessions, and failures on both sides. An equally plausible and pervasive metaphor for the realignment taking place is familial rather than military or commercial. Family quarrels never really end; time alters whatever accommodations have been worked out; and even the winners often feel like losers. Only by looking closely at these four linked careers as they unfold over time, by paying attention to the opportunities, triumphs, misunderstandings, and disappointments that characterized the different stages of the relationship, can we assess the achievements and the sacrifices. This is why I use not only the evidence of the works in prose and poetry that form the final accomplishment of these careers, but also as much of the biographical and contextual material as is readily available. I hope to insert their works back into their authors' lives, and into the transatlantic negotiation that often seems to give them shape.

These goals require a method that draws on cultural history, discourse analysis, literary criticism, and biography. The first three chapters offer an overview of the gradual shift in power from Britain to the United States, in which writers from both countries are treated as voices in an international conversation being carried on by powerful figures and the institutions they represent. I try to suggest how changing sociopolitical realities and shifts in consciousness create new literary opportunities, and also how writers help to bring those shifts about. The detailed accounts of the four careers that follow incorporate this historical material at many points but focus on the attempt by the four writers—Adams, James, Pound, and Eliot—to become significant actors in the cultural rapprochement taking place. I do not think of this as a slow but inevitable record of achievement, best surveyed from the perspective of the enduring works it produced. That may be the way we see retrospectively, but it is not the way it looked to these writers (or their readers) in the course of their lives. Rather, their careers seem more like a roller-coaster ride through alien territory, in which the major works are produced in the midst of perils, spills, and perpetual friction. Theirs was not a smooth passage to fame but generated a good deal of resistance among reviewers, editors, readers, and other writers in both countries who were indifferent or actively hostile to the cosmopolitan agenda being forced upon them.

To recapture this sense of flux, I stress process over product, the pressures of the moment rather than the view of posterity. In these career narratives, I use letters, early drafts, manifestos, suppressed works, ephemeral journalism, and other commentary both by the writers themselves and by their contemporaries. Cumulatively, this body of evidence seems to me to suggest how difficult the task they had set themselves was to achieve, and what it cost. A good deal of this material is recorded in private correspondence or remains buried in archives and unreprinted articles and reviews. Going back to these sources offers many rewards. Chief among them is the recovery of the troubled relationship between artist and audience, a clash of mentalities between the readers' expectations and the writers' methods and values.

This tension, so characteristic of the modernist movement, is greatly aggravated by expatriation, in which the writer moves out of familiar territory into a culture working by different rules. The record of this conflict, with its alliances and quarrels, its breakthroughs and setbacks, is very different from an account that highlights the final products, the "masterpieces." By reinserting the analysis of those works into the cultural and biographical matrix of their gestation and arrival, I hope to stress the difficulty of their coming into being and to help account for their final form. The smoother kind of literary history too seldom takes these birth pangs seriously and seems to give the canonical works a sense of inevitability they did not have when they emerged.

This does not of course mean that the modernist canon has remained fixed or that writers like the four here studied are now regarded with reverence. Very far from it. In fact over the last twenty-five years the reputations of all of them, but especially of James and Eliot, have been subject to a fierce revaluation. More often than not, they find themselves in the dock, accused of propagating attitudes and values seen by contemporary readers as deeply offensive—anti-Semitism and racism, patriarchal contempt for women, hostility to egalitarian ideals. There is a good deal of evidence for the prosecution, and the charges have stuck. In point of fact the pervasive questions of race, class, and gender that dominate present-day commentary were of major concern to all these writers as they tried to choose between America and Europe. That Britain still seemed, comparatively speaking, a society in which class distinctions were fixed, men in firm control, and the Anglo-Saxon legacy not seriously threatened by other races and religions made it more appealing to these disaffected writers in their flight. They were looking for the more stable, homogeneous culture they felt they had lost, one in which their Establishment status would be honored.

I have no wish to gloss over this aspect of their work or to explain it away. There are passages in their published writings, and even more in their letters and manuscripts, which I respond to with revulsion—particularly the attacks on the "alien" immigrants from eastern Europe polluting the purer racial strain of an America I never knew. I cannot read lines like Eliot's notorious "Rachel *née* Rabinovitch / Tears at the grapes with murderous paws" with equanimity. My father was born in Poland, my mother in Galicia, I myself in Germany. We came to the

United States as part of the wave of Jewish refugees in flight from the Nazis. America was my fourth country, English my fourth language. The last thing I would have wanted to hear was that "my kind" was undesired because unassimilable. Fortunately, it was not something I was often made to feel. It would be very easy to use these credentials as a license for revenge, to become the prosecuting attorney demonstrating with further damaging evidence that the parties in question are guilty as charged, and arguing that we are right to denigrate their works as instruments of oppression. The tone would be easy too—a mixture of irony, sarcasm, and righteous indignation, the superior stance of the enlightened examining the benighted.

The prospect strikes me as uninteresting. Stronger than my revulsion is my sense of astonishment. How could such patently brilliant writers—whose English I appreciated perhaps because my acquisition of the language was a struggle—have invested so much of their imaginative energy in such appalling attacks? What could account for their irrational fears, their nightmare visions of being under siege? What made these powerful figures see themselves as victims, the hunted rather than the hunters? Stronger than my indignation was my need to understand. The most urgent question was simply, Why? I have tried to answer it in this book by looking for causes and partial explanations—individual, familial, societal, historical, ideological. The larger the frame, the less idiosyncratic these writers appear, the less bizarre their words. They are of their time, of their place, of their familial heritage, even if others of the same time, place, and heritage reacted differently.

The banal formula so often invoked in such discussions—*tout comprendre c'est tout pardonner*—seems to me useless and inaccurate. Understanding, by which in this case I mean an honest attempt to get at the roots of offensive attitudes and actions, has no necessary connection with forgiveness. The fear of excusing the inexcusable can act as a brake on our healthy and restless curiosity. There is something to be said for separating our desire to know from our need to judge. This is especially true when we try to grasp the centers of imaginative energy in literary creation, because the fuel that makes the engine roar is so frequently polluted at the source. Anger, hatred, contempt are as often at the heart of great works as the more benevolent feelings, and are inextricably intertwined with their most idealistic, visionary elements. This has always been known, though not always advertised. The issue is further complicated when certain targets of satiric contempt that were once acceptable become proscribed. The Holocaust, for instance, has made *all* anti-Semitic feelings or statements seem equally dangerous and unacceptable. No comparable prohibition inhibits the most contemptuous caricatures of the rich and powerful, for example. We see with the ideological imperatives of the present and resist imagining a past different from it. This grows out of a complacency not so different, I think, from the confident assumptions of those we now patronize, even though in their time they had a similar cultural sanction. And it is unlikely, given the long historical record, that our progeny a century from now will fail to see *us* as ideologically misguided in ways that presently seem unimaginable.

For all these reasons, then, this particular chapter of our literary history deserves to be seen as it looked at the time to the actors involved, with as full and nuanced an understanding as we can muster. I try in the chapters that follow to enter into the thoughts and feelings that constituted the air these writers breathed. I want to see the world as it appeared to their eyes, even if only partially, within the limits of my powers of empathy. I must try to put my own values on hold for the duration. Consequently, this is the last time the words *I* or *my* will appear in this book outside of quotation marks.

I

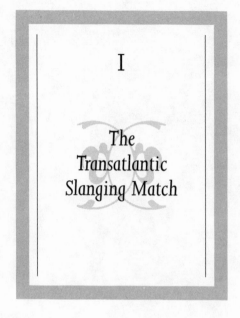

The
Transatlantic
Slanging Match

O N MAY 31, 1910, Theodore Roosevelt, fresh from a year's sabbatical spent hunting big game in Africa after he declined to run for a third presidential term, delivered an extraordinary speech to the dignitaries assembled in London's stately Guildhall. His subject was "British Rule in Africa." Those who came to hear him might well have expected words of praise from a statesman deeply committed to the idea of the imperial mission as he addressed the nation most certain of having faithfully carried it out. And Roosevelt does predictably congratulate both his own country and that of his hosts in celebrating the imperial partnership that had cemented their present alliance: "The dominion of modern civilized nations over the dark places of the earth has been fraught with widespread good for mankind," he reassures them; and he urges the countries engaged in this valuable labor to "treat one another with respect and friendship." Britain's task in the Sudan seems to him precisely the same as America's in building the

Panama Canal: Each is among "the great world works which had to be done" and which only "a great world Power" is capable of doing.

At this point, however, Roosevelt's celebratory rhetoric takes a decidedly unexpected turn. As he shifts to recent events in Egypt, where the reliably pro-British prime minister had been assassinated by an Egyptian nationalist, he tells his auditors "You have erred; and it is for you to make good your error." Roosevelt sharply criticizes Britain's conciliatory policies and what he takes to be her misguided efforts to hurry Egyptians toward self-government. And he continues with brutal frankness: "Now, either you have the right to be in Egypt or you have not; either it is or it is not your duty to establish and keep order. If you feel that you have not the right to be in Egypt, if you do not wish to establish and to keep order there, why, then, by all means get out of Egypt."[1]

What authority does this stripling imperialist from the former colonies have to address a venerable nation in such terms? Through what power does this foreign leader arrogate to himself the task of lecturing a distinguished body on how to run its country's affairs? In the weeks that follow, these questions are sharply debated in the British press and in Parliament. Although Sir Edward Grey, the foreign secretary, insists that the speech taken as a whole is "the greatest compliment to the work of one country in the world ever paid by the citizen of another," many of his fellow MPs disagree with him; and some are deeply offended. One notes that such criticisms, however just, are "unpleasant to hear from outside"; another calls Roosevelt's remarks "an insult to this country." But it is left to Sir Henry Dalziel to express the sharpest contempt. He calls the entire speech "the interference of a stranger in what was after all a matter of domestic policy," is outraged that the foreign secretary has not tried to prevent the former president from criticizing Britain's stewardship in Egypt, and concludes that the whole incident sets "a new and most dangerous precedent," one that licenses any foreign statesman to come to Britain and tell the country what to do. That this particular foreigner is an American is for Sir Henry the most offensive aspect of the whole incident, one more example, in his eyes, "of the attempts which are made in America to twist the lion's tail."[2]

Roosevelt's words have a striking interpretive confidence and the unmistakable tone of command. He lays out Britain's rights and duties, defines her options, cajoles and threatens, and ends by delivering an ultimatum. This is not the suavely indirect discourse of international diplomacy but the language of assumptive power. That the practical advice—which might be welcome if delivered in private, and in a different tone, to the proper authorities—is offered on a ceremonial occasion sure to receive international publicity only increases the offense. Yet perhaps the deepest cause for resentment is that it comes from an American and is accurately interpreted as a sign of the transformed power relations between the two countries. That the lion's tail can be so confidently twisted by Roosevelt and his countrymen means that the deference expected from Britain's "American cousins" has been replaced by an arrogant assurance of their own primacy. The British lion is no longer king of the jungle.

Roosevelt's 1910 address is only one instance of a transatlantic dialogue stretching over more than a century by British and American commentators engaged in surveying each other's country. The umbilicus, attenuated but never severed, still stretched across the ocean; the family relation was usually acknowledged on both sides; and the right to advise, evaluate, and correct, as well as to resent such intercessions, had not been surrendered. There are literally hundreds of books, and countless shorter pieces in nineteenth-century periodicals, that contribute to this continuing debate. Most are written not by important public figures like Roosevelt but by less well-known travelers eager to record their impressions of "the new republic" or "the mother country," social investigators, gentlemen (and sometimes ladies) with a curiosity about the world, literary pilgrims. Their reports are written for their compatriots and are meant to be informative. But what fuels them is not so much curiosity as an uneasy rivalry and mutual resentment. The Declaration of Independence is treated as a provisional rather than final document, to be reaffirmed (or perhaps even withdrawn) in succeeding generations.[3]

A rapid survey of this dialogue, seen first from the British, then from the American point of view, highlights a gradual shift in power. In the early and mid-nineteenth century, the voice of confident authority is clearly British, even though (or perhaps because) England has not succeeded in winning her two wars against the newer country. We hear it most strikingly when the subject is the culture or the manners of the

Americans rather than their unquestioned energy or native ability. So, in words that are often quoted and that once rankled as sharply as Theodore Roosevelt's nearly a century later, the Reverend Sydney Smith in 1820 asks—or rather taunts: "In the four quarters of the globe, who reads an American book? or goes to an American play? or looks at an American picture or statue?" The questions are rhetorical, the answers assumed to be obvious, the condescending tone unmistakable. There is no doubt about the relative positions of evaluator and subject. This is the perspective of interpretive authority that only a long-established and still expanding culture—certain that it knows what is happening in the four quarters of the globe—can claim. It is also the reproof of an aggrieved parent, disappointed by how little the combination of "British blood" and favorable circumstances has actually produced. Smith warns Americans to remember their roots and "make it their chief boast, for many generations to come, that they are sprung from the same race with Bacon and Shakespeare and Newton."[4] Nearly half a century after claiming to be adult, the prodigal child remains in the eyes of the parent hopelessly and helplessly dependent.

Nor are its manners fully formed. Frances Trollope's satiric account of them in her *Domestic Manners of the Americans* (1832) so deeply offended her American readers that three decades later her son, the novelist Anthony, tried to make amends in a far more conciliatory tome consciously designed "to mitigate the soreness" she had caused.[5] Frances Trollope's indictment of Americans is comprehensive: They are obsessed by money, inelegant of speech, coarse, disrespectful, ignorant, bellicose, lacking in probity, in leisure, in learning. Her standard of judgment is European refinement, decorum, and high culture, and she is appalled by the Americans' indifference to that standard. For these grubby and raucous savages, spitting their tobacco juice in private and public places, exhibiting "the entire rear of the person" in a theater, clapping and thumping their way through "Yankee Doodle," swallowing their drams of liquor standing up, nevertheless persist in considering themselves "more modern, more advanced than England. Our classic literature, our princely dignities, our noble institutions, are all gone-by relics of the dark ages."[6]

The voice is that of offended dignity; and although nothing in America makes Frances Trollope question the traditional standards with which she begins and ends her three-year stay, her anger suggests that the magisterial dismissiveness of a Sydney Smith has begun to evaporate in the heat of the argument. In later accounts, English superiority is often asserted rather than assumed. So Frederick Marryat, writing only seven years after Frances Trollope, needs to assure his British readers that "the American people are not equal in strength or in form to the English." He sees the two nations as competitors and predicts that "England with her immense resources is much more likely to surpass them than to be left behind." But even to make the claim rather than taking England's timeless superiority for granted concedes a great deal. Marryat reminds the American prodigals "that they are indebted to us, and the credit we give them, for their prosperity and their rapid advance; that they must still look to us for their literature and the fine arts; and that, in short, they are still dependent upon England."[7] In the century that followed the break, Americans were constantly told by Englishmen that the familiar document of separation did not include cultural independence.

Perhaps it was only the initially sympathetic British observer who could avoid the undertone of anxiety (Marryat's "must") in such accounts. An anthropological perspective might restore a shaky judgmental confidence. The most remarkable of these visitors from England is Harriet Martineau, whose *Society in America* (1837) is based on her respect for the egalitarian ideals of the Republic and her genuine curiosity to see how successfully they have been put into practice. Her cultural relativism is a deliberate investigative strategy to prevent herself from judging by her own society's absolutes. Martineau prepares herself for the journey by writing one of the first methodological guides to ethnographic investigation—*How to Observe. Morals and Manners*. In it she warns the traveler to "deny himself all indulgence of peremptory decision . . . even in his journal," and reminds him that "every man's feelings of right and wrong, instead of being born with him, grow up in him from the influences to which he is subjected."[8]

The Americans, Martineau insists in *Society in America*, "must be judged by their own principles, and not by the example of societies whose errors they have practically denounced"; and, in a sentence that would have baffled Frances Trollope, "No nation can pretend to judge another's manners; for the plain reason that there is no standard to judge by." But of course there *are*, by Martineau's principles, more reliable standards of judgment—those the foreign society itself professes. Her understanding of American ideals legitimizes her sometimes sharp critique of the United States. Although much in America's present and probable future state impresses her, she also freely criticizes what seem to her betrayals of the spirit of the Founding Fathers: slavery, of course; women's disenfranchisement; the political withdrawal of many citizens; the antidemocratic spirit of those who think themselves "the first people in Boston" and look down on their compatriots; and—most startlingly in a British observer—"the excessive reverence with which England is regarded by the Americans."[9] Martineau's judgments seldom sound the note of anxiety. She is apparently indifferent to the outcome of an Anglo-American contest for supremacy because she believes that national destinies must be worked out to a different timetable. Her cultural relativism gives her a pseudo-Olympian perspective on the acrimonious transatlantic debate. Yet her interpretive confidence, though different in tone from those of more anxious English observers, is if anything strengthened by her initial sympathy. And her methodological self-awareness recoups an imperiled evaluative authority. The claim to a supranational perspective becomes a powerful weapon in her nation's arsenal.

Like Martineau, Charles Dickens set out a few years later for his tour of the United States with an initial sympathy for her founding principles and an eagerness to praise her fledgling institutions: "No visitor can ever have set foot on those shores," he was to write in retrospect, "with a stronger faith in the Republic than I had, when I landed in America."[10] This is not exactly the spirit of disinterested inquiry, but it suggests an openness to the new and a willingness to judge by nonparochial standards. For Dickens, the United States is the principle of hope: Her claim to the world's respect lies in proving that the abuses of the older European societies that he works to expose are remediable.

Burdened with such great expectations, it is not surprising that he is deeply disappointed by what he finds. The two books to come out of his American sojourn, *American Notes for General Circulation* (1842) and the novel *Martin Chuzzlewit* (1844) are works of sharp disillusionment. The gap between Dickens's extravagant hopes and the realities he encounters makes him write to a friend even before he returns,

"This is not the Republic of my imagination. . . . In everything of which it has made a boast — excepting its education of the people, and its care for poor children — it sinks immeasurably below the level I had placed it upon."[11] He is outraged not only, predictably enough, by the conditions of slavery but by the scurrilous tone of American journalism, the bombastic rhetoric of public debate, the substitution of an aristocracy of money for one of rank, the country's refusal to tolerate any criticism of her failings. Like Martineau, he claims to judge by the original ideals of the Republic; but he is much more convinced than she is that America is moving in the wrong direction: "Year by year," he writes in *American Notes*, "the memory of the Great Fathers of the Revolution must be outraged more and more, in the bad life of their degenerate child."[12] In such harsh judgments, the familiar English role of admonishing parent is grafted onto an American identity so that the prodigal child can be more authoritatively reproved. And in *Martin Chuzzlewit*, Dickens sometimes mimics an outraged American patriotism, as in this attack on the cult of the dollar: "Make commerce one huge lie and mighty theft. Deface the banner of the nation for an idle rag; pollute it star by star; and cut out stripe by stripe as from the arm of a degraded soldier. Do anything for dollars! What is a flag to them!"[13] Americans were used to Englishmen harshly criticizing their country but must have been startled to find one of them wrapping himself in their flag for the purpose.

Yet Dickens's American patriotic fervor is not merely a rhetorical trick. It is based on his need to think of the country as the embodiment of his most passionately held social and political ideals and on his conviction that by betraying their heritage, Americans "put in hazard the rights of nations yet unborn, and very progress of the human race."[14] By using such visionary language, Dickens takes on the role of prophet rather than mere British observer. He never questions his powers of judgment nor sees beyond the present moment. This makes his conclusions timebound. Some of his observations show a surprising imaginative inertia, as when he describes the view from the Capitol in Washington as commanding a permanently empty prospect: "Spacious avenues, that begin in nothing, and lead nowhere; streets, mile-long, that only want houses, roads and inhabitants; public buildings that need but a public to be complete" — and confidently concludes, "Such as it is, it is likely to remain."[15] The myopia of Dickens's vision would soon become manifest, even to himself.

What occludes the sight of such observers is the lack of a historical imagination. An epistemological certainty too often taken to be final rather than provisional gets in the way. It is only after the passage of time that the more complex truths can be understood and acknowledged. So Dickens, returning to the country in 1867, a quarter of a century after his first sojourn, finds striking evidence of "improvement in every direction," is much more hesitant to reach conclusions, and rejects his earlier snap judgments: "It is a good sign, may be, that it all seems immensely more difficult to understand than it was when I was here before."[16] He now sees his earlier works as a kind of slander, and he takes the extraordinary step of writing a postscript testifying "to the gigantic changes in this country" since his initial visit and assuring its inclusion in all subsequent editions of his two American works.[17]

Such rueful revisionism, however, is possible only after a considerable passage of time, and after the grievances have been fully aired. Despite the gradual erosion of Britain's easy condescension toward the United States, the dismissal of the claims for an independent American culture is a hardy perennial of the nineteenth century.[18] It can be illustrated by juxtaposing two incidents, one from the 1820s, the other from the 1880s. In the early years of the century, the American novelist and journalist John Neal, temporarily resident in England, published a series of pioneering articles on American writers in *Blackwood's*, as well as a more general essay on the United States in the *Westminster Review*. Without Neal's knowledge or consent, and without illustrative support of any kind, the editor of the *Westminster* took it upon himself to insert the following passage in Neal's essay: "Violent exaggeration is the character of American literature at the present day, and, compared with the chaster and more rational style of our best writers, the style of the North American authors is usually the rant and unmeaning vehemence of a strolling Thespian, when placed beside the calm, appropriate and expressive delivery of an accomplished actor." Neal predictably exploded with anger, but he was powerless—the realities of Anglo-American cultural relations being what they were—to do anything but accept the fact that these words had achieved the authority of print in a journal whose prestige no American publication could then match.[19]

Close to the end of the century, such patronage surfaced yet again in the lectures Matthew Arnold delivered in America during his 1883–84 tour and the essays he wrote on his return. Like so many of his country-men, what he finds to praise in the United States is its promise of con-tinuing and extending English culture. Americans are simply trans-planted Britons, and he is anxious that they continue to see themselves in this light. He assures his listeners that they come "of about the best parentage which a modern nation can have."[20] And though he is ready to admit a few American writers, particularly Emerson, to the pan-theon, he is outraged by the thought that the country is beginning to consider her literature separate and unique. An advertisement for a book called *The Primer of American Literature* unleashes a tirade: "Are we to have a Primer of Canadian Literature too, and a Primer of Aus-tralian? We are all contributors to one great literature—English litera-ture."[21] Behind such thunder lies the fear of cultural devolution.

Most offensive to American readers is the retrospective essay Arnold publishes after his return, "Civilization in the United States" (1886). There he continues his attack on the notion that American literature is "a great independent power," ventures that the lack of cultural distinc-tion is due to the absence of "awe and respect" in the makeup of Amer-icans, and concludes that "a great void exists in the civilization over there; a want of what is elevated and beautiful, of what is interesting."[22] Such avuncular patronage could hardly go unchallenged. Mark Twain, infuriated by Arnold's attack, expends a considerable amount of energy over the next two years in trying to write a rebuttal, as well as a more general book to be called "English Criticism on America, Let-ters to an English Friend."[23] Although he never completes either pro-ject, his anger helps to shape his sharp satire of the crippling effects of *British* "awe and respect" in *A Connecticut Yankee in King Arthur's Court* (1889) as well as his defense of American journalism in *The American Claimant* (1891), which concludes that "a discriminating irreverence is the creator and protector of human liberty."[24] But by the late 1880s, Arnold's attack is in any case belated: The power relations between the two countries have changed; a pantheon of American writers with real claim to international recognition has emerged; and the American citizenry is increasingly drawn from non-Anglo-Saxon countries. More sophisticated American observers see Arnold's attempt to lay down the law as a pathetic vestige of Britain's former greatness and a sign of her present anxiety. So Henry Adams writes his friend John Hay after entertaining Arnold in Washington, "He is, between ourselves, a melancholy specimen of what England produces at her best; but we ought not to be harsh towards the poor little island. It would like to improve if it knew how."[25]

Adams's words suggest that condescension can be played as a competitive sport. The national inspectors, after all, did not come only in a westerly direction. For every British observer assessing the democratic experiment, an American writer set down comparable impressions of the mother country. And those impressions, also stretching from one end of the century to the other and beyond, were as likely to be fueled by grievance, wounded vanity, and entitlement as the British accounts. In the words of one historian of this dialogue, "Outraged American pride spawned a literature of self-defense."[26] What begins as a defensive game in the early nineteenth century, however, gradually becomes an offensive one as the nation's power grows; and even the earliest American participants sense that time is on their side in a match with an aging player. In his *Gleanings in Europe: England* (1837), for example, James Fenimore Cooper attacks every form of residual British power over the former colonies, from the patronizing tone of the quarterlies, to the need for an English imprimatur before American literary works are taken seriously at home, to the general "tendency to throw ridicule and contumely on the national character." But he also knows that such power is dependent on America's continuing cultural submission and that "Of all burthens, that of the mental dependence created by colonial subserviency, appears to be the most difficult to remove."[27] He is, however, sanguine about the future. In his anonymously published *Notions of the Americans* (1828), he confidently predicts that in fifty years the tables will be turned. He foresees a three-step historical process for Americans: "They have felt the degradation of being contemned; they are beginning to know the privileges of being respected; and they will shortly enjoy the advantages of being feared."[28] Though it took longer than half a century, Cooper's prophecy was eventually fulfilled.

This link between America's geopolitical power and her long-delayed cultural independence is essential to an understanding of the nation's growing confidence. British observers (like Dickens surveying the view from the Capitol) shut their eyes to the forces moving the world toward American dominance while Americans eagerly antici- pate them. Even Emerson, in his fundamentally respectful *English Traits* (1856), concludes that "British power has culminated, is in sol- stice, or already declining." Her heir, America, stands ready to take over at some not far distant time. The "prodigious natural advantages" the American landscape offers, combined with the vigor of the Anglo- Saxon heritage, will make the United States the inevitable "seat and centre of the British race"; and England, "an old and exhausted island, must one day be contented, like other parents, to be strong only in her children."[29] Such visions of an inevitable American victory in the gen- erational contest between the two nations take hold even in the minds of the most reverent literary pilgrims. Hawthorne's *Our Old Home* (1863), intended as an act of filial homage to England, nevertheless records his strikingly aggressive displacement fantasy "that we could annex it, transferring their thirty millions of inhabitants to some conve- nient wilderness in the great West, and putting half or a quarter as many of ourselves into their places."[30]

Hawthorne's fanciful vision echoes his nation's project of forcibly moving the indigenous peoples of the continent to western reservations. The various forms of "Manifest Destiny" that were transforming Amer- ica into a world power are connected. In the controversial 1845 essay by John O'Sullivan in which that fateful phrase is first used, the contest with England is seen as an integral part of a pattern of American expan- sion that will one day also swallow Canada, after that country has finally severed her ties "to the little island three thousand miles across the Atlantic."[31] By the end of the century, this patronizing image of "Great" Britain as a minuscule dot on the globe becomes a standard sign of America's present and future greatness. We recall Adams's "we ought not to be harsh towards the poor little island." Andrew Carnegie's con- tribution to an 1890 symposium on the question "Do Americans Hate England?" echoes Adams. Carnegie professes to find the notion that "the greatest manufacturing, commercial, and mining nation, and the wealthiest nation in the world" *could* be jealous of England touchingly absurd: "Jealousy of England! the dear little thing!"[32]

The connection between America's growth as a world power and her refusal to tolerate European patronage had been forcefully made a generation earlier in James Russell Lowell's classic essay, "On a Certain Condescension in Foreigners" (1871). Lowell saw the pervasive European sense of superiority to the United States as "an unpleasant anachronism," when it should already have become clear that "the young giant was growing, was beginning indeed to feel tight in its clothes, was obliged to let in a gore here and there in Texas, in California, in New Mexico, in Alaska, and had the scissors and needle and thread ready for Canada when the time came." He attacks the British delusion that the American is "a kind of inferior and deported Englishman"; and he urges the English to "give up *trying* to understand us, still more thinking that they do . . . [until] they learn to look at us as we are and not as they suppose us to be."[33] The vaunting, undiplomatic tone of these words is striking. Within a decade Lowell becomes Minister to the Court of St. James, but his official position does not change his attitude. He plays the game of competitive condescension with effortless assurance. So he can commend the master and fellows of Emmanuel College, Cambridge, on their proficiency in the language: "I must allow that, considering how long we have been divided from you, you speak English remarkably well."[34]

The English were unprepared to be on the receiving end of such mockery, though some American writers were trying to train them in the art. Henry James's comments on the reception of his story "An International Episode" (1879) suggest how reluctant his English readers are to see their themselves as satiric targets: "It is an entirely new sensation for them," James writes his mother, "to be (at all delicately) *ironized* or satirized, from the American point of view, and they don't at all relish it. The conception of the normal in such a relation is that the satire should be all on their side against the Americans."[35] Even more offensive is the new American idea that the great nineteenth-century English fiction writers are passé, that young practitioners can learn more from contemporary American novelists, or from the French. For William Dean Howells writing in 1882, James represents the future, Dickens, Thackeray, and Trollope the past. James's following among the young, Howells writes, is "more distinctly recognizable than that of any other English-writing novelist."[36]

Howells's words provoke an infuriated response in British journals, a reaction that delights James's friend John Hay, who exults that Howells "has made the British lion dance with rage." Hay is amused "to see

British dailies, weeklies, monthlies and quarterlies, stammering with fury at a little article in an American magazine."[37] The British prove as thin-skinned in their response to transatlantic criticism as the Americans had long been. The United States superior in the literary realm? The notion is unprecedented, absurd, insufferable. America's cultural submission to Britain had long been taken for granted. That the country of Chaucer and Shakespeare might not be able to live off her literary capital forever was a genuinely alarming idea, and few Britons could take it seriously. Nor would they be forced to do so until well into the twentieth century. American cultural dependency long outlasted the country's other forms of subordination (political, military, economic), despite the constantly voiced demand by American artists that it end. There is a significant time lag in which America's rapidly growing economic and geopolitical power is not yet matched by a comparable cultural authority.

Perhaps this delay was a safety valve in Anglo-American relations, a way of maintaining the family connection and even the deference—or "awe and respect," as Matthew Arnold has it—due one's elders in the face of the rapid shift in the balance of power.[38] As we will see, a number of forces converging toward the end of the nineteenth century made a strong link between Britain and the United States seem desirable to both countries. A sign of America's reluctance to break the habit of cultural dependence is the failure to enact an international copyright agreement until 1891, despite the articulated anger of generations of writers who understandably feel outraged that their works can be pirated by publishers on the other side of the Atlantic and thus rob them of half their royalties. So a Dickens or a Harriet Beecher Stowe could be read by millions across the ocean without receiving a penny for their labor. The domestic product can consistently be undersold, as unlicensed publishers compete with each other to print unauthorized editions of books certain to be popular. In the 1840s, one literary historian notes, "A cheap edition of a Dickens novel went for ten cents where a Cooper one cost fifty."[39] In 1890, a year before the international copyright agreement is finally enacted, a writer in the *North American Review* is still protesting "the unfair competition to which American writers have been exposed" and insisting that the artificial cheapness of English books has kept American literature "in thraldom to that of England."[40]

But if the law does not protect them, there are signs in the late nine-teenth century that American writers and editors are increasingly aware of the need to foster their own. So the *Century Magazine*'s influential editor Richard Watson Gilder writes in 1886 to the journal's London agent, his powerful English counterpart Edmund Gosse, that the *Century* must decline the proposal to publish a regular literary letter from a well-known English writer. Gilder explains "that the conviction is growing daily upon us that we must give place to our American writers rather than to foreign ones." And he asks, rhetorically, "Why should American magazines let American authors starve while they go seeking after strange gods?" Despite Gosse's vigorous protest against this new protectionism, he cannot change the American editor's mind.[41] The growth of the competitive spirit between the two countries undermines the long tradition of subservience in the one realm where English primacy has always been conceded.

This new cultural confidence rests on a solid material foundation. In other realms—economic, political, military—the rivalry is more obvious and the gradual shift in power undeniable. The half century between 1870 and 1920 is an era of unrelenting relative decline for Britain in its contest with the United States. England's often voiced scorn for America's worship of the dollar can be seen as a withdrawal from an unwinnable contest. The world's first industrial nation gradually but inexorably gives way to the more vigorous industries (and the unapologetic industrialists) of the new world.[42] One statistical study of this relative decline concludes that between 1870 and 1913 America's annual rate of growth is over three times that of Britain.[43] By the turn of the century, English books with alarmist titles (and even more alarming conclusions) like F. A. McKenzie's *The American Invaders* and William Stead's *The Americanization of the World*, both published in 1902, document the shift in power for British readers. McKenzie records and tries to account for the startlingly rapid American commercial and industrial takeover of the Western world, including British colonial markets. In industry after industry, he sees Britain trounced by a more alert, hardworking, less hidebound, more efficient competitor. The metaphor of war shapes the whole book: "America has invaded Europe not with armed men, but with manufactured products. . . . No nation has felt the results of this invasion more than England."[44] And

Stead warns his countrymen that "our definite displacement from the position of commercial and financial primacy is only a matter of time, and probably a very short time."[45]

In the United States, of course, this triumph is generally a cause for celebration, especially at the highest levels of power and influence, with which writers like Henry Adams, James, and Howells had intimate connections. In 1900, Brooks Adams (Henry's younger brother) publishes his *America's Economic Supremacy*, a book that impresses Theodore Roosevelt, who is about to succeed to the presidency. With such an ally in power, Brooks Adams felt that his country had reached "the moment when we won the great prize."[46] Sometime before the end of the First World War, America becomes the creditor, Britain the debtor nation: "The financial center of the world," John Hay writes in 1902, "seems passing to the Hudson between daybreak and dark."[47] At the same time, England's military supremacy is under challenge from an increasingly powerful American navy, and in the decade straddling the turn of the century Britannia ceases to rule the waves.[48] Her weakened power is reflected in the consistent pattern of major diplomatic concessions to America in these years: in the Venezuela crisis, in the Panama Canal Treaty, in the Alaskan boundary dispute. Though the London *Times* boasted that Britain did not "conclude treaties of surrender with any nation," one English diplomatic historian judges that this is precisely what happened: "In fact Great Britain signed what *were* virtually treaties of surrender on a number of occasions, but a very small amount of diplomatic camouflage apparently sufficed to conceal the fact."[49]

"The sun that never sets is setting," an American commentator on Britain's decline and his own country's ascendancy writes in 1909.[50] But there is an unexpected turn in this story. Although from the long perspective of their troubled relations over the previous century this power shift might be seen as a cause for celebration in America, that is not always how it is treated. For as American strength and confidence waxes, its appetite for the contest wanes. There are no winners and losers in family quarrels, at least in families determined to stay together. A belated recognition of that fact begins to sink in on both sides of the Atlantic while the transatlantic slanging match is still at its height. A countermovement of reconciliation, one that stresses mutual dependency, shared traditions, and a bedrock sense of racial and familial identity had begun before the decisive shift in power. It is based on the assumption that what Britain and America have in common is ultimately more important to both countries than what divides them. As we will see, a complex and powerful myth of unity develops out of the long-standing quarrel and for a time reconciles the opponents as it promises a new, supranational identity to them both: the Anglo-Saxon.

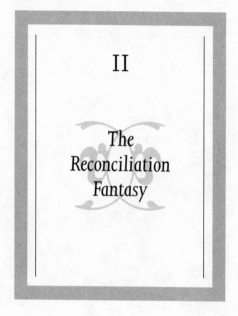

II

The
Reconciliation
Fantasy

America is becoming, not English merely, but world-embracing in the variety of its type; and, as the English element has given language and history to that land, America offers the English race the moral dictatorship of the globe, by ruling mankind through Saxon institutions and the English tongue.

Sir Charles Dilke, *Greater Britain* (1868)

A DEATH IN the family will often remind its feuding members of their common origins and shared life. A truce is called, the prodigal returns, divorced couples meet again, siblings and generations suspend hostilities, traditional words and gestures are offered as the cement of reconstruction. At the beginning of 1901, the aged Queen Victoria died; a few months later President McKinley was assassinated. The responses to these deaths in Britain and America suggest shared grief. The White House flag flew at half-mast for the queen, "the first time this had ever been done for a foreign sovereign."[1] When the president who ordered this tribute was himself cut down, King Edward's court went into mourning, with memorial services held under the highest auspices in Westminster Abbey and St. Paul's.[2] The following year brought the death of Lord Pauncefote, the long-serving British ambassador and architect (with John Hay) of improved Anglo-American relations. Once again, in the words of a contemporary observer, "The President personally gave orders that the flags of every public building in Washington should be half-masted. . . . The streets were thronged; the people in black. If he had been an American no deeper reverence could have been paid him, nor would the grief have been more genuine."[3] These expressions of mourning went well beyond diplomatic courtesies and seem more like signs of recovered family ties.

This displacement of a traditional Anglo-American rivalry and mistrust by a new spirit of concord was the product of many forces. The specifically literary voices were inextricably intertwined with political, academic, commercial, and scientific ones. The gradual shift in power from Britain to America around the turn of the century altered the tone of the transatlantic dialogue by transforming a slanging match into a conversation. It also created an opportunity for American writers to be taken seriously in England as a by-product of their nation's new authority. Henry Adams was as closely linked to his country's political establishment as anyone without public office could possibly be. But writers like James, Eliot, and Pound (about whom no such claim could be made) were also beneficiaries of, as well as contributors to, the emerging Anglo-American alliance. It is impossible to understand their impact on both sides of the Atlantic without grasping the larger international shift that was taking place. Although in this and the next chapter, their voices remain subsidiary, the accounts of their careers that follow will show the links between the new cultural authority to which they could lay claim and the geopolitical changes that gave them force.

The new Anglo-American amity would have astonished English and American observers of the previous generation. As recently as 1895, the two nations were on the brink of war, as President Cleveland invoked the Monroe Doctrine to threaten America's armed intervention in the boundary dispute been British Guiana and Venezuela. He told Congress that it was "the duty of the United States to resist *by every means in its power*, as a wilful aggression upon its rights and interests, the appropriation by Great Britain of any lands or the exercise of governmental jurisdiction over any territory which after investigation, *we have determined* of right belongs to Venezuela."[4] And many Americans would have remembered how close England had come to supporting the Confederacy in the Civil War. Despite her official neutrality, plans to sell British warships to the South were proceeding without government intervention. Adams, whose father was Lincoln's minister to Britain, would recall the showdown in *The Education of Henry Adams*, as his father confronted Earl Russell, the foreign secretary: "It would be superfluous in me to point out to your lordship that this is war!"[5] Although there was no war, Yankee bitterness about Britain's role lingered long after the event.

What then accounts for the changed relations between the two countries around 1900? How was the nation that had long followed George Washington's injunction "to steer clear of permanent alliance with any portion of the foreign world" induced to think of her traditional enemy as a partner in a special relationship? Underlying the possible answers to these questions is a sense of need, more urgent in Britain than in America, yet mutually acknowledged. The shift in power between the two nations transformed the tone and terms of the transatlantic dialogue. The era of Britain's expansion was over, and her more farsighted leaders saw that she needed a dependable ally. Her European neighbors had been her rivals in imperial expansion; the shifting structure of diplomatic accords could not paper over her deep mistrust of Germany, of Russia, of Japan; and her relative economic and military decline made a fantasy of a permanent Pax Britannica. At the same time, the era of America's international expansion had begun, and the British Empire was the available model for her unaccustomed role.

A solution to both countries' problems lay in rethinking the connection between them. In the last years of the century a closely linked group of political and industrial leaders, diplomats, and writers on both sides worked to bring them into accord: in Britain Joseph Chamberlain, Arthur Balfour, Julian Pauncefote, Rudyard Kipling, and Cecil Spring Rice; in America John Hay, Henry and Brooks Adams, Andrew Carnegie, Alfred Thayer Mahan, and Henry Cabot Lodge.[6] Theodore Roosevelt would eventually emerge as the pivotal figure in this transformation. As early as 1887, Cecil Spring Rice, the young English diplomat whose influence in Anglo-American affairs may have begun the previous year when he served as best man at Roosevelt's London wedding, wrote to a friend that Britain must make America forget their troubled relations since the Revolution: "There is a large amount of absolutely unreasonable hostility which time and a judicious treatment of political questions will soften down."[7] Spring Rice's intelligence, wit, adroitness, and charm allowed him to be on intimate terms with Roosevelt, Henry Adams, John Hay, and Henry Cabot Lodge—he was "Springy" in their circle—and finally brought him back to Washington as ambassador during Woodrow Wilson's presidency. He worked tirelessly for Anglo-American amity, but the basis of his crusade was *realpolitik*. Despite his deep American friendships there was never any doubt where his ultimate loyalties lay. He concludes in a letter to an English friend "That we can't possibly afford to quarrel, and that if we did, not only would it be an immense disaster, but we couldn't beat them. . . . I think the policy of Wolsey and Elizabeth towards France is the sort of line we should adopt. To keep friends at almost any cost."[8]

"To keep friends at almost any cost" is an admission of weakness. It would have sounded craven to an Englishman at the height of his country's prosperity. By 1900, however, it had become the basis of Britain's diplomatic relations with America. In giving up her treaty right to build a Central American canal in partnership with the United States, in accepting the Monroe Doctrine as though it had been promulgated by an international tribunal rather than by America alone, in surrendering to Roosevelt's will rather than defending Canada in the Alaskan boundary dispute, in conceding America's naval supremacy, Britain followed the policy of conciliating her new ally "at almost any cost." Admiral Fisher, Britain's First Sea Lord, concluded that a war against the United States was unwinnable, and that "it seems an utter waste of time to prepare for it."[9] Better to placate, even to appease.

This bitter pill would need to be thickly sugarcoated. Geopolitical necessity had to be translated into the language of high idealism. In 1898, a transformative event in American history made this possible. The Spanish-American War unexpectedly proved to be the real turning point in Anglo-American relations. John Hay called 1898 the annus mirabilis of that relationship; only a year earlier, in surveying the territory from his ambassadorial perch in Britain, he had written to Roosevelt: "There is never a civil word about England printed in America, and rarely a civil word about us printed in England."[10] The war against Spain was to change all that and to remind some Britons of their 1588 defeat of the Spanish Armada. When Dewey's troops sank the Spanish fleet off the Philippines and the Americans captured Manila, Spring Rice could barely contain his enthusiasm: "We have just received the

glorious news from Manila," he writes John Hay. "How curious it is—
the continuity of history, the struggle that began 400 years ago of which
we are seeing the last chapter." And he credits "the divine instinct
ingrained in the race" for these victories, four centuries separated (on
the slow-moving clock of racial history) by a mere instant of time.[11]

He was not alone in his enthusiasm. America's expansionist entry
onto the world stage seemed to pro-imperialists in Britain to confirm
the Anglo-Saxon mission of civilizing the dark places of the earth.
Ambassador Hay describes the popular enthusiasm to Senator Lodge:
"For the first time in my life I find the 'drawing room' sentiment altogether with us." Highly placed officials suggest that the British navy
might offer the Americans practical help; and the most frequently reiterated advice he hears is "I wish you would take Cuba at once. We
wouldn't have stood it this long."[12] The most unqualified support
comes from the colonial secretary, Joseph Chamberlain. In his Birm-
ingham speech of May 13, 1898, he sees the war as an opportunity "to
establish and to maintain bonds of permanent amity with our kinsmen
across the Atlantic." He stresses the links of race, language, law, literature, and the common commitment to world peace. And he ends with
a glorious vision of what this war might bring to birth: "I even go so far
as to say that, terrible as war may be, even war itself would be cheaply
purchased if, in a great and noble cause, the Stars and Stripes and the
Union Jack should wave together over an Anglo-Saxon alliance."[13]
Such rhetoric produced the most startling evidence of England's transformed sense of her former colonies. In 1898, Independence Day was
officially celebrated throughout Britain, and there were serious proposals that the Fourth of July should henceforth become an Anglo-American rather than merely American holiday.[14]

Such enthusiastic support, especially by contrast to the hostile or
guarded responses of other European powers, was deeply appreciated
and fostered a nascent Anglophilia among mistrustful ex-colonists.
Henry Cabot Lodge, the chairman of the Senate Foreign Relations
Committee, was one of them. He too saw 1898 as the turning point in
Anglo-American relations. England's support, he was to write in his
celebratory account of the Anglo-Saxon link, "did more to wipe out the
past and make the relations between the two countries what they
should have been long before than all the years which had elapsed

since the bitter days of the Civil War."[15] And most decisively, Theodore Roosevelt, whose vigorous part in the Spanish-American War was the turning point of his career, confessed that "I used to be rather anti-British in feeling . . . but England's attitude towards us in our war with Spain impressed me deeply and I have ever since kept it in lively and grateful remembrance."[16] Roosevelt's feelings about England and Anglo-Saxonism were complex, as we will see; but 1898 at least moved him in an Anglophile direction.

America's induction among the imperial nations, her new acquisitions in the Caribbean and the Pacific, strengthened the idea of an Anglo-American partnership. "The White Man's Burden," Kipling's somber celebration of the civilizing mission, was written in 1898, subtitled "The United States and the Philippine Islands," intended for Americans, and immediately sent off to Roosevelt, who promptly forwarded the poem to Lodge.[17] Though often read as a song of triumph, its tone is grim. In Kipling's vision, the torch is passed to the less experienced imperial nation with the warning that her selfless labor will only generate resentment among "the silent, sullen peoples" it is meant to benefit. The older power hands over the race's burden to the younger, in a painful but necessary ritual that replaces their "childish days" with a hard-won "manhood"; there is one consolation: The familial line will remain unbroken.[18] Kipling clearly sees Roosevelt as the heir. He hopes he will "go in for being a colonial administrator" and encourages him to "put all the weight of your influence into hanging on permanently to the whole of the Philippines," since America is "morally bound to build the house over again from the foundations."[19]

Grand claims were made for the inevitable triumph of this new imperial partnership. Well before 1898, propagandists for the cause had envisioned the joint conquest of the earth by what were variously called the English-speaking people, the Anglo-Saxons, or the English race. The influential American historian John Fiske assured an enthusiastic London audience in 1879 that the term "Manifest Destiny" did not refer to an exclusively American fate. He confidently predicted that "the English race" would not rest "until every land of the earth's surface that is not already the seat of an old civilization shall become English in its language, in its political habits and traditions, and to a predominant extent in the blood of its people."[20]

Such prophetic visions were not uncommon in the visionary phase of the imperial experiment in both countries. In England one finds comparable passages in Carlyle and Disraeli, later in the work of Charles Dilke and John Seeley.[21] By the turn of the century, they might emanate from America or Britain: The common vocabulary was one of the signs of the new entente. For Englishmen with a fear of their nation's decline, they promised immortality. So Spring Rice writes Roosevelt that even if Britain were to fall, her work would continue: "For whether the British Empire goes or not, the English people throughout the world will make such a power as can never be destroyed."[22]

Such imaginative leaps carry us into the realm of fantasy, religion, and myth. *Realpolitik* assumes the costume of destiny, the two nations united as by divine decree. John Hay was a master of the required rhetoric because he firmly believed in the vision. His 1898 speech "A Partnership in Beneficence" celebrates Anglo-American accord in mystical terms: "There is a sanction like that of religion which binds us to a sort of partnership in the beneficent work of the world." He sees Britain and the United States as "joint ministers of the same sacred mission of liberty and progress, charged with duties which we cannot evade by the imposition of irresistible hands."[23] No human agents construct this new imperial compact, only invisible and uncontrollable forces spinning the threads of a common fate. Hay provides the emollient to soothe a painful friction. If Britons and Americans can learn to think of themselves as a single people, fulfilling their joint destiny, the unpleasant *fact* of the passage of power from one nation to the other might be ignored. The glorious fate of the "English-speaking peoples" thus serves as a useful myth to assuage Britain's inevitable resentment, "allowing," as one historian of this rapprochement puts it, "a larger measure of concession than would have been possible without it."[24]

A recurrent fantasy of this historical moment is that the two nations will be reunited. It is surprising how often—and from what distinguished quarters—it surfaces. Cecil Rhodes's grandiloquent youthful vision of the British conquest of the earth ends with "the ultimate recovery of the United States of America as an integral part of the British Empire."[25] He suggests that an imperial parliament might meet alternately in London and Washington.[26] In 1893–94, the prestigious *North American Review* publishes a series of articles on Anglo-American reunion, with contributions by Andrew Carnegie, Alfred Thayer Mahan, and other luminaries. Surprisingly, most of these essays concern the timing and practical details of such a union, not its wisdom or viability.

In such fantasies, the flags of the two nations become interchangeable. In 1892, for instance, Henry Mortimer Durand (later the British ambassador during Roosevelt's presidency) publishes *Helen Treveryan or The Ruling Race*, a novel whose titular heroine falls in love with and marries a British colonel with strong Anglo-American sympathies. His wooing is carried on in passages like this: "I feel as proud of the Stars and Stripes as I do of the Union Jack. . . . I wish there were more room for the race to spread. There is no other to compare with it, none." To which the enchanted Helen can only respond, "I wish all Englishmen were like you."[27] And in one of Conan Doyle's stories of this time, Sherlock Holmes imagines a day when the Revolution is forgotten and the descendants of the original combatants have become "citizens of the same world-wide country under a flag which shall be a quartering of the Union Jack with the Stars and Stripes."[28]

After 1898, such visions multiply and descend to particulars. William Stead's *The Americanization of the World* (1902) foresees a merging of "the British Empire in the English-speaking United States of the World," in pursuit of "the great ideal of Race Union." The American primacy implicit in this verbal formula acknowledges a lost opportunity: "Unification under the Union Jack having become impossible by our own mistakes, why should we not seek unification under the Stars and Stripes?"[29] In 1903, John R. Dos Passos, a highly successful American lawyer and the father of the future novelist, offers a detailed blueprint for "a legal, constitutional and binding treaty between all of the English and American powers and colonies," an "imperishable instrument" he calls "*a second Magna Charta, or a second Declaration of Independence.*" In his book he refers to dozens of articles by eminent writers published since 1897 proposing an Anglo-American union.[30] As late as 1909, Arthur Balfour, then the leader of the Conservative Party, publishes an essay on "The Possibility of an Anglo-Saxon Confederation."[31] But by then the implausible elements in such proposals had begun to be recognized. And in 1930, Bernard Shaw could exploit their comic potential in his "political extravaganza," *The Apple Cart*, in which the American ambassador bursts in excitedly upon the British sovereign with the announcement that "The Declaration of Independence is cancelled. The treaties which endorsed it are torn up. We have decided to rejoin the British Empire." To which King Magnus gloomily replies, "This is the end of England."[32]

It is easy enough to see, with hindsight, that such plans were never even remotely plausible. They did not take into account that the "Anglo-Saxon race" was more a mythical construct than a biological fact, that the shared political structure and the common culture had diverged, that even the English language had split in two. Above all, they ignored the fact that increasingly with every passing year, America was becoming much more heterogeneous, its specifically British legacy rapidly losing primacy. Yet the pervasiveness of this visionary fusion reveals a powerful need for its existence. That it should have been voiced by imaginative writers as often as by statesmen suggests that it was tapping deep roots.

Those roots are uncovered when one sees that the vision of political union is often expressed in the language of familial reconciliation. Family terms had of course long been used to describe the relationship between the two countries. Lincoln was assassinated while attending a performance of the English comedy *Our American Cousin*. Britons often referred to their kinsman across the ocean as "Brother Jonathan." The nickname Uncle Sam, though of American origin, was quickly taken up in England. And Britain remained in the eyes of many Americans "the mother country." It is important that this whole range of familial identities was kept in play. The continuing viability of the family metaphor depends on its labile quality, and on the fact that power relations within a family change over time. As the *New York Tribune*'s enthusiastically Anglophile London correspondent writes toward the end of the nineteenth century, "Cousinship has given place to brotherhood."[33]

In the earlier prerapprochement phases, the American is still the prodigal son returning to his roots. Perhaps the most interesting literary attempt to explore this theme is the fragmentary, untitled novel Hawthorne had left unfinished at his death in 1864. Originally referred to as *Dr. Grimshawe's Secret*, Hawthorne's work has a young American heir returning to the home of his forebears to claim an ancestral family seat. Although Hawthorne's plan was for his American hero to reject his English legacy and return to the more vigorous United States, the most powerful passages in the manuscript record a plangent, irrational nostalgia for a mother country he has never before seen. On setting foot in England, Hawthorne's young American immediately begins to feel "the yearning of the blood within his veins for that from which it has been estranged." His essentially English ways, buried through two centuries of his family's American exile, are "now to be reassumed, not as a foreigner would do it, but like habits native to him, and only suspended for a season." He seems to *recognize* this strange world, as though he were recovering his "old, very deepest, inherent nature"— that of his English progenitor. In some passages of the manuscript, Hawthorne pulls out all the stops of a *nostos* fantasy that rewrites the *Odyssey* in a sentimental key: "The thought thrilled his bosom, that this was his home; . . . 'Oh home, my home, my forefathers' home! I have come back to thee! The wanderer has come back!'"[34] No wonder Hawthorne could never finish the novel. Its plot requirement that his hero return to America, as well as the patriotic imperative of the author, is in conflict with the intense Anglophilia at its root.

The story of an American heir to a British estate appeared in many versions. Henry James essentially produces a variant in the novella, *A Passionate Pilgrim* (1871)—an uncanny echo because Hawthorne's earlier fragment was only posthumously published long after the novella appeared. At the end of his career James was to leave unfinished in his turn yet another comparable tale, *The Sense of the Past.* Both works will be discussed in later chapters. Mark Twain published his own comic version, the novel *The American Claimant*, in 1892. The claimant is Twain's absurd Colonel Sellers, convinced he is the rightful Earl of Rossmore. In the meantime, the present earl's son, Lord Berkeley, has absconded to America incognito to seek his fortune in a democratic country without relying on the privileges of his station. Although the issue of who the rightful heir actually is remains unsettled, it hardly matters, since Twain resolves the conflict by marrying the earl's son off to the colonel's daughter. The two branches of the family, English and American, are reunited in a marriage that offers the happy opportunity, in Lord Berkeley's words, "to reconcile York and Lancaster, graft the warring roses upon one stem, and end forever a crying injustice which had already lasted far too long."[35]

Twain's comic reconciliation can be read as a knowing market exercise in pleasing both an English and an American audience. Its tone is not reminiscent of Hawthorne's anxious, unresolvable tale. He might well have been trying to match the fantastic success of a recent experiment in this genre, Frances Hodgson Burnett's *Little Lord Fauntleroy* (1886), one of the most popular books—and plays, in its later dramatic version—of the nineteenth century. Burnett's story of how the impoverished American-reared child of a British aristocrat and an American girl unexpectedly becomes the heir to an earldom "caused a public delirium of joy."[36] It delighted millions of ordinary readers in both countries but was also taken seriously in the highest circles. Both Gladstone, the prime minister at the time, and James Russell Lowell, the American minister to Britain, were enthusiasts, Gladstone assuring the author that "the book would have great effect in bringing about added good feeling between the two nations and making them understand each other."[37]

Burnett's book is an unalloyed romantic fantasy rooted in the desire to reunite the split Anglo-American family. It concedes nothing to reality, ignoring the likelihood of conflict between diametrically opposed class systems as well as the anger about the American takeover of British treasure. The old Earl of Dorincourt is cured of his passionate lifelong hatred of Americans by his grandson's and daughter-in-law's egalitarian manners, while the visiting Americans learn to love feudalism. Precocious Little Lord Fauntleroy has a clear sense of his political mission. He tells an American friend before reluctantly setting out for the old country, "If I have to be an earl, there's one thing I can do: I can try to be a good one. I'm not going to be a tyrant. And if there is ever to be another war with America, I shall try to stop it."[38] That such monosyllabic wisdom out of the mouths of seven-year-olds should have been taken seriously by prominent grown-ups in England and America suggests the powerful hunger for familial and national reconciliation it was intended to feed.

Nevertheless, Burnett's subject of the imminent passing of English power and treasure into American hands has its darker side, which she does not acknowledge but which others see. The family politics of this transfer are not always viewed in such benevolent terms but evoke the idea of generational rivalry. In the late book about England that

Hawthorne *did* manage to finish, *Our Old Home* (1863), he visits the sleepy Lincolnshire town of Boston, the ancestral home of the Puritans who carried the name to Massachusetts. He reflects with patriotic pride on the "mighty and populous activity of our own Boston, which was once the feeble infant of this old town;—the latter, perhaps, almost stationary ever since that day, as if the birthday of such an off-spring had taken away its own principle of growth."[39] In his version, the birth of the American heir enervates the mother, relegating her to a slow, inevitable decline. This more aggressive vision of generational displacement is also Andrew Carnegie's, who boasts in 1890 that the American son of the English parent "has made a great success since he left his father's roof," and that the "old gentleman" had better realize that the young man is ready to "work out his destiny after his own fash-ion, feeling that destiny to be something so grand that the world had never seen the like."[40]

The image of Britain as a baffled, geriatric old man or shrunken old woman replaces the traditionally reverent picture of the mother coun-try in the eyes of these new young masters of the world. Less idealisti-cally inclined Americans, like Brooks Adams, describe Britain's new desire for an Atlantic alliance in even harsher terms. Her need for American support if she were attacked by a Continental coalition, Adams writes in 1900, not only forces her to depend on the United States but reverses the traditional center and periphery: "Great Britain may, therefore, be not inaptly described as a fortified outpost of the Anglo-Saxon race, overlooking the eastern continent and resting upon America."[41] Here the British Isles are reduced to the fringes of an American archipelago spanning the Atlantic.

The harshness of the facts demanded compensatory myths, and of these the most potent was racial. It is impossible to separate theories of race from those of nation. The profusion of adjectives used in the dis-course of race in turn-of-the-century Britain and America, in which their peoples are variously called English-speaking, Anglo-American, Anglo-Saxon, Nordic, Germanic, Teutonic, Aryan, and Caucasian, is a measure of its intellectual incoherence. But as with shifting familial identities, the pliability of the terms made them more useful in meeting the new pressures exerted by shifts in power and circumstance. In the words of one historian of racial theory, "The fact that race has no precise meaning has made it a powerful tool for the most diverse purposes."[42] That a given racial label might serve for a primitive tribe, a nation, an international culture, a geopolitical alliance, or a biological species gave it a transhistorical air of mystery. The discourse of race could be opportunistically appropriated and modified to serve different ends.

The habit of thinking in racial categories in nineteenth- and early-twentieth-century England and America was nearly inescapable. Our present habit of condemning such practices as "rac*ist*" and of identifying them with mindless prejudice and mental pathology would have seemed incomprehensible to most serious thinkers a hundred years ago. Not only were racial categories pervasive in the academic, scientific, and ethical writings of the time; they were thought indispensable to an understanding of such diverse fields as biology, history and prehistory, literature, and comparative government. Every great academic institution in Britain and America boasted the presence of scholars whose research relied heavily on racial theory. It is impossible for us—aware of where such notions can lead and reared on a different set of received ideas—to understand the explanatory power of racial thinking. Characterizations of race were treated not as dubious hypotheses but as scientific facts; mental doors seemed to fly open; inexplicable historical or biological patterns suddenly made sense.

Behind the belief in racial categories lay the prestige of Darwin. His theory of natural selection was applied to human races, cautiously by Darwin himself, more enthusiastically by some of his followers.[43] The distinction between races, the "lower" doomed to disappear like other now extinct mammals unsuccessful in the struggle for survival, the "higher" to master the world, was rooted in evolutionary science.[44] Lending authority to theories of racial hierarchy were the reassuring conclusions of putatively exact research and measurement—the techniques of physical anthropology and anthropometry like the "cephalic index," paleontology, heredity and eugenics, comparative statistical studies of racial achievements, and so forth. Distinguished scientists confidently promulgated speculative ideas, as when the eminent zoologist Louis Agassiz—Henry Adams's favorite teacher at Harvard—argued that the account in Genesis could only refer to the creation of the white race, suggested that whites and Negroes might belong to different species, and stressed the scientist's "obligation to settle the relative rank among these races [since] it will not do to assume their equality and identity." For Agassiz, the Negro would always remain "submissive, obsequious, imitative," the Mongolian "tricky, cunning, and cowardly."[45] That such qualities might be by-products of a remediable powerlessness never occurs to him or his disciple. Adams recalls that at the time Agassiz's lectures "had more influence on his curiosity than the rest of the college instruction altogether."[46]

The discipline of history was equally reliant on theories of racial hierarchy. What came to be called the "Teutonic origins" school was highly influential in the writings of British and American historians. Major American figures like Parkman, Motley, and Bancroft—the leading historians of Adams's formative years—linked certain supposedly inherent Teutonic or Anglo-Saxon characteristics—rationality, judiciousness, self-control, a love of liberty and of self-government—to the race's triumphant progress.[47] Adams's own first major work as a historian (as well as that of his doctoral student at Harvard, Henry Cabot Lodge) was an edited volume in which the writers linked democratic government to the Germanic/Anglo-Saxon traditions of law and polity. *Essays in Anglo-Saxon Law* (1876) contains ambitious contributions by Adams and Lodge that connect modern republican institutions with the prefeudal political system of the Germanic tribes. That system, in Adams's words, "embraced every man, rich or poor, and in theory at least allowed equal rights to all. Beyond this point it seems unnecessary to go. The State and the Law may well have originated here."[48] In locating the omphalos of popular government there, Adams and his fellow historians are tracing an inevitable if interrupted line of racial continuity. That the centuries-long "break" of Norman feudalism can be relegated to a long parenthesis in the more inclusive sentence of Anglo-Saxon institutions suggests the power of the racial heritage and its capacity to triumph over temporary historical reversals.

It is not hard to imagine how simultaneously consoling and inspiring such visions must have seemed, both for those who feared the race's decline and those who eagerly anticipated its continuing triumph. In Anglo-American relations around the turn of the century, what was called a "patriotism of race" came close to replacing the traditional "patriotism of country."[49] The grandness of the claims made, the fusion of mystical assurance with scientific evidence, gave to Anglo-Saxon racial ideas the authority of revealed religion. We will see that in the first decades of the twentieth century this confidence evaporated, at least in America, and gave way to an intense Anglo-Saxon anxiety. But in the years of its greatest influence, Anglo-Saxonism became—like the fantasies of national and familial reconciliation—a powerful myth linking the fates of Britain and America. The political institutions and cultural patterns the Anglo-Saxon race had created might be taught to anyone: Indeed, this is the colonizing mission. But the racial identity and talent of the inventors cannot be passed on to other peoples. It is untransferable and transhistorical—a legacy that by the iron laws of heredity is rooted in the blood and can only remain in the family.

Exactly how do such racial and familial fantasies and myths enter the realm of practical politics? One might answer this question by looking closely at Theodore Roosevelt's complex appropriation of them. Roosevelt was the most significant actor in the redefinition of Anglo-American relations around 1900. His connections to many of the figures already discussed were exceptionally close. That he was significantly younger than Hay, Adams, and Lodge and not a countryman of Spring Rice gave him a certain critical perspective on them. But the sense of their common heritage was stronger. Like them, he was trained to move in the transatlantic social world in which a young patrician gentleman learned to be at ease anywhere. Through his family connections he had met many of the leading figures in English political and intellectual life, as well as those who would eventually rise to prominence. In America, the young Roosevelt was at Harvard when both Adams and Lodge were teaching there. In their set he was a known quantity even then, and the Adamses duly invited him to dinner in his freshman year. As he was later to write to Lodge, the Lodges, the Adamses, and Roosevelt's wife Edith, "all of you New England people . . . are more or less kin," though he playfully claims that in this close-knit circle he is "an alien outsider of uncouth antecedents."[50]

By the 1880s, the family party has reassembled in Washington, with the important addition of John Hay, Adams's closest friend. The Adamses and the Hays had built adjoining houses on Lafayette Square, a stone's throw from the White House. The easy intimacy of the set is suggested in an 1892 letter from Roosevelt to Spring Rice: "Henry Adams is back, and we have been there once or twice for the usual pleasant dinners and evenings . . . with perhaps John Hay—who is now in very good form and most amusing."[51] When Roosevelt unexpectedly succeeds to the presidency in 1901, virtually his first act is to make certain that Hay stay on as secretary of state, and their working partnership always implicitly includes Adams and Lodge and Spring Rice— "the kitchen ambassadorial circle," as Roosevelt calls it.[52] The circle later expands to include Brooks Adams, who became Lodge's brother-in-law. But the order of precedence has changed. As Hay ironically describes that new order to Henry Adams: "T[heodore] said the other day: 'I am not going to be the slave of tradition that forbids Presidents from seeing their friends. I am going to dine with you and H[enry] A[dams] and C[abot Lodge] whenever I like. But' (here the shadow of the crown sobered him a little), 'of course I must preserve the prerogative of the initiative.'"[53]

Yet despite the extraordinary intimacy of this circle, Roosevelt does more than preserve the prerogative of the initiative. He keeps a certain distance from their mental as well as social set. The sarcasm with which Adams and Hay think of their hyperenergetic friend in power is matched by Roosevelt's misgivings about them. From his perspective there is something essentially wrong with their whole tone, as this is manifest in Adams's pessimistic mockery, in Hay's abject worship of England, and in their friendship with decadent expatriates like Henry James: an absence of energy, a lack of the patriotic fervor appropriate to this unprecedented moment in American history. Despite his early admiration for Hay, Roosevelt concludes that Hay's career was compromised by his unswerving loyalty to Britain: "The fact was that Hay could not be trusted where England was concerned," Roosevelt writes to Lodge. And he is outraged when reading Hay's letters to find that America's secretary of state had written to Balfour when he became prime minister in 1902 that he had assumed "the most important official post known to modern history." What business had an American of the twentieth century to use such words? Hay's Anglophilia is for Roosevelt a sign of his too close association with Henry Adams and Henry James, men "wholly lacking in robustness of fiber," from whom he caught "the tone of satirical cynicism" that had compromised his usefulness as a representative of America's new world power.[54]

As Roosevelt's criticism of Hay's Anglophilia suggests, the president was not a true believer in the Anglo-Saxon myth, though he could make use of it when it suited his purposes. His optimistic vision of America's present and future greatness is not dependent on the continuity of the Anglo-Saxon line, and this is not only because his own Dutch colonial ancestry links him to a different European family. Roosevelt is eager to strengthen the partnership with England, but only on condition that the older country acknowledge (in action, if not in words) that America has become the senior partner in the firm. If that is accepted—as it came to be in the years of his presidency—the rhetoric of benevolence might continue to flow. Roosevelt's appropriation of the familial language can only be understood with this condition in mind. Although British imperialism is seen as a plausible model for American expansion, Roosevelt treats this legacy as a final bequest, in valedictory language that firmly associates British greatness with the past. England for him is "the archetype and best exemplar" of "the great expanding peoples which bequeath to future ages the great memories and material results of their achievements."[55] But the next stage in this glorious history will be dominated not by England but by "the English-speaking race in all its branches."[56]

Roosevelt's use of the adjective "English-speaking" rather than Anglo-Saxon or Anglo-American is no accident. In fact he has little use for the term "Anglo-Saxon," which he describes as "loose and meaningless."[57] He is keenly aware that the European roots of America's new citizenry are far more tangled than a generation earlier, and that the "English-speaking race" in America will soon include a majority of people whose background is not British, or even northern European. He welcomes this fact, believing firmly in the power of the melting pot to dissolve these differences and blend the heterogeneous European immigrants into an entirely new entity. He sees Americans as "a people different from all of the people of Europe, but akin to all," and he celebrates the mingling of nations to create a "new national type."[58]

But though the new national type is not Anglo-Saxon, there is no doubt that it is white and must remain so. Roosevelt's own brand of racial hierarchy idealizes a pan-European people, now primarily speaking English, though they might trace their origins to Britain or Holland or Italy or Poland or Russia. This sets him apart from many of the more conservative members of his class in America. But it does not fundamentally differentiate him from the impassioned visionaries eager to take up the white man's burden. And so, despite his distrust of Anglophilia and his doubts about the Anglo-American family connection, he is perfectly willing to see the future in terms relatively congenial to a British imperialist.

This is nowhere more apparent than in the Romanes Lecture Roosevelt delivers at Oxford in 1910. "Biological Analogies in History" is the closest he comes to acknowledging the Darwinian roots of his own ideas about race: In fact he specifically invokes "the great name of Darwin." His words are meant to reassure an English audience as well as his own increasingly heterogeneous compatriots. Roosevelt tries to accomplish this feat by consciously stressing the analogies among species, races, and nations and by assuring his auditors that if only they think of themselves not as Englishmen but as members of an extended family consisting of "peoples of European blood," they can take pride in the achievements of the future as well as of the past and present. For four centuries, "the people of European descent" have triumphantly managed "an ethnic conquest" of the world. In the face of this tremendous achievement of the white race, petty distinctions among European national stocks scarcely matter. They are in any case merging into "the English-speaking peoples" scattered throughout the world and swaying "the destinies of teeming myriads of alien race." In Roosevelt's visionary peroration, this order of things lasts indefinitely, as "our children and children's children to endless generations shall arise to take our places and play a mighty and dominant part in the world."

The language is mystical, the promise a divine covenant. But in both the Darwinian and the biblical models Roosevelt's rhetoric invokes there is a downward as well as an upward curve. Species and races ascend, triumph, decline, and perish. To everything there is a season: a time to be born, and a time to die. And Roosevelt is conscious that the race he sets out to celebrate is in the eyes of many already in decline. His words give voice to this anxiety: "Is our time of growth drawing to an end? Are we as nations soon to come under the rule of that great law of death which is itself but part of the great law of life?"[59] And he enumerates the symptoms of decline in the white race—the sharply falling birth rate, the love of ease and luxury, all the signs of decadence Europeans had been taught to note and fear at the fin de siècle.

Roosevelt's answer to these questions in 1910 is meant to reassure, and his own vigorously optimistic spirit gives it the ring of conviction: Through strenuous effort, "our seed [shall] inherit the earth," he predicts.[60] But like the other myths and fantasies on which the new Anglo-American partnership relied, his vision of the future is built on the need to deny conflicts others knew to be powerfully present. On the Continent, "the peoples of European blood" are preparing to spill it in great quantities. And in his own country, the confident faith in the assimilative fusion of different peoples in the melting pot is threatened by a sense of panic among "the Anglo-Saxons" that their country has been invaded by alien hordes. The fantasy of a reconciliation and amalgamation of the dispersed European family was in fact giving way to the reality of a deepening mistrust among rival claimants and to the fratricidal conflict that was about to begin.

III

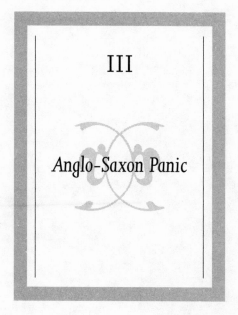

Anglo-Saxon Panic

THE UNEASINESS that pushed England and the United States toward reconciliation around the turn of the century had different causes in the two countries. But each was urgent, and each had its roots in a fear of decline. This is anomalous, since it seems unlikely that rivals fighting for supremacy should both be convinced they are losing ground. The sense of anxiety was felt on each side, however, though the particular fears were distinct. Britain, as we have seen, was acutely conscious of her relative decline as a manufacturing and trading nation, and of her loss of military and geopolitical supremacy. The United States, confident in the abundance of her natural resources, astonishing economic growth, and new power and influence on the world scene, was deeply troubled by what seemed like a catastrophic change in the composition of her people.

The very rapid growth in the U.S. population around the turn of the century (which more than doubled between 1880 and 1920, from fifty to over a hundred million) should have been a cause for celebration. America was a vast country, and there was certainly plenty of room. New European immigrants had long been eagerly welcomed, not only because they were needed for the country's westward expansion but because their arrival in great numbers was treated as an international vote of confidence in the democratic experiment. Yet the optimistic spirit that took for granted America's ability to absorb and assimilate vast numbers of strangers and turn them into productive, loyal citizens—Whitman's faith in an inexhaustible "teeming nation of nations" which "rejects none," which "permits all"[1]—seemed suddenly to evaporate.

What had changed was the composition of the immigrant pool. In 1882, for instance, over three-quarters of the arriving immigrants had come from "Nordic" countries like Britain, Germany, and Scandinavia, while those from southern and eastern Europe accounted for only about an eighth of the total. By 1905, the proportions were nearly reversed, with over three-quarters emigrating from countries like Italy, Austria-Hungary, and Russia and less than a quarter from northern and western Europe. In the year 1907, nearly a million of these "new" southern and eastern European immigrants poured into the country.[2] Clearly if this trend continued—and there was every reason to think that it would—America would no longer be able to call herself an Anglo-Saxon nation. The increasing alarm with which this significant shift was met in some influential circles was fueled both by an instinctive fear of people who seemed alien and by the pervasive theories of racial hierarchy that had also shaped the fantasies of Anglo-American reconciliation. We now know that such distinctions of superior and inferior races could and did lead to genocide, to our century's greatest atrocity. It is therefore exceptionally difficult to permit ourselves to look at their roots with a genuine curiosity about their original appeal. But the imaginative effort must be made if we are to understand how the past looked to itself.

The shockingly alien quality of the new immigrants from southern and eastern Europe is not hard to grasp. They spoke strange tongues; they worshiped strange gods; some were illiterate and few had immediately marketable skills. Many had little interest in becoming Americans but sent their wages "home" and planned eventually to return to their native countries. In addition, the late-nineteenth-century urban explosion and the gradual displacement of agriculture by manufacturing meant that the new immigrants clustered in crowded ghettos rather than fanning out across the nation. This slowed the process of assimilation and increased the sense of visibly separate groups—of enclaves like the Jewish Lower East Side of Manhattan, with its packed tenements and swarming streets of exotic-looking, incomprehensibly articulate people, carrying on a vigorous community life whose alien character made the native American observer feel like an unwelcome intruder. There had, of course, been such ethnic communities before 1900—the Irish in Boston, the Germans in Milwaukee, for example. But it is the confluence of the unfamiliar elements of language, religion, class, physiognomy, and dress in a single people and their concentration in a tiny pocket of a great city that makes the Jews of the Lower East Side seem unassimilable. Henry James describes them in *The American Scene* (1907) as "the representatives of the races we have nothing 'in common' with," apparently at their ease in a world of their own making.[3] The antithesis between "we" and "they" in his sentence reveals a chasm felt by many native observers.

As James's remark suggests, race is at the heart of the perceived problem. A new set of racial labels is invented to distinguish the various European groups now making their way across the Atlantic. In order to understand it, we have to abandon the prevalent idea of a single "white race." People who were once called "whites" or "Europeans" or "Caucasians" in contrast to the peoples of other continents now come to be categorized in a more regional and potentially divisive way. In *The Races of Europe* (1899), a book that has a significant impact on American immigration policies, William Ripley, an economist at MIT, subdivides the peoples of the European continent into three distinct "races"—the northern Teutons (or Nordics), the central Alpines, the southern Mediterraneans. In addition there were the Slavs, straddling Europe and Asia. These races are said to have different cranial shapes and characteristic strengths and weaknesses, a typology that could be and eventually was interpreted hierarchically, though Ripley himself resists the temptation. He insists that "there is no single European or white race of men," that despite intermarriage the European races are distinct and readily recognizable, but that the differences between them are as much the product of "physical and social environment" as of biology.[4] When Ripley's categories are appropriated by more inflammatory race theorists like Madison Grant and Lothrop Stoddart, the role of environment is minimized, and the biological superiority of Teutons or Nordics over the other European races heavily stressed.[5]

The result is an increasingly urgent discrimination between more and less desirable European immigrants. Not only are the Teutons or Nordics of northern and western Europe identified with the earliest American settlers and therefore linked by blood and tradition to the nation's founders. The new typology insists that they are biologically superior—in brain size, for example. The displacement of the original immigrants by the biologically inferior races of southern and eastern Europe is therefore a national disaster that will deeply compromise the country's future. And the biological basis of the distinction undermines the traditional American faith in her power to absorb and transform the alien. Assimilation is an environmental process and a temporal inevitability, as the immigrants and their children are exposed to the shaping power of American schools and other institutions. But if the "new" immigrants are genetically inferior to the older settlers, they will not take the imprint of existing American culture. Not only will they remain permanent aliens, but their significantly higher birth rates will allow them to remake America in their own image.

Such agitated visions engender a kind of Anglo-Saxon panic. One senses it in the imagery regularly used to describe the new immigrants. The mere titles of contemporaneous essays and books on the subject register the sense of alarm: *The Alien Invasion* (1892), "Alien Degradation of American Character" (1893), "The Overtaxed Melting Pot" (1903), "Immigration the Annihilator of Our Native Stock" (1904), *The Immigrant Tide* (1909), *The Immigrant Invasion* (1913), "Social Deterioration of the United States from the Stream of Backward Immigrants" (1914).[6] They picture a country helpless to withstand the onslaught of hostile forces bent on its destruction. Such writers often rely on metaphors of flooding and invasion. One of them sees the dikes breaking and warns that "this country is in danger of being swamped by alien elements, and stands in need of reenforcement."[7] Another writes that America is being "deluged by the truly alien hordes of the European east and south" and warns that "the immigrant tide must at all costs be stopped and America given a chance to stabilize her ethnic being."[8] The images of inundation—of tides, swamps, deluges—suggest overwhelming forces that no melting pot, no matter how capacious, could even hold, let alone transform.

The closely associated comparison of the immigrants to barbarian invaders plays on similar fears, as in Thomas Bailey Aldrich's notorious poem "Unguarded Gates" (1895), which Henry Cabot Lodge quoted to persuade his fellow senators to restrict immigration:

> Wide open and unguarded stand our gates,
> And through them presses a wild motley throng—
> Men from the Volga and the Tartar steppes,
> Featureless figures of the Hoang-Ho,
> Malayan, Scythian, Teuton, Kelt, and Slav,
> Flying the Old World's poverty and scorn;
> These bringing with them unknown gods and rites,
> Those, tiger passions, here to stretch their claws.
> In street and alley what strange tongues are loud,
> Accents of menace alien to our air,
> Voices that once the Tower of Babel knew!

Inevitably, to Aldrich's mind, the invaders recall "the thronging Goth and Vandal [who] trampled Rome."[9] At stake for such observers is the survival of civilization itself, or rather the particular civilization in which they themselves had prospered.

The Nordic race will be mongrelized or bred out. This fear is treated as incontrovertible fact by eugenicists and other experts. Lodge the professionally trained historian informs his congressional colleagues that "if a lower race mixes with the higher in sufficient numbers, history teaches us that the lower race will prevail. The lower race will absorb the higher," and the inferior characteristics of the new immigrants will annihilate the great qualities of the first settlers by "breeding them out."[10] Some writers on this subject express a deep anxiety about miscegenation, though the races involved are all white. Madison Grant, whose *The Passing of the Great Race* (1916) is the most important work to give these ideas intellectual respectability in America, uses the fear of mongrelization to attack the very ideal of the melting pot. "What the Melting Pot actually does in practice," he argues, is to produce an inferior race with an "incapacity for self-government. . . . Whether we like it or not, the result of the mixture of two races, in the long run, gives us a race reverting to the more ancient, generalized and lower type."[11] One might call this theory the survival of the *unfittest*, yet its contradiction of Darwin does not give these new experts pause. Though Madison Grant was not a trained scientist, the title page of his book offers his claim to authority: Chairman, New York Zoological Society; Trustee, American Museum of Natural History; Councilor, American Geographical Society. This is hardly the voice of a lunatic fringe but of a bedrock intellectual respectability.

The alarmism of this vision of racial decline is crystallized in the phrase "race suicide." First used in a 1901 essay on "The Causes of Race Supremacy" by the distinguished and prolific sociologist Edward Ross, it rapidly gained currency. Ross attributes the triumph of the lower race to its fecundity and ability to tolerate lower living standards. As a result, the higher race withdraws from the contest: It "quietly and unmurmuringly eliminates itself rather than endure individually the bitter competition it has failed to ward off from itself by collective action." Its "race suicide" takes the form of delaying marriage and restricting family size below replacement levels—a short-term solution that preserves the old standard of living for one or two generations but increases the likelihood that the higher race "might wither away."[12] By 1914, as the problem gains urgency, Ross's rhetoric heats up. He warns that "the blood now being injected into the veins of our people is 'subcommon,'" that "the Caliban type" is taking over, and that if the old colonial stock continues to have so few children, it will deserve "the extinction that surely awaits it."[13]

Ross's phrase quickly becomes a familiar slogan, and his warnings are taken seriously at the highest levels. Theodore Roosevelt is a veritable Cassandra on the subject. "All the other problems before us in this country, important though they may be, are as nothing compared with the problem of the diminishing birth rate and all that it implies," he warns in the year Ross publishes his influential essay: "When a race commits suicide it is not of the slightest consequence what are the qualities which it would have possessed if it had lived." Therefore,

Roosevelt argues, it is the duty of every fertile married couple of "native American descent" to have at least four children to prevent "race suicide." Those who "refuse to have children sufficient in number to mean that the race goes forward . . . are criminals."[14] The race and class anxiety behind these warnings becomes increasingly urgent. In 1907, J. R. Commons warns that "the 'race suicide' of the American or colonial stock should be regarded as the most fundamental of our social problems."[15] By 1916, Madison Grant is ready to recommend stronger measures "to attack race suicide," a problem that cannot be solved "by encouraging indiscriminate breeding." He preaches a new eugenic gospel that a modern reader can hardly take in without a shudder of recognition: "the elimination of defective infants and the sterilization of such adults as are themselves of no value to the community." And he proposes "a rigid system of selection through the elimination of those who are weak or unfit," a group that includes the "ever increasing number of moral perverts, mental defectives, and hereditary cripples."[16]

Most striking in such radical proposals is the loss of confidence they betray. Gone is Roosevelt's faith in the triumph of "our seed." The survival of the fittest can no longer be entrusted to the process of natural selection. The problem has become not national but international, since the first great contest of the twentieth century is pitting the Nordic race against itself and creating a new meaning for the phrase "race suicide" that its inventor had not foreseen. Madison Grant's radical prescription grows out of his despairing sense that "Nordics" are not only being bred out in America but destroying each other by the million on the western front. *The Passing of the Great Race* was published in the year that brought the mass slaughter of trench warfare. In his eyes, the Great War is not a contest between nations but "essentially a civil war" between members of a single race, the "mutual butchery and mutual destruction between Nordics," or "class suicide on a gigantic scale."[17] (It is worth noting how often the terms *race* and *class* are used interchangeably in such writing.)

Grant's disciple, Lothrop Stoddart, sees the war as even more decisive in *The Rising Tide of Color* (1920), the inflammatory book that translates Grant's ideas for popular consumption. The European "homeland, the heart of the white race" had met its Armageddon in the war, but it was particularly "the Nordics—the best of all human breeds—who suffered far and away the greatest losses."[18] Stoddart's book is essentially an acknowledgment of defeat. The war has shown that Nordic suicidal tendencies are uncontainable and that those attempting to reverse the pattern are fighting a losing battle. At best one might preserve the race's influence in a few countries through an aggressive program of exclusion. Stoddart calls for an immigration policy that is frankly racial in intent, to put a stop to the uncontrolled migration that is "filling our own land with the sweepings of the European east and south."[19] As we will see, this is precisely the solution the United States adopts in the 1920s.

It is useful to go back for a moment to the mid-nineteenth century to see how much has changed. Of course American nativism and the hostility to certain immigrant groups was not born in the 1890s. The mass migration of the Irish to America after the Great Famine exacerbated invidious distinctions between European immigrant cohorts, since they too seemed alien at first—Catholics in a largely Protestant country, poor, parochial, unskilled. The idea of Anglo-Saxon superiority gained currency in the earlier nineteenth century not only to justify America's appropriation of Indian and Mexican territory but to distinguish the Celtic Irish settlers from the dominant group. The hatred and violence this opposition spawned in mid-nineteenth-century America should not be minimized.[20] Nevertheless, there is a different quality to the exclusionary theories and blatant panic of the turn of the century. In the earlier period, despite the strength of the nativist Know-Nothing Party in the 1850s, faith in the American melting pot had remained largely intact, and the country's openness to different peoples was still a matter of national pride.

One only has to go back to Emerson and Melville (and of course Whitman) to see how self-confident this celebration of American inclusiveness once was, and how wide the net was cast. Emerson writes in 1845 that "in this continent,—asylum of all nations,—the energy of Irish, Germans, Swedes, Poles and Cossacks, and all the European tribes,—of the Africans, and of the Polynesians,—will construct a new race, a new religion, a new state, a new literature, which will be as vigorous as the new Europe which came out of the smelting pot of the Dark Ages."[21] His catalog makes no distinction among Europeans, nor between Europeans and settlers from other continents. Melville's novel *Redburn* (1849) rhapsodically voices a similar optimism and national pride: "Settled by the people of all nations, all nations may claim her for their own. You can not spill a drop of American blood without spilling the blood of the whole world. . . . No: our blood is as the flood of the Amazon, made up of a thousand noble currents all pouring into one." There is no fear of inundation here; nor any anxiety about alien tongues. Melville foresees the American language ending the curse of Babel by incorporating into a single tongue not only the languages of western Europe but those of "the dwellers on the shores of the Mediterranean, and in the regions round about; Italians, and Indians, and Moors."[22] Rather than anxiously distinguishing and ranking races, such inclusive visions reject the very concept of the alien. No assimilative task is too difficult for the melting pot—or "smelting pot," as Emerson calls it, a variant that emphasizes the precious metal extracted from this process. John Higham, the leading historian of American nativism, calls the pre–Civil War period "The Age of Confidence," and the words of the midcentury writers powerfully reflect that feeling.[23]

A later generation of prominent Americans will treat this optimistic faith in America's assimilative powers as naive, and so in one sense of the word it is, since it has not been tested by experience. Theodore Roosevelt is perhaps the last confident assimilationist in a position of power, and even he expresses concern. We have seen that he has no use for the narrow concept of the Anglo-Saxon breed and that unlike many members of his class he believes in a pan-European migration of settlers whose mixed blood will strengthen the "American race" it is bringing into being. He despises nativist prejudice against the new immigrants, and he repeatedly insists that no distinctions should be made between Americans of different ethnic and religious stock. The ideal immigrant, he tells Congress in his 1905 annual message, should not be judged by such labels: "We cannot afford to consider whether he is Catholic or Protestant, Jew or Gentile; whether he is Englishman or Irishman, Frenchman or German, Japanese, Italian, Scandinavian, Slav, or Magyar."[24] Roosevelt's writings are full of such passages, particularly during World War I, as he is pressed to declare America's kinship with Britain in the European conflict. He writes to one Anglophile correspondent that he cannot support England on these grounds: "England is not my motherland any more than Germany is my fatherland. My motherland and my fatherland and my own land are all three of them the United States."[25]

But although Roosevelt refuses to distinguish between different European "races" (and in fact rejects the whole idea that they exist), although he appoints the first Jew to a cabinet position and consistently supports the rights of the more recent immigrants, he is troubled by the parochialism and sense of divided loyalty among the increasingly heterogeneous American population. His own anxiety about whether or not the process of assimilation is working takes the form of a relentless battle against what he calls "hyphenated Americans," those unwilling to surrender their original identity to become entirely and irrevocably American. He calls a plan to open a center in New York "to foster the Russian language and keep alive the national feeling" in Russian immigrants "utterly antagonistic to proper American sentiment, whether perpetrated in the name of Germany, of Austria, of Russia, of England, or France or any other country." Nostalgic feelings for the country one has left creates divided loyalties: Russo-American or Anglo-American or Jewish-American. "But a hyphenated American," Roosevelt insists, "is not an American at all. . . . Our allegiance must be purely to the United States." If the people of America ignore such warnings, the country will be "split into warring camps" and the "great democratic experiment on this continent will go down in crushing overthrow."[26] Roosevelt's coercive rhetoric ("must" is one of his favorite words) and his vision of imminent national disaster suggest how little even he shares the serene confidence of earlier believers in assimilation. In his eyes, the melting pot is a pressure cooker about to blow up.

Roosevelt's anxiety about the divided loyalty of immigrants and the threat they pose to the assimilative ideal, however, pales beside the responses of his close associates. Brooks Adams, for example, sees the eastern Europeans as not European at all: "The Russians are Asiatic, and therefore less vigorous, energetic and inventive than Western races."[27] But the most determined of the exclusionists in Roosevelt's circle is Lodge, whose campaign for European immigration restriction is unrelenting from before his election to the Senate in 1893 to the final enactment of ethnically based immigration quotas in 1921. He sees the handwriting on the wall as early as 1891, in an essay in which he argues that because the new immigrants do not share "community of race or language, or both" with the earlier settlers, they will be much harder to absorb. And because they come from "races most alien to the body of the American people and from the lowest and most illiterate classes among those races," their increasing numbers will "tend to lower the quality of American citizenship."[28] His solution is to exclude such undesirables by discriminating among the immigrant groups in favor of those that had originally peopled the country. It is worth noting that a verb like "discriminate" is used by restrictionists in its almost forgotten positive sense: to select the best.

Lodge is certain that northern and western European settlers are "the best" by any measure. He goes through Appleton's six-volume *Encyclopedia of American Biography* page by page in order to establish the "race-extraction" of the thousands of eminent men and women it lists. The statistics he compiles demonstrate to his own satisfaction that "the immigration from Great Britain has contributed three-fourths of the ability furnished from outside sources." If one adds settlers from Germany, France, the Netherlands, and Scandinavia, virtually all the eminent Americans since the country's founding are accounted for. Of the 14,243 biographical subjects, only 19 have roots in southern or eastern Europe.[29] Perhaps more remarkable than this conclusion (since the arrival of the new immigrants is much too recent to affect the historical record) is that a man of Lodge's ability and importance should even have undertaken such a numbing task in the first place. But he is a trained historian as well as a crusader, and he needs hard evidence.

The evidence he finds apparently supports both the theory of Nordic superiority and the policy of rejecting alien races unlikely to assimilate to the existing population. For Lodge, the great strength of the United States lay in her Anglo-Saxon heritage and in the intrinsic qualities of that race. He idealizes an America that is fully formed rather than still defining herself. The United States, he tells his fellow senators, "have attained a fixity and definitiveness of national character unknown to any other people." The Anglo-Saxon race that accounts for this character is notable for its "will power," for "an unconquerable energy, a very great initiative, an absolute empire over self, a sentiment of independence pushed even to excessive unsociability, a puissant activity, very keen religious sentiments, a very fixed morality, a very clear idea of duty."[30] A more skeptical observer might note the rigidity and self-righteousness implicit in this catalog of virtues, and point to the absence of imagination, communal spirit, tolerance, humor, modesty, and grace. But such qualities would only dilute the puissant legacy Lodge wants to preserve. Better to close the unguarded gates than to admit the bacillus.

Lodge is not speaking only for himself but for his class; and here again race and class merge as they so often do in writings on this subject. The Harvard-educated Boston Brahmin culture of which he is a distinguished representative prides itself on its colonial ancestry, its hereditary castelike status, its civic-mindedness. It is often described as America's untitled aristocracy, its achievements multigenerational, its marital patterns endogamous. Lodge could have found many bearers of the same name in his survey of Appleton's *Encyclopedia*, just as a reader of today's *New Columbia Encyclopedia* will find entries for two Henry Cabot Lodges, two Oliver Wendell Holmeses, two Henry Jameses, and many, many members of the Adams and Eliot clans.

This New England patriciate is closely associated with the movement to restrict immigration. Although there are some significant exceptions to the Brahmin hostility to the "alien" (most prominent among them William James and President Eliot of Harvard), the most powerful organization working for the Anglo-Saxon cause has close ties to this group.[31] The influential Immigration Restriction League was founded in 1894 by several graduates of Harvard College determined to reverse the tide of southern and eastern European immigration. It soon becomes the voice for a movement that gradually gains force in other eastern cities and eventually affects public attitudes and legislation.[32] Its writings back up the racial stereotypes of Anglo-Saxonism with statistical, scientific, anecdotal, and frankly speculative "findings" that make the principle of immigration selection by race follow like an inevitable conclusion. So Prescott Hall, the league's secretary, warns that "in the long run heredity is far more important than environment or education" in determining the quality of a people; and that therefore America should treat the power to discriminate among potential immigrants as "a unique opportunity to exercise artificial selection on an enormous scale."[33]

For a variety of reasons too complex to analyze here, the necessary legislation took a quarter of a century to enact. But when in 1921 the Johnson Bill finally became law (and even more when it was modified in 1924 and 1927), it had clearly been shaped by the Anglo-Saxon panic at its root. The forty-two-volume Dillingham Report of 1910 had provided a mountain of evidence to support the theory of racial hierarchy; the Chinese Exclusion Act of 1882 offered a precedent for such legislation; and a majority of the American people were at last ready to support it. Henceforth immigration was to be drastically cut (from close to a million a year to 165,000 after 1924), and the basis of selection was to be national origin. The revised 1924 act allotted the available places according to a formula based on the statistics of the 1890 census: 2 percent of the foreign born of each nation living in the United States *at that time* would be allowed to enter the country every year. The choice of 1890 is highly significant, since that year antedated the great influx from southern and eastern Europe that began in the nineties. The 1924 law is essentially nostalgic, seeking to restore the status quo ante—the American people as they had been before the deluge.

The quota system for immigration selection proved to be remarkably successful in achieving its aims. In the years before World War I, immigrants from southern and eastern Europe had accounted for nearly 80 percent of the arrivals; after the 1924 act went into effect, their proportion was reduced to one in eight. In sheer numbers, the drop was even more dramatic—from over 600,000 a year to 20,000. With relatively minor adjustments, this system was to stay in place until well after World War II and was indirectly responsible for America's failure to provide sanctuary for more than a small fraction of the Jews trying to flee eastern Europe.[34] No longer were the gates unguarded. For the ethnic groups the Anglo-Saxonists considered "alien," they had virtually shut.[35] Whitman's vision of America as a "Union holding all, fusing, absorbing, tolerating all" had come to seem a relic of the distant past.[36]

We have seen that the New England patriciate played a major role in reversing the country's long-standing tradition of welcoming the outcasts of other nations. Their zeal was linked to their sense that their prominent role in the affairs of their country was threatened. Many felt that their tradition was in irreversible decline. The downward slide had begun long before the influx of the new immigrants but was speeded along by it. The two groups were moving in opposite directions, one up, one down. This Brahmin bitterness was alternately directed against the newcomers and against themselves. Henry Adams's notorious description in the *Education* of his return to America in 1868 after a seven-year absence fuses these reactions:

> His world was dead. Not a Polish Jew fresh from Warsaw or Cracow—not a furtive Yacoob or Ysaac still reeking of the Ghetto, snarling a weird Yiddish to the officers of the customs—but had a keener instinct, an intenser energy, and a freer hand than he—American of Americans, with Heaven knew how many Puritans and Patriots behind him, and an education that had cost a civil war. He made no complaint and found no fault with his time; he was no worse off than the Indians or the buffalo who had been ejected from their heritage by his own people; but he vehemently insisted that he was not himself at fault. The defeat was not due to him, nor yet to any superiority of his rivals. He had been unfairly forced out of the track, and must get back into it as best he could.[37]

Adams's reaction is a historical anachronism. Although he is ostensibly writing about the period immediately after the Civil War, his terms of reference (and his anxiety) are patently the product of the early twentieth century, when his retrospective words are actually written. In the powerful displacement fantasy they record, the energy and initiative that had belonged to the Puritans and Patriots from whom he is descended and that had carried his great-grandfather and grandfather to the White House are dissipated. The nation's original settlers are overwhelmed by a new uninhibited and ambitious breed, eager to seize power and ready to relegate Adams and his kind to the dustheap of history. He treats this change as inevitable—makes no complaint, finds no fault, even treats it as a kind of poetic justice. Yet his words ring with outrage: *unfair!* And his anger against those who have driven him and his people from power unleashes a demonizing tirade directed at a surprising target—the raw Jewish immigrants who were in fact only to arrive more than a generation later. They prove to be convenient scapegoats for Adams and many of his contemporaries and successors, including Eliot and Pound, as we will see.

The restrictionists needed a symbol that combined alien identity with ambition and success. The Jews were nicely adapted to this purpose because they came in two guises: the impoverished inhabitants of

ghettos whose history of deprivation really did make them look like inferior biological specimens; and the successful merchants or financiers or
writers who could be seen as usurpers. So John Hay in a very early diary
entry (1867) describes the Polish-Jewish ghettos of Vienna as "squalid
veins and arteries of impoverished and degenerate blood"[38]; and Henry
Adams is overwhelmed by a phantasm of Jewish malignancy: "The Jew
has got into the soul. I see him—or her—now everywhere, and wherever he—or she—goes, there must remain a taint in the blood forever,"
he writes in 1896.[39] As these new citizens begin to make their mark individually rather than collectively, the sense of their presumption grows.
Barrett Wendell, the Harvard professor and author of *A Literary History
of America* (1900), protests that these interlopers have the audacity to
claim parity with the older settlers. His description of Mary Antin's sympathetic treatment of the new immigrants in her autobiography *The
Promised Land* (1912) perfectly conveys the Brahmin outrage: "She has
developed an irritating habit of describing herself and her people as
Americans, in distinction from such folks as Edith and me, who have
been here for three hundred years."[40]

Wendell's insistence on that distinction throws light on the growth
of nativist societies around the turn of the century. Pride in colonial
roots, once a private matter, is institutionalized. Most of the organizations that celebrate colonial ancestry were only founded in the 1890s,
almost certainly as a way of distinguishing "Edith and me" from the
newcomers: the Colonial Dames (1890), the Daughters of the American Revolution (1890), the Society of Mayflower Descendants (1894),
the Baronial Order of Runnymede (1897), and the like.[41] There is a
concomitant passion for genealogical research, especially to establish
Anglo-Saxon lineage, a version of what the English historian Eric
Hobsbawm calls "the invention of tradition."[42] The American past is
made to serve the present by denying entry to those without roots in it.

But to celebrate the past is also to withdraw from the present. The nostalgia intrinsic to the whole enterprise is a tacit confession that the great
days are over. That this was so in New England at any rate was a received
idea by the turn of the century, which is why the attack on the new immigrants seems oddly belated. The flowering of New England had turned
into "a harvest of leaves," as George Santayana put it.[43] Much has been
written about the late-nineteenth-century decline of New England cul-

ture, and it is not necessary to rehearse it here. The important point, however, is that it is acknowledged at or near the time it occurs by those who might have been most reluctant to do so. Brooks Adams, for example, could be describing his own heritage when he writes in 1896 about "families who have been famous in one century sinking into obscurity in the next" and attributes this decline to the fact that "the energy of the race has been exhausted."[44] And even Barrett Wendell, whose ambitious *Literary History of America* was retitled by one waggish rival *A Literary History of Harvard University, with Incidental Glimpses of the Minor Writers of America*, confesses that ever since the 1870s New England culture "has been tending to lapse more and more into provincial isolation."[45] Most pointed is Henry Adams's tragicomic lament to an English friend: "Our class is as defunct as the dodo."[46]

It is interesting that Adams addresses this confession to an Englishman, his kindred spirit and lifelong friend, Charles Milnes Gaskell, a member of the civic-minded, liberal, intellectually sophisticated, hereditary elite of England whose own political ambitions had come to very little. Anglophile Boston was the city in America toward which English travelers gravitated and in which they felt most at home. The area was not called *New* England for nothing. Surely the English could sympathize with those who lamented its decline. They recognized the symptoms and might understand. Even British travelers not looking for a copy of their own culture in the United States instinctively grasped what had happened. H. G. Wells, for example, visiting Boston in 1906, had a sharp sense of the city's lost cultural centrality after 1875.[47]

In that same year Henry Adams, then a young instructor at Harvard, records his new awareness of Boston's increasing provincialism and his own need to escape. As he writes to Henry Cabot Lodge, "I yearn, at every instant, to get out of Massachusetts and come in contact with the wider life I have always found so much more to my taste."[48] His escape route leads him first to the new power center of Washington and later to Europe. In that same year, his friend Henry James takes the decisive step of leaving his family home in Cambridge and moving abroad—briefly to France, then to England. As he writes his parents on his arrival in London, in a sentence that rings with a new American colonizing power, "I take possession of the old world—I inhale it—I appropriate it!"[49] Although the choice of expatriation has often been interpreted as a defeat, it can also be seen as a way of achieving abroad what no longer seems possible at home. The echo of American imperial expansion is not lost on William Dean Howells, who writes in 1902 that the literary exiles ought to be seen as the "vanguard of the great army of adventurers destined to overrun the earth from these shores, and exploit all foreign countries to our advantage."[50] Manifest Destiny can claim high culture as well as territory and travel back across the Atlantic.

As the United States becomes less congenial to such displaced patricians, the alternative of Europe, and more particularly of England, becomes more appealing. Here is a world in which their own kind is not yet threatened by alien intruders, in which a rich cosmopolitan culture can dispel their fear of provincialism, in which the threat of an increasingly heterogeneous society can be ignored. So Oliver Wendell Holmes predicts in 1887, "The time may come when a New Englander will feel more as if he were among his own people in London than in one of our seaboard cities." He foresees an increase in American expatriation to Britain, or rather "re-migration"—a striking coinage.[51] Certainly James is more in his element in London than when he briefly returns to Massachusetts in 1905 to find that even Boston Common has been taken over by a polyglot populace from whose lips "no sound of English, in a single instance, escaped."[52] The need for community among such writers, their desire to be central rather than marginal players in a global game, is met by working toward Anglo-American unity. Like the public figures committed to a political entente between England and America, they are eager for a cultural rapprochement based on Anglo-Saxon identity. So James writes his brother William in 1888 that he thinks of England and America as "a big Anglo-Saxon total" whose common culture is "continuous or more or less convertible."[53]

Behind this ideal is the awareness that year by year England was becoming a more plausible place to celebrate Anglo-Saxon unity than America. Britain was no teeming nation of nations but a more stable, monolingual culture with a deep distrust of "abroad." Her immigrant pool was tiny compared to that of the United States, and likely to remain so. When the increasing presence of "undesirable" aliens was first felt around the turn of the century, the government quickly appointed a Royal Commission on Alien Immigration (1902) and in 1905 enacted legislation in line with that body's recommendation to restrict their arrival.[54] A member of the commission published a book on *The Alien Immigrant* in the following year that suggests both the similarity of attitude and the difference of magnitude in the English and American situations. Like the American restrictionists, the British perfected a highly charged metaphorical vocabulary of alarm: The Jews of London's East End are called "a race apart, as it were, in an enduring island of extraneous thought and custom," or "an army of locusts, eating up the English inhabitants or driving them out." Yet the actual numbers of eastern European immigrants to Britain highlight the difference: In 1902, the year of the commission's report, there were twenty-one thousand.[55] The ethnic composition of the population had remained remarkably stable: Between 1861 and 1931, over 99 percent were born in the British Isles, in striking contrast to the American scene.[56]

From a comparative perspective, then, Britain looks essentially monocultural. As Price Collier, an American writer sympathetic to Anglo-Saxonism, observes in 1909, English exclusionary policies should be the model for the United States, since they maintain stability and national unity: In his eyes, "the homogeneity of the race makes for mutual understanding and solidarity."[57] In such an atmosphere, the displaced American patricians might well feel more at home than in one of their own seaboard cities. For some, *England* proves to be the promised land. James celebrates a very different melting pot from the one bubbling away at home when he writes that England and America are "destined to such an amount of melting together that an insistence on their differences becomes more and more idle and pedantic."[58] Given their bedrock Anglo-Saxon loyalties, and the felt need among certain communities on both sides of the Atlantic to strengthen the ties that bind the two nations, it is no wonder that Americans like Adams, James, Pound, and Eliot find easy entry into London's highest social and intellectual circles, circles that had long treated Americans as barbarians. But a common fear of decline, a shared anxiety, brings the wary combatants into accord. They work hard to create what Winston Churchill was to dub the "special relationship" between the two countries. The transatlantic cosmopolitanism that gradually displaces the slanging match of the nineteenth century not only shapes a number of important American literary careers but renegotiates the terms of the old divorce to create a seemingly invincible new form of cultural authority.[59]

IV

Henry Adams's
Baffled Patriotism

I

THE WORK OF renegotiating the terms of the cultural connection between the United States and Britain is at the heart of four closely linked careers, those of Adams and James in one generation, of Eliot and Pound in the next. They form a single line of affiliation and descent, as they themselves realize. They are engaged in a group project, the goals of which only gradually become clear. But the sense of a shared identity and a cumulative group achievement (and defeat) are felt early, as the two generations overlap. "We all began together, and our lives have made more or less of a unity,"[1] Henry Adams wrote his friend Henry James in 1911 on the occasion of William James's death, in the decade that would also end the careers of the two Henrys. The kinship between the Jameses and Adamses and beyond them to a tight network of eastern upper-class artists and intellectuals who had by 1900 distinguished themselves in various fields is clearly grasped, the unity becoming clear as the superficial distinctions evaporate. Or so it struck

Adams as he sought perspective on his own long life. Born in 1838, he had been leading what he called a posthumous existence since his wife's suicide in 1885 and never expected to survive into the twentieth century. And he had poured so much energy into inventing the myth of his failure that the idea of his own achievement was literally unthinkable. It seemed easier, and more accurate, to retreat into his original group identity and make no individual claim.

The most striking example is a 1903 letter to James in which Adams tries to define that group and coins the phrase that gives this book its title. He is responding to James's biography of the expatriate Boston sculptor William Wetmore Story, a book that is so completely recognizable that he playfully insists he wrote it. Story strikes Adams as an alter ego, the "type bourgeois-bostonien"—molded by Boston, Harvard, and Unitarianism; shallowly educated, introverted, self-conscious, yet apparently successful; contesting his provincialism in "irritable dislike of America, and antipathy to Boston." As Adams thinks of the young men brought up in such circumstances in mid-nineteenth-century New England, they fuse into a single type: "Improvised Europeans, we were, and—Lord God!—how thin!" His friend has written "not Story's life, but your own and mine."[2] James's reply to this extraordinary letter acknowledges the essential accuracy of Adams's judgment and confesses that his covert autobiographical work did indeed "begin with me, myself . . . though pushing me to conclusions less grim, as I may call them, than in your case."[3]

Their essential kinship is acknowledged at this stage, their divergent life choices masking a deeper affinity. An ocean separated them, but their friendship had deep roots: James knew Clover Hooper long before she became Mrs. Henry Adams and thought she embodied the best of American young womanhood. Writing from a British spa in 1870, he praised Clover's "intellectual grace" and contrasted her with the stiff, dowdy Englishwomen surrounding him. Her marriage cemented the friendship; they were inseparable whenever their paths crossed; and Clover's tragic death set the relationship in amber. This explains Adams's first response when he hears of James's death in 1916. He writes his confidante Elizabeth Cameron, "Not only was he a friend of mine for more than forty years, but he also belonged to the circle of my wife's set long before I knew him or her, and you know how I have clung to all that belonged to my wife."[4]

Yet clearly their paths had diverged, and part of the attraction was that each represented for the other the road not taken. One stayed single, the other married; one had a clear, undivided sense of vocation, the other moved restlessly from one commitment to another; one left his native country, the other made his home there despite the lure of Europe. Whenever the friends met, their bedrock affinity allowed them to tease each other about their mistaken choices. So James writes when the Adamses visit him in 1879, "I sat up with them till one o'clock this morning abusing the Britons. The dear Britons are invaluable for that."[5] And Clover mockingly concludes that it was "high time Harry James was ordered home by his family. . . . He had better go to Cheyenne and run a hog ranch."[6] When James later visits the Adamses in Washington, he is amused and appalled by their way of life. They become the exclusive Bonnycastles in his satirical story "Pandora" (1884), a couple who "had taken upon themselves the responsibilities of an active patriotism" but who exercise it chiefly in patronizing the president and other knuckleheads in power.[7] As Adams mockingly explains to an English friend, "poor Henry James" considers their Washington life "revolting in respect to the politics and the intrigues that surround it."[8]

The ridicule has a cutting edge. Behind the banter each needs to defend the choices he has made and deny the attractions of the alternatives. Most highly charged was the choice of expatriation. The temptation and opportunity were there for both men. As products of the cosmopolitan East Coast patriciate, each had spent much of his youth in Europe. Their years abroad, with their families or on the American version of the Grand Tour—designed to "finish" a young gentleman by teaching him European manners and the chief Continental languages—had made them familiar with the major cities and provided an entrée to various exclusive circles. Their class identity overrode their country of origin. As Adams recalled in the *Education*, "The Paris of Louis Philippe, Guizot, and de Tocqueville, as well as the London of Robert Peel, Macaulay, and John Stuart Mill, were but varieties of the same upper-class *bourgeoisie* that felt instinctive cousinship with the Boston of Ticknor, Prescott, and Motley."[9]

This international class was small enough to recognize its members instantly. It subsumed distinctive elements of national or individual identity under shared social rituals—letters of introduction certifying a new member, at-homes, luncheons, dinner parties, country weekends, the life of the club. It was not difficult for a presentable American with the right credentials to enter this world. James had clearly mastered the art when he ruefully noted at the height of the 1879 London season that he had "dined out almost every night for two months—*je n'en peux plus*"[10]; but his experience was not unique. The Adamses on their 1873 wedding journey were as much in demand, and when they returned for an extended London stay in 1878–79, Adams announced that they were retreating to Spain "to recover our nerves after nine months of dinners."[11] By the end of the century—an era of unprecedented affluence for American cosmopolites—the annual European journey had become routine: Adams calls it "the regular migration which characterises aquatic animals."[12]

So Adams might easily have made James's choice. His whole life reveals a pattern of vacillation between patriotic rootedness and expatriate flight. With an independent income, a circle of European friends, an easy familiarity with various foreign capitals, he might have followed the pattern of his numerous New England contemporaries who took up European residence or divided their time between the two continents. But for the decades of his prime (1870–1890) he deliberately chose another path. A male Adams, after all, was more than a member of a class: A special destiny inextricably bound him to the fate of America. This familial obligation to serve his country had been inculcated early into every son. Their particular line was diplomatic and other government office. Henry's father Charles Francis Adams was following the example of his own father and grandfather in becoming Minister to the Court of St. James, a position in which he rendered distinguished service during the Civil War. It seemed plausible that he would also follow his progenitors to the White House: In 1872 he was almost nominated for the presidency. Henry wrote an English friend that "my father commands much the most powerful support for the nomination, and it is not improbable that all parties may combine on him."[13] It was largely fortuitous that this did not happen.

What mattered, however, was not necessarily attaining high political office but serving the nation; distinguished stewardship was not optional for an Adams. The training could be coercive, and continued long into adulthood, as in John Adams's letter to his twenty-seven-year-old son,

John Quincy: "You come into life with advantages which will disgrace you if your success is mediocre. And if you do not rise to the head not only of your Profession, but of your country, it will be owing to your own *Lasiness, Slovenliness* and Obstinacy."[14] A patrilineal dynastic ambition fused with the welfare of the Republic. John Quincy Adams passed the family seal with which his father had ratified the 1783 peace treaty with England to his son Charles Francis with instructions to bequeath it to "a descendant worthy of him to whom the Seal first belonged."[15]

Under such a dispensation, training (or "education") was instrumental—strictly a means to an end. An Adams went abroad only to represent his country, or to prepare himself to serve it. Beyond that, "abroad" was a dangerous lure. Henry Adams was to remember sardonically in the *Education* that his father "felt no love for Europe, which, as he and all the world agreed, unfitted Americans for America." For a latter-day Puritan youth, it was of course the land of primrose paths, in the sensuality of Paris and points south, in the trifling habits, the dilettante sophistication of an urbane existence. So Adams recalls a time in his London years when he "felt himself catching an English tone of mind and processes of thought," as though these were communicable diseases.[16] As a young man with literary ambitions, he fears the loss of the American idiom. He catches himself using Anglicisms like "an 'awful swell' and 'such a funk' as calmly as though I were native to the language" and knows this will make him a comic figure to his countrymen.[17]

There was also the alarming example of his adored elder sister Louisa, married to a man without ambition and leading the useless existence (as her parents saw it) of a permanent expatriate. Her death at thirty-nine in Bagni di Lucca as a result of a carriage accident must have seemed like a judgment. Her chosen path was to be shunned, although—or perhaps because—she appeared to be entirely happy. So the young Henry had tried to prevent his brother John from coming abroad on his wedding journey because he might follow their sister's example in choosing "pleasure" over "duty." Henry himself feared contagion: "As a matter of pleasure of course both she and I and everyone else would prefer Europe . . . not because it's gay or because it's amusing, but because one is free and one's own master."[18] Most tellingly, Henry writes his brother Charles during his own extended European sojourn in the 1860s (even though at the time he was not free but serving as his father's private secretary), "I tell you frankly, three more years of this, and I shall never pass my life in America, nor permanently anywhere else."[19] A prolonged European stay unfitted Americans for America, made them lose touch with their own language, and choose pleasure over duty; it turned them into grasshoppers unable to settle and take up the serious business of life. For Adams, the siren call of the "Cunard steamers stretching in a long line to the horizon . . . offering to take him away"[20] contended with the stronger voice of his ancestors heard unto the third and fourth generation. Whether or not he was to inherit it, he had clearly received the full impress of the family seal.

The seriousness of this conflict was not clear to the twenty-three-year-old Adams when he accompanied his parents to London in 1861. Lincoln had appointed his father minister to England as the Civil War began, and Charles Francis Adams needed a trustworthy private secretary. Given the importance of the mission, the dignity of the position, and the prospective delights of a long London residence, there was reason to expect that the assignment would combine duty with pleasure, as father and son worked for Anglo-American accord. This hope failed to anticipate England's response to the war and the intolerable position in which it placed the family. Although Britain had abolished slavery in her own colonies three decades earlier, her government and governing class did not side with the Union against the Confederacy. British textiles needed Southern cotton, and a unified America was likely to be a more powerful rival than a divided one. The widespread support for the South that the Adamses encountered despite England's official neutrality is described at length in *The Education of Henry Adams*. The former colonies were being taught a lesson, and the American minister and his family felt their hosts' overt and covert hostility to their government.

Adams's recall in the *Education* of his response to this shock records his outrage: "He wanted nothing so much as to wipe England off the face of the earth. Never could any good come from that besotted race!" The experience awakened his dormant patriotism and briefly turned him into a crusader—a response alien to his cosmopolitanism and his complex, judicious, and ironic temperament. But there was no room for complexity in politics, it seemed. Of Palmerston, Russell, and Gladstone, Adams writes, "Complex these gentlemen were not"; and of Gladstone in particular, "Never in the history of political turpitude had any brigand of modern civilization offered a worse example."[21] The terms are moralistic rather than analytic, the tone outraged and unnuanced. They reflect Adams's reflex patriotism as the nation's survival becomes uncertain, while his brother Charles is fighting for the Union and he himself is marooned in what seems like hostile alien territory. After the disastrous Union loss at Bull Run, he writes in desperation to Charles, "Our flag, what has become of it? Who will respect it? What can we ever say for it after this."[22] The later turn of the tide in the North's favor, Lincoln's emancipation of the slaves and 1864 reelection, only confirm Adams's patriotic fervor, now couched in assured rather than despondent terms: "I never yet have felt so proud as now of the great qualities of our race, or so confident of the capacity of men to develop their faculties in the mass. . . . Europe has a long way to go yet to catch us up."[23] The survival of the *United* States confirms the success of the American experiment as a model for the eventual worldwide triumph of democracy.

Adams's patriotic fervor informs his first venture into print. In 1861–62, he published without his father's knowledge a series of unsigned articles in the *New York Times*, giving American readers a detailed account of England's reaction to the war. Based in part on his access to confidential information, their authorship had to be kept secret. Adams abruptly stopped writing them when he feared his identity would be exposed and his father embarrassed.[24] He expresses dismay at Britain's apparent indifference to the outcome, insisting that the English people are betraying "their natural allies" by remaining neutral: "Neutrality in a struggle like this is a disgrace to their great name."[25] His alarm increases when he realizes that this neutrality is benign compared to the outright hostility to the Union regularly expressed in the "needlessly insulting" and "wantonly malignant" tone of the London *Times* and other conservative papers.[26] When he understands that war may actually break out between the two nations, Adams—though working for reconciliation—inflames his American readers by describing a British political establishment "bent upon forcing a war, with the expectation of breaking America down, and putting an end to our Republican institutions."[27] There is a youthful bluster and unreflecting jingoism in these words, but the patriotic outrage would be confirmed by the mature Adams, not only in the *Education* but in an 1896 letter to Charles: "The idea that the upper class alone was hostile, is a total mistake. It was the hostility of the middle-class which broke our hearts, and turned me into a life-long enemy of everything English."[28]

Yet Adams's retrospective claim of lifelong enmity toward England is simply not accurate. It is his deep affection for the country that triggers his violent response to the sense of betrayal. Even in the early 1860s, as soon as the threat of war between the two nations passed, his love affair with England blossomed. Despite his frequent complaints about the patronage and snobbery of the British (a lifelong theme), despite his mocking self-portrait in his letters and in the *Education* as a social wallflower, he was in fact soon caught up in the hectic social whirl that his class and family and individual identity assured.

Adams's appointment books for the London years, writes his biographer Ernest Samuels, "tell of an almost endless succession of interviews, calls, breakfasts, dinner engagements, balls, teas, and at homes; and the record glitters with the names of Englishmen and their wives who were helping to make him a man of the great world."[29] The hostility of much of the upper class to the Union cause may even have served him, since it protected him from establishment bores and made English liberal and radical sympathizers eager to welcome him into their midst. The list of his friends grew, and one was destined to become a lifelong intimate—Charles Milnes Gaskell, a young Liberal with political ambitions who eventually followed his father into Parliament. Gaskell became the recipient of some of Adams's most important letters. The education Harvard had failed to provide was carried on extramurally by such figures as John Stuart Mill, Sir Charles Lyell, Browning, Dickens, Swinburne, met not on the page but in the flesh.[30] How could the theoretical notion of "perfidious Albion" compete against such a glittering company or challenge Adams's own sense of his rapid mental growth? England was reinventing him, putting him in touch with the most vital intellectual currents of his time.

As early as 1863, Adams was "getting to be of Dr. Johnson's opinion that nothing is equal to Fleet Street."[31] He would not have endorsed Johnson's dictum that "when a man is tired of London, he is tired of life; for there is in London all that life can afford" but would have understood it. He felt attracted not only to the city but to the whole spirit of the age it embodied: "Young England, young Europe, of which I am by tastes and education a part," as he writes to Charles.[32] This acknowledgment is the real beginning of Adams's maturity; in retrospect he saw himself in those years as "a young man who felt at home in England—more at home there than anywhere else."[33] The man of thirty who returned to America at the end of his father's ministry was no longer the flaming patriot of twenty-three bearing witness for his cause and country and damning the British for failing to support them. The description of his departure in the *Education* fuses the puritan-parental evaluation of Europe as the fallen world with the image of a lost Eden: "London had become his vice. . . . He lived deep into the lives and loves and disappointments of his friends. When at last he found himself back at Liverpool, his heart wrenched by the act of parting, he moved mechanically, unstrung."[34]

Adams's London years formed a kind of large receptacle in his memory that held a potent brew. Never again—not even in his late years in Paris—was he to find a city that offered so much nurture. "I gravitate to a capital by a primary law of nature,"[35] he said of himself; but London in the 1860s was not just any capital. It was the seat of history's greatest empire near its zenith, palpably the center of a deeply interesting political and intellectual life. It offered a rich, cosmopolitan culture open to a socially adept, observant, intellectually voracious young man like Henry Adams. No American city could compare, either then or later, not only because the United States was still relatively weak and provincial, but because America *had* no metropolis combining such disparate elements. Boston was still the intellectual capital, Washington the seat of government, New York the financial heart. But London was all of these, and the combination attracted hundreds of brilliant foreigners, from Karl Marx to Henry James, and prevented the English mind— which Adams called slow, eccentric, unsystematic, and illogical[36]— from dominating the culture of this cosmopolitan city.

This is why Adams as often recalls his London years with nostalgia as with bitterness, and why in his darkest moments he treats his 1868 return to America as a kind of exile. A year and a half after his immersion in the corrupt atmosphere of President Grant's Washington, he can hardly wait to get back. He writes his friend Gaskell, "I shall experience three months of civilisation again, and wash the dirty linen of my mind. . . . I want to meet everybody, talk with everybody, and know everybody."[37] The London sojourn does not disappoint him. Even the coal dust smells sweet; the pompous architecture of the commercial streets, the glitter of the fashionable world cast their spell, and his response elicits a tortured confession in the *Education:* "He loved it all—everything—had always loved it!"[38] He returns to spend much of his 1872–73 wedding journey introducing his bride to his friends and old haunts, since he still feels "more at home in London than in any other great city."[39]

This was not, however, how his bride felt. Clover Adams was not descended from presidents or foreign ministers, but in New England the Hoopers and the Sturgises were almost as venerable as the Adams clan, and she was not used to being treated as an unknown. The slightest hint of British condescension unleashed her fierce patriotic pride. In a letter home she recounts having "to tomahawk an offensive baronet who took me down [to dinner] and made sneering remarks about America. I laid him out stiff."[40] She considers herself the representative of a morally superior and crescent country amid the effete and moribund remnants of a once great culture living on borrowed time. Her friend Henry James saw through to the uneasiness that English patronage of Americans covered over, but she could accept neither the condescension nor James's tolerance. James's version of the story is that Clover preferred Washington to London because she was "someone" there and "nothing" in Britain.[41] Adams was caught in the middle and was partially sympathetic to both sides. But though he returned to London for an even longer stay in the late seventies, when working in European archives for his *History of the United States,* his wife's critical response permanently colored his attitude to the city. The pageantry and ceremony of English life simply confirmed her American identity. She writes her father, "I rejoice that I am alien & belong to a race who kicked out of this old harness so long ago."[42] Until Clover's death in 1885, "home" was the world the Adamses made for themselves in Washington.

This does not mean, however, that Adams was ready to write off the English connection. His father, grandfather, and great-grandfather had all been ministers to Britain, and this had created a long family tradition of working for Anglo-American accord. Even in the darkest days of the

Civil War, he and his father "clung to the idea that there would come a day . . . when our Government and theirs should act in harmony on large and liberal principles."[43] This was a transgenerational goal. "For a hundred years," in the words of the *Education*, "the chief effort of his family had aimed at bringing the Government of England into intelligent cooperation with the objects and interests of America."[44] Although Adams welcomes the shift in power that turns the United States into the dominant partner, he is not eager to see Britain's eclipse. "I am deranged by the rapidity of England's decline," he writes his brother Brooks in the middle of the Boer War; "I do not speak merely of her economics, but of her relative place in the world. . . . England, of course, means *we*."[45] And when in 1917 America finally joins the Allies, Adams writes his lifelong friend Gaskell, "Here we are, for the first time in our lives fighting side by side and to my bewilderment I find the great object of my life thus accomplished in the building up of the great Community of Atlantic Powers which I hope will at least make a precedent that can never be forgotten."[46] From this perspective, the transatlantic slanging match is over at last, and the common cause of the Anglo-Saxon nations made plain.

II

BEFORE ADAMS could see his mission in such global terms, however, he had to spend two decades trying to set his own country's house in order. He knew early on that he was born to write—but write what? for whom? and to what purpose? How might his intensely private sense of vocation serve the national interest? No Adams could evade such questions without a fear of self-indulgence. Unlike James, Adams had to find forms of writing that accommodated his conflicting needs: to satisfy his private literary vocation, and to be worthy of his illustrious public ancestors. This conflict produced one of the most discontinuous careers in American letters. He was a reforming journalist, a medievalist and academic, a historian of America, a novelist, a biographer and autobiographer, and—not least—the author of some of the finest letters in the language. His collected works would fill a long shelf. Toward the end of his life he persistently called himself a failure. The private and public goals he set himself did not fuse; his "career" did not add up as those of his less self-divided friends did. His deep interest in stages or phases—of history and of individual lives—may well have grown out of his awareness that he himself had passed through so many.

This sense of restless, inconclusive experiment is occluded in the magisterial but evasive *Education of Henry Adams*, more or less completed by 1907 but published only after his death in 1918. In this late attempt to order his life, a pattern of inevitable failure is superimposed on the long record of experimentation, and crucial parts are left out entirely, most shockingly the two decades between 1871 and 1891. Even when read only as an account of Adams's education (rather than his life), the book reveals some of the blindness of hindsight. This has long been recognized. The vital chaos of his career can, however, now be recovered by reading the fugitive pieces he chose not to reprint as well as the splendid six-volume edition of his letters. Following his work sequentially shows us just how far the late pessimism of the *Education* is from the spirit of his earliest writings. Van Wyck Brooks's conclusion that Adams was "all but born discouraged"[47] mistakenly takes the words of the elderly memoirist at face value.

The young Henry Adams was filled with a confident sense of private and public mission. Both before his departure for England and after his return, he was sure he had an important role to play. What he was learning from "young England, young Europe" might be applied to the reconstruction of his own country after the war. He sees himself playing a major part in that national undertaking. Even earlier, in 1860, he writes to Charles that the goal they must set themselves is that of Goethe and Schiller and Horace Mann—to educate their countrymen: "Our people are educated enough intellectually but it's damned superficial and only makes them more willful; our task so far as we attempt a public work, is to blow up sophistry and jam hard down on morality."[48] The terms here are vague, the tone callow; but the basic premise that they might lift their countrymen to a higher plane is confidently embraced and not soon abandoned.

Less than three years later, Adams's vision has crystallized, in great part as a result of his London life. He now sees the task as a group project for himself, Charles, and others of their age and upbringing: "We want a national set of young men like ourselves or better, to start new influences not only in politics, but in literature, in law, in society, and throughout the whole social organism of the country. A national school of our own generation." The model is the sort of metropolitan culture Adams has been living in: "In England the Universities centralize ability and London gives a field. So in France, Paris encourages and combines these influences." Although America has no comparable center and no clustered elite, it is the mission of their generation to make up the deficiency: "We ought to have a more concentrated power of influence than any that now exists."[49] The labor is collaborative, though individuals might work separately. Adams's first published book, *Chapters of Erie, and Other Essays* (1871) is such a venture, Charles contributing three essays, Henry four, with another jointly authored with Charles A. Walker. Most of the pieces had been previously published in British and American periodicals. Adams's first academic work, *Essays in Anglo-Saxon Law* (1876), which he edited and wrote in collaboration with his Harvard graduate students, is also a joint project.

His choice of the essay form is significant. It is discursive and purposive, not likely to be seen as self-indulgent; and it can be tailored for different audiences. Adams had no intention of becoming a journalist; he concluded at twenty-one that writing for the papers is "one of the most dangerous beginnings that a man can make."[50] Yet as we have seen, it was the beginning he *did* make, though his anonymous pieces for the *Times* might well have confirmed his sense of peril. But there are higher forms of journalism than newspaper reporting. Adams settled on the longer essay designed for the prestigious quarterlies in Britain and America, the *North American Review* in the United States, the *Edinburgh* and *Westminster* in Britain. He saved his most ambitious essays for these periodicals. The quarterlies had small circulations but enormous influence, and more than one writer's reputation — Macaulay's, for instance — had been made in their pages. The *North American Review* had only a few hundred subscribers, but it was close to being the house organ of America's intellectuals, and its impact was out of all proportion to its circulation. Adams's early essays in such journals are the product of a reforming zeal. He is more interested in his own country's welfare than in seeing it from the supranational perspective of his later years.

The "concentrated power of influence" Adams sought for himself and his associates stressed the importance of an intellectual elite. The nation's thinkers were to be what Coleridge had called a "clerisy": "the immediate agents and instruments in the great and indispensable work of perpetuating, promoting, and increasing the civilization of the nation."[51] In order to write honestly about America's problems, they needed a forum for critical thought. Tocqueville was Adams's god; he called *Democracy in America* "the Gospel of my private religion."[52] Like Tocqueville, he believes in the potential greatness of the United States but fears its potential for cultural leveling. He sharply criticizes an essay by Charles as pandering to the uneducated reader; perhaps his brother had decided that more refined methods would fail, but, Henry writes, "You have no business to say it without first trying the better way—and the trial ought to last your life."[53]

The experiment did not last Henry Adams's life; but he allowed it a good run, and he was proud of his early success. The three long essays on historical and economic topics he published in the *North American Review* and reprinted in *Chapters of Erie*, as well as the important piece on Lyell's *Principles of Geology*, established him as a trenchant and lucid writer on difficult topics, and won him the respect of intellectuals. But his real breakthrough came with the highly critical 1869 and 1870 *North American* essays called "The Session." The product of his return to Washington, and of his new confidence, these pieces established him as "the ranking censor of Congress."[54] He exulted to Gaskell, "For once I have smashed things generally and really exercised a distinct influence on public opinion by acting on the limited number of cultivated minds."[55]

The trickle-down effect he describes is at the heart of Adams's early theory of audience. He echoes it in more impersonal terms in the *Education*: "The difference is slight, to the influence of an author, whether he is read by five hundred readers, or by five hundred thousand; if he can select the five hundred, he reaches the five hundred thousand."[56] There is no question that at the time he *had* reached both elite and popular audiences. The 1869–1870 "Session" essay was reprinted and distributed by the Democratic Party in 1872 as a campaign document under the very un-Adamsish title *The Administration—a Radical Indictment! Its Shortcomings. Its Weakness, Stolidity. Thorough Analysis of Grant's and Boutwell's Mental Calibre. No Policy. No Ability.*[57]

Muckraking rhetoric was hardly Adams's chosen mode, but his indictment of Grant's administration and his exposure of corruption in high places, his claim that power has passed from individual politicians once guided by honor and principle to political parties and industrial "rings" or "special interests" does not mince words. "A network of rings controls Congress," he charges.[58] A supine president has surrendered his power and authority to the legislature and is reduced to bargaining for its support: "The success of any Executive measure must now be bought by the use of public patronage in influencing the action of legislators. The Executive has yielded without a protest to this necessity, which it has helped to establish."[59] Such writing falls well within the family tradition of serving the nation and does not yet suggest alienation.

At the time Adams wrote these reformist essays, he was convinced that such exposés might turn the tide, that the trend to corporate and party domination of American politics was a temporary aberration, not a permanent change. The spirit of these attacks is optimistic, the faith in republican institutions untouched: "We can see no reason why a democracy should be necessarily corrupt . . . and we maintain that the first and last duty of Congress and the President is to draw from the expression of the last ten years a lesson as to the PRINCIPLES OF REFORM."[60] The reforms he envisages are essentially conservative—a return to the Constitution's strict separation of executive, legislative, and judicial power; the creation of a class of civil servants appointed solely on the basis of merit, rather than as a political reward; legislators and judges who are not for sale; a president with an unshakable loyalty to the Republic willing to use his office to appeal directly to the people when its principles are subverted. Behind these ideals Adams still feels a bedrock faith in the ultimate wisdom of the citizenry. "The true policy of reformers," he writes in an 1869 essay, "is to trust neither to Presidents nor to senators, but appeal directly to the people."[61] As governmental corruption is exposed, the sense of popular revulsion will force reform.

This is Adams at his most sanguine. Only a year later, the confidence in immediate redress already seems dubious, though the ultimate faith in his mission remains intact. In the second of "The Session" essays, he sees the problems as long-term. The debate about reform, he says, "will occupy generations," and the reformer "must make his appeal, not to the public opinion of a day or of a nation, however large or intelligent, but to the minds of those persons who in every age and in all countries attach their chief interest to working out the problems of human society."[62] Yet his sense of mission and the faith that such problems *will* eventually be worked out are not yet touched. They are connected to his obligation to carry on the family tradition of stewardship. He describes the erection of "a comprehensive and solid structure of reform" as "a work not inferior in quality to that of the Republic's founders," and he considers it "an aim high enough to satisfy the ambition of one generation"—namely his own.[63]

Adams's patriotism, sense of vocation, and feeling of familial obligation are inextricably linked in this reformist enterprise, and its eventual failure explains his massive disappointment. Later, he writes as though the two years spent in Washington (1868–70) before taking up his Harvard position were decisive and the extinction of his hopes complete. So in the *Education* he dismisses these years entirely: "Every hope or thought which had brought Adams to Washington proved to be absurd. No one wanted him; no one wanted any of his friends in reform; the blackmailer alone was the normal product of politics as of business."[64] And in a 1911 letter to Charles, he insists that "Grant wrecked my own life, and the last hope or chance of lifting society back to a reasonably high plane. Grant's administration is to me the dividing line between what we hoped, and what we have got."[65]

Yet these are the inaccurate catastrophic reconstructions of a much later time. For much of Grant's presidency (1869–77), Adams not merely contributes to but edits the *North American Review*, a position that comes with his Harvard offer. He uses his editorial power to solicit contributions from writers interested in the cause of government reform, even though he himself no longer has the leisure to write such long essays.[66] And when Adams resigns from Harvard and returns to Washington in 1877, he remains sanguine about his cause and the role he and his friends might play. The future of the nation still seems bright to him, he writes Gaskell: "As I belong to the class of people who have great faith in this country and who believe that in another century it will be saying in its turn the last word of civilisation, I enjoy the expectation of the coming day, and try to imagine that I am myself, with my fellow *gelehrte* [men of learning] here, the first faint rays of that great light which is to dazzle and set the world on fire hereafter."[67]

A mocking faith may be a contradiction in terms, but this is the precarious balance of Adams's feelings at this point. It is also worth noting that his optimism is now focused on the distant future.

Certainly the present moment offered little reason to rejoice. The immediate post-Grant hopes of liberal Republican reformers were embodied in the ultimately disappointing figure of Carl Schurz, whom Adams warmly supported. An 1876 letter to Schurz reveals an energetic Adams working behind the scenes to create a reformist alternative to the anointed Republican nominee. He considers the possibility of founding a third party or temporarily bolting the Republicans in order to teach them a lesson.[68] When Schurz finally returns to the Republican fold to support Rutherford Hayes, Adams temporarily cuts off his own involvement in electoral politics. A week after Hayes's nomination, he writes Henry Cabot Lodge, "Politics have ceased to interest me. . . . The caucus and the machine will outlive me."[69] But politics had *not* ceased to interest Adams, then or ever, though the meaning of the word "interest" had changed. He no longer saw himself as a political activist, and nothing he wrote was ever again used by either—or any—party. His farewell to active politics is the 1876 essay with Charles called "The 'Independents' in the Canvass," a plague-on-both-your-houses piece in which the brothers argue that there is no difference between Democrats and Republicans, and that the two party platforms recall Swift's comic vision of politics in *Gulliver's Travels* as a contest between the "big-endians" and "little endians."[70]

Despite this momentary cynicism, Adams's 1877 resignation from Harvard and move to Washington signaled his growing fascination with people in power. Though appointed as a medievalist, he had also taught American history. His restlessness in provincial Boston, his love of capitals, his decision to devote himself to writing American history (and the need to work in government archives) all contributed to the move. But most important was the magnetic attraction of the nation's power center. Adams's decision to live across Lafayette Square from the White House (and to build a house with a direct view of it) is hardly a sign of alienation from political life. Though Adams was never to hold (or to seek) elective or appointive office, he wanted to be in the orbit of those who did. Given his personal gifts and family credentials, he could easily meet anyone who interested him. The exclusive political salon the Adamses established soon became legendary, a social and intellectual center that separated those they considered worth talking to in public life from the hacks. He had an early sense of the influence such a center might exert. When his father was elected to Congress in 1860, he had urged his mother to make *her* salon "the first in Washington" and predicted that her drawing-room would "hatch all the Presidents for the next twenty years."[71]

His 1876 farewell to political involvement had been premature. Five years later Adams was still working behind the scenes as well as through the reformers' "recognised mouth-piece," Carl Schurz.[72] James's visit in 1882 and his friend's disapproval of the atmosphere of political intrigue that dominated the salon made Adams realize how much he depended on this stimulant. "To me its only objection is its over-excitement," he writes to Gaskell; "Socially speaking we are very near most of the powerful people, either as enemies or as friends."[73] He loved the sense of access his position gave him, as well as the freedom he gained by not seeking office. He was the Olympian spectator, knowing all but keeping his hands clean.

From first to last Adams claims that he has no interest in power. "You work for power. I work for my own satisfaction," he writes to Charles in 1869.[74] And in the well-known formulas of the *Education*, "Every friend in power is a friend lost"; "Power is poison."[75] But the word is ambiguous, and some of its meanings coincide with what Adams did want. In a democracy power can mean holding office, making administrative decisions, enacting legislation, directing bureaucracies, being in the public eye: None of these interest Adams. His vow never to make a speech or run for office is kept; it is his way of refusing to "follow the family go-cart."[76] But power can also mean exerting public influence, shaping minds and policies, molding national consciousness, and these aspects certainly did interest him. If, as Dennis Wrong defines it, *"Power is the capacity of some persons to produce intended and foreseen effects on others,"*[77] Adams in his middle years was still pursuing it. He writes to a correspondent in 1879 "that one man may reasonably devote his life to the effort at impressing a moral on the national mind, which is now almost a void."[78] His language is semicoercive and reminds a modern reader of Joyce's Stephen Dedalus, who vows to "forge in the smithy of my soul the uncreated conscience of my race." The two ambitions fuse patriotism with patronage, and both suggest the imposition of the will. There is less faith here in the people's wisdom than in Adams's early reformist phase, but the desire to influence and the expectation of success remain.

His interest in power becomes that of a detached historian rather than of a reformer and participant. Adams's vicarious involvement in past and present politics is inescapable. What has changed is his vehicle. He stops writing the reformist essays that first brought him to public notice. He uses his training as a historian to see his country's destiny from a long-range perspective. The genre of history is more likely to fulfill his personal ambition to be a writer who will be read long after any given administration has departed. Like the essay, it is discursive and potentially purposive—a legitimate continuation of the family legacy. "Our house needs a historian in this generation," Adams writes Charles, "and I feel strongly tempted by the quiet and sunny prospect, while my ambition for political life dwindles as I get older."[79] History was a recognized branch of letters, and writers like Bancroft, Motley, and Prescott had paved the way for a Massachusetts-born, Harvard-educated man to make his mark. Adams knew that such a career could lead to great rewards. In encouraging his student Henry Cabot Lodge to take up the profession, he writes from Boston, "Anyone who has the ability can enthrone himself here as a species of literary lion with ease, for there is no rival to contest the throne. With it, comes social dignity, European reputation, and a foreign mission to close."[80] Both Bancroft and Motley had served, like Adams's progenitors, as Minister to the Court of St. James.

What interested him more than the public rewards was the power to "impress a moral on the national mind." If reform was indeed to be the work of generations, Americans needed a clearer sense of their own history. He embarked on the decade-long project that produced the *History of the United States of America During the Administrations of Thomas Jefferson and James Madison* (1889–91), a work in nine volumes that set a new standard in American historical writing. The sheer length tacitly assumes the importance of the nation, since Adams devotes to sixteen years of her administrative history nearly as many words as Gibbon needed to describe *The Decline and Fall of the Roman Empire*.

Gibbon and Macaulay and Bancroft were all very much in his mind; his ambition matched theirs.[81] But long before he thought in such terms, Adams had seen himself as an annalist of America. In Washington in 1860, when he was only twenty-two, he wrote Charles a series of letters designed to record for posterity the decisive events of the time: "I want to have a record of this winter on file, and . . . would like to think that a century or two hence when everything else about us is forgotten, my letters might still be read and quoted as a memorial of manners and habits at the time of the great secession of 1860."[82] His words are imbued with a sense of history in the making, and with the greatness of America's destiny; but they claim for Adams himself no more than the authority of an immediate witness and scribe.

The *History of the United States*, on the other hand, was hardly a modest undertaking, either in scope or in interpretive authority. The project was the vehicle for the shift in Adams's sense of mission. In the words of J. C. Levenson, "As an historian, he made politics his subject, not his career."[83] He thus reshaped not only his patrilineal imperative but the legacy of earlier American historians, who had largely worked in the epic mold. What he was writing, as the lumbering full title of his work suggests, was not a panoramic history of the country but an account of its administrative leaders and their decisions in office. He sharpens the focus to concentrate on the elements of the American experience that most engage him personally. He also dismisses the more comprehensive kind of history as unwieldy and superficial. "The microscope will be a more valuable instrument than the field glass," Adams writes in a highly critical review of a historical work that took the opposite tack.[84]

With the exception of its wide-ranging introductory and concluding chapters, Adams's *History* focuses on the behavior of men in power. He is interested in the force and frustrations of office, in the methods of diplomacy and in the battles of the War of 1812. At this stage in his career he wants to record public actions and decisions, not the pattern of ordinary lives, nor the movements of consciousness, nor the transformation of the land as the settlers move westward and the villages become cities. Executive, diplomatic, legislative, and military power are his subject. He is as fascinated by the nation's European antagonists (like Napoleon and Canning) as by Jefferson or Madison. Writing this detailed account puts Adams in the presidential seat day by day, contemplating options, weighing consequences, making decisions. It also makes an armchair warrior of a man who had missed the Civil War. The chronicle quality of his work, its immediacy and staggering richness of detail, his heavy reliance on primary sources and the actual words of the participants, seats Adams inside the councils of state while giving him the detached vantage of posterity.

The *History* is also a vehicle for Adams's patriotism, his choice of America over Europe. The particular era he chooses, after all, is that of the ruinous Napoleonic Wars. His primary interest is Jefferson's conviction that America could demonstrate her new independence and commitment to peace by refusing to join the conflict. At stake is the idea of American exceptionalism, the conviction that his country's special destiny would exempt her from the tragic patterns of European history. The secular version of this idea stressed America's geographical isolation, unlimited room for expansion, abundant resources, and freedom from established power and precedent. For all these reasons, the United States might evade the history of war and civil strife that had dominated Europe. By the middle of the nineteenth century the ideology of American exceptionalism had achieved a "presumptive consensus," in the words of a recent commentator; the country "could escape historical change" and "would not follow Europe into a historical future."[85]

Adams's *History* is a reluctant challenge to that consensus. The possibility that America might escape the pattern of the European past is deeply attractive to him but also becomes a hypothesis his narrative tests. The presumption of experience, which the new nation cannot afford to accept, is "that what had ever been must ever be." Yet Americans as an independent people ought not "to waste time in following European examples, but must devise new processes of their own."[86] So Adams begins. Yet by the end of Jefferson's presidency, his pacifist strategy for keeping America out of the vortex of the European conflict is bankrupt. War with Britain or France, or possibly both, seems inevitable. And Adams grimly concludes that the United States "must bear the common burdens of humanity, and fight with the weapons of other races in the same bloody arena; that she could not much longer delude herself with hopes of evading laws of Nature and instincts of life; and that her new statesmanship which made peace a passion could lead to no better result than had been made by the barbarous system which made war a duty."[87] So much for the country's unprecedented destiny.

The United States becomes a helpless pawn in the contest between England and France. Adams's account of the War of 1812, which takes up most of the Madison volumes, is no epic tale. The conflict seems futile and purposeless, a tragedy of errors with here and there a glorious victory. America's occasional triumphs are mere episodes in the prevailing pattern of confusion and internal dissension, unpreparedness, and plain incompetence. The war ends in a stalemate, in futility and mutual exhaustion, and the Treaty of Ghent (which Adams's grandfather had helped to draft) is essentially a return to the *status ante bellum*. How could a young country, with a new set of national imperatives, have become enmeshed in the dusty spiderweb of European politics? The answer must be that America was not after all exceptional, that her destiny was inextricably linked to Europe's, that she was subject to the same factionalism and political opportunism, the same temptation to expand her territory without scruple, as other countries, that she was not in fact exempt from the "laws of Nature and instincts of life."

This fatalistic conclusion does not prevent Adams from voicing his impatience with European precedents and contrasting the "lithe young figure" of the free American with the "decrepitude" of the European, locked into a system in which church, state, and hereditary privilege inhibit energy and initiative. "The average American," he writes, "was more intelligent than the average European, and was becoming every year still more active-minded as the new movement of society caught him up and swept him through a life of more varied experiences."[88] There are many such passages in the *History*, expressing Adams's patriotism and his desire to please his American readers. And his Jefferson is a man of cultivation, vision, and principle. The failure is neither in the people nor in the leadership but in the political process itself. Power transforms the man, or fatally compromises his original ideals. So even the democratic Jefferson, who once received official visitors in corduroy overalls and rode his own horse from the White House to the Capitol, assumes royal prerogatives. In forcing through the Louisiana Purchase without constitutional authority, he "made himself monarch of the new territory, and wielded over it, against its protests, the powers of its old kings."[89] Madison's seizure of West Florida in 1810 is similarly an "arbitrary act," a "usurpation which no other country was bound to regard."[90] Adams is no propagandist for America's Manifest Destiny; he sees such actions as the opportunistic abandonment of principle by men in power. Even Jefferson had confessed that the Louisiana Purchase made "blank paper of the Constitution."[91]

Yet Adams's reluctance to accept the disturbing implications of his own narrative is suggested by the idealistic chapters that bracket it at either end. They contain most of his more patriotic passages, and they encapsulate his vision of America's promise; but they seem strangely out of keeping with what follows or precedes. So the famous early chapter on "American Ideals" captures a Whitmanesque vision of the country: "Who would undertake to say that there was a limit to the fecundity of this teeming source?" Adams asks rhetorically. And he foresees a future in which widespread education and his countrymen's creative power might move them "to the level of that democratic genius which found expression in the Parthenon."[92] The peroration of the Madison volumes echoes this patriotic vision: "The American, in his political character, was a new variety of man"; and it was unlikely that "America should under any circumstances follow the experiences of European development."[93] But despite these optimistic echoes of the exceptionalist argument, the *History* ends with a set of disturbing possibilities and unanswered questions. Although Americans might escape "the violence and extravagances of Old-World development," the Tocquevillean alternative Adams imagines is not much preferable: "The inertia of several hundred million people, all formed in a similar social mould, was as likely to stifle energy as to stimulate evolution." And his final words raise troubling questions about the future: Could America avoid the corruptions of ease, the loss of idealism attendant on physical content? Adams concludes, "For the treatment of such questions, history required another century of experience."[94]

At the heart of the book, then, Adams's patriotic idealism conflicts with his darker vision of America's destiny in the century that followed his chronicle, much of which he had lived through, and which had steadily eroded his early patriotic zeal. This explains his later disen-chanted sense that the *History*, conceived in the 1870s but long in the making, "belongs to the *me* of 1870; a strangely different being from the *me* of 1890. There are not nine pages in the nine volumes that now express anything of my interests or feelings; unless perhaps some of my disillusionments."[95] This internal conflict, reflected in the narrative as we have it, accounts for the very different interpretations that Adams's serious readers have offered. On the one hand, Ernest Samuels concludes that "The *History* reflected much of the patriotic optimism of 1876"; and J. C. Levenson sees Adams's account of the war as proof that "America not only faced trial by combat successfully, but came from it with moral integrity." Barbara Miller Solomon, on the other hand, treats the *History* as "a swan song to the American dream" that shows that Adams "had lost faith in the criteria of his parents long before he admitted it"; and George Hochfield concludes that the work answers negatively the implicit question asked by the chapter on "American Ideals": "Can these ends be realized?"[96] Evidence for both an optimistic and a pessimistic reading can readily be found in the body of the *History*, and Adams himself suggests that the later stages of writing were in effect alienated labor.[97]

But how might such divided purposes serve Adams's desire to "impress a moral on the national mind"? He himself is far from certain what conclusions to draw from his story, and in the course of writing it he gives up the prerogative of confident interpretation. The reception of the *History* was one of his greatest disappointments; the "national mind" was not impressed. It sold a respectable 1,500–2,000 copies and was highly regarded by Adams's fellow historians, who elected him to the presidency of the American Historical Association. But the popular audience of a Gibbon, a Macaulay, a Bancroft permanently eluded him, even in the "continent of a hundred million people fifty years hence"[98] he claimed to be addressing. He knew he was telling a tale more likely to offend than inspire his countrymen. He predicts that "the American public will growl, for I have some unpleasant stories to tell of them." And he compares his failure to interest the larger audience with its hostility to James: "As you know," he writes an English correspondent, "the American public growls a good deal at having its face slapped; even poor Henry James was a victim."[99] If the *History* had more consistently celebrated American triumphs and achievements, it might have matched the popularity of Macaulay's *History of England*, which had sold 140,000 copies and remained in print for generations.[100] But Adams's increasingly unreliable patriotism, in which the nation's progress is constantly undermined by its tendency to repeat historical precedent, was inevitably disturbing to American amour propre. In

Adams's own disillusioned words, "Man refuses to be degraded in self-esteem, of which he has never had enough to save him from bitter self-reproaches. He yearns for flattery, and he needs it."[101]

Adams's increasingly critical sense of America's destiny initiated a crisis of confidence about audience that was never resolved. He began with the expectation of finding a responsive American readership, and he undertook the *History* at a moment in his life when this hope was still vital. By the time the work was finished, his expectation of being read had evaporated and he was no longer sure for whom he was writing. His uncertainty anticipated and was confirmed by the disappointing reception of the *History*. His letters all through the 1880s reveal his increasing uneasiness about the likelihood of reaching a large audience, either directly or through the funnel of a chosen elite.

What disappears is not only his faith in the ultimate wisdom of the people but in "the influence on public opinion" that a "limited number of cultivated minds" might exert, as he had earlier put it. His vision of the coterie changes. It is no longer a link to the larger culture but a fortified island within it. Its nucleus is "the five of hearts," the intimate circle that included the Adamses, John and Clara Hay, and the geologist Clarence King. It is based in Washington but admits a few of the like-minded from other places, either in the United States or England.[102] Adams stresses its exclusiveness. As he only half-mockingly writes Hay, who is abroad meeting what might be called its English branch, "The universe hitherto has existed in order to produce a dozen people to amuse the five of hearts. Among us, we know all mankind. We or our friends have canvassed creation, and there are but a dozen or two companions in it."[103] The coterie becomes not a group of exceptional "improvised" or actual Europeans but a transnational aristocracy of intellect. Adams writes William James, "A few hundred men represent the entire intellectual activity of the whole thirteen hundred millions."[104] He relegates his interest in reaching a wider audience to the distant past: "Twenty years ago, I was hungry for applause. . . . Today . . . the public is as far away from me as is the celebrated Kung-fu-tse [Confucius]."[105] The "concentrated power of influence" Adams had once sought for himself and his colleagues is seen as a delusion. For all his arrogance about the influence of his circle, he is aware that his earlier democratic idealism lay in ruins.

From the 1880s on, Adams deliberately severs his ties to the audience. Most of the books he wrote between 1880 and his death in 1918 were published anonymously or pseudonymously or privately printed for distribution to "worthy" readers by Adams himself. The *History of the United States* and the collection of his *Historical Essays* (1891) are the exceptions to what became a rule: ignore the public audience. So *Democracy: An American Novel* (1880) was published anonymously; *Esther* (1884) appeared under the pseudonym of Frances Snow Compton; his book on Tahiti, *Memoirs of Marau Taaroa* (1893), was privately printed, as was its heavily revised and retitled 1901 version; even the late classics through which most readers know him, *Mont-Saint-Michel and Chartres* (1904) and *The Education of Henry Adams* (1907), were available for a decade only in minuscule private editions intended for the chosen few. Adams deliberately withheld or refused to acknowledge the works to which he devoted his major intellectual energy. It was only by separating himself as a writer from himself as a public figure (especially an Adams) that he might write as he pleased and ignore the demands of popular taste and the Adams family imperative of national stewardship. Anonymity made him a free agent.

This is suggested by *Democracy*, a book that appeared in 1880 but whose authorship was not disclosed until after Adams's death: It was one of the best kept secrets in American literary history. Though it was written quickly while Adams was working (officially) on the *History of the United States*, and though it was published a decade before the completion of that major work, Adams's bitter novel came closer to expressing "the *me* of 1890" than the magnum opus completed in that year, which, as Adams said, was closer to "the *me* of 1870." *Democracy* gives voice to his intense disillusionment with American political life. "I bade politics good-bye when I published Democracy,"[106] he writes his brother Brooks in 1902. Like many of Adams's retrospective statements, this is not strictly true. His interest in politics persisted, and his involvement revived during the years of the Roosevelt presidency, as we will see. But *Democracy* does record the permanent break between Adams's fascination with politics and his idealism. His shift from the discipline of fact to the freedom of fictional invention was an escape from family tradition—a kind of self-indulgence. This is one of the reasons he could not acknowledge authorship.

Democracy records its author's unpatriotic conclusion that the Republic is doomed to reenact the failures of earlier forms of government. Although it is often interpreted as a roman à clef rooted in Adams's shocked response to the Grant administration, its terms are generic and timeless rather than local, contingent, and particular, from the title and subtitle — *Democracy: An American Novel*, rather than, say, "The Gilded Age" or "Washington Corruption" — to the categorical statements of its confident narrator, or the assured conclusion of its heroine, Madeleine Lee: "She had got to the bottom of this business of democratic government, and found out that it was nothing more than government of any other kind."[107] Adams deprives his country's experiment of its uniqueness. At stake, again, is the idea of American exceptionalism. Words like "court" and "dynasty" describe the world of democratic politics; there are flatterers and petitioners for office; monarchical forms are aped in the capital, as in the reception for the English princess, at which two thrones command opposite ends of the ballroom, one for royalty, the other for the president.[108] And political corruption is treated not as a temporary and remediable offense but as a predictable reenactment of an ancient pattern. As the jaundiced European diplomat Baron Jacobi sarcastically puts it: "You Americans believe yourselves to be excepted from the operation of general laws. . . . Rome, Paris, Vienna, Petersburg, London, all are corrupt; only Washington is pure!" Yet corruption, he insists, is no stranger to the United States: "Everywhere men betray trusts both public and private, steal money, run away with public funds." And he predicts that in another century the United States will be "more corrupt than Rome under Caligula; more corrupt than the Church under Leo X; more corrupt than France under the Regent!"[109] The more tentative final questions of the *History* about the fate of the democratic experiment are thus preemptively answered.

Adams the consummate Washington insider invents an outsider surrogate in Madeleine Lee — an observant, sophisticated young widow who initially knows nothing about Washington but wants to learn how her country is governed: "What she wished to see, she thought, was the clash of interests, the interests of forty millions of people and a whole continent, centering at Washington; guided, restrained, controlled, or unrestrained and uncontrollable, by men of ordinary mould; the tremendous forces of government, and the machinery of society, at work. What she wanted was POWER."[110] But not at any price, since she rejects the offer of marriage from Senator Ratcliffe, the corrupt but intelligent and charming legislator who is likely to become the next president. Her refusal expresses her revulsion as she grasps his sordid methods of seeking and holding on to public office. She retreats fastidiously from the defilement American political success apparently entails. She will remain a spectator rather than a participant, like the Adams whose new detachment from the political scene she gradually comes to represent.

Spectatorial distance dominates Adams's perspective. He describes the arena of Washington politics as precisely that—an arena. On view below is the performance of normal politics—the inauguration of a new president, the scramble for offices, the contest for power and loot. But the reader's seat is nowhere near the action. Along with Mrs. Lee, we remain detached observers. She views the Senate from the specta-tors' gallery. The speeches delivered below are performative rather than substantive and are never quoted directly. Invited to the White House, she leaves the reception line before meeting the president and is led to an eyrie from which she can survey the scene below. Her com-panion is the British ambassador, aptly named Lord Skye; together they watch what Adams calls "the slowly eddying dance of Democ-racy." Metaphors of performance—of dance, opera, theater—domi-nate the narrative and suggest that the whole political world is at best an illusion. Adams's other metaphorical cluster is scientific: Politics is an "organic disease"; Ratcliffe is a laboratory "specimen," to be used "as young physiologists use frogs and kittens"; the coming catastrophic demise of democracy is an event in space visible only through a tele-scope.[111] The images create emotional distance between observer and observed and prize spectatorship over involvement.

In this world, no cause is worth fighting for, reform is a delusory hope, retreat into political quietism the only honorable option. Madeleine Lee's newly gained knowledge shocks her; she is not yet hardened. But the narrator's tone is as cynical as Baron Jacobi's, as in this description of the White House and Capitol on the eve of the inauguration: "This is the moment when the two whited sepulchres at either end of the Avenue reek with the thick atmosphere of bargain and sale. The old is going; the new is coming. Wealth, office, power are at auction. Who bids highest? who hates with most venom? who intrigues with most skill? who has done the dirtiest, the meanest, the darkest, and the most political work? He shall have his reward."[112] The pattern is as recurrent and inexorable as the seasons. Far from being an aberration, Senator Ratcliffe is the quintessential politician, and Adams occasionally permits him to make a real case for his brand of *realpolitik*. He may be a crook, but he is not a liar.

Democracy is a postmeliorist work: The political abuses it exposes are seen as structurally inevitable.[113] The only escape is into alienation or expatriation—a withdrawal from the *polis*. At the end of the novel, Mrs. Lee is bound for Egypt, as far away from her own country as she can safely travel: "Democracy has shaken my nerves to pieces. Oh, what rest it would be to live in the Great Pyramid and look out forever at the polar star!"[114] She is in flight toward an imaginary goal where the sordid reality of contemporary life is simply expunged.

Unlike his heroine, Adams was not yet ready to leave the country. But then virtually no one knew him as the author of this national libel. Adams refused permanently to acknowledge *Democracy* as his, even after it had become an international *succès de scandale*: Nine printings were called for in the first year,[115] and the book was massively pirated in Britain and translated into French. He would have lost his easy access to people in power if he were known as its author. The professional politician's response can be imagined from Adams's mimicry in an ironic letter to Hay—one of the few people in on the secret: "We regard [*Democracy*] with loathing, as must be the case with every truly honest citizen. . . . Every virtuous citizen must join in trampling on these revolting libels."[116] The novel's vogue in England, which the Prince of Wales helped to fuel by calling it "the first American book he has read which seems true all round,"[117] must have made Adams even more reluctant to reveal himself. He kept the secret even from his English intimates, as well as from his brother Charles, who opined that the author must be "coarse" and "half-educated."[118] That Adams was aware of the perils of exposure is suggested by an 1897 letter to his young friend Bay Lodge, the son of Senator Lodge and a budding writer: "I have the material for an American novel that would make your literary fortune and oblige you to live in Europe forever."[119]

The connection between telling unpleasant truths about America and beating a retreat to foreign parts becomes clearer after Adams finishes the *History of the United States*. While he is writing it all through the 1880s, he suspends the revulsion from America expressed in the most bitter passages of *Democracy*. Only toward the end of his labors can he acknowledge the erosion of his faith in America's future, the disappointment of his hopes for molding the national consciousness, and his alienation from his country. As he contemplates his nearly completed work, he describes the pattern of his narrative and its probable reception to Hay: "All my wicked villains will be duly rewarded with Presidencies and the plunder of the innocent; all my models of usefulness and intelligence will be fitly punished, and deprived of office and honors; all my stupid people, including my readers, will be put to sleep for a thousand years." His revulsion extends to his entire involvement with national politics, past or present. As he writes in 1888 to an English friend, "Politics have been the single uncompensated disappointment of life—pure waste of energy and moral."[120]

The approaching end of his labors frees him to leave. Brief trips to Japan and to Cuba had restored his taste for travel, seen now as escape rather than renewal. He recalls his feelings in Cuba: "I had not one wish ever to see Washington or home again. My only instinct was to run away."[121] There was nothing to keep him in that city, or in America, any longer. He was a childless widower; his long historical task was done, his future a blank. The publication and reception of the *History*—its failure to find a larger audience—strengthened his sense of the bankruptcy of his earlier goals. To found a "national school of our own generation" that might exert a "concentrated power of influence" on the country? To use his writings "to impress a moral on the national mind"? Words, words, words. The future looked bleak, but there was an alternative. A British review of *Democracy* had linked the author's vision to a new pattern of American upper-class life: "We cease to wonder at and can scarcely condemn the flight of the elegant exiles disgusted by a system so hopeless."[122]

Adams was eventually to join them. In 1890 he undertook a long journey to the South Seas and from there to Europe that had neither a clear goal nor a contemplated end. He had no itinerary and no sense of when, if ever, he would be back: "My return is wholly indefinite," he writes to Charles, his early collaborator in the abortive attempt to found a national school of their generation. His flight is linked to his new, distinctly unpatriotic feelings about his country: "You and I have had our minds fairly soaked with the kerosene of American ideas and interests, until we can neither absorb more, nor even retain what we have. Nausea has set in, and we might as well wash the nasty stuff out of us now, as let it make us sick. . . . Whenever the nausea leaves me, I shall come straight home."[123] Here was the "irritable dislike of America" Adams was to identify as a prime attribute of his "improvised Europeans." As we will see, the nausea never left him, and the meaning of "home" became more and more of a mystery.

V

Adams Adrift,
1890–1918

Thick foliage
Placid beneath warm suns,
Tawn fore-shores
Washed in the cobalt of oblivions;
. . . .
A consciousness disjunct,
Being but this overblotted
Series
Of intermittences;

Ezra Pound
Hugh Selwyn Mauberley

I

LIKE POUND'S Mauberley, Henry Adams in the 1890s allows himself
to drift. The strict discipline of the decade that produced the *History of*
the United States is abandoned. The very idea of a task, historical, literary, or practical, becomes repugnant. Duty, drilled into him from earliest childhood, is simply shrugged off. He strips his life of obligations
and stops working toward a goal. He is a free agent: His tomes are completed, his wife and parents dead; he has no children; he holds no
office and owes allegiance to no institution; he can go anywhere and
not count the cost. Nothing holds him.

If absence of restraint were liberation, Adams might have qualified.
But all those negatives—no, no, no, not, nothing—tell a story of
emptiness rather than freedom and fulfillment. His odyssey is centrifugal, a goalless quest driven by the need to escape. Even before the voyage that sends him round the world in 1890–92, he is feverish to take
his leave. A trial journey to Japan in 1886 had given him a taste for

97

flight, the farther the better. He writes Gaskell on his return that he has vowed "to close up everything here, finish history, cut society, foreswear forever strong drink and politics, and start in about three years for China, never to return. . . . Sooner or later, if health holds out, I shall drift there; and once there, I shall not soon drift back."[1] This is hardly a plan: to allow oneself to drift is to surrender control.

He never gets to China, but between 1890 and the beginning of the First World War, he spends more time out of America than in it.[2] He travels to the South Seas, Australia, Ceylon, Mexico, and the Caribbean, to eastern and southern and northern as well as western Europe, to Egypt and Turkey and Russia. By the end of the nineties he establishes a routine, leaving Washington in the spring, returning as winter begins. Eventually he sets up a second home in Paris, where he spends half the year. But the word "home"—connoting stability, rootedness, belonging, being native not foreign—seems inappropriate. He has no home. His uprootedness recalls his prediction during the London years: "Three more years of this, and I shall never pass my life in America, nor permanently anywhere else."[3] He had stayed in England six years longer, and the family curse— that Europe unfits Americans for America—belatedly falls upon him.

His letters convey an unmistakable sense of hysteria. Even before his departure he writes Gaskell, "The object of such long expeditions about the Pacific is to tire myself out till home becomes rest." Once on his way, he warns him, "Of my plans, I can say nothing. . . . I may make a sudden bolt, and turn up in India, in China or even in England, without notice." But the journey round the world does not cure him; the grasshopper cannot rest. He understands his own incoherence, and even his formerly balanced sentences now mirror the chaos: "I want to go—go—go—anywhere—to the devil—Sicily—Russia— Siberia—China—only keep going," he writes Elizabeth Cameron in 1899; "At moments I have shivered on the verge of—I wont say melancholia, but chronic depression, and have looked about me rather desperately for some means of escape."[4]

Elizabeth Cameron was in part the cause of this anxiety, and would never be the cure. Married to but emotionally estranged from Senator Cameron of Pennsylvania, her home was a Washington social center, where the beautiful young wife held court. It was a political salon too, though its tone was less elevated intellectually than the Adamses' had

been. By the 1890s he was hopelessly in love with her, hopelessly not
because she failed to respond but because separation, divorce, flight
from Washington—a radical break with convention—seemed emotionally impossible. Their impeccably correct courtship, carried on in
letters or in full public view, made Adams suffer the tortures of Tanta-
lus. He wanted more intimacy than she could give, and leaving Washington was an alternative. His letters from abroad are intense, the gap
of miles releasing the passionate words, since they cannot lead to
actions. "I suppose no woman can have the heart to object to being
made love to, if the offender remains ten thousand miles away,"[5] he
writes with self-lacerating irony from Tahiti. When and whether he
comes back he leaves to her discretion. It was an impasse, though
eventually they work out a modus vivendi, and Paris becomes an
attractive alternative to Washington because special relationships like
theirs were not so special there.

But Adams's romantic friendship with Elizabeth Cameron is not
the primary cause of his alienation from his native land, though it certainly intensifies it. He is more and more out of sympathy with the
late-nineteenth-century transformation of America and often plays the
scolding role of Thersites. He writes her in 1895 that he is glad to be
out of the country: "The behavior of our government and monied-men
irritates me, wears on my nerves, and makes me talk much more than
is wise or virtuous. Away from America I am always more human." He
becomes obsessed by the changes he is witnessing, particularly the
shift in power to the new plutocracy. "My country in 1900," he writes
Gaskell, "is something totally different from my own country of 1860. I
am wholly a stranger in it."[6] That the adjective "own" should be
attached to the earlier but not the later period speaks volumes.

Ownership is a significant part of the problem. The nation that had
once belonged to him—to his family, to his class—had passed into
other hands. The civic-minded, moralistic patriciate of the eastern
seaboard, long used to wielding power and exerting influence, was
rapidly being displaced by two intruders—the plutocrat and the new
immigrant, alike raw, energetic, fiercely ambitious, temporarily indifferent to the public weal. They had not come into life with hereditary
advantages, after all, and had to make their way. The two groups gradually fuse in Adams's mind despite their obvious differences; together

they threaten the ancien régime he had come to feel he represented. He avidly reads Saint-Simon's *Memoirs* and sees the decline of his own class mirrored in the French nobleman's pages.

Adams had been counting the days since the late 1860s, when he and Charles first saw a speculative fever replacing the productive labor of the prewar years. Many of his early essays emphasize economic issues, though they use ethical terms. So in "American Finance, 1865–69" he describes the veterans returning from the battlefield "to plunge into the profligate and swindling transactions of the stock-exchange and the gold room." The great corporations simply buy the laws and judicial decisions they need from corrupt elected officials. America under plutocratic rule squanders the "advantages left to it by a past and purer generation."[7] That Adams publishes this hard-hitting essay anonymously in a British journal and never reprints it in his own country suggests a fear that he had gone too far. His classic attack on the plutocrats, however, pulls no punches. In "The New York Gold Conspiracy" (1870) the attempt by Jay Gould and Jim Fisk to corner the gold market represents the cynical opportunism and contempt for civic responsibility that threatened the nation. Adams's brilliant satire links Gould and Fisk to the railway magnates Vanderbilt and Drew and by extension to a whole generation of speculative capitalists—a new autocracy, "an empire within a republic." "Cormorants," he calls them, with "no conception of a moral principle." The control of vast corporate riches by a few individuals becomes a direct threat to the state: "Over this wealth and influence,—greater than that directly swayed by any private citizen, greater than is absolutely and personally controlled by most kings, and far too great for public safety in a democracy or in any other form of society,—the vicissitudes of a troubled time placed two men in irresponsible authority."[8]

The phrase "a troubled time" suggests that Adams in his reformist days sees this arrogation of power as temporary and believes such muckraking exposés will help end it. "The New York Gold Conspiracy" closes reassuringly: "Messrs. Gould and Fisk will at last be obliged to yield to the force of moral and economical laws. . . . The United States will restore a sound basis to its currency, and will learn to deal with the political reforms it requires."[9] With what bitter derision the Adams of the 1890s would have read this example of his youthful optimism. By then the battle was lost; the plutocrats had won. One of the losers was his brother Charles, forced out of the presidency of the Union Pacific Railroad by that same Jay Gould.[10] Though Adams himself had no more interest in a business than a political career, he realized that his comfortable *rentier* status had relegated him to the past. In the 1901 poem "Prayer to the Virgin of Chartres," he sees himself, "dethroned," a

> Fossil survival of an age of stone,
> Among the cave-men and the troglodytes.[11]

His letters of the time are full of attacks on plutocratic America, "fat and greasy with wealth," and of protests about his class's relative poverty. There is something absurd in this complaint of a man who by 1900 is worth close to a million dollars, spends less than half his income, and is not in the least greedy, lamenting his failure to acquire an enormous fortune: "For the first time I begin to feel poor and peevish, like a child left out of a game," he writes Elizabeth Cameron; "Not to have fifty millions is to feel oneself conspicuous for pride and incapacity." And to Gaskell: "Of course this country is rotten with wealth, which means that my class is poorer than ever." Though they can afford anything they want, they have become "relatively paupers." In this new political economy only great wealth brings real power and influence; not to have it spells extinction: "Our class is as defunct as the dodo,"[12] he writes Gaskell.

Increasingly, he thinks in terms of class rather than national or personal identity. It is as though the patriciate's training unfitted them for victory in the new contest. He notes that virtually none of his Harvard classmates, "with all their immense advantages, seem to have got or kept their proportional share in the astounding creation of power since 1850." And he concludes, "Unless one makes money in some way, one has no place in our world." When the speculative mania spreads to the established class, the results can be disastrous. They have no gift for it, or too many scruples. The 1893 Panic nearly wipes out the Adams family fortune; though Henry has invested more conservatively and is not personally affected, he returns from Europe to oversee the rescue operation.[13] "My generation has been cleaned out," he claims; but there is no escape: "Where Wall Street rules, there I die ... seeing that our American so-called society is simply Wall Street and nothing else."[14]

Everywhere he looks he sees symptoms of decay—common enough in the fin de siècle, of course; yet Adams's version is specifically linked to the decline of patrician power. There is leisure-class *ressentiment* in his laments, a volatile mix of envy, contempt, rage, and plangency. Brooks Adams saw it as the inevitable historical eclipse of once prominent families, "because a certain field of activity which afforded the ancestor full scope, has been closed against his offspring."[15] But Henry Adams could not manage such philosophical detachment and needed a more exalted vocabulary. In 1901 he saw Wagner's *The Twilight of the Gods* for the first time. He calls the experience "world-shaking," and is amazed that "fifty years ago a great artist should have said all I have since learned." Finally, he sees the shift in power as unalterable: "My class is not one which is now likely to furnish what government needs," he writes as he contemplates the ascent to greatness of "the Hebrew Barney Baruch."[16]

In Adams's mind, the Jews and the Irish are linked as the inheritors. These recent immigrants are filling the economic and political power vacuum left by the exhaustion of his own class. The Irish displace the Adams family even from local office in their Quincy ancestral home, as they fan out from Boston to the villages that become its suburbs. Henry's brother Charles laments the decay of the little town, as the "ignorant and credulous" race sweeps "the native New Englanders" aside.[17] In 1884, Boston elects an Irish Catholic mayor,[18] the first in a long line. And in 1910, Henry Adams writes contemptuously of the most recent successor: "Poor Boston has fairly run up against it in the form of its particular Irish maggot, rather lower than the Jew, but more or less the same in appetite for cheese."[19] There is a supreme historical irony, which Adams might well have appreciated, in the fact that this new mayor was "Honey Fitz" Fitzgerald, destined to become the grandfather of America's first Irish Catholic president. That the grandson and great-grandson of presidents should have greeted the grandfather of another in such terms suggests that Adams's outraged sense of class displacement, offensive as it now seems, had some basis in fact.

He sees the Irish and the Jews as working clannishly to undermine the established, more cohesive dispensation. As he puts it in the *Education*,

"The foreign element, especially the Irish, held aloof, and seldom consented to approve anyone; the new socialist class, rapidly growing, promised to become more exclusive than the Irish." A Brahmin protest against Irish and Jewish "exclusiveness" has its comic aspect. And Adams's official language remains guarded, compared to the frankness of his letters: "The foreign element" is more seemly than the "Irish maggot," "the new socialist class" avoids identifying the culprit in ethnic terms, though the notorious passage on the "furtive Yacoob or Ysaac still reeking of the Ghetto, snarling a weird Yiddish to the officers of the customs" clearly abandons decorum.[20] One can trace the sentiment far back in Adams's career, to the description of Jay Gould in "The New York Gold Conspiracy": "dark, sallow, reticent, and stealthy, with a trace of Jewish origin."[21] But the figure of the Jew gradually becomes more and more malignant, and letters allow him to vent his anger without fear of reproach. As early as 1879, he describes Spain's 1492 expulsion of the Jews as expressing "a noble aim," though the passage is still hedged by "playful" irony and not yet related to his fear of displacement.[22]

As that anxiety grows, the fantasies become more violent, fusing Adams's hatred of speculative capitalism with his nativist fear of engulfment. He describes America in the wake of the 1893 Panic as "a society of Jews and brokers, a world made up of maniacs wild for gold." A year later he longs to see the end of his time, "with all its infernal Jewry. I want to put every money-lender to death, and to sink Lombard Street and Wall Street under the ocean." And the arrival of the new immigrant "hordes" in the first years of the new century unleashes fantasies of drowning in the flood: "A hundred million Slavs and Jews have bought steamer tickets here." As in the other displacement fears—by the plutocrats, by the Irish—Adams is troubled by the erosion of his class's power. Of the pervasive "Jew atmosphere" he writes to Gaskell, "We are still in power, after a fashion. Our sway over what we call society is undisputed. We keep Jews far away . . . ; yet we somehow seem to be more Jewish every day."[23]

If such disturbing sentiments had been peculiar to Adams, one might dismiss them as idiosyncratic pathological symptoms. But as we will see, they are echoed by the other writers in this study—James, Eliot, Pound; and they are not limited to this circle of "improvised Europeans." One ought to ask, repeatedly, why are they necessary?

what purpose do they serve? There is no uniform answer, but for Adams, all such hostile group identities are useful as a way of absolving himself from blame. If he does not—in the words of John Adams to his son—"rise to the head not only of your Profession, but of your country," it is emphatically *not* owing to his "own *Lasiness, Slovenliness* and Obstinacy." The doors open to John Quincy Adams had been shut in Henry Adams's face by a conspiracy of outsiders who robbed him of his birthright, even of his chances. The failure was not personal but communal, inevitable.

It was a consoling myth, but that it *was* mythical is shown by a career Adams had tracked since its Harvard beginnings—Theodore Roosevelt's. Although Roosevelt was descended from the New York Knickerbocker aristocracy, he and Adams were members of the same affluent, established class; their Harvard training and early exposure to Europe were comparable. Nor was he indifferent to his colonial heritage: "I speak as one proud of his Holland, Huguenot, and Covenanting ancestors, and proud that the blood of that stark Puritan divine Jonathan Edwards flows in the veins of his children," he writes in his autobiography. Independently wealthy, he early determined to use his economic freedom to pursue a political career. His income, he writes, gives him the luxury of ignoring any "pressure to barter his convictions for the sake of holding office." But he has no use for patricians who think themselves above vulgar politics, and he dismisses the warnings of his fastidious peers that political life is a brutal trade not fit for a gentleman. The judgment merely convinces Roosevelt "that the people I knew did not belong to the governing class, and that the other people did—and that I intended to be one of the governing class."[24]

The extraordinary political career these decisions enabled need not be recounted here. It was based on many of the convictions Adams and his family held. Like them Roosevelt is a reform Republican, sympathetic to the muckrakers, suspicious of corporate power, determined to keep the new economic forces in check and root out government corruption. But unlike Adams, he is willing to start at the bottom and eager to pursue elective or appointive office, including such unglamorous posts as head of the New York Police Board, within a party framework and with all his native vigor. And he has a more realistic sense of the inevitable rough-and-tumble of American politics. His path to the presidency is not smooth. He is defeated for mayor of New York, cynically chosen by the Republicans as McKinley's running mate to get him out of the New York governorship, and toward the end of his political life fails to regain the presidency. His succession at the age of forty-three upon McKinley's assassination could hardly have been predicted, but it required no great prescience to foresee that he would one day occupy the White House.

What *was* unpredictable is Adams's response to his elevation. He had known Teddy as a Harvard freshman and was on cordial terms with him in the early stages of his Washington career, offering the young family his house during his voyage round the world when Roosevelt—"the poor wretch"—is appointed Civil Service commissioner. This hardly prepares us for Adams's reaction when "the poor wretch" is catapulted to the heights of power. "So Teddy is President! Is not that stupendous! Before such a career as that, I have no observations to make," he writes Elizabeth Cameron. And to John Hay, "Then, curiously, behind all, in my mind, in all our minds, silent and awful like the Chicago express, flies the thought of Teddy's luck!" That the supremely articulate Adams can be struck dumb is an event. That the professional ironist resorts to exclamation points is rare. But that someone who delights in condescending to presidents and documenting their frustration in office should call Roosevelt's accession "luck" is revelatory. "You must never let yourself down to the level of these Presidents," he once advised his young niece, playfully recommending that invitations to the incumbent might read, "Miss Mabel Hooper requests Grover and Mrs Cleveland to do themselves the honor of dining with her."[25] But this was at a time, which Adams thought would last forever, when his kind were out of power.

Adams's intense response to the "stupendous" news of "Teddy's luck" reveals that his scorn for high office is a veneer, and that the spectacle of a member of his own class wielding supreme power deeply excites him, stirring up envy, buried ambition, forgotten idealism, and undermining the alibi that the failure of *his* generation of Adamses had been inevitable. The fault was not in their stars but in themselves that they were underlings. This is a truth he could not acknowledge. Roosevelt's presidency (1901–08) forcefully resurrects Adams's early political engagement, though its method shifts from journalism to behind-the-scenes influence. The change really begins three years earlier when John Hay becomes McKinley's secretary of state, an office Roosevelt insisted he continue to hold. Hay was Adams's next-door neighbor and closest friend; the two went for a daily walk or ride in the years Hay and Roosevelt presided over the transformation of America into a world power; this gave Adams an unprecedented direct access to statecraft. If T. S. Eliot's judgment that Adams "was born to exercise governance, not to acquire it"[26] is right, here was his chance.

He alternately deprecates and boasts of his influence. On his relation to power Adams is a bundle of contradictions, barely in control of his feelings. On the one hand, he presents himself only as a "stable-companion to statesmen," a "political atheist," an amused spectator who "wants to listen at the key-hole." He writes to Gaskell, "my triumvirate friends—Roosevelt, Hay and Lodge" are "running our foreign affairs . . . in my house at the cost of my comfort."[27] This is Adams's familiar amalgam of boasting and complaint. On the other hand, in the *Education* he recalls his early interest in power quite differently: "One began to dream the sensation of wielding unmeasured power. The sense came, like vertigo, for an instant, and passed, leaving the brain a little dazed, doubtful, shy." And that exact phrase recurs in his description of Roosevelt as president, "wielding unmeasured power with immeasurable energy."[28] In the Roosevelt years, Adams's letters record fantasies of acquiring such power played out like other unacknowledgeable desires, as extravagant invention: "My wild ambition sees already the republican party broken up; Theodore reelected on a platform of pure anarchy that I shall write; and a Cabinet which I shall rule."[29]

These contradictory impulses are unresolvable, felt simultaneously or alternately in equal measure. He is the accomplished Machiavel behind the scenes in the months that settle the fate of Cuba and the Philippines, and those leading up to Hay's intervention in China. He virtually dictates the terms of the peace treaty with Spain.[30] Diplomats and congressmen beat a path to his door; Lodge and Hay and Roosevelt listen to his counsel; he often feels the impact of his words. But he is also revolted by the whole spectacle—by Roosevelt's incredible egotism, Lodge's coercive single-mindedness, Hay's exhaustion under the burdens of office. His thoughts crystallize into the lapidary sentences of the *Education*: "Power is poison"; "Every friend in power is a friend lost."[31]

The alternating attraction and repulsion turn Adams into a political voyeur, fastidiously detached from those in office while exerting covert influence. This is how he tries to keep his hands clean, himself unpoisoned. As the reality of America's new global power sinks in, his feelings are equally divided. He is delighted that no country—especially Britain—can now condescend to the United States, that Euro-American power relations have shifted. But he is appalled that America, like earlier empires, will work by naked takeover: "The octopus is stretching its tentacles everywhere, quite blindly," he writes to Brooks in 1900; "As for traditions, constitution, principles, past professions, and all that, the devil has put them back into his pocket for another thousand years."[32]

These conflicted feelings explain why Adams feels at home neither in nor out of America, why he divides his time between Washington and abroad. He is compulsively addicted both to flight and to return and uses them as antidotes for each other. The "nausea" he had described in his 1890 letter to Charles alternates with homesickness, and he drifts on the unstable tide of his emotions. When he first begins his voyages in the 1890s, he looks for a radical alternative to modern industrial America in the South Seas and the Caribbean. "I love the tropics," he explains to Gaskell, "and feel really at ease nowhere else."[33] He wants to escape from what he would later call the "dynamo" and from his Puritan training.

The months spent in Samoa and Tahiti and Cuba awaken responses linked to nineteenth-century primitivism and follow the route of artists like Melville, Gauguin, and Robert Louis Stevenson. He is fascinated by Stevenson, another close friend of Henry James, whom Stevenson had called "the Prince of Men,"[34] visiting him in Samoa, where the Scottish novelist had settled after drifting around Polynesia. Stevenson does not understand why anyone "who is able to live in the South Seas, should consent to live elsewhere." Adams is tempted but cannot finally "go native." Yet he does not merely take in the scenery, gawk at the "old gold maiden," and rest content with his first impression that this is "an ideal archaic Arcadia."[35]

Even in Tahiti he resurrects his professional training to write the history of the island's displaced aristocratic rulers, and he is literally adopted into the Teva clan. One of its survivors recounts the impact of the English and French colonizers on Tahiti's traditional culture.

Although Adams had come to the South Seas as an escape, without a writing project in mind, he is spellbound by the story told by "the old chiefess" Arii Taimai and her daughter Marau Taaroa. He listens to them by the hour and later publishes his version of their narrative in the 1893 privately printed *Memoirs of Marau Taaroa Last Queen of Tahiti* and in a 1901 revision. What interests him in their story is the unexpected echo of his own. Tahiti became a French colony in 1880, and his visit coincides with the last vestiges of the island's independence. As the modern editor of what he calls simply *Tahiti* notes, "Arii Taimai's proud memories of the Teva clan and its genealogy could hardly fail to meet a responsive hearer in the descendant of Presidents whose policies had been repudiated by the march of events."[36] It is a meeting of displaced aristocrats, and the adoption suggests that the "instinctive cousinship" Adams had sensed in Europe with other disempowered patricians could also be felt in the South Seas.

His sympathies lie entirely with the old order; he treats both the English and French settlers and the Tahitian puppet "kings" they install with contempt. His hostility is filtered through Arii Taimai. She speaks of "English gunpowder, which had been as great a curse as every other English thing or thought had been."[37] And she compares her world's demise to the later stages of the French Revolution, an analogy the avid reader of Saint-Simon finds appealing. The decimation of the native population is directly attributed to the colonizers: "Everywhere the Polynesian perished, and to him it mattered little whether he died of some new disease, or from some new weapon, like the musket, or from the misgovernment caused by foreign intervention."[38] The book reveals Adams's distrust of the myth of the "civilizing mission," which his own country would soon appropriate. That he should have devoted so much time to this work, have published two versions at his own expense with no audience in sight, merely to record the story for posterity, suggests how alienated he had become from what Matthew Arnold had called "the young light-hearted masters of the waves" about to intrude upon a vulnerable preindustrial culture.[39] Yet despite his attraction to the South Seas, Adams is too divided to follow Stevenson's example. As he ruefully confesses to Elizabeth Cameron, "I was born under the shadow of Boston Statehouse, and I prefer my beans without saffron."[40]

II

FOR ALL HIS exploratory drifting, in the tropics and elsewhere, Adams
gradually realizes that for him Europe is the only alternative to Washington. But where? Could he belatedly make James's choice and settle
in England? His wife had disliked it, and after her death he had written
to Gaskell, "I can't go to Europe. It is full of ghosts." But that had been
six years earlier, and in 1891–92 Adams certainly considers the possibility. He returns from the South Seas via Europe and stays for several
months in Britain. James's path is open to him and he is tempted to
follow it. He discovers to his delight that his old friendships are intact
and feels that "London is curiously homelike to me, even after so
many years of absence." Finally back in Washington, he confesses, "I
have never ceased to debate within myself whether the return was
wise, and whether I should not be in a better situation now if I had
stuck it out alone in England."[41]

But if America near the turn of the century bears no resemblance to
"my own country of 1860," Adams might have said the same about
Britain. London is no longer the site of "young England, young
Europe, of which I am by tastes and education a part." It seems geriatric. A moribund imperialism was not preferable to a nascent one.
Adams's descriptions of Britain around 1900 predict her impending
demise. "As for England," he writes his Anglophile friend Hay, "there
is no longer a possibility, that I can see, of preventing a sweeping financial, social and political collapse, that can hardly fail to leave her a
second-rate, lower-middle-class, democracy." He perpetually sings
Britain's swan song for her, particularly during the Boer War. He sees
the great expatriate artists who settled there, "The generation of Harry
James and John Sargent . . . already as fossil as the buffalo." By contrast, the American century is just beginning, the "centre of human
energy" has shifted there, and the years 1898–1903 have swept England
"out of our path as completely as the Roman Empire."[42] His "our"
reveals national pride. This is the voice not of the disaffected Adams
but of the companion to the country's leaders and the fiery patriot of
old. He cannot help it. The tone of English life, to Adams still so com-
placent when the reasons for self-satisfaction had vanished, resuscitated his youthful jingoism. He would often visit, but he could not live

there. Unlike James, unlike Hay, and despite his family's transgenerational task, Adams could never quite master the tune of Anglo-American harmony.

The viable alternative to Washington proves to be Paris, not London, though this is not immediately apparent. When Adams first arrives from the South Seas to meet Elizabeth Cameron there and to see where they stood, the signs are not immediately promising. He is "hit over the head by an apocalyptic *Never*," as he puts it in a letter to her; not even in Paris can his longing for intimacy be satisfied: "I must always make more demand on you than you can gratify, and you must always have the consciousness that, whatever I may profess, I want more than I can have." Washington's prying eyes had little to do with it. The inhibition lay in themselves, as Adams's conventional response to "decadent" French literature suggests. He is scandalized by contemporary writers, though he assiduously reads Zola, the Goncourt brothers, Maupassant, and attends the theater until he is "thoroughly saturated with all that is best in French decadence. . . . The last show is a rape and abortion to be performed on the stage at the Theatre Libre." He force-feeds himself this unsavory fare to stay current, "but, do what I will, the gorge rises." New England speaks in his conclusion that "of all the people in the world, the French are the most gratuitously wicked."[43]

From these unpromising beginnings he is rescued by a new friend, destined to become the center of his Paris life—Edith Wharton. He is impressed by her intelligence and familiarity with French society and culture, though he is not at first aware of its strict limits. She offers entry to an atmosphere of connoisseurship, pleasure, and luxury, where American upper-class expatriates mix with the French aristocracy. They are of the same class, though Wharton's more worldly New York patrician background allows her to respond to Paris in the belle époque less puritanically. As his initial shock wears off, and as the relationship with Elizabeth Cameron gradually turns less emotionally exhausting, Paris becomes the cosmopolitan center Adams had longed for. In the *History of the United States* he had described "the liberal, literary, and scientific air of Paris in 1789" as the one atmosphere the versatile Jefferson could "breathe with perfect satisfaction."[44] A century later an American whose interests were nearly as wide ranging can still fall under the spell.

By the mid-1890s a long stay in France becomes part of Adams's routine. He "slowly began to feel at home in France as in other countries he had thought more homelike," as he recalls in the *Education*.[45] In 1903 he is furnishing his apartment at 23 Avenue du Bois de Boulogne in the style of the ancien régime and threatening to hold his "first reception in bed." Yet Adams's Paris was less French than American. His European existence is decidedly "improvised" rather than rooted in local custom. His circle is dominated by his compatriots, many also in flight from an America they find unappealing. It is a class migration—in two senses of the word *class*: "The sun shines as bright on the Champs Elysées as it did under the Empire, and all my schoolmates who were here with me then, are here with me now." His original community has drifted to Europe and is regrouping in Paris, which, he pronounces, "has become an American city, as much a matter of course as New York. The American has no longer a standard here but himself." As he writes to Gaskell of his "little American family-group," centered on Wharton: "We are rather sufficient to ourselves."[46]

His social world is sharply bounded. R. P. Blackmur has suggested that "Adams had a familiarity with the streets of Paris which must have equalled Henry James' with those of London,"[47] but this hardly acknowledges the narrowness of his perimeter: *rive droite* and the Faubourg St. Germain, the starred restaurants rather than the bistros, the galleries and museums, not the ateliers. The contemporary explosion in painting, music, dance that set a younger generation on fire largely remained outside his ken. Whistler and Rodin are his limits. When one reflects that at the same time his compatriots Gertrude and Leo Stein are buying Cézannes, Picassos, and Matisses, one gets a sharp sense of his relatively conventional tastes. Of course by this time the old age he had been courting for twenty years has finally come upon him. And he confesses with disarming frankness, "My horizon stops at Ritz's."[48]

But although this was true of his social existence, it does not describe his intellectual life. As in the South Seas, what had begun as escape becomes an occasion for serious exploration and writing. Paris's sophisticated air was not France's only attraction. In 1895 he accompanies the Lodges to revisit Normandy, sees the cathedrals of Coutances and Chartres as well as Mont-Saint-Michel for the first time, and awakens as from a long sleep. These masterpieces of religious architecture silence his reflex cynicism and misanthropy and reawaken the forgotten idealism of his youth. The medieval cathedral is "the greatest single creation of man," he writes excitedly to Elizabeth Cameron. "The more I study it, the more I admire and wonder. I am not disposed to find fault. The result was beyond what I should suppose possible to so mean an animal as man."[49]

The experience initiates Adams's first ambitious writing project since the *History*. He begins to read voraciously in the fields of medieval poetry and history, art and architecture, religion and philosophy. He visits the surviving monuments again and again. That he should turn back to the European Middle Ages, his specialty during the Harvard years, and abandon the field of American history he had made his own shows the gap between his late-career needs and the life of modern America. The violence of his rejection is powerfully suggested in a 1909 letter to Brooks linking his revulsion from American history to his contempt for the forces now dominating the country. He describes his "nauseous indigestion of American history, which now makes me physically sick, so that only by self-compulsion can I read the dreary details. . . . The unhealthy atmosphere of the whole age, and its rampant meanness even in violence; the one-sided flabbiness of America; the want of self-respect, of education, of purpose; the intellectual feebleness, and the material greed—I loathe it all."[50] Only a temporally distant, European world seen as the antithesis of what he was leaving behind could rekindle his desire to write history at all.

The work that eventually emerges from this new obsession, *Mont-Saint-Michel and Chartres*, is conceived from the first as a critique of the United States, though the antithesis is seldom explicit. Adams's need to find an imaginative alternative to mercantilist America is the book's emotional root. Medieval Normandy is seen as precapitalist. It does not leave the "greasy taste," the "mercantile and gold-bug trail" of other monuments, and he returns to it "with the relief of an epicure who has had to eat pork." Like Adams's early *Essays in Anglo-Saxon Law*, *Mont-Saint-Michel and Chartres* tries to forge a link between medieval Europe and colonial America, the stage from which he now dates his country's long decline. His first sight of Coutances links the two cultures. As he writes to Brooks, "I have rarely felt New England at its highest ideal power as it appeared to me, beatified and glorified, in the Cathedral of Coutances. Since then our ancestors have steadily declined and run out until we have reached pretty near the bottom. . . . So we get Boston."[51] He considers himself a spiritual descendant of the Normans who built these masterpieces stone by stone without a thought to their own gain.

He fancifully invents a Norman progenitor, a medieval craftsman or prince—it hardly matters which—engaged in the communal labor that built Chartres and Mont-Saint-Michel, and whose descendants had long ago crossed the Atlantic. The voyage to America is conceived as an abandonment of the nurturing Virgin in quest of plunder and imperial conquest:

> Crossing the hostile sea, our greedy band
> Saw rising hills and forest in the blue;
> Our father's kingdom in the promised land![52]

Adams's rediscovery of Chartres, the world of the Mother, is a prodigal's return. In this fantasy, the "episode" of the Norman conquest of Britain is simply passed over; the first colonists choose New England because it reminds them of their older ancestral landscape. To an American, the Normandy coast "recalls the coast of New England," Adams writes in *Mont-Saint-Michel and Chartres*; "the relation between the people who live on each is as hard and practical a fact as the granite itself"; the Norman eleventh century is "the starting point of American genealogy."[53] Adams's version of the Nordic myth now stresses the role of France rather than England or the Germanic tribes in the founding of America. Like the other variants it implies that the more recent immigrants are eroding the granitic integrity of the first settlers.

Adams's stress on the integral community of medieval Normandy, united by religious belief, recalls early theocratic New England. Normandy had of course been Catholic rather than Protestant; Adams celebrates the inclusiveness of Mary's love over the sternness of a Calvinist deity. But this only strengthens the overarching social, religious, and aesthetic unity of Normandy and the colonies. Unlike fragmented turn-of-the-century America, as well as the Europe of the same era, the medieval world has no fault lines. Those it has are minimized or ignored to highlight the contrast between past and present. Self-censorship strengthens this impression. So Adams cuts short his account of a conflict between medieval peasants and burghers: "The efforts of the bourgeoisie and the peasantry to recover their property, so far as it was recoverable, have lasted to the present day and we had best take care not to get mixed in those passions." Class conflict, hardly unknown in medieval Europe, is passed over to highlight Adams's myth of unity. What impresses him even more than the product Chartres Cathedral is the communal project of its building, with thousands of the poor, the middling, and the rich and powerful contributing to the work. The director of the project is imagined to be Mary, "and nowhere any rival authority; one sees her give orders, and architects obey them." Artists and artisans are mere instruments of a single will; their work is not their own but their community's and their faith's: "Beneath the throne of the Mother of God, there was no distinction of gifts; and above it the distinction favoured the commonalty."[54]

The antithesis to the dog-eat-dog rivalries, the factions, the disharmonies of the modern industrial and political world is implied in every word and finally made explicit. The last remnants of medieval single-mindedness are now "yielding before the daily evidence of increasing and extending complexity." Unity gives way to "multiplicity, variety, and even contradiction."[55] The lines of force diverge; society becomes incoherent. Adams invents a world-historical explanation for his overwhelming sense of the fragmentation of his culture and of his own psyche. His picture of the Middle Ages, like those of his contemporaries Ruskin and Morris, was to have a powerful imaginative impact and would influence literary works by his successors, like Pound's *The Spirit of Romance* and Eliot's *Four Quartets*.[56] Its deep subject, however, is not the medieval world but Adams's intense sense of loss in the present day, as he imagines the Virgin "looking down from a deserted heaven, into an empty church, on a dead faith."[57]

For whom was this book written? What purpose did this fatalistic work serve? Writing was a means to public ends, or so Adams had treated it in the earlier stages of his career. But by the time he finishes the book in 1904, his fear of self-indulgence has virtually disappeared. He denies that *Mont-Saint-Michel and Chartres* could possibly be of interest to anyone except himself and the handful of "nieces," either literal or "in wish," who sometimes accompanied him on his travels.[58] The history of the book is bizarre, though it sets the pattern for Adams's final phase, in which his works are not so much published as privatized. A hundred copies are printed, at his own expense, to be sent to the few people he thinks might value it—friends and relations, a handful of carefully picked historians. To one of them he writes that he considers the book "only my private folly" and insists, "I could not publish it if I would." He keeps it out of the hands of those unlikely to read it with sympathy, including most professional medievalists, since their approach must be objective while for him the medieval world "has somehow to be brought into relation with ourselves," even at the cost of factual accuracy.[59]

The book nevertheless circulates in an early version of samizdat, despite Adams's perhaps disingenuous efforts to restrict access. He takes pride in creating an artificial scarcity. In 1911, another hundred copies are printed, again for private circulation, though a number of them go to academic libraries. It is only in 1913, nearly a decade after the manuscript was finished, that he finally agrees to let the book be published, but even then the arrangements are idiosyncratic. Pressed urgently by the architectural historian Ralph Adams Cram to grant permission to the American Institute of Architects to sponsor publication, Adams agrees, on condition that he receive no royalties and that Cram and the institute attend to all details. The book is published under these conditions by Houghton Mifflin, with an introduction that records Adams's disavowal: The reluctant author "expressly stipulated that he should have no part or parcel in carrying out so mad a venture of faith—as he estimated the project of giving his book to the public."[60]

Publication—the act of seeking an audience rather than preselecting one—is treated as a doomed experiment. Behind Adams's reluctance to engage in it lies his bitter disappointment with the reception of the *History*, his last "public" venture. With what he took to be its failure, he abandoned forever the project of finding American readers.[61] His sense of the shrunken modern audience for serious work contrasts with his vision of the Middle Ages, where works like the *Chanson de Roland*, he claims, were "known by heart, from beginning to end, by every man and woman and child, lay or clerical."[62] He idealizes the artist's ability to express the essential vision of his culture. This has vanished in modern America, where the gap between artist and audience seems to widen continuously. Impossible to imagine the writer now recording what Pound was to call "the tale of the tribe."[63]

Adams's sense of his potential audience shrinks with each passing year. He had not yet written the retrospective passage in the *Education* about the assumption behind his early reformist journalism, that it made no difference whether an author was read by five hundred or five hundred thousand, since "if he can select the five hundred, he reaches the five hundred thousand."[64] But he already knew that he no longer believed it. Even the modest number five hundred comes to seem inflated. When Brooks in 1905 calls *Mont-Saint-Michel and Chartres* the "crowning effort of our race" and begs his brother to publish a commercial edition, Henry replies that "five hundred [readers] do not exist,—nor half that number—nor a quarter of it." By 1910, he reluctantly treats this shrunken audience as a form of cultural continuity: "Our only chance is to accept the limited number of survivors—the one-in-a-thousand of born artists and poets—and to intensify the energy of feeling within that radiant center."[65] As we will see, this theory of a tiny, cosmopolitan cultural remnant becomes a central assumption of modernist art and is often linked to the expatriate impulse.

Although Adams's terms and numbers do not distinguish between one country and another, he saves his angriest diatribes for the total indifference of the American audience. "No one ever cares," he complains to one correspondent in 1908. "Nothing diverts the American mind from its ruts." And in the following year he writes to Barrett Wendell, "My favorite figure of the American author is that of a man who breeds a favorite dog, which he throws into the Mississippi River for the pleasure of making a splash. The river does not splash, but it drowns the dog."[66] Such bitter comments are testimony to the disappointment of Adams's early ambitions, particularly of making his intense writerly vocation serve a public, political purpose. His refusal to publish, his inability to imagine a sympathetic response to his later work, his use of the letter as a major expressive form, all demonstrate his loss of faith in the power of his words to influence his society.[67]

"I write for myself and strangers," Gertrude Stein's tentative formula in *The Making of Americans,*[68] would have struck Adams as excessively optimistic. There were no strangers. There was only the coterie. He emphasized the point in his 1911 biography of George Cabot ("Bay")

Lodge, the senator's son. Even in his brief life, the young writer had discovered that "the gap between poet and citizen was so wide as to be impassable." His real country was not America but the tiny transatlantic world of his own kind—in the older generation, for instance, Adams himself, Henry James, Edith Wharton, all among his mourners. For Lodge being unpopular was a sign of artistic purity. His class markings as well as his literary ancestry show perfectly in the rhetorical question he asks his mother: "Whom, in this age of universal machine-made cheapness, whom more than James with his immense talent and his small sales, are you going to respect?"[69]

Lodge's question takes as inevitable, and even celebrates, a state of affairs the older generation responded to with dismay. If the American audience and contemporary American life are simply to be despised, and if neglect is certain to be the fate of "immense talent," then one might as well sever all links with American culture, whether as an expatriate or an internal emigré. As a result Lodge's actual poetic and dramatic work—as against the legend of his heroic failure that Adams needed to propagate—is very thin gruel indeed. It represents the worst defects of what George Santayana called "the genteel tradition," the work of "cultivated writers" whose "culture was half a pious survival, half an intentional acquirement," whose "head did not belong to the trunk."[70] Lodge is crippled by his sense of the venerableness of European tradition and the contemptible lowness of the American world around him, whose defiling touch he needs to escape. He settles for pale imitations of the classic writers, in closet dramas like *Herakles* that would never be performed. In such disciples, Adams's myth of failure becomes, simply, failure—though his role as official biographer makes it impossible for him to say so outright.

The late style of vaunting self-denigration that Adams himself perfected is a much more complex and interesting response. He too might have linked small sales to genius; but despite his refusal to publish, he could not resign himself to the situation. And as his last major work shows, he remains deeply interested in the culture he has come to despise and will not surrender his right to examine and judge its defects (and his own) with supreme interpretive confidence. He becomes a detached spectator, even of someone called "Henry Adams." What Santayana says about James's way of escaping the crippling effects of the genteel tradition also applies to Adams. James manages it, according to Santayana, "by adopting the point of view of the outer world, and by turning the genteel American tradition, as he turns everything else, into a subject-matter for analysis."[71]

This is so even though the outer world would not read *The Education of Henry Adams* until long after it was written. Like *Mont-Saint-Michel and Chartres*, it is privately printed and remains a coterie work until after Adams's death in 1918. In 1907 one hundred copies are produced for circulation among his inner circle. But since so many of them are also characters in Adams's autobiographical narrative, he disingenuously insists that the copies be returned with corrections and with any offensive sentences crossed out. He imagines the venture as a collaborative effort to record the group history of these "improvised Europeans," designed for publication (or perhaps archival storage) in the distant future. This is like his attitude toward James's *William Wetmore Story and His Friends*, the biography in which, he tells James, he has written "not Story's life, but your own and mine."[72] Since Adams has remained a private person, the *Education* can only be justified as social history rather than autobiography. Despite his request, and not surprisingly, only a handful of copies come back to the author.[73] The rest are not only kept but circulated and quoted, so that Adams's book is known beyond his circle long before it is actually published.

Even when the *Education* finally becomes available to the public, it appears with a flurry of disclaimers. Adams had asked Henry Cabot Lodge to act as his agent but also to sign an "Editor's Preface" that Adams himself had actually written.[74] It is a curious document, full of preemptive self-criticism and pretending to recount "the author's" failed efforts to suppress the book. It claims that although Adams wanted to leave the work unpublished, the "Massachusetts Historical Society has decided to publish the 'Education' . . . not in opposition to the author's judgment" but to make it accessible to students.[75] The elaborate pretense of disclaiming significance for his own life is continued in Adams's signed preface by never using the word "I" and by presenting the author as an egoless tailor's "manikin," on whom the clothes of his education are draped to see if they fit.[76] And in the body of the book, Adams consistently writes about himself in the third person, as a specimen to be examined. All these rhetorical choices suggest his disclaiming responsibility for himself. They recall the Kansas editor Ed Howe's witty comment that Adams was "the only man in America who could sit on a fence and watch himself go by."[77] Long before, he had imagined such a cloak of invisibility: "My ideal of authorship would be to have a famous *double* with another name, to wear what honors I could win."[78] The double has the same name but is treated as a stranger.

The anonymity and modesty of *The Education of Henry Adams* are steadfastly maintained; the author's personal insignificance is repeatedly stressed. This, among other reasons, is why the twenty years of Adams's prime are expunged from the record, the career at Harvard, his marriage, the Washington salon. We hear nothing of his successes, only of his failures. Yet few readers are likely to be taken in by this charade. *The Education of Henry Adams* is not a modest book. In expunging his private self and denying his own achievement, in stressing his spectatorial distance, he lays claim to an objectivity no confessional writer could command. His formulaic self-deflation, a version of Socratic irony, becomes an attack on established authority: I know nothing; therefore I am wiser than those who claim to know everything. Above all, the nearly three-quarters of a century he covers gives him a historian's perspective on the gap between past and present and allows him to grasp what Adams the *participant* had passed through in a way that person never could. As we will see, James in *The American Scene*, finished in the same year, also uses the authority of long experience to record how America has changed.

Adams exaggerates this historical distance, claiming that his education was that of an eighteenth- rather than a nineteenth-century child, in order to strengthen the radical disjuncture between the ideals of colonial America (in which he had been trained) and the requirements of the modern world. The gulf between the two is emphasized in categorical statements like "The American boy of 1854 stood nearer the year 1 than to the year 1900"; or "His world was dead"; or "The moral law had expired—like the Constitution." They heighten the drama of his disinheritance by attaching it to agentless historical shifts, for example in his description of "the whole mechanical consolidation of force, which ruthlessly stamped out the life of the class into which Adams was born, but created monopolies capable of controlling the new energies that America adored."[79]

If Adams could show that the old-fashioned probity of his class training was now a crippling *dis*advantage, a hopeless impediment to
advancement in the America he had putatively inherited but actually
lost, he need feel no sense of guilt or inadequacy. The Puritan heritage
of being accountable for one's failures made it difficult to blame anyone or anything else. Adams's strategy in the *Education* is to pay lip service to the idea of personal responsibility by repeatedly calling attention to his inadequacy but finally to exonerate himself by widening the
gap between his "troglodytic" ancestral training[80] and the spirit of the
age. *The Education of Henry Adams* might have been called *Apologia
Pro Vita Sua,* if Newman had not appropriated the title.

But Adams is not satisfied with self-exculpation. He also wants to
understand and assess—to master—the alien forces that changed his
world; and here the surface modesty of the *Education* evaporates completely. The moral law that had supposedly expired, and that unfitted
him to compete in the land of political opportunism and monopoly
capitalism, is resuscitated by Adams the hanging judge. His fierce
attack on the forces that sent him packing is delivered in Olympian
thunder: The Grant administration "smirched executive, judiciary,
banks, corporate systems, professions, and people, all the great active
forces of society, in one dirty cesspool of vulgar corruption"; "the blackmailer alone was the normal product of politics as of business."[81] There
is nothing tentative in the tone of such sentences. The unsettled drifter
can still call his society to account.

Adams's effort of mastery does not stop there. Despite the rearguard
nature of his formal and familial education, he sets himself the task of
grasping the forces at work in contemporary politics, economics, industry,
and international affairs. He keeps his eyes and ears open, studies the
behavior of those in power rather than the antiquated principles of governance, reads widely in science and mathematics, studies the triumphs
of technology at the Chicago and St. Louis world's fairs as attentively as
he had looked at the masterpieces of medieval architecture. Despite his
nostalgia, he is determined to live in the chaotic present. He needs to
understand the dynamo's force as much as the Virgin's. He refuses to
become a relic: "His single thought was to keep in front of the movement, and, if necessary, lead it to chaos, but never fall behind."[82]

This eagerness to keep up suggests how unwilling Adams is to surrender his connection to power, no matter how menacing he finds its contemporary scientific embodiment. The passages about the dynamo in the *Education* are worshipful: "Before the end, one began to pray to it; inherited instinct taught the natural expression of man before silent and infinite force." And for all his alienation he sees himself as "bound to accelerate progress; to concentrate energy; to accumulate power; to multiply and intensify forces."[83] In imaginatively attaching himself to industrial dynamism, Adams tries to reconcile his atavistic desire to occupy a position of power with the new order relegating him and his kind to the past.

His "solution" is to invent a science of history whose laws are as authoritative as the laws of physics. In the penultimate chapters, "A Dynamic Theory of History" and "A Law of Acceleration" (and in two later essays, "A Letter to American Teachers of History" and "The Rule of Phase Applied to History"),[84] Adams lays down the laws of historical development in a way that allows him to predict the future as well as order the past. If his scientific formulas worked, "The mathematician of 1950 should be able to plot the past and future orbit of the human race as accurately as the November meteoroids. Naturally such an attitude annoyed the players in the game, as the attitude of the umpire is apt to infuriate the spectators."[85] His attempts to use science to predict future development have never been taken seriously by historians. But it is the ambition that is interesting. If he cannot reform his society he can foresee its future. Not content with the role of powerless spectator, he claims the office of umpire, or final arbiter. The ambition reveals just how unacceptable he finds the new marginality of his class. His ambition and interest in power have survived every disappointment. The irony, the trademark self-mockery, the Socratic disclaimers, the admission of failure are all camouflage. Behind them stands the habit of authority.

The authority gained force during the years of semiexpatriation. His decades of drifting, to other countries and to other centuries, gave him an outsider's perspective on the United States of his day. In the words of R. P. Blackmur, "His pilgrimage was prodigal and its riches were in the return."[86] His book is designed to teach succeeding generations how the original promise of a nation "so conceived and so dedicated" was compromised by forces now spinning out of control. It is often said that history is written by the winners. Adams's record of his times is history by a self-proclaimed loser. He contends that his criticism of his own inadequate education is designed "to fit young men, in universities or elsewhere, to be men of the world."[87] But his deeper object is to alert them to how much they will have to surrender to become successful operators in America's new world order. In this the *Education* confirms the vision of *Mont-Saint-Michel and Chartres*. Adams had conceived the two books from the first as complementary, one describing medieval unity, the other modern multiplicity.

Did he have any intimation of how successful a failure he was destined to become? The reception of *Mont-Saint-Michel and Chartres*, when it was published in 1913, might have given him some inkling. The advance sale broke all records for a Houghton Mifflin book, his biographer tells us, "and belied all of Adams's pessimism about American taste."[88] But even this could not foretell the critical and popular acclaim that greeted the posthumous publication of *The Education of Henry Adams*. It won the Pulitzer Prize and stayed at the top of the best-seller list for two years.[89] Given its dense and allusive style, this is remarkable enough. Although it was written before World War I, it deeply influenced the modernist generation because it anticipated the postwar mood of disillusionment—a war, it should be added, whose disastrous consequences Adams had clearly foreseen. The book turned out to be both a relic and a portent.

In 1911, he had written a valedictory letter to Charles that records his conviction of their group's failed promise. "The task of suitably putting our generation to bed, and tucking them all nicely in, so as to rest in quiet for eternity, is one which much needs to be done by us, for I see no reason to suppose that our successors will concern themselves about it." And he concludes, despondently, "We leave no followers, no school, no tradition." This echoes the letter to Charles, written nearly half a century earlier, in which Adams envisions a "national school of our own generation" prepared "to start new influences not only in politics, but in literature, in law, in society, and throughout the whole social organism of the country."[90] He was right to conclude that such a school had never materialized; nor did he any longer believe that the country even *was* a social organism. Yet in a way that the septuagenarian author could scarcely have imagined, his despair was unwarranted. The words he had written impressed the seal of an Adams deep into the consciousness of his countrymen. The nineteenth-century "improvised Europeans" with whom he associates himself become the models for more than one generation of artists who need distance from their society to free themselves from what they consider its baleful influence. The parallel careers of Adams and James become alternate models for America's cosmopolitan, disaffected, hypercritical expatriates and deracinated artists. This enormously influential school was their legacy. For better or worse, their progeny would dominate transatlantic cultural discourse for many years to come.

VI

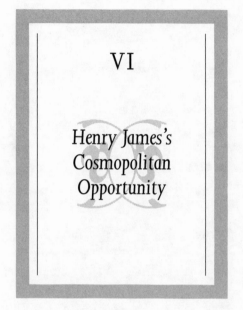

Henry James's
Cosmopolitan
Opportunity

I

UNLIKE ADAMS, Henry James has always been treated as the writer for whom the label expatriate might have been invented. As we have seen, Adams shuttles back and forth between his country and Europe and never settles for good anywhere. Although his family's traditional imperative is to strengthen Anglo-American ties, he is no passionate pilgrim, longing for a return to his Anglo-Saxon roots. His feelings about London, though intense, are deeply divided. And his sense of vocation is much more fragmented and incoherent than James's. His life plans alter constantly, so that the pattern is one of aborted experiments, fresh starts, unexpected opportunities, and apparently accidental achievements.

James seems by contrast on a single track that stretches straight across the length of his life. He sets himself sharply defined goals and pursues them almost without interruption. The focus is clearly literary, the chosen vehicle fiction, the ideal audience international, and the center a European capital, soon identified as London. These early ambitions crystallize in his own mind in 1888, nearly a quarter of a century into his career, when he writes his brother William, "I have not the least hesitation in saying that I aspire to write in such a way that it would be impossible to an outsider to say whether I am, at a given moment, an American writing about England or an Englishman writing about America . . . and so far from being ashamed of such an ambiguity I should be exceedingly proud of it, for it would be highly civilized."[1] This is anything but the goalless quest of Adams's later years, and it brings many of the expected rewards of such concentrated labor—relatively early fame on both continents, the unmistakable sense of having an impact on his contemporaries in the field, and the recognition that he has made the very subject of the Euro-American connection his personal property and exploited it for all it was worth.

Yet despite these contrasts, the two writers and close friends have a great deal in common. Both are hyperconscious of and determined to use the shift in power between the old world and the new and seize the opportunities newly available for Americans of their cosmopolitan background. Like Adams, James might have said "I gravitate to a capital by a primary law of nature."[2] He felt the same impatience with provincial Boston and arid Cambridge. The Adams family warning—that long residence in Europe unfitted Americans for America—applied especially to James. Their sense of kinship had been instantaneous; James describes Adams when he first meets him as "a youth of genius and enthusiasm." That James should have known and admired Clover Hooper, who embodied for him "the genius of my beloved country," long before Adams married her seems unsurprising. Their social and intellectual circles overlap; and when James first settles in London in 1876 he makes good use of the letters Adams provides: "Your introductions rendered me excellent service," James writes him; "Lord Houghton has been my guide, philosopher and friend. . . . I have seen, under his wing, a great variety of interesting and remarkable people."[3] Adams's London intimates help to launch James's career in English society. The two men remain close for the rest of their long lives even though the Atlantic usually separates them.

Yet to be born a James rather than an Adams was a much less exacting fate. A James had the advantages of money and high social position but was free of the historical baggage that came with a familial tradition of serving the nation. Henry James's grandfather, William James of Albany, as he is usually called, had assured his large family's continued affluence by his far-sighted investments in land at a time when upper New York State was wilderness. He died in 1832 one of the richest men in the young country and left an estate sufficient to support each of his nine surviving children in luxury for the rest of their days. "Leisured for life" Henry James Sr. declared when he learned of his share of his father's estate. In the words of the James family's most recent biographer, he was "a man who in his twenty-seventh year began to live on an income that today would be in excess of $300,000 a year before taxes."[4] Nothing he did for the rest of his days was determined by financial necessity.

Instead, Henry James Sr. used his affluence and leisure to live a life of perfect freedom—freedom to study and to write, even if his philosophical and religious works found few readers; freedom to take his wife and five children to Europe for years at a time, or to live in New York, Newport, or Boston; and—in the fullness of time—freedom to provide his adult children with similar undirected opportunities. The exploratory stage of young adulthood was stretched to the limit for his more gifted sons, William and Henry; they were free to try anything before making final choices or becoming financially independent. William, who was far less single-minded than his younger brother, studied painting with William Morris Hunt, then pursued a scientific career, then trained in medicine though he never practiced, then spent a year in Germany. He lived with his family in Cambridge until his marriage at thirty-six. That he eventually became a philosopher and psychologist rather than pursuing his earlier goals would not have struck his parents as a poor return on their investment. Money existed to make such exploratory freedom possible.

It also served to enlarge the range of the children's experience. The extraordinary nomadic existence of the James family between 1843 (the year Henry the future novelist was born) and 1866 when the senior Jameses finally settled in Cambridge largely served educational ends—to make the children multilingual, to broaden their experience and make them feel at home anywhere. Whatever "at home" meant! The bicontinental itinerary of the young Henry James made this a nice question. Born in New York City, he was almost immediately taken off to Europe for a two-year stay. The family returned to live in Albany from 1845 to 1847 and in New York City between 1847 and 1855 before resuming their travels: Europe 1855–58, Newport 1858–59, Europe 1859–60, Newport 1860–62, at which point the nineteen-year-old Henry briefly studied law at Harvard. Nor were the European years more stable: Paris, Geneva, London, Boulogne, Germany, Switzerland. This was the pattern a bitter Alice James would later call "our rootless & accidental childhood."[5]

But as the nomadic career of the senior Jameses finally ended, their restless spirit could be seen to have infected their son. In 1869–70 Henry undertook the Grand Tour that was his leisure-class birthright, exercised earlier by William and later by Alice. But Henry's plans for an extended European stay were not satisfied by tourism. The task of his twenties and early thirties was not to identify his calling—unlike William he knew early what he wanted to do, despite the abortive experiment of legal study—but to discover a way to practice it in Europe. In the 1870s he would try Rome, Paris, and London as possible centers, returning to Cambridge or New York to remind himself of the alternatives. His cultural vision was essentially cosmopolitan, but he had to decide which city offered the best conditions for his projected work.

James's quest for a supranational identity was a quintessentially American product of his time. It was made possible by the global shift in power that altered the early Anglo-American relationship. His native country's expansion and new wealth engendered a confidence in her capacity to incorporate vast stretches of territory and her moral right to make them her own. The divine destiny of a young nation whose capacity to endure had been tested by civil conflict was manifest: to inherit the earth. Far from rejecting this grandiose vision, James may be said to have translated it into literary terms. His earliest ambitions are both personal and national, couched in language that shows no trace of modesty. He writes a friend in 1867 that his chance of success "is to let all the breezes of the west blow through me at their will," a phrase in which the promise of the American West fuses with the legacy of English poetry from the medieval "Western Wind" to Shelley's great ode. He looks upon his national origin as a blessing, because unlike Europeans Americans "can deal freely with forms of civilization not our own, can pick and choose and assimilate and in short . . . claim our property wherever we find it." Because their country remains undefined, American writers are able to force "a vast intellectual fusion and synthesis of the various national tendencies of the world."[6]

The takeover mentality behind such pronouncements is unmistakable. James's ambition is unapologetically linked to interpretive power and confidence. The American continent, he writes Charles Eliot Norton in 1871, "will yield its secrets only to a really *grasping* imagination"—one like his own. As he takes up European residence for good, he confidently announces to his family, in a gesture that could be called a speech-act: "I take possession of the old world—I inhale it—I appropriate it!"[7] As Leon Edel says of this sentence, "No conquistador, planting a flag of annexation, could have sounded a note more genuinely triumphant."[8] The aggressive animus in these declarations is evident in James's verbs: to claim property, fuse and synthesize, grasp, take possession, appropriate. All suggest the impatience of an heir who has waited too long for his share of the estate, a latter-day Heathcliff, long despised by his "betters," finally getting the better of *them*. James speaks for his long patronized countrymen—writers, political figures, tourists, ordinary citizens. As he predicts ominously in an 1878 essay, "On the whole, the American in Europe may be spoken of as a provincial who is terribly bent upon taking, in the fullness of ages, his revenge."[9]

To the victor belong the spoils. This is the standard vengeance exercised by James's American conquerors. They do indeed claim their property wherever they find it—increasingly in the treasure houses of Europe. Far from lamenting this new rape of Europa, James treats it sympathetically, though he knows the would-be possessor is sometimes foiled. The triumphs and failures of his American collectors become one of his recurrent subjects, from Christopher Newman in *The American* seeing the world as "a great bazar, where one might stroll about and purchase handsome things" to Adam Verver in *The Golden Bowl* sitting like "Alexander furnished with the spoils of Darius" amid the European masterworks he has unerringly chosen for his museum in American City.[10]

There is irony in such passages, of course, but James does not see his inheritors as unworthy recipients. In his early *New York Tribune* reports from Paris, he confesses an "acute satisfaction in seeing America stretch out her long arm and rake in, across the green cloth of the wide Atlantic, the highest prizes of the game of civilization."[11] Americans are more fit to own such treasures than the Europeans who neglect or take them for granted. An exquisite Botticelli in "a mean black frame" hidden in an obscure corner of a Florentine museum deserves a better fate: "What a pity that it should not become the property of an institution which would give it a brave gilded frame and a strong American light!"[12] And in *The Portrait of a Lady*, Daniel Touchett, with a "real aesthetic passion" for his Gardencourt, the stately home once familiar to Queen Elizabeth and to a long line of distinguished names, is unreproved for thinking "that the latest phase of its destiny was not the least honourable."[13] James's animus allows him to see the legacy of Europe as ripe for appropriation and to treat his more discriminating countrymen as deserving heirs. They also press their claim to—or choose to pass up— the old world's ornamental human treasures, like the French, English, and Italian aristocrats in *The American, The Portrait of a Lady, The Ambassadors, The Golden Bowl*.

These are the material rewards of winning. A more subtle form of James's revenge lay in becoming a world-class competitor in the game of international condescension, a contest Adams had mastered early and Eliot and Pound would carry on in their time. This was hardly a cosmopolitan response, though it drew on the cosmopolite's breadth of experience. Eliot coolly asserts the superior knowledge of an American of this class, and unapologetically carries on the condescending tradition, in one of his essays on James: "It is the final perfection, the consummation of an American to become, not an Englishman, but a European—something which no born European, no person of any European nationality, can become."[14] James often made a similar claim. The real provincials, from this perspective, are the Europeans, "defined, imprisoned, if you will, by their respective national moulds," as he puts it in an early essay. Their American observers, on the other hand, are still molten shape-changers, "not hardened yet into the old-world bronze."[15]

The interpretive confidence—or arrogance—of such assertions is breathtaking. James would not have retracted them in later life, though he might have put them more suasively. They were based, despite their national categories, on the Jameses' untypical life experience. As William concluded many years later, Henry had remained "a native of the James family, and has no other country."[16] The younger James in effect acknowledges this as he first settles into his expatriate existence: "To tell the truth I find myself a good deal more of a cosmopolitan (thanks to the combination of the continent and the U.S.A. which has formed my lot) than the average Briton of culture." But his idiosyncratic experience becomes the basis for national stereotyping. He mocks the "insular and ignorant" British abroad, who persist in putting English stamps on their letters no matter where they are posted, and concludes, "I often think that we Americans are more 'European' than they."[17]

In James's 1878 novel *The Europeans*—the title itself is a homogenizing act—Felix informs his uncle that he, like his sister, is essentially "a European."[18] Neither acknowledges a more local identity; their father was born in Sicily of American parents, Felix in France, his sister in Vienna; she is the wife of Prince Adolf of Silberstadt-Schreckenstein, a comic German principality that would probably fit into Rhode Island with plenty of room to spare. Yet that they have no real roots apparently gives them the right to call themselves Europeans at a time when few residents of that continent would have identified themselves in this way, any more than most "Orientals" in the early twentieth century or inhabitants of the "Third World" in more recent times would choose so to label themselves. Naming becomes an act of incorporation. Leon Edel suggests that even in his earliest adulthood James "had become a cosmopolite without ever having been a provincial."[19] But his frequently reiterated claim to cosmopolitanism is also the reassuring form his often uneasy rootlessness takes. A true cosmopolitan, as one of James's early skeptical interpreters observed, "is at home even in his own country!"[20]

His peripatetic existence in the 1870s is fueled by an anxiety about where he might belong. He worries early about the eventual price of expatriation. "I know that if I ever go abroad for a long residence," he writes in 1870, "I shall at best be haunted and wracked, whenever I hear an American sound, by the fantasy of thankless ignorance and neglect of my native land."[21] The conviction that he could thrive and prosper in London followed a decade of restless experimentation. Unlike his father, he was not "leisured for life," though his family was patient and generous in its sponsorship. He was determined to earn his living as a professional writer and not to dig into the family purse forever. He needed to support a serious literary vocation without writing journalism or formula fiction, and he wanted to hold on to an American audience from abroad. It took more than ten years of steady application before James solved these problems. In that period he worked in a variety of commercial genres—reviewing, travel writing, stories tailor-made for the magazines, even weekly journalism. He had to produce his more ambitious novels in the interstices and sometimes to take dictation from well-meaning editors who knew just what their readers wanted.

The path is not smooth nor the triumph assured. He tries Rome, New York, and Paris before at last finding London. James's letters home in the 1870s are full of apologies for continuing to draw on his letter of credit, anxious anticipations of his financial independence, plans for bringing it about. When he decides in 1874 to return to the United States after his frustrating two-year stay in Italy, the reasons are in great part financial. He needs interested publishers and a sympathetic audience. He writes his father that he hopes to find "a better market for my wares . . . than in this faraway region." He decides to try New York, as he tells his mother, "because I can find more abundant literary occupation by being on the premises." His sense of the literary marketplace is urgent and he can talk shop. But the New York experiment fails. The city is more expensive than Europe and offers largely literary hackwork. And after his long stay in Italy he detests New York: "*Hideous* is the most amiable word I can find to apply to it." His earlier conviction that his "salvation, intellectually and literarily" required him to live abroad has only been strengthened by the failed experiment of returning.[22]

But James had other reasons for giving up Italy. His initial response to the country had been orgiastic: "At last—for the first time—I live!" he wrote in 1869 when he first set foot in Rome. When he came back from his Grand Tour he had vowed to return "not for months but years." But those years, 1872–74, ended by convincing him that the seductive charm of the place was no substitute for the supportive cultural community he needed. He felt intellectually lonely, though his life was filled with engagements and he appreciated the city's sybaritic pleasures. There seemed to be no exit from the wealthy expatriate American colony, dominated by figures like the successful (but for James vain and pretentious) sculptor William Wetmore Story, whose official biography he later wrote. Story lived in a fifty-room apartment in Rome, held court, received commissions for his "classical" pieces, but was fatally out of touch both with modern Italy and with contemporary culture in general. Here was Santayana's "genteel tradition" in the pure state. The past was more vital than the present; there seemed no opening to the present day. James sees the American colony as sterile: "Limited and isolated, without relations with the place, or much serious appreciation of it, it tumbles back upon itself and finds itself of meagre substance."[23] His first attempt to live abroad had proven a failure.

Perhaps as a result, the Americans he sends off to Rome or Florence in his fiction encounter great misfortune: Roderick Hudson's genius is snuffed out, Daisy Miller dies of the Roman fever, Isabel Osmond returns to her incarceration in the elegant Palazzo Roccanera. The tales set in Italy tell a similar story. The expatriate artist in "The Madonna of the Future" (1873) wastes his life in trying to paint a worthy successor to the madonnas of the past. The Florentine masters he worships seem to mock his efforts; his canvas remains permanently blank, as he laments, "We are the disinherited of Art!"[24] In "The Last of the Valerii" and "Adina" (1874), the American protagonists lose the battle of wills with their Italian antagonists. But the most catastrophic story is told in *Roderick Hudson* (1875). Roderick's Roman initiation is an artistic and personal liberation from the stifling atmosphere of his New England childhood, and he rapidly produces a group of statues worthy of his genius. But his passion becomes a raging fever; he works only by fits and starts; he becomes infatuated with the illegitimate daughter of an American mother and an Italian cavaliere, a young woman who even describes herself as "corrupt, corruptible, corruption!"[25] The passion proves fatal. James's novel ends by reinforcing the New England vision of Catholic, decadent Rome as a wilderness of temptation. Roderick finds no solid basis on which to build a new life. In the fiction of the 1870s, Italy and America prove irreconcilable and James's cosmopolitan goal remains elusive.

When he tries again in 1875 he settles in Paris. "I feel as if I had struck roots into the Parisian soil, and were likely to let them grow tangled and tenacious there," he writes to Howells. But the roots are shallowly sunk and the soil not nutritive. Despite his keen interest in French literature, his instant intimacy with Turgenev, and his apparent acceptance into Flaubert's Olympian *cénacle*, where he encounters Zola, Daudet, Maupassant, Edmond de Goncourt, and other luminaries, the initial enthusiasm soon fades. He feels like an intruder and in some ways prefers to remain one. He is shocked by the frankness of French naturalism, for example by the subject of Edmond de Goncourt's latest novel: "A whore-house *de province*." But the real failing of French culture for James is its parochial quality. Of Flaubert's disciples he writes, "They are extremely narrow and it makes me rather scorn them that not a mother's son of them can read English. But this hardly matters, for they couldn't really understand it if they did."[26] In *French Poets and Novelists* (1878), the critical book he addresses to an Anglo-American audience, he attacks this linguistic and cultural provincialism and criticizes the pervasive habit of intellectual discipleship: "Everything in France proceeds by 'schools,' and there is no artist so bungling that he will not find another to call him 'dear master.'"[27] Once again, the animus is clear, and James plays the game of competitive condescension with the stacked deck his transatlantic youth provided.

After a year of this life, despite his success in at least gaining entry to various exclusive literary and social circles, he bolts for London. To William he confesses his "weariness and satiety with the French mind and its utterance. . . . I have done with 'em, forever and am turning English all over."[28] His revulsion echoes many of his misgivings about Rome. His residual puritanism discovers a pervasive immorality; he fears he will remain a permanent outsider despite the *politesse* of his hosts; the shallowness of the Paris branch of the American colony appalls him, and he is afraid of being sucked into it because other doors are closed. As he puts it in a retrospective account in his notebooks, "I couldn't get out of the detestable *American* Paris. . . . I saw, moreover, that I should be an eternal outsider."[29] As we will see, T. S. Eliot would try the same experiment in the next generation, and reach the same conclusion.

All these reactions find their way into *The American*, the first fruit of James's failed Paris experiment. Not for another quarter of a century, in *The Ambassadors*, could he bear to resurrect his first enchantment with the place in a major work. In the immediate aftermath of his disappointment he produces a novel that can be read as a national indictment. His American protagonist hardly seems like a surrogate. Unlike James, Christopher Newman is a westerner, a Civil War veteran, a self-made man, uneducated and unsophisticated, who confesses that "he had never read a novel." Nevertheless, like his creator, he is intelligent, confident, ambitious, full of an initial curiosity about and attraction to the French people he meets. He lives by a strict moral code and has no interest in the empty life of his expatriated countrymen. Despite appearances, he is right to call himself "a highly civilized man."[30]

These admirable qualities will not gain him entry to the closed aristocratic world of the Bellegardes, whose daughter he is wooing. They finally decide that they cannot derogate from their ancient principles and admit this rich bourgeois gentleman into their midst. Their house is built to exclude (as well as to enclose the inmates). Like the others in the Faubourg St. Germain, it presents "to the outer world a face as impassive and as suggestive of the concentration of privacy within as the blank walls of Eastern seraglios."[31] As James's simile hints, it has been the site of dark doings. These include broken faith, forced marriages, even murder; the real barbarians are those within the gates who claim an ultimate refinement. James's melodramatic novel is his revenge against French exclusiveness, a story—as he put it in the later preface—of "some robust but insidiously beguiled and betrayed, some cruelly wronged, compatriot: the point being in especial that he should suffer at the hands of persons pretending to represent the highest possible civilisation and to be of an order in every way superior to his own."[32] It is a moralistic and patriotic indictment, rooted like *Roderick Hudson* in James's frustrated cosmopolitan hopes. At this stage in his career, the Continental centers are too strong for his American protagonists, with a communal power to defeat them that they will no longer have when he comes to write his last novels in the twentieth century. For the present, Paris proves to be no easier to conquer than Rome.

The viable alternative is London, to which he at first responds with all the eagerness of a rejected lover on the rebound. "I take very kindly indeed to London, and am immensely contented at having come here," he writes his mother, though he is sitting alone on Christmas Eve, 1876, looking out on "the deadly darkness" of an English winter. He concludes, "I must be a born Londoner."[33] But unlike Rome and Paris, this is no infatuation. As James recalls half a dozen years later, after he has committed himself to staying in London for life, "It has succeeded beyond my most ardent hopes. . . . It is not a pleasant place; it is not agreeable, or cheerful, or easy, or exempt from reproach. It is only magnificent."[34]

As Adams had already proven, there were no barriers to acceptance for a young American with their credentials. The common language helped, of course, though their affinity with what Noel Annan has called "the intellectual aristocracy"[35] was more decisive. Respectable Americans also benefited from their anomalous position in the English social hierarchy: They were not easily placed. James's insistence that he was a stranger saved him from the cubbyholes of the English class system. As Daniel Touchett tells Isabel in *The Portrait of a Lady*, "I never took much notice of the classes. That's the advantage of being an American here; you don't belong to any class."[36] There was little danger of being relegated to an American ghetto. Within weeks of James's arrival, as the seeds planted by the letters of introduction from Adams and others sprouted and spread, he had met such prominent figures as Sir Charles Dilke, Lady Pollock, Andrew Lang, Browning, Froude, Kinglake, Trevelyan, F. T. Palgrave, and James Bryce. And this was before the season had even begun.

Unlike Paris, London was not compartmentalized by profession. James had easy access to an extraordinarily heterogeneous Establishment. That England had only one metropolis or mother-city, and that it was relatively open to interesting outsiders, proved highly important. It allowed James to do extensive fieldwork on the natives without impediment. Like Adams before him and Pound and Eliot after, he was in search of a city to which all roads lead. There was no such place in America, a country whose literary, commercial, and political centers were distinct. But in London he could find it all.

The familiar story of James's extraordinary social triumph in his adopted home has been well told by Leon Edel, who traces his expanding network of associations from his arrival.[37] It was based on his blend of eager curiosity and sophistication, his status as an attractive bachelor, his exceptional powers of conversation. James was fortunate to arrive in London at the end of his long apprenticeship. None of his books had been published in England when he arrived, though four had appeared in America. His early expatriate years had been enormously productive.

When James belatedly finds an English publisher, his accumulated works appear in dizzying succession; between 1877 and 1879, eight books: *Roderick Hudson, The American, French Poets and Novelists, The Europeans, Daisy Miller, The Madonna of the Future, Confidence, Hawthorne.* Little wonder that his name is on everyone's lips or that he dines out 140 times during the 1878–79 London season.[38]

But there is a deeper reason for his brilliant success than his social skills or his productivity. He begins to define himself not as an American, not as a European, not even as a cosmopolite, but as an Anglo-Saxon. His publishing debut in England—very much by design—is *French Poets and Novelists.* James offers himself as a cicerone for Englishmen and Americans interested in French culture. He regularly uses phrases like "the Anglo-Saxon reader" to associate himself with his intended audience's shared assumptions and values. "We of English speech" are uncomfortable with Gautier's frankness about the body, but that writer pays "scantiest attention to our English scruples." James's "we" and "our" conflate his English and American readers: In contrast to the alien French, "we" are of one mind and spirit. George Sand's sexual frankness is intolerable: "From our point of view . . . her discretion is simply non-existent." In contrast to "us," the French are "they." "They have the psychological passion," James writes; "but in dealing with people of this race and society . . . we Anglo-Saxons are constantly reminded of the necessity of weighing virtues and vices in an adjusted scale."[39] The Anglo-Saxons, in other words, are a single people—united in their moral seriousness, reticence, and judiciousness; lacking passion, perhaps, but serenely confident in their maturity. James anticipates the Anglo-American rapprochement on the horizon, and helps to create it.

His Anglo-Saxon racial pride is deep-seated and increasingly linked to his highest ambitions. "It seems to me many times the strongest and richest race in the world," he writes Charles Eliot Norton in 1878; "my dream is to arrive at the ability to be, in some degree its moral portrait painter!" There is an unmistakable political resonance to this faith. James identifies with the greatness of the British Empire and regrets its decline on the world scene. He mourns the loss of England's international prestige and hopes for the revival of her military prowess no matter what the cost: "I almost wish she would fight in a bad cause, if only to show that she still can." And he laments "the political decadence of our mighty mother-land."[40] The family metaphors stress filial devotion rather than resentment or rivalry.

These quotations are from James's letters, but his published works are, if anything, even more Anglocentric. His essays of the late seventies and eighties are full of a romantic imperialism and regularly treat London as "the capital of our race," or, by a seemingly effortless extension, "the capital of the human race." London is the new omphalos, round which the reverent American tracing his roots can see "the total of the English-speaking territories of the globe as the mere margin, the fitted girdle." James verges on sycophancy in his celebration of "the greatness of England," a phrase that has a romantic sound to an American "who remounts the stream of time to the head-waters of his own loyalties." He describes the Thames estuary as "remind[ing] you of nothing less than the wealth and power of the British Empire at large; so that a kind of metaphysical magnificence hovers over the scene."[41] A modern reader will recall a remarkably similar passage at the beginning of a work by another Anglophile expatriate, Conrad's *Heart of Darkness:* "What greatness had not floated on the ebb of that river into the mystery of an unknown world! . . . The dreams of men, the seed of commonwealths, the germs of empires."

Is it any wonder that such attitudes would have earned James an initial sympathetic hearing in his new home? An apparently faithful colonial is expressing his allegiance to the mother country. But this is not just the clever strategy of an ambitious applicant for admission. It is perfectly genuine. James had expressed such sentiments in the more complex medium of fiction long before he settled in England, in "A Passionate Pilgrim" (1871), one of the few tales he rescues from his first decade as a writer and uses as the title story of his first published collection. James's tale is saturated with Anglo-Saxon nostalgia and is a plea for the reconciliation of the two major branches of the family. Clement Searle, its Anglophile American protagonist, is forty, seriously ill, but determined to see the England of his ancestors. He also has a claim on the ancient Searle estate, owned by his distant cousin Richard, a childless widower who lives there with his unmarried sister. We have seen that tales of "the American claimant" also captured the imaginations of Hawthorne, Twain, and Frances Hodgson Burnett. Like them, James longs for Anglo-American reconciliation. Clement's response on setting foot in England suggests that he has found his true home. We are told that the roots of this reaction "are so deeply buried in the virgin soil of our primary culture" that it makes an American's pilgrimage to England "fatal and sacred." The dream of reconciliation is pursued in his attraction to Richard Searle's sister, a virgin spirit who seems destined for him. When Clement begs her to pay his claim to the estate "from your heart," she replies, "If I marry you . . . it will repair the trouble."[42]

It is all fantasy, of course. Clement is ill and unlikely to survive; and Richard Searle is outraged when he learns of the plot. He throws his American kinsman out of the house and screams at him that in any suit concerning the estate, "you shall be beaten—beaten—beaten!"[43] That James's American intruder is a moribund aesthete and his Englishman a vigorous opponent plays against type and offers reassurance to British readers fearful of the threat posed by these American invaders. But though the estate will remain in English hands, this is treated as a loss. As the disappointed Clement lies dying, Miss Searle visits him, dressed in mourning. Her brother has been killed in a riding accident, has left no other heirs, and she will now almost certainly never marry. The murderous rivalry between the English and American heirs to the Anglo-Saxon legacy has killed them both. If they had reconciled the line might have been carried on, strengthening both countries. The story can be read as a political allegory urging Anglo-American rapprochement, though James retains the trappings of romantic fantasy. "If only" is part of that fantasy. This early tale continued to be important to him despite its obvious crudeness. It was the only one of the many stories he wrote before his first expatriate experiments that he included in the career-defining New York Edition. But then, it had been his first love letter to the country he was destined to marry.

II

James's successful courtship of his English audience shows not only his passion but his tactical shrewdness. He knows (or quickly learns) exactly what it wants to hear and tailors his early expatriate work to meet those expectations. At the same time, he needs to hang on to his American readers, to make sure that this Anglo-American relationship is nurtured on both sides of the ocean. There is no want of effort or lack of opportunity. The effort was unremitting and the opportunity there for an American-born writer in the last quarter of the nineteenth century. A sophisticated transatlantic go-between was suddenly in great demand. The shift in Anglo-American power relations created a good deal of uneasy curiosity. The newly affluent class of American travelers whose annual invasion or long-term European residence increased dramatically in these years required intermediaries. The Baedeker and Murray guidebooks could identify the starred masterworks. But they were not much help in interpreting the puzzling mores of the alien Europeans.

Even a reasonable command of the foreign tongues, including English as distinct from American, did not guarantee an understanding of the puzzling customs and habits of mind that differed, sometimes so alarmingly, from American ones: the unfamiliar class system, gender roles and family structure, the rules for courtship and marriage, for what one might and might not say or do. Every major European city soon contained an American colony—"contained" in several senses of the word. One might beat a safe retreat to these higher-class ghettos, like many minor characters in James's fiction. But the more adventurous want to master the alien code. When Isabel Archer's aunt, in *The Portrait of a Lady*, informs her that she cannot with decorum stay up late into the night talking to Lord Warburton even with her cousin Ralph as chaperone, Isabel is guardedly grateful for the information:

"I always want to know the things one shouldn't do."
"So as to do them?" asked her aunt.
"So as to choose," said Isabel.[44]

The scene suggests the options that confront the Jamesian characters who come to Europe knowing only the mores of their native land. Isabel's bafflement and determination to judge for herself are paradigmatic.

There is a comparable need to understand on the other side. Who were these strange Americans now visible (and audible!) in all the cities and pleasure spots of Europe? The obstacles that kept out the socially dubious did not succeed in barring the Americans. In some cities they had even become the vogue. London's highest social circle, presided over by the Prince of Wales, signaled their astonishing success. His youthful visit to the United States had given him a taste for the freedom his own restricted life had lacked. Once he came of age he opened his Marlborough House set to people notable for their vivacity rather than their prominent place in British society, and Americans—especially American women—were conspicuous among them. Great wealth even if recently acquired and freedom from the deadly propriety of Victoria's court attracted the future monarch; and here the American invaders had a clear edge over the prince's peers.[45]

The fascination with Americans filtered down to less august circles. British curiosity had long been satisfied by writers and entertainers who fed the primitivist taste for the American frontier. The 1880s triumphal European tour by Buffalo Bill's Wild West Show only confirmed the image of Americans as reassuringly barbarian; and Bret Harte churned out his increasingly inauthentic tales of the California gold rush for years after he settled in London. As James asks pointedly in 1898, "Has he continued to distil and dilute the wild West because the public would only take him as wild and Western?"[46] But the Americans now becoming socially visible in Europe were not cowboys or outcasts of Poker Flat. They lived by some code that had to be cracked, but to which the British lacked the key. So Jenny Churchill, the American-born mother of the future prime minister and a prominent figure in the Marlborough House set, recalls late in life that "In England, as on the Continent, the American woman was looked upon as a strange and abnormal creature, with habits and manners something between a Red Indian and a Gaiety Girl. . . . No distinction was ever made among Americans: they were all supposed to be of one uniform type."[47]

There was a need for a writer who might define and distinguish the new American types by embodying them in compelling literary works. As early as 1862, Trollope had complained that the emergent American entrepreneurial capitalist remained a mystery, though he might "be a great man to all posterity, if only he had a poet to sing of his valour."[48] James could be said to have applied for the position: His portrait of Christopher Newman in *The American*, though it was in prose, might have been produced to meet Trollope's specifications. Perfectly conscious of which aspects of American behavior puzzled Europeans, James was the ideal native informant.

The use of this anthropological term seems appropriate, since the kind of information his fiction provides was often treated as ethnographic. James calls his tales of the clash of cultures his "*études des moeurs*,"[49] and so they were often received—as scientific studies of national customs. A contemporary reviewer of *The American* and *The Europeans* sees James studying "the human specimens, which he has first carefully selected," and concludes that both books "illustrate the different types of character and manners produced by European and American civilization." Another congratulates him on having invented the new literary genre of "romantic sociology." A third concludes that his museum of characters "has rather an anthropological than an artistic interest." However inadequate these early estimates of James may be, they illustrate how some of his first readers used his work. His fiction is instrumental; it provides helpful information. In one of the earliest overviews of James's career, an English critic notes the "extraordinary minuteness and detachment of vision" with which he has studied his countrymen and assesses the impact of his work on the English mind, "which, contrasting its knowledge of America now with what it was some twenty or thirty years ago, perceives how largely, among other causes, Mr. James has contributed to that knowledge."[50]

A great deal of James's early work is self-consciously produced to satisfy this market need and designed as a guide for the perplexed. His peripatetic childhood had alerted him to national differences, and he often stresses group identity and locale over individuality, as some of his titles suggest: *The American, The Europeans, The Bostonians, Washington Square,* "The Siege of London," "A New England Winter," "A London Life." And even in *Daisy Miller*, the named character is no individual but a national type—in this case, the American Girl. Ethnological typecasting is the primary method of characterization in James's early fiction. The psychological depths of his later portraits are rarely plumbed before the 1880s, in part because his readers' curiosity is focused not on the individual psyche but on the divergent manners and morals of identifiable groups.

The young Henry James knew he had stumbled on a mother lode. As he reflects on this early career phase three decades later, he notes sardonically, "It was as if I had, vulgarly speaking, received quite at first the 'straight tip'—to back the right horse or buy the right shares. The mixture of manners was to become in other words not a less but a very much more appreciable and interesting subject of study."[51] James's early fiction unashamedly feeds this market interest by defining its characters typologically. This is our introduction to Christopher Newman in *The American* (1877); his every characteristic—including, of course, his name—reinforces his generic identity: "An observer with anything of an eye for national types . . . might have felt a certain humorous relish of the almost ideal completeness with which he filled out the national mould. The gentleman on the divan was a powerful specimen of an American."[52]

This reliance on "specimens" or "types" is not limited to the title character. The French are similarly labeled. Their puzzling behavior is explained to Newman (and indirectly to James's American readers) by a Paris-based friend. She says of the aristocratic world of Claire de Cintré, whom Newman is courting, "It is the skim of the milk of the old noblesse. Do you know what a Legitimist is, or an Ultramontane? Go into Madame de Cintré's drawing-room some afternoon, at five o'clock, and you will see the best-preserved specimens." They represent the displaced titled aristocracy of the ancien régime, as Newman embodies a crescent one that lays claim to qualities the moribund one has lost: great wealth, power, largesse, valor, probity. A sympathetic member of Claire's family sees him as "an American duke, the Duke of California." That Claire rejects Newman at her mother's insistence, though she loves him and sees him as her deliverer, should not surprise us if we have been following the novel's anthropological perspective. As Newman's confidante explains, "In France you must never say nay to your mother, whatever she requires of you. . . . With those people the family is everything; you must act, not for your own pleasure, but for the advantage of the family."[53]

This combination of national stereotyping and ethnographic lore is found in most of the novels and tales of the 1870s: *Roderick Hudson* (1875), *The Europeans* (1878), and in the contemporaneous collections of the shorter fiction: *A Passionate Pilgrim and Other Tales*; *Daisy Miller: A Study. An International Episode. Four Meetings*; *The Madonna of the Future and Other Tales*; *The Diary of a Man of Fifty and A Bundle of Letters*. It is a carefully calculated career decision. James had been publishing stories in American journals for over a decade, but these tales attached little importance to the sense of place. He casually abandons more than a dozen of them in putting together his first collection. A letter about his plan for this book reveals how carefully he considers the market: "What I desire is this: to make a volume, a short time hence, of tales on the theme of American adventurers in Europe, leading off with the *Passionate Pilgrim*. I have three or four more to write."[54] He had found his subject after years of writing fiction that was now irrelevant to his opportunity—to become the taxonomist of the new internationalism.

This is the role that made him famous on both sides of the Atlantic. His 1878 tale *Daisy Miller* enjoyed an extraordinary vogue and gave permanent life to a new American type, so that for years "a Daisy Miller" was a shorthand way of categorizing a disturbing new model of young womanhood: a naive, brash, vulnerable, provincial American girl who seems sexually provocative—not bashful, not modest, willing to meet a man's gaze—but who is actually quite innocent. Daisy is the victim of conventional people who see her unorthodox freedom of movement and speech, her unchaperoned life, as proof of her fallen state. Her behavior puzzles and disturbs her Europeanized compatriot Winterbourne because he has lost touch with his country's emerging types. He is attracted to her but cannot act because he cannot fit her into a standard category. Her "inscrutable combination of audacity and innocence" confuses him, and when he lectures her on the need to "go by the custom of the place" while she is abroad, she protests against this abridgement of her freedom: "I have never allowed a gentleman to dictate to me."[55] When Winterbourne sees her late at night in the Colosseum with a handsome Italian, he confidently writes her off as tainted goods. But he is wrong; despite appearances, Daisy is as fresh as her name. Though she contracts the Roman fever, the *mal aria*, it is the breath of scandal and Winterbourne's rejection that kills her. She is the victim of a fatally erroneous diagnosis. James tries to protect the Daisy Millers from such ignorant malpractice by characterizing the newly emergent condition of women she represents. He wants to isolate and analyze a new phenomenon, a new type.

The clash of opposed national types is not necessarily tragic. James also exploits the comic potential of crossed cultural codes in some of his tales and in *The Europeans*, a novel in which the conflict takes place on American soil. In bringing his "Europeans"—actually the adult son and daughter of Europeanized Americans—to visit their long estranged New England family, he creates endless opportunities for comic perplexity, as the rigidly puritanical Wentworths try to fathom the bizarre behavior of these charming, sophisticated, and devious extraterrestrials, the bohemian Felix and his brilliant, complicated sister Eugenia, the Baroness Munster. Eugenia's ambiguous marital status as the morganatic wife of a minor European prince, whose marriage may be dissolved for reasons of state, is totally bewildering to the Americans. Her earnest uncle Mr. Wentworth lies awake anxiously wondering, "Was it right, was it just, was it acceptable?"[56]

But it is not just the European visitors' circumstances but their performative conversation that baffles their American kin. Their style is courtly, self-mocking, theatrical—anything but straightforward or purposeful. Mr. Wentworth—who to Felix's eyes looks "as if he were undergoing martyrdom, not by fire, but by freezing"—reacts with uneasy confusion. His response to Eugenia's witty persiflage is the apprehensive thought, "This was the cleverness, he supposed; the brilliancy was beginning." And as he and his sober daughter Charlotte listen uncomprehendingly to Felix's chatter about the "charming" sense of "duty" he sees in a less reliable member of their family, they "both looked at him as if they were watching a greyhound doubling."[57]

Their conversations are not communication but antiphonal responses in different languages. Although Felix convinces his more rebellious cousin Gertrude to marry him and live in Europe, the two branches of the family fail to find a common tongue and part in mutual bewilderment. Even when his uncle agrees to the marriage, he has no idea what is happening. His failure is a sign of his American provincialism: "the old man felt himself destitute of the materials for a judgment. It seemed to him that he ought to find them in his own experience, as a man of the world and an almost public character; but they were not there, and he was ashamed to confess to himself . . . the unfurnished condition of this repository."[58] James's novel is both an entertainment that capitalizes on the shared bafflement of his national types and a bicultural dictionary designed to teach each party the alien tongue. But its ideal audience is the cosmopolitan readership that can easily cross cultural boundaries.

James exploits the satiric opportunities of juxtaposing national stereotypes in a series of linked tales produced for this market—"The Pension Beaurepas," "A Bundle of Letters," and "The Point of View" (1879–82). All are plotless stories that place their characters in a neutral setting (a pension, an ocean liner). The taxonomic spirit is primary, and the comedy grows out of the failure of these ill-assorted national types to make sense of each other. Their meetings only confirm their initial prejudices; despite its reputation, travel narrows. In these stories, the individual gives way to the type. Of the jaded Mme. Beauregard, who has seen every sort pass through her pension, James writes, "as regards individuals, she had neither likes nor dislikes; but she was capable of expressing esteem or contempt for a species."[59] Both "A Bundle of Letters" and "The Point of View" are written in epistolary form, which allows James to mock his benighted characters, as he shifts like a ventriloquist from one to another. In "The Point of View," for example, he allows first a contemptuous Frenchman, then a superpatriotic American to describe the Capitol in Washington. The Frenchman sees only cultural poverty: "No functionaries, no door-keepers, no officers, no uniforms, no badges, no restrictions, no authority—nothing but a shabby people circulating in a labyrinth of spittoons." The proud American interprets the same facts as a parable of democratic access: "The doors were gaping wide—I walked all about; there were no door-keepers, no officers, nor flunkeys."[60]

As James's title suggests, everything one sees is determined by one's "point of view." Or at any rate everything these marionettes see. The characters in these stories, as well as many in the novels contemporary with them, are shaped by the author's illustrative design. They are "specimens" pure and simple, collected by a more cosmopolitan, Olympian intelligence to mock the narrow vision of provincials. No one has depth or can grow or need be taken seriously. The real point of view is that of an arrogant satirist who sees his fellow creatures as bits of speaking matter to be mimicked and classified. Such fiction can be amusing; it can be superficially informative; it can help readers master the new internationalism. But it cannot be moving; and this James gradually comes to understand.

He is finally not content to put his brand on various national types, nor to be seen forever as "the Author of *Daisy Miller*," which is how he was often identified. He has ambitions that go beyond the realm of

"romantic sociology." To satisfy them he has to abandon the static conception of character intrinsic to his immediate enterprise. His escape
comes through writing the novella *Washington Square* (1880), in
which he goes back to the New York of his youth, before restless wandering had become his lot, and to a tightly enclosed domestic world in
which the highly charged emotions of family life take precedence over
the shallow observations of travel. The brilliant, imperious Dr. Sloper
does take his formerly pliable daughter Catherine to Europe for two
years to make her forget her passion for Morris Townsend, her charming, mercenary suitor. But the sights of Europe are mere background
scenery in the working out of her complex relations with her father
and her lover.

The whole story serves as a critique of James's own patronizing tendency to read types with epistemological confidence. As a physician,
Dr. Sloper is proud of his diagnostic skill and boasts of his ability to see
through Morris in a single encounter. As he tells Morris's sister, "You
see I am helped by a habit I have of dividing people into classes, into
types." He is not wrong about Morris, who is indeed the heartless fortune hunter Dr. Sloper takes him for. But he is hopelessly mistaken
about Catherine, the plain, stolid daughter he sees as "a weak-minded
woman." Catherine may initially have been docile and foolish, but as
she grasps her father's contempt for her and Morris's perfidy, her resistance stiffens and she grows through her multiple disillusionments
into a figure of commanding dignity and self-reliance. *Washington
Square* reveals the blindness and arrogance of a too confident typecasting. When Catherine's mature response gives Dr. Sloper "a sudden
sense of having underestimated his daughter," he is not pleasantly surprised but angry, because her growth challenges his analytic authority.
In tracing Catherine's gradual, convincing transformation, James suggests that no character—no matter how initially unpromising—can be
written off as static. She is capable of change, of *re*vision, as when she
sees her romantic suitor with new eyes: "It was the old voice; but it had
not the old charm. . . . It seemed to be he, and yet not he; it was the
man who had been everything, and yet this person was nothing."[61] As
Catherine's mind grows, her father's contracts, until he can no longer
understand his daughter at all. In constructing such a narrative of
changes, James put his own diagnostic pride and his patronizing atti-

tude toward his more easily typecast and supposedly fixed fellow mortals under a humbling scrutiny.

This self-questioning allows him to shape *The Portrait of a Lady* (1881) out of different clay. On the surface the story also records the encounter of Americans and Europeans; but although some figures like Isabel Archer's persistent suitors Lord Warburton and Caspar Goodwood are still conceived as static national stereotypes, the characters who affect her life most deeply are not. They amalgamate different national traits. Her uncle Daniel Touchett has retained his American identity despite decades of living in England. When his son Ralph complains that he has never mastered the art of English reticence, Mr. Touchett replies with easy confidence, "I say what I please." His strong sense of individuality accounts for the fact that "It had been for himself so very soluble a problem to live in England, and yet not be of it." His wife and son are similar hybrids. Though educated at Harvard and Oxford, Ralph is the product of neither country: "His outward conformity to the manners that surrounded him was none the less the mask of a mind that greatly enjoyed its independence, on which nothing long imposed itself." And Mrs. Touchett counters Isabel's innocent question about whether her point of view is American with the impatient rejoinder, "American? Never in the world; that's shockingly narrow. My point of view, thank God, is personal!"[62]

But the least easily placed characters are Madame Merle and Gilbert Osmond, the mysterious pair who jointly trap Isabel into a disastrous marriage. They too are impossible to characterize on the basis of their origins. Isabel's attempt to classify Madame Merle only leads to confusion. She first decides she is French because she speaks the language flawlessly; but before long she speculates that "Madame Merle might be German—a German of rank, a countess, a princess."[63] In point of fact, Madame Merle was born in the Brooklyn Navy Yard, married a Swiss businessman, lives in Italy, and is as much at home in England or France as anywhere. At the end of the novel she plans to go back—if that is the right word—to America. The impression she gives of unfathomable depths is closely tied to her cosmopolitan experience.

An even more baffling figure is her intimate friend Gilbert Osmond, and this is not merely because the two have a secret—that they were lovers when each was married, and that Pansy Osmond is their unacknowledged child. James's introduction of Osmond offers a striking contrast to his confident typecasting of Christopher Newman in *The American:* "You would have been much at a loss to determine his nationality. . . . He was one of those persons who, in the matter of race, may, as the phrase is, pass for anything." His aura of mystery deepens his interest. Ralph tells Isabel, "I don't know his antecedents, his family, his origin. For all I know, he may be a prince in disguise." It is precisely this opacity that fatally attracts Isabel: "He resembled no one she had ever seen; most of the people she knew might be divided into groups of half-a-dozen specimens. . . . Her mind contained no class which offered a natural place to Mr. Osmond—he was a specimen apart."[64]

James's terms here offer an indirect critique of his earlier reliance on stereotypes (groups, classes, specimens) and a signal that such short-cuts are no longer helpful. All these characters (and in the long run, Isabel herself) use their expatriation as a form of freedom to construct an idiosyncratic identity independent of any given social order. What they make of this freedom is not necessarily attractive. They challenge stable expectations and institutions. They can be willful, irresponsible, devious, elusive, dangerous. They take liberties and risks, and their lives are strikingly experimental. But they are neither simple nor dull, and we want to know what they will do next.

Such characters are capable of change over time, and the capacious, slow-moving narrative is constructed to highlight this fact. The stages of Isabel's growing awareness are patiently narrated, and the notoriously inconclusive ending of the book (so frustrating for readers requiring resolution) suggests that her growth will not stop merely because the novel does. She remains a mobile character perpetually in transit. In his later preface, James notes that Isabel's consciousness, not a plot or situation, was the "single small corner-stone" of "the large building" he had constructed. The heart of his narrative lies in the maturation of her sensibility, and its most significant action is mental—the "extraordinary meditative vigil" in the middle of the book in which a solitary Isabel reflects on the decay of her marriage and the growth of her understanding in the chapter James justifiably saw as "obviously the best thing in the book."[65]

Isabel's growth alarms her friends and relations. "O Jupiter!" exclaims her impatient brother-in-law, "I hope she isn't going to develop any more!"

And her friend Henrietta Stackpole laments, "She is not the bright American girl she was. She is taking different views, and turning away from her old ideals." Even Ralph, who fosters her growth and eagerly watches from the sidelines, is not happy with the changes he observes: "The keen, free girl had become quite another person; what he saw was the fine lady who was supposed to represent something."[66] But all these complaints hypostatize an essential, innocent Isabel whose fall into darker knowledge is regrettable. James's sense of her is different. Experience and suffering do not ennoble her but increase her understanding. They make her a competent interpreter of a world of tangled desires, of illusions and disillusionments whose complexity she can finally assess even to her own cost.

In this deepened vision, the moral categories for evaluating people become as useless as her initial national stereotypes. Can Madame Merle conceivably be called *"wicked,"* Isabel wonders, considering how cynically she had manipulated her newly rich friend into marrying her ex-lover? As Isabel reflects on Madame Merle's motives—her desire to give her unacknowledgeable daughter a mother as well as the chance to make the kind of marriage that had eluded *her*, and as she imagines how Osmond must be treating the agent who had engineered his present misery, she can only murmur, "Poor Madame Merle!" The same empathetic imagination allows her to see beyond the easy dismissal of her husband as a deceitful fortune hunter, of the Morris Townsend type. He is that, of course; yet his love for her had originally been genuine enough, and it was fed by her own unintentional deception of him: "She had effaced herself, when he first knew her; she had made herself small, pretending that there was less of her than there really was." She sees herself in retrospect as "hypocritical" and reflects on how cruelly he must have been awakened to her true, fiercely independent nature. What she had kept from him "was the whole thing—her character, the way she felt, the way she judged."[67] *The Portrait of a Lady* is full of deceptions and seems to follow the simple typecasting of fairy tales—the wicked enchanter, the innocent maiden. Its complex vision challenges these stereotypes by simultaneously accepting and questioning them. Although our sympathies lie with Isabel in her conflict with her husband, we also come to understand that Osmond was merely the less deceived of the two, and that Madame Merle's heart had its reasons.[68]

Even more strikingly, James makes it possible for us to see Isabel's behavior as a kind of adultery—not physical, like her husband's, but emotional. She is consistently disloyal to his wishes while pretending she is working on his behalf, as in her sabotaging of Warburton's plan to propose to Pansy and her encouragement of Ned Rosier's suit. Osmond's jealousy of Ralph, his dislike of Henrietta, are after all well founded. He knows intuitively that the secrets of their marriage will be betrayed to these intimates, as in fact they are. When Isabel tells Henrietta of her unhappiness, her friend advises her to leave her husband. And the narrator comments drily, "It was not surprising that Gilbert Osmond should not have taken comfort in Miss Stackpole; his instinct had naturally set him in opposition to a young lady capable of advising his wife to withdraw from the conjugal mansion." Of Ralph's relations with Isabel we learn that "He tried and tried again to make her betray Osmond; he felt cold-blooded, dishonourable, cruel almost, in doing so." But he persists and is rewarded on his deathbed, when Isabel acknowledges her marital misery, lets Ralph tell her that he loves her, and confesses in turn, "I don't care for anything but you."[69]

That our sympathy for Isabel should survive such betrayals is not so much the product of changed attitudes toward marriage—in which "till death us do part" has become optional; nor is it a response to the monstrous conspiracy of which she was a victim. In fact the belief in marriage as a sacred, indissoluble bond is something Isabel and her husband share; and the conspiracy, as we have seen, has trapped the conspirators as well as their target. Nor does the victim remain helpless. Her initiation into knowledge makes her a formidable antagonist, able to dispatch Madame Merle to America, possessed of as much power as the husband she returns to confront. James's deepened sense of individual identity and need, of the inevitability of human conflict and growth, of the uselessness of group standards for judging behavior, all work to create the heterodox, unstable moral environment the alert reader must negotiate. Here the essential differences are not between Americans and Europeans or the wicked and the innocent, as they so often were in the earlier fiction. National and moral categories are constantly in play, but they serve primarily to distinguish the simpler characters from the more complex. The binary oppositions that dominated works like *The American* and *The Europeans*, and that proved so useful as a guide to perplexed provincials, are here abandoned. Introduction to Cosmopolitanism has been displaced by the advanced course.

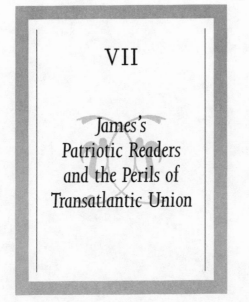

VII

James's
Patriotic Readers
and the Perils of
Transatlantic Union

We are each the product of circumstances and there are tall
stone walls which fatally divide us.

James to Howells, 30 March 1877

I

JAMES SET himself two goals in his first expatriate years—to choose
and settle in a European metropolis with a rich, cosmopolitan culture
to which he could secure entry; and to find a way of writing serious fiction that gained him a new European readership without alienating
the American audience he was leaving behind. His early career seems
constructed according to some strict architectural timetable: identify
the site, draw up plans, secure funding, build the foundation, proceed
step by step until the whole grand edifice is triumphantly in place. And
if one reads the record selectively, this more or less corresponds to
what actually happened. The confidence in his long-range objectives
sustains him through the inevitable setbacks any writer faces, as well as
while he produces the evanescent work that came—and helped to
pay—his way. Journalism, travel writing, stories, and reviews bought
him time. In the dozen years before he publishes his first books, James
contributes about two hundred pieces to periodicals. But he does not

allow himself to be deflected from his more ambitious goals by the requirements of pleasing a popular audience. This is a luxury his family's long financial sponsorship makes possible.

His decade-long apprenticeship finally earns him the freedom to devote himself to writing a novel about Americans abroad. His friend Howells, the editor of *The Atlantic*, agrees to publish and pay for the parts as James writes them; and so *Roderick Hudson* is born. With the publication in rapid succession of that book and *The American*, both of which appeared first as serials in the *Atlantic*, then as books from the Boston firm of James R. Osgood, James had established himself as an American writer with a following in his own country. Osgood had already published A *Passionate Pilgrim and Other Tales*, the deliberately delayed collection of his short fiction organized around "the theme of American adventurers in Europe." But though copies of these editions were available in London, he had not yet found an English publisher. This was clearly the next task for an American writer who hoped to make that city his home. In 1877 he submits the collection of his essays on French writers to Macmillan & Co., assuring them that "I should like to publish the book in England; I have taken, and propose to take, no steps to its appearing in America."[1] Despite misgivings, Macmillan accepts, largely in the hope of becoming the English publisher of James's fiction. His reputation had crossed the Atlantic.

From this point on, James juggles his commitments to the two literary markets, but there are signs that he favors the English one. He is so delighted to have *Daisy Miller* accepted by the *Cornhill*, the distinguished British literary journal edited by Leslie Stephen, that he neglects to make copyright arrangements in America. As a result, James's most successful tale is pirated by two periodicals in his own country and loses him a good deal of revenue. Nevertheless, *Daisy Miller* makes his name in both countries, largely because of his shrewd sense of the cultural politics at stake. As we have seen, it feeds the transatlantic interest in national typecasting. But it also balances the English curiosity about this odd new type with the American need to exonerate her. Detached clinical analysis (the full title is *Daisy Miller: A Study*) combines with the case for the defense. No final verdict is necessary because James kills Daisy off before anyone has to take up the challenge of her heterodox code and conduct. Despite her immaturity, she is on the way to becoming what was soon to be called "the new woman." But she is not allowed to grow into a woman. Cut off in her youth: curious, affecting, but not alarming. It was a clever debut for what promised to be a mainstream career, and James became the lion of the hour: This was the season of the 140 dinner parties.

The belated English publication of his earlier books reinforced the sense of achievement, rather than of mere promise. How delightful to meet Mr. James! And the early novels and tales could all be read, like *Daisy Miller*, as unthreatening. That passionate pilgrim Clement Searle dies before pressing his claim to the ancestral estate or to its English heiress; Roderick Hudson, like Daisy, is killed off in his youth; Christopher Newman declines to use the damaging evidence of the Bellegardes' crimes to avenge himself; the disturbingly complex Eugenia in *The Europeans* does not divorce her prince to marry Robert Acton, the ornamental bachelor of the New England circle she briefly invades.[2] In all these works, the arrival of the adventurers from abroad does not threaten the stability of the established order.

This reassuring vision helped to cement James's relations with both his American and English audience for a time. After *Daisy Miller* and *The Europeans* he had no difficulty in publishing his work serially in both England and the United States, a profitable arrangement that promised to make him financially independent for good. *Washington Square* and *The Portrait of a Lady* came out simultaneously in British and American periodicals, followed shortly by their appearance in London and Boston in volume form. There was nothing accidental in this success. He worked hard to appeal equally to the audiences of his native and adopted countries and to anticipate and defuse possible offense. He allows Isabel to reject Lord Warburton, but he gives her reasons "at the risk of making the reader smile." And he continues, a little anxiously, "Smile not, however, I venture to repeat, at this simple young lady from Albany, who debated whether she should accept an English peer before he had offered himself, and who was disposed to believe that on the whole she could do better."[3] Every word of this artfully constructed sentence is chosen to balance the presumptuousness of Isabel's decision against its legitimacy.

Such labors brought the expected rewards. On the eve of James's departure for an extended stay in America in 1881—his first in six years—he writes his London publisher that he sees copies of the *Portrait* in every bookshop window, "which makes me feel as if I had not only started but arrived." And in his own country, he finds that he is "someone" there at last.[4] He is lionized in Boston, New York, and Washington. His triumphal tour culminates in a Washington dinner in which the other guests include President Arthur and a distinguished circle of the country's political, diplomatic, and business leaders.[5] And when James returns to London from a second American trip in 1883— the last, as it will turn out, for more than twenty years—Macmillan is bringing out an inexpensive collected edition of his works in fourteen volumes, a shilling each in wrappers, a guinea for the entire set in cloth.[6] Truly, the forty-year-old author might be said to have arrived.

THIS IS THE familiar sanguine version of James's "conquest of London." But there is a more ominous tale to tell, in which this half decade of glory shows early signs that the Pax Anglo-Americana James had negotiated so carefully will not hold. He finds to his surprise that readers on both sides of the Atlantic are considerably more thin-skinned than he had anticipated. The tide of praise meets a powerful undercurrent of hostility. The British response is far from uniformly favorable. Who *was* this young American meteor lately descended on British soil? What gave him the right to regard the native inhabitants with a level glance, or worse, from a superior vantage? The first sign of trouble came in the British reception of "An International Episode" (1878), the early version of the Isabel Archer–Lord Warburton courtship plot, in which an intelligent but presumptuous American girl of no obvious importance has the temerity to reject the proposal of the heir to a dukedom. Lord Lambeth is handsome, good-natured, empty-headed, and much smitten with Bessie Alden, the "serious" young woman from Boston who, upon reflection, finds him "distinctly dull."[7] James was unprepared for and disturbed by the hostile British reaction to this tale. As he writes a friend, "So long as one serves up Americans for their entertainment it is all right—but hands off the sacred natives!" The English are not prepared to be "*ironized*," he tells his mother, and he vows not to repeat the experiment, since he likes them too much "to go into the satire-business or even the light ironi-cal."[8] But of course he only compounds the offense in *The Portrait of a Lady* by making Isabel's rejection of her peer an important event in a major novel.

In James's courtship of the British he can never quite keep the mockery out of his voice. Some of his readers quickly recognize that this is less a game than a power contest. He challenges the sense of decorum. His English reviewers are alert to the politics embedded in such narratives. In the words of an 1882 essay in *Blackwood's*, James has set out to record "the predominance of the great American race, and the manner in which it has overrun and conquered the Old World." His American intruders "overshadow altogether the background against which they pose, and make London and Paris and Rome into Western settlements, with the most easy consciousness that they are lords of all."[9] *The Spectator* complains that it is humiliating "to find that this son of the New World regards England in very much the same light as we regard Italy—as a museum."[10] The anger mixes with fear that power is passing from England to America, as it had once passed from Italy to Great Britain.

But the most comprehensive attack on the presumptuousness of James and other would-be cosmopolites appeared in 1883 in a *Quarterly Review* essay on American novelists. To read this outraged response gives us a sense of what kind of resistance James and other expatriate artists faced. The *Quarterly* reviewer regards them as poaching on pri-vate property. They should stick to their own sphere—the description of their native country and its colorful inhabitants. The American novels worth reading are only ones that, like Charles Brockden Brown's, offer "true and picturesque sketches" of America—those by Cooper, William Gilmore Simms, Hawthorne, Bret Harte, the anonymous author of *Democracy* (that brilliant book about Washington), and "Mr. George W. Cable, who is doing for the State of Louisiana what Nathaniel Hawthorne did for New England."[11]

The works of Mr. Henry James, on the other hand, can hardly even be called American, the *Quarterly* tells its readers. His characters are removed from their native habitats and seem singularly unattractive. In depicting such morally ambiguous figures as Daisy Miller he "has done scant justice to his countrywomen." He "comes almost as a stranger to make his 'analyses' of Americans." James's geographical and interpretive distance from his native land makes him an unreliable commentator on the disturbingly hybridized Americans to be found abroad and on the Europeans they encounter. Such writers should heed the advice their country offers its new immigrants: go west. If only they would follow it, "we should see less of the plaster images brought back from Venice, Paris, or London, and more of the living men and women who inhabit the American continent."[12]

James's compatriots could be just as suspicious of his motives and goodwill, and equally reluctant to become satiric targets, especially for the benefit of an international audience. His American portraits are scrutinized for lapses in patriotic spirit and the jury is quick to find him guilty. Even "The Point of View," in which *all* the characters, European, American, and Europeanized American, are subjected to an equal irony, is seen as a national betrayal. John Hay describes the reaction to Howells: "How James is catching it for his 'Point of View'! . . . The worst thing in our time about American taste is the way it treats James." Hay is certain that the reaction is based less on his work than on his decision to live abroad: "If he lived in Cambridge he could write what he likes, but because he finds London more agreeable, he is the prey of all the patriotisms."[13] The satiric license granted the native observer is withdrawn when he defects to alien soil.

Such chauvinistic responses shaped the way James's work was read by his countrymen and the demands made of him. The dispute over the ending of *The American*, in which our hero gets neither the girl nor his revenge, has nothing to do with plausibility or artistic propriety, though James himself would later find the book flawed by its melodramatic departures from realism. At the time it is serialized in the *Atlantic*, however, what concerns his American readers is that Newman be rewarded. Howells urges the author to marry Newman off to Claire. James prevails by protesting that "they would have been an impossible couple, with an impossible problem before them," since neither understands the shaping forces in the other's world.[14]

But though James refuses to give way on this occasion, his later negotiations with Howells are more accommodating; he learns to subvert expectations in more subtle ways. The wholesale matrimony at the end of *The Europeans* was the payment of a promissory note; as he explains to a friend, "the offhand marrying in the end was *commandé* . . . a part of the bargain with Howells." When he outlines the plot of *The Portrait of a Lady* for Howells long before he sits down to write it, he presents it in mock-reassuring patriotic terms: "My novel is to be an *Americana*— the adventures in Europe of a female Newman, who of course equally triumphs over the insolent foreigner."[15] James's tone suggests both his contempt for the demands of his American readers and his inability to ignore them. The book he writes will not in fact meet those standards, but the tension between his wishes and the audience's is always in play. It prompts him to write a notoriously ambiguous ending. Isabel rejects her American suitor Caspar Goodwood and goes back to Rome and her loveless marriage. But in the final sentences, Henrietta reassures him: "'Look here, Mr. Goodwood,' she said; 'just you wait!'"[16] Is this a promise of Isabel's future liberation or another sign of Henrietta's cock-eyed optimism? The author shrugs it off: Let the reader decide.

James's most serious conflict with his American audience, however, had less to do with fictional formulas than with the status of American culture itself. In what became a notorious passage from his 1879 critical book, *Hawthorne*, he seems to doom not only that writer but all American stay-at-homes to provincialism by insisting that "the items of high civilization" needed for a great literature are missing from their country. He enumerates them in a sort of catalog aria that outraged American readers: "No sovereign, no court, no personal loyalty, no aristocracy, no church, no clergy, no army, no diplomatic service, no country gentlemen, no palaces, no castles, nor manors, nor old country-houses, nor parsonages, nor thatched cottages nor ivied ruins; no cathedrals, nor abbeys, nor little Norman churches; no great Universities nor public schools—no Oxford, nor Eton, nor Harrow; no literature, no novels, no museums, no pictures, no political society, no sporting class—no Epsom nor Ascot!"[17]

The passage is based on a similar lament in Hawthorne's preface to *The Marble Faun*, but that did not save James from the fury of his countrymen. Hawthorne had only said that the absence of such elements in what he called "my dear native land" made it hard to write the genre of romance. He did not attack the possibility of American culture; nor did he praise institutions his fellow citizens would see as oppressive—king and court, an established church, hereditary privilege. James questions the very foundations of the country and then trivializes the issue by juxtaposing such "items" against the mere picturesque—thatched cottages, ivied ruins. How could he have been naive enough to think that this might pass? Perhaps because he was in the most passionate phase of his love affair with England and could not hear his obsession forcing its way through his otherwise measured prose. A letter to his father before *Hawthorne* was published shows him unprepared for the response: "I should think the tone of the book gentle and good-natured enough to disarm reprobation."[18]

Hawthorne illustrates better than anything else that the idea of a unified Anglo-American audience was a myth. The book was commissioned by a British publisher and clearly written for English readers. It was the first volume in the English Men of Letters Series devoted to an American writer. The other thirty-eight titles advertised in the original edition of this prestigious series range from Chaucer to Thackeray, and James has no doubt that Hawthorne belongs in their company. Of *The Scarlet Letter* he writes, "Something might at last be sent to Europe as exquisite in quality as anything that had been received, and the best of it was that the thing was absolutely American."[19] But because Hawthorne is the first *American* "English Man of Letters," and because his interpreter is a fellow countryman, James is anxious to make no grandiose claims and to explain Hawthorne's deficiencies— his narrow range, his relatively slim output—by linking them to impoverished cultural roots. The offensive catalog is intended for English readers who wonder why Hawthorne had not accomplished more, given his extraordinary gifts. But the same words would not be read in the same spirit in the two countries, and the book's hostile American reception is James's first awakening to that fact. He is stunned by what he calls "the vulgarity, ignorance, rabid vanity and general idiocy" of the reviews and concludes, "What a public to write for!—what an inspiration in addressing them! But let us hope that they are not the real American public. If I thought they were, I would give up the country."[20]

He does not give up the country, but he never again writes a major study of an American author. Each of his later critical books contains only a single essay on an important literary compatriot. He no longer trusts himself to speak directly about his native land, at any rate until he returns to it a quarter of a century later and writes *The American Scene*. The reception of *Hawthorne* disturbs him profoundly, but its immediate effect is to make him carry on his increasingly rocky transatlantic courtship in the less nakedly revealing language of fiction. There the internal conflict between his American and European loyalties can be expressed in a more subterranean fashion, without forcing him to speak out directly. Fiction, unlike discursive prose, offers a whole wardrobe of costumes, some of which might serve the purposes of disguise while allowing James to satisfy his most urgent expressive needs. Somehow the demands of the market must fuse with the author's private preoccupations.

II

"LONDON IS ON the whole the most possible form of life. I take it as an artist and as a bachelor." So James wrote in his "American Journal" when he looked back in 1881 on his first five years in his adopted city. He notes how stimulating London's sheer size and variety are to the literary artist, calling it "the biggest aggregation of human life—the most complete compendium of the world."[21] There is no mystery in such an appeal, particularly for a writer who thinks of himself at this time primarily as a social observer. But "as a bachelor"? What could that mean?

When James wrote those words, he was thirty-eight years old. His brother William had married three years earlier, and James had long been urged to do the same, especially by his mother. In 1874, he responds to a letter in which she has apparently pressed the matter by thanking her for her "advice that I take a wife," advice he is clearly not disposed to follow. "I will bore a hole in my nose and keep it down with a string," he replies sarcastically, "and if you will provide the wife, the fortune, and the 'inclination' I will take them all."[22] A suitable young lady might be found by others, but the "inclination," as he is perfectly aware, has to be his. In the courtship practices of the period, the man declares himself before the woman even searches her feelings. James is warning his mother that he cannot feel that inclination.

The absence of heterosexual desire does not prevent him from using his bachelor status as a social asset, especially in securing entry to London society. He plays the role of eligible young man for years and does little to discourage the rumor mills from grinding out gossip of his attachment to this woman or that. But when any really plausible candidate appears, he quickly backs off. The women whose beauty or wit he praises are either safely married or many years older. This allows him to express his genuinely warm feeling for them; he was no misogynist. But his affections are *inhibited* rather than encouraged by sexual opportunity. He feels no "inclination." By 1880, he is not only certain he will never marry but willing to say so, jokingly but confidently, to his friends. "The only important things that can happen to me are to die and to marry, and as yet I do neither," he writes Howells. "I shall in any case do the former first; then in the next world, I shall marry Helen of Troy." And to Grace Norton in the same year: "I am too good a bachelor to spoil."[23]

If so, he had come to the right place. A generation earlier Herman Melville had published his powerful story "The Paradise of Bachelors and the Tartarus of Maids" (1854). The first of these locales is upper-class London, the second a grim New England paper factory. Melville's juxtaposition contrasts the affluent, male, professional, civilized world of London with the poverty-stricken, female, working-class, brutalized world of industrial America and suggests that the privilege of one is dependent on the deprivation of the other. The maids produce the paper on which the professional bachelors indite their lucrative or elegant words. Despite his critique, Melville is obviously attracted to the seductive social rites of male companionship in London: "Sweet are the oases in Sahara; charming the isle-groves of August prairies; delectable pure faith amidst a thousand perfidies: but sweeter, still more charming, most delectable, the dreamy Paradise of Bachelors, found in the stony heart of stunning London."[24]

In James's time too, London was a male bastion like no other city he had known. The cultural life of Boston seems to him dominated by women. When he returns to America in 1881, he writes to decline the honor of addressing "an audience of seventy young women at the Saturday morning club" on a topic of his choosing. This image of Boston culture under genteel petticoat government would crystallize in his novel *The Bostonians* (1886), in which money, influence, and power are all in the hands of the female characters, who must be outwitted by James's poor but aggressive male protagonist. The cultural life of

Rome, Florence, and Paris, especially in the expatriate colonies James knew too well, also seemed dominated by women. As he wrote to William from Italy during his long sojourn there, "An intelligent male brain to communicate with occasionally would be a practical blessing. I have encountered none for so long that I don't even know how to address yours." And the literary salons of Paris had long been under female sponsorship. Though James was welcomed into Flaubert's distinctly male *cénacle*, he spent more time in Paris visiting the salons of Henrietta Roubell, the Princess Ourousoff, and Mme. Blaze de Bury. He writes in disgust to Howells, "There are no men here to see but horribly effeminate and empty-pated little *crevés* [fops]. But there are some very nice women."[25]

London is entirely different. It offers James the chance to meet many of the illustrious men of English society in a male setting free of the performance rituals of mixed social life. The institution that caters to these needs is the London club. It proves indispensable to him, and within three months he has guest privileges at the Athenaeum, the Savile, and—through the offices of Henry Adams's friend Lord Houghton—an invitation to the Cosmopolitan, "a sort of talking-club, extremely select, which meets on Wednesdays and Sunday nights." The Athenaeum he calls "a little heaven here below. It transfigures the face of material existence for me."[26]

These clubs offer James access to the professional world of the society he wants to enter, not segregated by field of interest, but mixing prominent figures across the whole spectrum. They extend his horizontal, if not vertical field of observation and make him feel that he need never again settle for an expatriate colony in place of the vital life of the host country. They also allow him to reciprocate elegant hospitality without relinquishing his modest bachelor quarters. When, less than two years after his arrival—a fraction of the usual wait—he is elected a life member of the venerable Reform Club, he writes in triumph to his father, "*j'y suis, j'y reste*—for ever and a day. It is a precious good thing for me . . . and makes me feel strangely and profoundly at home here."[27] Uncannily, this event coincides with the announcement of William's forthcoming marriage. The brothers are settled at last, their divergent paths defined by the institutions they are about to enter, the haven of matrimony, the paradise of bachelors.

He writes in congratulating his brother, "I believe almost as much in matrimony for most other people as I believe in it little for myself—which is saying a good deal."[28] But one could not reach such a conclusion from reading James's works. Though the subject of courtship and marriage dominates his fiction from the earliest moment, long before he settles on the international theme, his treatment does not suggest much belief in either phase of heterosexual relations for anyone. There was more than one reason to suppress the stories he had written in his twenties. James was right to call them thin. But they also offer an insight into his obsessions that a more guarded, slightly older writer might well want to disguise.

Almost all the stories in the first volume of the *Complete Tales*, published when James was between twenty and twenty-five, deal with compromised courtships and blighted marriages. Their spirit is virulently antiromantic and deflationary, their consistent target the illusions of young love. Whether couched in the language of realism or romance, they all uncouple love and marriage. Real passion sometimes proves fatal (as in "A Tragedy of Error," "De Grey," and "The Romance of Certain Old Clothes"). Courtship is full of professions of fidelity debunked by the reality of fickleness ("The Story of a Year" and "The Story of a Masterpiece") or the juggling act of keeping alternate suitors in reserve ("Poor Richard"). Marriage is often a calculated act of survival or desperation ("A Landscape-Painter" and "My Friend Bingham"). James regularly links romantic passion with fatal disease, or with the compensatory model he uses much later in *The Sacred Fount* (1901), where the blossoming of one lover is paid for by the withering of the other.

These tales are the work of a young man deeply reluctant to join the inexorable march to the altar. But because of his misgivings about the institution of heterosexual love and marriage, he is able to see its imperfections (including the gender stereotyping and disparities in power on which it is so often based) in a way most of his American contemporaries are reluctant to do. At the same time, the stories are seriously flawed because James is producing "realism" more out of inchoate fantasy than lived experience. The lovers seldom have substantial identity, and the settings are sketchy at best. With one or two exceptions the stories might take place anywhere: They are rooted less in carefully observed social detail than in the murkier regions of

James's imagination. This will change, perhaps because he becomes aware that he is revealing too much.

In the meantime, the early stories paint a dismal picture of the illusions, compromises, and rude awakenings of courtship and marriage. In "The Story of a Masterpiece" (1868), for example, John Lennox, a thirty-five-year-old wealthy widower, courts the charming, beautiful, but penniless Marian Everett. During their engagement, he finds out that she had been passionately in love with a poor young painter, whom she had dropped in search of more lucrative proposals. Lennox comes to think of her as "the most superficial, most heartless of women." But he marries her anyway, in a chilling gesture that detaches matrimony from romance: "His love's vitality had been but small, and since it was to be short-lived it was better that it should expire before marriage than after."[29] Other stories, like "A Landscape-Painter" or "My Friend Bingham," shift our sympathy to the woman in the couple. But in either case, we are asked to regard the whole courtship ritual as fraud and opportunism followed by weary compromise.

James's cynical vision shapes his first novel. This was not *Roderick Hudson*, the book that begins the collected New York Edition, but a work he very much wanted to forget. *Watch and Ward* appeared in the *Atlantic* in 1871, was not published in volume form until 1878, and then only in America. James in effect repudiates it when in the preface to *Roderick Hudson* he calls this later work "my first attempt at a novel."[30] *Watch and Ward* is certainly no neglected masterpiece. James dismisses it in a letter to his father as "very thin and as 'cold' as an icicle."[31] But there is a good deal of heat at the heart of this chilling tale. It is a revealing and disturbing book that seems fundamentally out of control.

Watch and Ward is a version of the Pygmalion-Galatea legend in which a twenty-nine-year-old bachelor, Roger Lawrence, adopts a helpless twelve-year-old orphan in order to form her into his ideal mate. Nora knows nothing of his plans and responds with deep affection to his loving sponsorship. Only when she is a "finished" young lady, with all the accomplishments Roger's money and concern have provided, does she discover his covert intentions. The shock of his proposal is compounded when she is shown a letter written when he adopted her outlining his plan to make her into "a perfect wife." Far from being grateful, Nora is appalled: "Her immense pain gushed and filtered through her heart, and passed out in shuddering sobs. . . . Why had he never told her that she wore a chain!"[32] She flees the house, seeks protection from a cousin, then from another admirer, finally tries to find work. Each of these alternatives fails: The cousin tries to extort money from Roger to reveal her whereabouts, the admirer turns out to be engaged, her search for employment is fruitless. Absolutely humiliated, marriage to Roger becomes her only alternative. In the novel's disturbing climax Nora crushes her rebellion, takes all the guilt of her flight upon herself, and gratefully accepts his offer. The cage snaps shut as the prisoner consents to her bondage. In *Watch and Ward*, the neutral phrase "the marriage plot" takes on sinister new meaning.

Unlike all the novels that follow, James's first long fiction has no densely realized social context. There is no world, no society, beyond the characters and outside the author's imagination. They are colliding atoms, not representative figures standing for a particular culture, city, or nation. Nora spends her adolescence with Roger in a country setting that has no real local identity. The experiment of raising her is carried on in an isolated domestic laboratory, a forcing-house in which anything can happen. James's metaphors suggest the sexual object behind the educational agenda, as when Roger reflects that "the petals of the young girl's nature, playfully forced apart, would leave the golden heart of the flower but the more accessible to his own vertical rays." However such passages were read by a late-nineteenth-century audience, James is playing a dangerous game. He cannot go too far in criticizing power disparities between the sexes or a system that routinely encourages a man of thirty-five to marry a girl of eighteen. What he produces is a "happy ending," in which Nora in a kind of narcotic haze after the shock of her discovery and her fruitless search for an escape sees Roger as her savior. He seems the embodiment of "the secret of the universe, and the secret of the universe was, that Roger was the only man in it who had a heart."[33]

The ending is fraudulent and produces an incoherent book, morally experimental at first yet at last deeply conventional. This was not only because James was a beginner, but because he could not yet see an alternative to the *fictional* tyranny of "the marriage plot," with its inescapable resolution. The narratives he invents—both here and in the early stories—reveal more about his uncontrolled hostility to matrimony and his bedrock feeling that men and women were incompatible than he could afford to acknowledge. It was only much later, in *The Awkward Age* (1899), that he summoned the courage to describe the whole process of manufacturing a marriageable young girl and the tragedy of substituting an older-man/guardian for her desired lover without resorting to a fantastic happy ending. For the moment, what he needed was a thicker disguise.

There was one to hand in a social phenomenon that became increasingly visible in the 1870s and thereafter, just as James was embarking on his first expatriate experiments: the marriage of American heiresses to European aristocrats. This was a subject he was to make his own: One contemporary reviewer called him the Homer "of the invasion of Europe by American women."[34] But James was not the only writer to pay close attention, and so his focus on transatlantic marriages could not be seen as a private obsession. The phenomenon was real and widespread enough to attract a great deal of notice, whether celebratory or hostile. In Arthur Conan Doyle's "The Adventure of the Noble Bachelor" (1892), the marriage of a British peer to the daughter of an American millionaire is described with asperity in the society papers: "There will soon be a call for protection in the marriage market, for the present free-trade principle appears to tell heavily against our home product. One by one the management of the noble houses of Great Britain is passing into the hands of our fair cousins from across the Atlantic."[35] In addition to James and Conan Doyle, such writers as Anthony Trollope, Gertrude Atherton, Frances Hodgson Burnett, and Edith Wharton were all to seize on the subject.

Among the "dollar princesses," as they were often called, were some of the most prominent women in British society—Jennie Jerome, wife of Lord Randolph Churchill and mother of Winston, described in a contemporary journal as "The Most Influential Anglo-Saxon Woman in the World"[36]; Consuelo Yznaga, who married the heir to the duke of Manchester; her goddaughter Consuelo Vanderbilt, who became the duchess of Marlborough; Mary Leiter (Henry Adams's friend) who as Lady Curzon, vicereine of India, found herself playing what her biographer calls "the greatest role of any Englishwoman but one, and she was not even English."[37] And these were only the most notable. In 1902, a British writer noted that "four English statesmen of Cabinet rank have married American wives."[38] By 1915, the edition of *Titled Americans*, published annually in New York, listed close to five hundred such unions.[39]

By the time Edith Wharton came to write about the subject in her unfinished novel *The Buccaneers*, she could see the vogue in historical terms. In her proposal for the book, she notes that it would be set in the 1870s (sixty years back), "the first time the social invasion had ever been tried in England on such a scale."[40] But of course James was living there at the time, was acquainted with some of the invaders, and could describe the phenomenon at first hand. In both Paris and London, he met a number of such couples.[41] The subject proves a godsend for him; it allows him to combine his interest in observing national types with his private revulsion from the rituals of courtship and marriage. It provides a cover story for his more subversive observations and gives a realistic societal identity to the generic combatants of his earliest fiction. The all but inevitable tensions and misunderstandings of such unions, perfectly plausible on the literal level as the clash of expectations fostered by different social systems, become a metaphor for a more fundamental estrangement of the sexes. James focuses on the fault lines in these marriages, sure to create havoc when the predictable quake comes.

This is how he differs from other writers who take on the subject. Trollope's *The Duke's Children* (1880), for example, also offers an American Isabel as a major character, and a peer to propose to her. She is Isabel Boncassen, daughter of a wealthy, urbane man of letters, granddaughter of a man who had risen from the working class; he is Lord Silverbridge, son and heir to the Duke of Omnium. Silverbridge, like James's Warburton, is attracted to Isabel's vitality and irreverence, and sees her as "alive to all that was going on." Trollope presents this merger of British aristocrat and American commoner as unproblematic, even desirable given new geopolitical alignments. Silverbridge, unlike his hidebound father, knows "that there were certain changes going on in the management of the world" which by this time make it fitting "that an American girl should be elevated to the rank of an English Duchess." It is a domestic confirmation of the transatlantic political rapprochement. Isabel, despite her independent mind and republican training, can respond in harmony: "To be an English Duchess! Oh—yes; her ambition understood it all!"[42] Beyond such simple responses her feelings are a blank. Trollope gives us virtually no access to her mind, though he records the inner lives of his English characters. His resolution of this concluding Palliser novel is blandly reassuring. The marriage is a step toward revitalizing the decaying English aristocracy. Accommodation is in the air.

The blanks in Trollope's novel were James's opportunity. He may have read *The Duke's Children:* It appeared in serial form as he was working on *The Portrait of a Lady.*[43] But whether he did or not, his vision of such unions was different. *His* Isabel of course refuses her peer. Warburton's proposal seems to her an act of aggression: "What she felt was that a territorial, a political, a social magnate had conceived the design of drawing her into the system in which he lived and moved. A certain instinct, not imperious, but persuasive, told her to resist—it murmured to her that virtually she had a system and an orbit of her own."[44] The words make the amiable Warburton sound like a predatory threat to her freedom. Throughout James's international fiction, he focuses attention on such conflicts between different "systems." Though he was as committed to Anglo-American reconciliation as Trollope, he had a deeper investment in recording the mutual bafflement—or worse—these heterogeneous courtships produced. He will not let them thrive.

On the Continent, the transatlantic liaisons bring disaster. Claire de Cintré flees from Newman, from her family, from marriage itself by immuring herself in a convent. In James's tale "Madame de Mauves" (1874), his American heroine's revulsion from the profligate ways of her French aristocratic husband, and from his cynical suggestion that she discreetly take a lover to console herself for his infidelity, initiates a tragic action that finally makes him blow his brains out. He wanted "to have the comfort of feeling that his wife was as corruptible as himself,"[45] but he does not get it, and he cannot begin to understand her puritan training. Their codes are simply incompatible. Many years later, when James returns to this theme in *The Golden Bowl*, his Italian prince will be just as bewildered by his American wife, though by then the relatively simple moral framework of *The American* and "Madame de Mauves" will have given way to a much more ambiguous sense of conflicting values.

James's English stories of international courtship stress mutual bafflement above moral conflict. He had foreshadowed this response in Newman's reaction to Claire's refusal: "Why, why, why?" he demands in their final interview; she replies "Nothing that you can understand"; and he concludes, "You are a mystery to me."[46] In the English stories, such cognitive dissonance is primary and doesn't necessarily prevent the marriages. Stories like "The Siege of London" (1883) and "Lady Barberina" (1884) exploit the comic rather than tragic potential of the subject. Mrs. Headway, in the earlier tale, is an ambitious, wealthy, much-divorced westerner bent on transforming herself into a socially respectable woman by bypassing the exclusive circles of New York and carrying off a baronet, Sir Arthur Demesne. This innocent young man is fascinated by her exotic ways. He has never seen anyone like her, and he has seen entirely too many proper young ladies of his station: "She was like an Hungarian or a Pole, with the difference that he could almost understand her language." Mrs. Headway makes certain that he does not master it. When she wants to confide in an American friend, she gets rid of her admirer by saying, "We are going to talk American; you wouldn't understand us!" Once she grasps its appeal to the British, she shamelessly uses her "fund of Californian slang" to play the child of nature. It is all part of an aggressive campaign, and James emphasizes her military strategy: She puts London under siege and is making "headway" in her plan "to take possession."[47] Despite her shady past, despite the disapproval of the baronet's family, she succeeds in eloping with him and becoming Lady Demesne. She can no more make him out than he can understand her. But the social position she craves is finally hers; and her fluid identity will take the shape of its new container. What becomes of her instrument, the hapless baronet, is left to the reader's imagination.

James also emphasizes this American capacity to remake oneself when necessary in "Lady Barberina." The stereotypical identities in such international experiments are reversed: Here it is the woman who is titled, the man who has the money. This had also been true of the major courtship in The American and The Europeans, but here the experiment works; or at least the marriage takes place. Yet the sense of mutual incomprehension is as complete. Lady Barberina, daughter of Lord Canterville, is an entirely conventional member of the British aristocracy, comfortable in her world and unable to see beyond it.

That she is genuinely attracted to her American suitor, Jackson Lemon, is anomalous. He is a millionaire and a confident, educated man, a doctor with a deep sense of vocation. But she cannot begin to understand why anyone with such financial resources would choose to work at all or to live in New York, a city of "commoners" with unmemorable names. The experiment of living in America after their marriage is a disaster. She is "ravaged" by homesickness, utterly baffled by the people she meets and even by her husband, whom she persists in considering a "foreigner."[48] Her passive resistance to the experiment finally succeeds, and Dr. Lemon agrees to give up his practice, move to London, and live a version of the aristocratic life. It is a marriage of permanent strangers, "an unnatural mixture," an example of "social incoherence," as James calls these tales in his later preface to them.[49]

What keeps the couple together is a sense of racial identity that overrides their differences. Dr. Lemon is first attracted to Lady Barberina because she embodies his sense of Anglo-Saxon physical characteristics at their most refined. In his outline for the story, James writes that his protagonist "must be a great admirer of the physique of English race and think her a beautiful specimen of it."[50] He imagines her as the mother of "children, in whom the look of race should be conspicuous. He should like his children to have the look of race." Various characters treat the marriage as a symbolic union of England and America, for example the American-born Lady Marmaduke, who tries to build a social bridge across the Atlantic: "It was her belief that an ultimate fusion [of the two countries] was inevitable, and that those who were the first to understand would gain the most." Lady Barberina's father agrees: "They were all one race, after all; and why shouldn't they make one society—the best on both sides, of course?"[51] These idealistic platitudes barely mask a naked calculation and also mirror the Anglo-American realignment.

James's story anticipates the political rapprochement of the two countries and underlines the class compact between new money and aristocratic position that helped cement it. But while "Lady Barberina" seems to work toward Anglo-Saxon racial harmony, it subversively expresses James's deeper sense of marriage as the product of rivalry, self-betrayal, and opportunism. And his final picture of the "happy couple" is chilling. A superficial accord covers over their essential estrangement: "Jackson Lemon has a house in London, and he rides in the park with his wife, who is as beautiful as the day, and a year ago presented him with a little girl, with features that Jackson already scans for the look of race—whether in hope or in fear, to-day, is more than my muse has revealed. He has occasional scenes with Lady Barb, during which the look of race is very visible in her own countenance. . . . He is exceedingly restless."[52] James studiously avoids recording the marital conflicts, but these dark hints make them vivid enough. Such saturated reticence is his way of negotiating between his Anglo-American readers' optimistic expectations and his own grimmer vision.

It is possible to see these tales as distorted pictures of matrimony written by someone permanently hostile to that condition who uses his art to undermine its authority. But there is also plenty of evidence that James's sense of such international marriages was realistic. The celebratory vision of dream unions combining the best of the old world and the new is belied by the historical record. Most of them were frankly calculated business arrangements in which the social ambitions of the plutocracy were matched to the impecuniousness of an improvident aristocracy needing an infusion of cash: title for wealth. In the pithy formula of Trollope's *The Way We Live Now* (1875), "Rank squanders money; trade makes it;—and then trade purchases rank by re-gilding its splendour." There was a market for international marriages, with its own go-betweens, as one American journalist discovered when she was deluged with replies to a false advertisement placed in a London paper: "A young American Lady of means wishes to meet with a chaperon of Highest Social Position, who will introduce her into the Best English Society. Liberal Terms. Address, 'Heiress.'"[53]

Behind "the glitter and the gold," as the Duchess of Marlborough entitles her autobiography, there often lay a darker story James might well have invented. The marriage of Consuelo Vanderbilt to Britain's ranking peer was viewed as one of those fairy tales come true, and the newspapers on both sides of the Atlantic treated it in this fashion. The reality was more like a nightmare. After the Duchess produced the obligatory two sons to ensure the continuity of the line, and the Vanderbilt millions restored Blenheim Palace to its former glory, she and the Duke separated. In truth they had both been pawns in the hands of their ambitious families. The grounds stated in the annulment were

Theodore Roosevelt, 1903: portrait by John Singer Sargent.
(White House Collection, copyright White House Historical Association)

Uncle Sam jeered by "ethnics": cartoon originally printed in Frank Leslie's *Illustrated Newspaper*, 1888.

"Spoiling the Broth": cartoon from the *Los Angeles Times*, 1921.

Immigrants arriving on the *Patricia*, 1906. *(Library of Congress)*

Hester Street pushcart market, New York,
from H. Idell Zeisloft, *The New Metropolis* (1899).

"Blood Thicker Than Water," *Punch*, 26 March 1898.

"Jonathan Shopping," *Punch*, 8 May 1901.

AMERICANA.

First Millionairess. "No, we've not started so far. But I guess we're going shopping in Bond Street this afternoon."
Second Millionairess. "Better choose another locality. Reckon you'll be a bit late for Bond Street. We're doing Bond Street this morning!"

"Americana," *Punch*, 24 July 1907.

"The World's Constable," cartoon from *Judge*, 1905.

Henry Adams, c. 1860.
*(Courtesy of the Massachusetts
Historical Society, Boston)*

Henry Adams, 1914:
drawing by John Briggs Potter.
*(Courtesy of the Massachusetts
Historical Society, Boston)*

Henry James at Newport, age 20.
(*By permission of the Houghton Library, Harvard University*)

Henry James, 1906:
photograph by Alvin Langdon Coburn.
(*Courtesy George Eastman House*)

Ezra Pound, 1913:
photograph by Alvin Langdon Coburn.
(Courtesy George Eastman House)

Ezra Pound, 1916.
*(Photography Collection, Harry
Ransom Humanities Research Center,
The University of Texas at Austin)*

T. S. Eliot outside the offices of Faber and Gwyer, 1926. *(By permission of the Houghton Library, Harvard University)*

T. S. Eliot at his desk as editor for Faber, 1926. *(By permission of the Houghton Library, Harvard University)*

that the nineteen-year-old bride had been married against her will, by her imperious mother. The Duke too confessed that he had given up "the girl he loved," since "a sense of duty to his family and to his traditions indicated the sacrifice of personal desires."[54] They were mere instruments, links in the chain; their happiness did not matter in the face of family imperatives. Even the most successful of these marriages demanded major sacrifices. Mary Leiter, who adored her Curzon and was deeply loved in return, had to remake herself completely to fill her new role. Her husband detested Americans as a breed, and she never again saw her native country nor most of the friends who had formed her extraordinary circle in Washington: Mrs. Grover Cleveland, Henry Adams, John Hay, the Roosevelts.[55]

Such relationships offered rich material for writers interested in the international theme. Lady Curzon might have been taking the advice offered one of the "dollar princesses" in Gertrude Atherton's novel *American Wives and English Husbands* (1898): "To live comfortably with an Englishman you've got to become his habit, and to be happy with him you've got to become his second self." Atherton's heroine reluctantly agrees to the terms, at the cost of her individuality, since she is convinced "We represent the fusion of the two greatest nations on earth."[56] But such Anglo-Saxon unions, the complex product of geopolitics, social mobility, racial theory, and personal inclination (or the lack of it), were burdened with far more excess baggage than most marriages and offered an exceptional opportunity to a novelist dubious about the institution itself. The subject gave James a way of translating his private anxiety, hostility, and sexual panic into public terms. This is why he fastened upon it so avidly, and why he became its most critical interpreter.

He made the most of his opportunity, and he might have gone on writing tales of international alliances for years. But after the definitive triumph of *The Portrait of a Lady* he found himself more and more reluctant to go back to a subject he had made his own; and nearly two decades were to elapse before he returned to it with a sense of new possibilities. He was coming to understand the price he had paid for becoming the Homer of the American invasion of Europe. As he wrote to his brother a few years later, when the sentiment had crystallized, "I am deadly weary of the whole 'international' state of mind—so that I *ache*, at times, with fatigue at the way it is constantly forced upon one as a sort of virtue or obligation."[57] The subject had become formulaic. He feared it as an ambitious actor fears being identified with a career-defining role.

Just as he came to dislike his reliance on national stereotypes, so he came to distrust the imperatives of the courtship plot. The one flattened character; the other created predictable and, given his own skepticism about marriage, fraudulent resolutions. The subversive undercurrent allowed him in analyzing the tensions of international unions did not reverse the direction of the inexorable tide. There is a fundamental scorn—for the reader's expectations, for the formulas of the marriage plot, for heterosexual relations—in James's submission to the discipline. Why, he seems to ask, must I go through this dreary exercise? He sometimes has trouble disguising his contempt for the whole subject. In a disturbing novel that has completely dropped out of the canon, *Confidence* (1880), James tells the story of how a passion for the same woman nearly wrecks the intimate friendship of two men who are turned into murderous rivals by what one of them calls "the marital monopoly."[58] The novel is a disastrous failure, because like the earlier *Watch and Ward* it attaches a fraudulent comic resolution to a narrative that explores irreconcilable conflicts, in this case between powerful male bonds and heterosexual desire.

An impatient need to speak in his own voice was threatening to unmask the urbane inventor of the international courtship plot, with all its elaborate disguises. When we think about all the readerly expectations James is expected to satisfy—to provide information about national types, avoid offending either his American or his English readers, bring international conflict toward harmonious resolution, not abandon the institution of matrimony—we can understand why the whole experiment begins to unravel and why he comes to feel trapped in a machine of his own making. There had always been a disparity between the demands of a transatlantic audience and his own expressive needs, and the ingenious but brittle compromise he had worked out was in danger of snapping.

Nothing suggests this tension so well as the ending of *The Europeans*, which does not entirely follow the formulas of comedy. James had promised Howells a connubial feast to make up for the *Atlantic* audience's disappointment with the ending of *The American*, and marriages there are aplenty. All three of the Wentworth children are to be wed: the rebellious Gertrude to her Europeanized cousin Felix, the conventional elder daughter Charlotte to her solemn admirer Mr. Brand, young Clifford to his pert sweetheart Lizzie. We even hear of the engagement of Robert Acton, but not to Eugenia, the woman he has been wooing—or torturing. Acton is the most interesting male character in the novel. Although he is a New Englander born and bred, on intimate terms with the Wentworths, he is not a provincial but a man of wide experience and sophistication. He has lived abroad; his house is filled with the treasures of Asian art he has collected in his travels; and his mind and spirit do not seem constrained by the anxious and anxiogenic melancholy of his puritanical neighbors. When the Baroness Munster meets her American relations for the first time, Robert Acton is present. The Wentworths are uneasy and embarrassed to encounter this perplexing foreigner who is nonetheless their kin. But Acton is not: He "met Eugenia's eyes; he appeared to appreciate the privilege of meeting them. Madame Munster instantly felt that he was, intrinsically, the most important person present."[59]

This is how their doomed courtship begins—as the meeting of equals across a level gaze. It is of course bound to be highly irregular. Eugenia is still the wife of the younger prince of a tiny European country. She is about to be cast aside so that her weak-willed husband can make an advantageous second marriage in accord with the master plan of his brother the reigning prince. All she has to do is sign a letter of agreement to secure an annulment. She is potentially a free agent, and it is clear that whatever emotional bonds once tied her to her husband are broken. But to break the legal one would leave her marooned—a painfully isolated figure in an exposed, ambiguous position. This is hardly the sort of girl one brings home to mother, and in fact Acton's gentle mother, to whom he introduces her, is utterly baffled by this fascinating, unreadable woman, though she senses her son is deeply attracted to her. His attraction is a tribute to his apparent freedom from the conventional wisdom of his sect, in which the qualities a man looks for in a wife are innocence, malleability, and a heightened sense of duty. Eugenia is a mature, experienced woman in her early thirties; Acton finds her deeply interesting precisely because she is a match for his own complexity and sophistication. Can marriage be a form of spiritual kinship, a union of equals? Acton is described as a man with a capacity "for showing a larger courage, a finer quality of pluck, than common occasion demanded."[60]

In the event, this impression proves unfounded. His unconventionality takes the form of toying with Eugenia, proposing, for example, that they become lovers, that they take a trip to Niagara together. He treats her not as a human being in an exceptionally difficult situation who would respond to the empathetic understanding of which he is capable, but as a curious phenomenon requiring an icy analytic attention: "He was constantly pondering her words and motions; they were as interesting as the factors in an algebraic problem." His cross-examination of her is for him "the pursuit of the unknown quantity." In their last scene, he goes to what even he thinks of as "the limits of legitimate experimentation" in order to trap her into letting down her guard. Once he "solves" the algebraic problem of Eugenia by identifying her unknown quantity as dishonesty and thus puts her beyond the limits of his moral calculus, he can perhaps get her out of his system. It is the end between them. Despite his sophistication, Acton embodies a kind of scientific puritanism that works within the limits of the old code in searching eagerly for evidence of guilt, like Chillingworth in *The Scarlet Letter*. His heterodoxy is of the surface. At heart he remains loyal to his original training, and the announcement that after his mother's death "he married a particularly nice young girl"[61] only confirms his retreat to the conventional, though many of the book's American readers would not have seen it that way.

James is playing a double game in toying with the audience's expectations. To read the Eugenia-Acton plot as primary is to bypass the requirements of the novel's original readers and to ignore the wholesale marriages he provides for what Shakespeare's Touchstone sarcastically calls "the rest of the country copulatives." But this broken courtship, and the mistrust across the divide of gender and culture it illustrates, interests James far more than the happy couples crowding to the altar. The Eugenia-Acton plot was decidedly not what Howells had bargained for. It represents James's sense of the humiliation rituals so frequently found in courtship and the frustration of trying to please an audience that did not really want to hear about them. Both are examples of the "tall stone walls which fatally divide us,"[62] Americans and Europeans, men and women, author and reader.

He had begun with the dream of constructing an Anglo-American language that could be mastered by a transatlantic audience not bound by the ideological imperatives of their local training. As Richard Poirier suggests, *The Europeans* "is addressed to those of high and assured cultivation, to readers free from any provinciality about specifically European or American aspects of what is presented."[63] But James was to find in the course of his career that few such readers actually existed—not enough, certainly, to make up a reliable audience for his fiction. He could not push the rest toward heterodoxy without setting off the alarm bells and exposing himself. In introducing Europeans to Americans and vice versa, he was capitalizing on an international curiosity his work did much to satisfy. But how much he needed to explain and to suppress, and how little sympathy for differences he could take for granted! Like Adams, he would have to come to terms with his increasing impatience with the audience, and the audience's disappointment in him. As this hard fact sank in, he began to understand that his cosmopolitan freedom had deprived him of a sympathetic community and that being a citizen of the world might only be a glamorous name for homelessness.

VIII

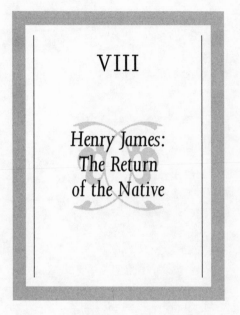

Henry James:
The Return
of the Native

Instances will occur to everybody of American writers in particular who have written with the highest discrimination of our literature and of ourselves; who have lived a lifetime among us, and finally have taken legal steps to become subjects of King George. For all that, have they understood us, have they not remained to the end of their days foreigners?

Virginia Woolf

I

IN THE EYES of most of his contemporaries, Henry James's career peaked at forty, then went into steep decline. That he writes a series of ambitious novels and tales for the next three decades, some now considered his masterpieces, owes little to the encouragement of his first audience. He encounters a general bafflement and hostility; he contrasts the upward trajectory of his first two decades as a writer with the subsequent downward slide, which increasingly seems irreversible. "I have entered upon evil days," he writes Howells in 1888; the commercial failure of his panoramic novels, *The Bostonians* and *The Princess Casamassima* (both 1886), "have reduced the desire, and the demand, for my productions to zero." By 1895, the literary world's indifference seems final: "Every sign or symbol of one's being in the least *wanted*, anywhere or by any one, have so utterly failed."[1]

The shift becomes self-perpetuating as James reluctantly tailors his style and subject matter for an elite rather than popular audience. Its original cause was his abandonment of "the contrast of manners," his patented subject. His cosmopolitan ideal—the hope "that it would be impossible to an outsider to say whether I am . . . an American writing about England or an Englishman writing about America"[2]—does not commit him to mixing national types. And so *The Bostonians* is set on the East Coast and concerns Americans, while *The Princess Casamassima* has a European cast. Boston and London dominate these novels, and James assumes both will be read as the observation of an insider.

He is dismayed when he is denied authority to speak as a Bostonian *or* a Londoner. His ambiguous status makes him suspect on both sides. Like a petitioner in a legal dispute whose claim is not recognized by the court, James is refused "standing." His readers question both his accuracy and his right to criticize. For Americans, his expatriation revokes his license to judge his country. James is shocked that Howells's *The Rise of Silas Lapham* (1885), also set in Boston, is praised despite its sharp critique while his own novel is attacked. "They don't revile Howells when he does America, and such an America as that, and why do they revile me? The 'Bostonians' is sugar-cake, compared with it," he laments.[3] The American reviews of *The Bostonians* are so hostile that the New York agent of James's London publisher warns the home office to expect the worst: "I must say that I never knew of a book being more thoroughly condemned."[4]

James congratulated himself on producing a study of Boston that was "probably rather a remarkable feat of objectivity."[5] But this is not how his depiction of late-nineteenth-century American feminism has been read. The power of *The Bostonians* to offend is rooted in its subjective elements, including James's critical attitude toward the political movement he describes. Nor was objectivity what his countrymen wanted of him, since it subjected them to the clinical scrutiny of a detached observer. They wanted sponsorship, reassurance. James's analytic mode and his disturbing treatment of the barely disguised lesbianism of Olive Chancellor, his major representative of the women's movement, are hardly reassuring. *The Bostonians* did more to alienate James's American readers than any work since *Hawthorne*.

Perhaps the solution was to write about his adopted country instead. In 1890 he tells Howells that he wants to "do" England in fiction, since he now knows it best, and since "America fades from me." He nearly writes off his native land: "As she never trusted me at best, I can trust *her*, for effect, no longer."[6] But James's English readers did not trust his vision either. One reviewer of *The Princess Casamassima*, while treating his description of London as an impressive debut, notes errors of observation and concludes "that the whole minute and conscientious picture is painted from the outside."[7] This image of James as a permanent alien recurs in the response to the novels set in England: *The Tragic Muse* (1890), *The Spoils of Poynton* and *What Maisie Knew* (1897), *The Awkward Age* (1899), *The Sacred Fount* (1901), and others. As with *The Bostonians*, James's readers were less disturbed by his local inaccuracies than by his analytic scrutiny and treatment of disturbing subjects—radical politics, class and familial conflicts, promiscuity, adultery, and divorce—without offering solutions. Such pitiless accounts of the disintegration of Victorian England might have been tolerated even though not welcomed from an English writer, but were intolerable coming from a foreigner.[8]

This questioning of James's interpretive authority in both countries helps to explain the evaporation of the audience of his international fiction. Beyond the territory he has made his own he is treated as an intruder and unreliable witness, a response that dismayed him. James never wanted to write for a coterie. Nor could he have predicted that a century after they appeared most of his books would be in print in many languages. He wanted the career of a Balzac or a Dickens— ambitious, voluminous writers whose genius was immediately recognized. In his autobiography he recalls with envy how the world took Stowe's *Uncle Tom's Cabin* to its heart. That novel had "the extraordinary fortune of finding itself, for an immense number of people, much less a book than a state of vision, of feeling and of consciousness."[9] James knew that he did not have Stowe's democratic temperament. But he was reluctant to settle for the shrunken audience of five or ten thousand readers destined to be his lot.[10]

His rebellion against this fate involved a five-year-long flirtation with the theater, which ended in the failure of his play *Guy Domville* (1895), at whose premiere he was jeered off the stage. It is a defining moment in James's career. The audience's response divides along class lines: the enthusiastic applause of the stalls, the rude hoots of the gallery. He knows from then on that he will never have the popular audience of a

Dickens or a Stowe. His account of the disastrous event shows how easily James blames the audience: "All the forces of civilization in the house waged a battle of the most gallant, prolonged and sustained applause with the hoots and jeers and catcalls of the roughs. . . . Obviously the little play, which I strove to make as broad, as gross, as simple, as clear, as British, in a word, as possible, is over the heads of the *usual* vulgar theatre-going London public." He concludes that "the stupid public is the big public, and the perceptive one the small."[11]

It never occurs to him that his contempt for the popular audience might be recognized and reciprocated: "broad, gross, vulgar, stupid." Writing plays is a conscious form of literary prostitution. The compromises he refuses in his fiction he permits in his theatrical ventures to earn the large rewards of a successful West End run (followed by an American one). The temptation grows with the commercial failure of his fiction. Unlike his father, he was not "leisured for life" but largely dependent on his literary income. He calls himself "a penniless toiler," in contrast to Henry Adams, "a man of wealth and leisure, able to satisfy all his curiosities." He agrees to turn *The American* into a play with "a happy denouement"—an ending he had resolutely refused to provide for Howells.[12] In this 1890 version, Claire de Cintré, rather than taking the veil, melts into Newman's arms with the words, "You've done it—you've brought me back—you've vanquished me!"[13]

The cynicism is born of desperation; it doesn't work because it goes against the grain. From this point on, James reluctantly resigns himself to writing for his coterie, the ardent transatlantic group willing to follow "the Master" along the unexplored paths of his later experimental fiction. He also gradually withdraws from his expensive London existence to a relatively frugal life in the seaport town of Rye.[14] He treats the burst bubble of his early reputation as typical. In the story "Broken Wings" (1900), two artists, one a formerly acclaimed novelist, the other a fine but forgotten painter, compare notes. The writer leaves the painter "in full possession of all the phases through which in 'literary circles' acclaimed states may pass on their regular march to eclipse and extinction."[15]

The melancholy fatalism suggests that James is at best resigned to his new coterie status. He tells Whistler in 1897 that "One writes for one's self alone—one has accepted, once for all, the worst." When the ardent young disciples of his later years arrive, he greets them with pathetic relief, as when he calls the novelist Hugh Walpole's fan letter a "rare and blest revelation . . . that I enjoy the sympathy of the gallant and intelligent young." A few months later he asks his new disciple to call him "'*Très*-cher Maître,' or 'my very dear Master.'"[16] It is worth recalling the scathing irony with which James described the Paris coteries around the "maîtres" of his youth: "There is no artist so bungling that he will not find another to call him 'dear master.'"

Was James's increasing isolation related to his estrangement from his native land? It is striking that between 1882–83, when he had last visited America (and buried both his parents), and 1895, the year of his theatrical debacle, there is not a single mention in his published correspondence of a wish to return, even for a visit. This is strange, since most of James's intimates lived in the United States. In the following years, however, the idea of a return germinates and grows. By 1897, he writes to an old friend about New England summers with a sensuous nostalgia: "I envy you—for I see you in the mind's eye at Beverly—the element of wide verandah, cut peaches—I mean peaches and cream, you know—white frocks and Atlantic airs. You make me, my dear Fanny, in these high lights, quite incredibly homesick."[17]

In the following years, these exilic feelings become more urgent and express a wish to reconcile his divided attachments. They have a political as well as personal dimension. This is the era of the Anglo-American rapprochement, and James is touched by the new accord, especially as he realizes that the days of the British Empire are numbered. His response to Britain's early losses in the Boer War is elegiac: "I gloom and brood and have craven questions of 'Finis Britanniae?' in solitude." As he sees the United States take on the imperial mission Britain is abandoning, he hopes the younger country will prove worthy of the great "civilizing" tradition. What interests him is "human Anglo-Saxondom, with the American extension, or opportunity for it."[18] In such ways, geopolitics becomes cultural and personal.

But by 1900 he feels out of touch with "the American extension," wants to refresh his memory and learn what has happened to his country in the intervening decades. The America of his youth seems legendary, prehistoric, the present state of the country even more unreal. As he writes Oliver Wendell Holmes, "*All* reports of the land of my birth, however, are, to me, bewildering now, and I know not what to think of anything." He is torn between the feeling that this is his last chance—before age robs him of his power of fresh observation—and the fear that he is already too late. The return is an opportunity for artistic renewal, he writes William in 1903, in a desperate letter arguing against his brother's dissuasion. He calls the trip "the one chance that remains to me in life of anything that can be called a *movement*: my one little ewe-lamb of possible exotic experience, such experience as may convert itself, through the senses, through observation, imagination and reflection now at their maturity, into vivid and solid *material*, into a general renovation of one's too monotonised grab-bag."[19] His need to return overrides William's gloomy prediction that the new America will appall him and rob him of his remaining patriotism. His homesickness is linked to regret. "I have never been more curious of it," he writes Grace Norton, "nor more interested in it, nor more sensible of loss by absence from it."[20] By the summer of 1904 he is on his way. It would be nearly a year before he set foot in England again.

His return in body had been anticipated by a return in spirit. His countrymen again become his major fictional protagonists. In 1901–1904 he goes back to the subject that made him famous—the international theme. For the first time since *The Portrait of a Lady*, he devotes his primary energy to the encounter between Americans and Europeans. These are the years that produced *The Ambassadors*, *The Wings of the Dove*, and *The Golden Bowl*.[21] The reversion marks the defeat of James's ambition to become the authoritative interpreter of various sets without regard to national origin. He resurrects the subject long associated with his name. But a simple market explanation takes no account of his reconceptualization of the Euro-American relationship.

James acknowledged that in the earlier stage he had "written himself out as far as the international novel is concerned," as one of his reviewers had put it in 1884.[22] But the "contrast of manners," the ethnological impulse that dominates the earlier fiction, is no longer prominent in the late novels. James goes back to his earlier theme because he now sees it differently. A full-scale comparison of the two phases is unnecessary and is in any case familiar ground. *The Ambassadors* is often treated as a reworking of *The American*, for example.[23] But two overarching differences between his early and late treatments help to account for his renewed interest: his increasing moral casuistry, and the changes in Euro-American power relations.

James must have felt, as he reread his early accounts of American innocents trapped in the European web of intrigue, convention, and decadence, that he had schematized simplistically. The puritan strain in those works, for example Newman's consignment of the budding *grande horizontale* Noémie de Nioche to outer darkness, is replaced in the later novels by a more sympathetic treatment of illicit sexuality. The last novels are all concerned with infidelity, but the "guilty parties"—Chad and Madame de Vionnet in *The Ambassadors*, Kate Croy and Merton Densher in *The Wings of the Dove*, the Prince and Charlotte Stant in *The Golden Bowl*—are treated with much greater empathy. This was recognized at the time. A reviewer of *The Wings of the Dove* notes that "the puritan dualism" of the earlier fiction has given way to a more complex view in which our "sympathies are entangled with both sides." Surprisingly, James "comes to bend his intensest and finest light upon the archconspirator, who nearly supplants her intended victim in tragic and intellectual interest."[24] Such revisionism suggests that James looks critically at the group typecasting and brash judgmental confidence of his youth, and now wants to treat heterodox sexual experiments with more open sympathy than he had previously allowed himself.

James also returns to the subject to record the changes in the relative power of his Americans, Europeans, and Europeanized Americans. The Americans can now dictate terms, and this alters all the relationships in these novels and in tales contemporary with them. For example, "Miss Gunton of Poughkeepsie" (1900) revives a hoary Jamesian formula—the rejection of a European aristocrat by an American girl. But in this version Lily Gunton breaks off her engagement to an Italian prince when she is told that his family requires her to pay court to her future mother-in-law (as Christopher Newman had unprotestingly done). She will have none of this obeisance. In *her* society, she explains, the girl is instantly welcomed "on her engagement, before anything else can happen, by the family of her young man."[25] Her decision is irrevocable and incomprehensible to her European friends, including the baffled prince, who no more understands her than the Prince in *The Golden Bowl* will understand *his* American mate. James's new breed of Americans get their way. He had first shown their new power in "The Siege of London," as Mrs. Headway carries off her baronet; but the desperate vulgarity of this combatant is very different from the Americans' confidence in the later fiction. The passionate pilgrims or desperate petitioners are replaced by commanding figures of authority.

In all the last novels, the unreconstructed Americans win the contest against their European or expatriate rivals. In *The Ambassadors*, it is only a matter of time before Chad Newsome abandons his French mistress and returns to Massachusetts to run the family business and make a suitable marriage. Milly Theale's victory in *The Wings of the Dove* may be Pyrrhic but is nevertheless decisive. Densher will remain true to her memory and never marry Kate Croy. Milly's "stupendous" will (in both senses of the word "will") controls the lives of her survivors from the grave. And in *The Golden Bowl*, Maggie and Adam Verver separate the Prince from Charlotte Stant and settle them on different continents. Maggie hears in her father's voice "the note of possession and control" and could echo it as her helpless Prince confesses "I see nothing but *you*."[26]

In these novels, the European or Europeanized will bends to American power. James records this shift without celebrating it. This is clearest in *The Ambassadors*, in which he consciously politicizes the international conflict, beginning with the book's title. In 1893, to accord with its increasing geopolitical importance, the United States "changed the ranking of its diplomats from ministers to ambassadors."[27] No longer would the country's representative to Britain be called "Minister to the Court of St. James," which suggests deference to a higher authority, though three generations of Adamses had accepted the title with pride. He was the United States Ambassador. This magnification of American power is everywhere apparent in *The Ambassadors*. James's most brilliant stroke is to make the real potentate of this world invisible. The formidable Mrs. Newsome, a frail but steel-willed wealthy widow living quietly in Massachusetts, is the novel's unmoved mover. She dispatches her fiancé Lambert Strether to bring her reprobate son Chad home from his sexual entanglements in Paris to run the family's "big brave bouncing business." The firm is on the verge of becoming a monopoly if it regains the leadership once exercised by her husband and her father, both rather unsavory characters associated with the "infamies" of the robber barons.[28]

Mrs. Newsome is a regal force: "she looked, with her ruff and other matters, like Queen Elizabeth," Strether muses; he confesses he is "a little afraid of her." Her power is suggested by his reflection that "he had literally heard her silent." Strether is her first ambassador, the recipient of her detailed daily instructions. When his mission falters as he becomes caught up in the seductive ambiguities of Chad's situation, he is given an ultimatum and then dismissed. Replaced by Mrs. Newsome's daughter Sarah, he ruefully tells Chad, "I feel like the outgoing ambassador . . . doing honour to his appointed successor." His replacement "had come to receive his submission." When he defends himself and questions Mrs. Newsome's sense of Chad's situation, Sarah "let fly at him as from a stretched cord." Seeing her in conversation with Chad's mistress, the Countess de Vionnet, Strether concludes that it is Sarah "who most carried out the idea of a Countess."[29] James's metaphors throughout suggest that the Newsome campaign— with its awesome confidence and readiness to do battle—echoes the strategy enunciated by their nation's new leader in the year *The Ambassadors* was written: "Speak softly and carry a big stick."

For all his apparent unreliability, Chad is cut from the same cloth. As with his mother, his invisibility increases our sense of his power. He evades Strether for weeks, and when he unexpectedly turns up he is unrecognizable as the gauche young man who had left America some seven years earlier. He glides into the box at the Théâtre Français in which Strether and his companions are watching a performance like a man used to making a late entrance. And they realize with a shock that "they were in presence of Chad himself." The phrase suggests the descent of royalty. Though Strether is old enough to be Chad's father and can remember him as a chubby boy in knickerbockers, this twenty-eight-year-old man is a formidable stranger. With his *savoir-faire*, his sense of command, his hair prematurely streaked with gray, Chad "had been made over." Strether instantly senses Chad's power, "latent and beyond access, ominous and perhaps enviable," and asks himself if he had "carried himself like a fool." When he protests at what the young man's long absence and silence has put him through, Chad replies serenely, ominously, "Oh I haven't put you through much—yet."[30]

The prodigal son is well on the way to taking up his filial duties, as Shakespeare's Prince Hal dismisses his unsuitable companions and dons the robes of office. Although the novel leaves Chad in Paris, supposedly heeding Strether's unexpected advice not to abandon Madame de Vionnet, his thoughts are elsewhere. He comes back from London intensely excited about the new "art of advertisement," which he sees as "the great new force" that can revolutionize business practice "with the right man to work it." Clearly, he is the man. Even Marie de Vionnet, desperate to keep him, feels that Chad has "the makings of an immense man of business." And Strether ruefully agrees: "There it is. He's the son of his father!"[31]

The real casualties in this contest are the Europeans and Europeanized Americans. Madame de Vionnet, the charming, beautiful, outwardly confident aristocrat, is reduced to sobbing for her American lover like "a maidservant crying for her young man." She knows that she will be "the loser in the end" and is finally compared to Madame Roland approaching the guillotine. Maria Gostrey must contemplate a solitary future when Strether turns down her offer of companionship. And Strether himself, a man adrift, without a country or a vocation after betraying Mrs. Newsome's commands, has only the consolation of his arid probity: "Not, out of the whole affair, to have got anything for myself."[32]

Our sympathies are with the vanquished. We are given little chance to look through the eyes of the victors, though it is easy to imagine how the Newsomes feel about the defection of their trusted ambassador or about their promising son and brother's liaison with a married woman ten years his senior who keeps him from his home and work and prevents him from producing a legitimate heir. That is not, however, the perspective from which the book is written. Mrs. Newsome's voluminous dispatches to Strether are never even quoted. The striking *absence* of sympathy for the loyal Americans makes one wonder if James himself has not by this point "gone over." The U.S. diplomatic corps regularly transfers its representatives from country to country to make certain of their continuing loyalty. When *The Ambassadors* was published, James had been living in Britain without "home leave" for exactly twenty years. It was time—it was well past time—for him to renew his ties to his native land.

II

JAMES'S AMERICAN journey has two goals—to recapture a past that is fading from memory, and to expose him to the forces relegating that past to oblivion. He responds with pained shock: so much is unrecognizable, and he cannot make his peace with what has displaced his remembered world. But not all his impressions are negative. His response to New York, to Chicago, to California is intense, in full recognition of American vitality. He is overwhelmed by New York and can barely make sense of his conflicting feelings about "the horrific, the unspeakable, extraordinary, yet partly interesting, amusing, and above all fantastically *bristling*" metropolis. Chicago is even more startling and confirms the country's new vigor. Like Adams contemplating the dynamo, James is stunned by "the sense of *power*, huge and augmenting, power, power (vast mechanical, industrial, social, financial) everywhere! This Chicago is huge, *infinite*." Even California, not the most plausible candidate for Jamesian enthusiasm, "has completely bowled me over—such a delicious difference from the rest of the U.S. do I find in it."[33] These reactions show that James's responsiveness is intact, that he doesn't simply reject the unfamiliar, as people in their sixties often do. He sees America as he had once seen Europe—as a land of mystery and romance. In *The American Scene* (1907), the important book that grows out of this journey, he writes that his long absence, while making him miss "a thousand stages and changes," now offered him a country with "a perfect iridescence of fresh aspects, [that] seemed more and more to appeal to the faculty of wonder."[34]

His journey is also recuperative. He visits the memorial sites of his childhood and youth in a spirit of filial piety: Albany and lower Manhattan, Newport, Cambridge. The images he recaptures, whether in fact or memory, reinforce his sense of pre–Civil War America as a lost paradise. He describes his childhood in New York and Albany as a pastoral cornucopia. This image dominates the autobiography he writes on his return to England: "What did the stacked boxes and baskets of our youth represent but the boundless fruitage of that more bucolic age of the American world?" Even the cities are prelapsarian: "Broadway must have been then as one of the alleys of Eden."[35]

The heart of this return is his visit to the James family graves in Mt.

Auburn cemetery, an orgasmic experience that breaks the dam of his contained familial love and justifies the whole journey: "It was the moment; it was the hour, it was the blessed flood of emotion that broke out at the touch of one's sudden *vision* and carried me away," he writes in his notebooks. "I seemed then to know why I had done this; I seemed then to know why I had *come*—and to feel how *not* to have come would have been miserably, horribly to miss it."[36] As we will see, the climax of one of James's most powerful late tales, "The Beast in the Jungle" (1903), anticipated the revelatory response in such a setting. There is a connection between his longed-for and actual return to his native land and the recovery of suppressed feelings, as though his expatriation had frozen over a large tract of his emotional life.

Yet the past is barely recoverable; there is a conspiracy in twentieth-century America to obliterate it. James feels that his country is deliberately expunging the vestiges of the past that hamper what passes for progress. The omnipresent power and energy is destructive as well as creative. To make it new, scrap the old. To *conserve* anything—churches, meeting halls, gracious old houses—seems an alien concept. Why bother? America is on the move. Her eye is on the future. "What was taking place was a perpetual repudiation of the past," he writes in *The American Scene*. The spirit of New York is the spirit of a permanent provisionality: "I build you up but to tear you down."[37] The private homes of his youth have been smashed to make way for apartment houses, the apartment houses for skyscrapers. It is going, going, gone.

The rhetoric is conservationist, the politics behind it conservative. Not only buildings are being displaced, but a class—James's own class of established wealth and position. *The American Scene* is not a travel book but a work of social history by a "brooding analyst" who records the decline of his caste, and the ascendancy of two groups displacing them from power—the plutocrats and new immigrants. The point of view is close to Adams's, and there are countless parallels between James's book and the *Education*. Of the two agents of change, the plutocracy is the more sinister in James's eyes. *These* are the people who are tearing down the old to make way for their gaudy mansions. He describes the "white elephants" at Newport that have displaced the more modest "cottages" of his youth—"the time of settled possession," as he calls it, without saying whose—mansions already deserted as their restless proprietors move on to the next fashionable resort.[38]

The eager pursuit of money is the agent of change. The atmosphere is so thick with it that it fills the lungs: "There was gold-dust in the air," James writes; "money in the air, ever so much money." Mere comfortable affluence is displaced by Veblen's conspicuous consumption. The ubiquitous businessman is in control. This is the first impression that "assaults the arriving visitor."[39] Such images of pollution and aggression express James's anxiety. Can his kind still breathe in this environment? His grandfather might have found it congenial. His father, who had cultivated the life of leisure, would have sought shelter. James himself, filled with resentment in being relegated to the middle class as both the family's capital and his literary income shrink, feels set aside, and with more reason than Henry Adams.

The other agents of change are the new immigrants from southern and eastern Europe. James's return coincides with the cresting of this migration. Between 1900 and 1903, their numbers double from 300,000 to 600,000 annually. By 1907, when *The American Scene* is published, over 900,000 arrive.[40] There is no end in sight. What hope is there for the continued "Anglo-Saxon" domination of America, or for an Anglo-American alliance, in the face of such an invasion? James is intensely conscious of how his childhood world has been altered by these new inheritors. Inheritance, succession, possession, and displacement are the terms he uses to register their impact. His response is more complex than Adams's, but their sense of dispossession is shared. James's long account of his visit to Ellis Island in *The American Scene* records his fear of the alien intruder. He compares himself to a "privileged person who has had an apparition, seen a ghost in his supposedly safe old house."[41] He will use this image of the invasion of a domestic retreat in two of his last works, "The Jolly Corner" and *The Sense of the Past*.

James is stunned by the confidence of the new proprietors. For him, "the great fact" about the Jews of the Lower East Side, "foreign as they might be, . . . is that they were *at home*." And he records with amazement "their note of settled possession . . . ; so that *unsettled* possession is what we, on our side, seem reduced to." His "we" makes it clear which group he is addressing. He is disturbed but not repelled by the Yiddish culture of the streets and theaters and keeps returning to understand what is going on. His genuine curiosity is different from

Adams's revulsion. Such alien intruders are now encountered every-where. In the New Hampshire hills, he fruitlessly asks directions of a young man he meets—in English, in French, in Italian. "What *are* you then?" James demands; "'I'm an Armenian,' he replied, as if it were the most natural thing in the world for a wage-earning youth in the heart of New England to be." Even in Salem, where he asks the way to Hawthorne's "house of the seven gables," his question meets with an indifferent shrug from an Italian resident.[42] Strikingly, it is James, not the "alien," who is lost.

These disturbing experiences involve the erosion of English linguis-tic primacy. Unlike Adams, James is not an anti-Semite. He was a Dreyfusard, a sponsor of Emma Lazarus, a frequent guest at Roth-schild country houses in Britain; the sympathetic Miriam Rooth is a major character in his novel *The Tragic Muse*. What worries him about the Jews and other non-Anglo-Saxons settling on the eastern seaboard is their *culture*, not their race. He grasps their intellectual and imagina-tive power, even in the midst of their poverty. In the coffeehouses and Yiddish theaters, James sees a vital cultural dispensation and audience preparing to take on, possibly to take over, "the living idiom." He has a remarkably prescient sense of the future of his own Anglo-American language and culture: "The accent of the very ultimate future, in the States, may be destined to become the most beautiful on the globe and the very music of humanity (here the 'ethnic' synthesis shrouds itself thicker than ever); but whatever we shall know it for, certainly, we shall not know it for English—in any sense for which there is an exist-ing literary measure."[43] Here is the rivalry at the heart of James's anxi-ety. The authority of his own culture, which he has devoted his life to propagating, is imperiled. It might have appalled, but would not have surprised him that of the six most recent American recipients of the Nobel Prize for Literature—Saul Bellow, Isaac Bashevis Singer, Czes-law Milosz, Joseph Brodsky, Derek Walcott, Toni Morrison—only one was born in the United States and none could qualify as an Anglo-Saxon. The "ethnic synthesis" he foresaw and feared has arrived.

He could hardly welcome its coming, since it signaled the eventual demise of his own world's cultural centrality. Has any such group *as* a group ever relinquished control without a fight? He sees the immi-grants wiping out his dispensation, eradicating the past like "a huge applied sponge, a sponge saturated with the foreign mixture and passed over almost everything I remembered and might still have recovered."[44] He works to slow down the process but knows he cannot stop it. His alarmist Bryn Mawr address (later published as "The Question of Our Speech") pleads for the preservation of "a common language," essential to "a coherent culture." It is being undermined by the divergence of colloquial and formal speech, and by universal public education as it accommodates the alien tongues. Assimilation and acculturation are not one-way streets. The immigrants are the language's new owners and will make alterations as they see fit. James concedes that they "have just as much property in our speech as we have, and just as good a right to do what they choose with it." Yet he describes the amalgamation not as creative but polluting, as the foreigners "dump their mountain of promiscuous material into the foundations of the American."[45] What Spenser had once called "the well of English undefiled" in harking back to Chaucer is being contaminated. His anxiety is rooted in an Arnoldian fear of cultural devolution and ignores the long history that had already made American English a distinct and constantly changing language.

The Bryn Mawr talk is James's first intemperate response. His considered judgment, in *The American Scene*, is more complex and accommodating—"a shifting mixture," in Irving Howe's words, "of curiosity, admiration, disdain, withdrawal, respect, animus."[46] These opposing reactions reflect the conflict between James's instinctive recoil and his more judicious historical imagination. There is no denying his anger and contempt. He acknowledges "no claim to brotherhood with aliens in the first grossness of their alienism." But future generations will be different: "*They* are the stuff of whom brothers and sisters are made." Furthermore, James asks rhetorically, "Who and what is an alien, when it comes to that, in a country peopled from the first under the jealous eye of history? . . . Which is the American, by these scant measures?—which is *not* the alien?" James's fellow Anglo-Saxonists would not have made such a concession. Finally, his tolerance is a survival tactic, a way of avoiding the extinction a purely hostile attitude toward the new virtually guarantees. "To recover confidence and regain lost ground, we, not they, must make the surrender," James warns his readers. "We must go, in other words, *more* than half-way to meet them; which is all the difference, for us, between possession and dispossession."[47] We would now call such a strategy preemptive. James might have called it the fostering of cohesion.

The sense of imperiled national unity was, after all, the defining experience of his early adulthood. He was eighteen when the Civil War began; two of his brothers fought in it; one nearly died of his wounds. The slow recovery of national identity during his middle years once again seemed threatened, not by war but by the pace of immigration. In his autobiography, James sees the period 1900–1910 as the moment "where our national theory of absorption, assimilation and conversion appallingly breaks down," where the communal sense is blighted, where "the old, the comparatively brothering, conditions" of the America he remembers have ceased to exist.[48]

This nostalgia for an unrecoverable past and fear of the present make James feel less American than ever. Like Adams, he has lost his place. The fictional and discursive works he writes after his return mourn the lost world and lament his incapacity to grasp the shaping forces of change. Past and present seem unconnected because of his long absence. The chasm separating them structures these works—*The American Scene*, the autobiography, stories like "Crapy Cornelia" and "The Jolly Corner," the unfinished novel *The Ivory Tower*. Change is not gradual but catastrophic. All are variants of Washington Irving's fantasy, in "Rip Van Winkle," of a man who sleeps through major events in his country's history and awakes to find it altered for the worse.

"The repentant absentee," as James refers to himself in *The American Scene*, is a complex figure in these works. He longs for the restoration of the vanished world and refuses consolation. Nostalgia for a lost Arcadia is the dominant emotion. The time frame is entirely unrealistic, as in this Proustian reliving of his childhood journeys from New York to Albany: "Here, in the stir of the senses, a whole range of small forgotten things revived, things intensely Hudsonian, more than Hudsonian; small echoes and tones and sleeping lights, small sights and sounds and smells that made one, for an hour, *as* small—carried one up the rest of the river, the very river of life indeed, as a thrilled, roundabouted pilgrim, by primitive steamboat, to a mellow, mediaeval Albany."[49] Albany was never medieval, of course; James's dislocated time sense conveys the huge gap he feels. It recalls Adams's equally fanciful claim that "he was born an eighteenth-century child," that his mid-nineteenth-century education fitted him more for the year 1 than the year 1900.[50]

The feeling provokes a need to recapture (or invent) the distant past: Adams's medieval cathedrals, as well as his earliest memories in the *Education,* James's detailed recovery of his childhood and youth, or his fantasy, in *The Sense of the Past,* of a modern American who changes places with a progenitor. His autobiography recreates the lost social and familial worlds of his earliest years. It differs from most such ventures because it isn't teleological: There is no present to which it leads. The finished volumes—*A Small Boy and Others* and *Notes of a Son and Brother* (1913, 1914)—simply recreate minutely the New York of the 1840s and 1850s, the Newport, Boston, and Cambridge of the 1860s, the London of the 1870s. He must record these vanished eras as the survivor—the last of his generation of Jameses after William's death in 1910. The past is gone; but a writer with an evocative memory can give it a kind of afterlife.

More disturbing are the characters in James's late fiction who cannot live in the present. In "Crapy Cornelia" (1909), his refined middle-aged bachelor, White-Mason, has the choice of joining in "the music of the future" by marrying a dazzling, vivacious woman of present-day New York, or of growing old with Cornelia Rasch, the faded friend of his youth, "as conscious, ironic, pathetic survivors together of a dead and buried society"—their genteel world of old New York. Yet his aversion to the "harsh and metallic" sound of modernity is so strong that he really has no choice. He proposes to Cornelia that they "make over and recreate our lost world" by retreating into the shade of their shared memories, photographs, stories.[51] The word "pathetic" acknowledges defeat, but they are allergic to the harsh medicine that might cure them of their debilitating nostalgia.

That a refusal to live in the present is something like a mental illness is suggested in James's unfinished novel *The Sense of the Past,* in which his young American protagonist, Ralph Pendrel, inherits a gracious old house in the heart of London from a distant relative and abandons his country (and Aurora Coyne, the woman he has been courting) to live in it. "The sense of the past," Aurora reminds him as he leaves, "was the thing in life you desired most to arrive at." As her name suggests, she has no such need; she sends him off in the hope he will eventually return to

America, to the present, to her, to his senses. Ralph is a passionate pilgrim, like the hero of James's early tale, who also had a claim on an English estate. But Ralph's legacy proves a disaster.

The Sense of the Past is a ghost story in which Ralph's spirit is possessed by one of his own ancestors, who looks out at him from a family portrait in the London house. Ralph suddenly finds himself living out of his own time and place. We are to understand this as a kind of derangement, though James writes from inside Ralph's fantasy. Even from that perspective, however, being transplanted to the past proves intolerable. The initial feeling of wonder gives way to revulsion as he takes in the conditions of family life, the need for deference and servitude in the older English world. And he is terrified, as James puts it, "that he is going to be *left*, handed over to the conditions of where and what and above all *when* he is; never saved, never rescued, never restored again, by the termination of his adventure and experience, to his native temporal conditions, which he yearns for with an unutterable yearning." What he comes to feel is an "unspeakable homesickness for his own time and place."[52] More than any of James's works, *The Sense of the Past* raises the disturbing possibility that his major life choices—of expatriation over staying home, of tradition over modernity—were terrible mistakes. This may be why he never finishes it. It remains not only a fragment but a work of fancy rather than imagination. Too much is at stake for James to invest himself in this story. He cannot afford the price.

III

"A man always pays, in one way or another, for expatriation, for detachment from his plain primary heritage," James writes in *William Wetmore Story and His Friends* (1903), his biography of the nineteenth-century American sculptor who settled in Rome.[53] He attributes the conclusion to Story but acknowledges its truth. This was the book Adams read with such intense identification. He accused James of writing a crypto-autobiography or group portrait of the "improvised Europeans" to which they belonged—Story, Adams, James, and others of the "type bourgeois-bostonien."[54] It tells of loss rather than triumphant achievement, surprising in an official biography commissioned by Story's family. James agrees to do it only on his own terms. And he treats his individual subject as a test case, an early experiment on the effects of artistic expatriation.

The results are not encouraging. James acknowledges that Story achieves international recognition. He is in demand for large public projects designed for the America he has abandoned. The enthusiastic London reception of his sculpture gives him the right credentials. But he has paid a heavy personal and professional price. He is intellectually marooned among the American sybarites in Rome. He complains that he has "no friends, no one with whom I can . . . walk any of the higher ranges of art and philosophy. This for me is a terrible want." The absence of stimulus, of talents and ambitions striving to create a new artistic language, undermines his achievement. He is out of touch with the vital forces of the present, too much under the spell of his European precursors. His work becomes safe, conservative, forgettable. Story never ventured into the realm of "shockability," James writes, but venerated traditional subjects and styles. "The general lesson" to be learned from this "case of the permanent absentee or exile," he concludes, is that "Story *paid* — paid for having sought his development even among the circumstances that at the time of his choice appeared not alone the only propitious, but the only possible." He sees the whole decorous career as a mistake, based on a "frank consent to be beguiled."[55]

Were such judgments crypto-confessional? Obviously there are major differences between the two careers. James finds an intellectual community in London; although he never achieves popular success, he is honored by his peers; he transforms the novel and does not surrender his power to shock; his work lasts. For all that, his feelings often startlingly echo Story's. The deepest fact about himself, he writes a friend in 1900, is the *"essential loneliness of my life."* And though this feeling antedates his decision to expatriate, it is greatly intensified by it. He begs Edith Wharton, embarked on her own expatriate career when he encounters her, to study "the American life that surrounds you." In a remarkable 1902 letter, written upon reading *The Valley of Decision,* her historical novel set in early-nineteenth-century Italy, he exhorts her to "profit, be warned, by my awful example of exile and ignorance" and urges her to seize hold "of the *American subject* — the immediate, the real, the ours, the yours, the novelist's that it waits for." He offers three words of advice—perhaps the most fruitful advice an older writer ever gave a younger: "*Do New York!*"[56] The command saved Wharton from Story's fate by legitimizing the unvenerable subject of novels that would count among her greatest achievements: *The House of Mirth, The Custom of the Country, The Age of Innocence,* all set in New York.

James becomes increasingly aware of the price *he* has paid for expatriation. The midwestern novelist Hamlin Garland records a melancholy talk with James after his return from America, in which James laments his flight. The accuracy of Garland's later published account (in his *Roadside Meetings,* 1930) has been questioned by Leon Edel, who compares that frequently cited version with the less dramatic record of the conversation in Garland's notebook. Yet the notebook entry is decisive enough. In it James tells Garland, "if I were to live my life again I would be American—steep myself in it, know no other," and he concludes that the "mixture of Europe and America is disastrous."[57] His late disenchantment recalls a letter to his brother, imploring William not to impose on *his* children their parents' disorienting cosmopolitan experiment. Allow them, he pleads, "to contract local saturations and attachments in respect to their *own* great and glorious country, to learn, and strike roots into, its infinite beauty, as I suppose, and variety."[58] The "as I suppose" painfully acknowledges his own uninitiated state.

The American journey makes him aware of his missed chances. Though often appalled by the changes, he is intensely interested. He wants to write about the new forces in American life but fears his long absence unfits him for the task. As he hears the "alien syllables and sounds" of America's new citizens, he vents his frustration in being barred entry: "My imagination, on the great highways, I find, doesn't rise to such people, who are obviously beyond my divination. . . . Abysmal the mystery of what they think, what they feel, what they want, what they suppose themselves to be saying."[59] Though he is testily impatient with "such people" for remaining beyond his ken, he criticizes his imaginative failure to rise to or fathom them.

Nor can he understand the newly dominant culture of accumulation and display. He notes the rich literary material waiting to be explored in "the typical American figure" of the businessman, "whose song has still to be sung and his picture still to be painted."[60] He had made a stab at it in his portrait of Christopher Newman and tries again in the figure of Adam Verver. But we know virtually nothing about how either *made* his money. Both are implausibly unworldly for men who had relentlessly pursued success, and their business careers—unlike Silas Lapham's, for instance—remain blank.[61]

James blames his "fatally uninitiated state" for his imaginative failure. To be initiated means to secure entry to an exclusive mystery. In *The American Scene* he laments his inability to penetrate the closed doors of Wall Street, "behind which immense 'material' lurked, material for the artist, the painter of life, as we say, who shouldn't have begun so early and so fatally to fall away from possible initiations."[62] This ignorance is as much a product of James's family training as of his expatriation. The Jameses' leisure-class training was a "monstrous exception" to the American cult of acquisition. He describes the family's "helpless ignorance" about money: "Business in a world of business was the thing we most agreed (differ as we might on minor issues) in knowing nothing about."[63] But this freedom was also a formula for social inconsequence. To a writer whose model was Balzac—"the father of us all," with his enviable panoramic grasp of his society—such ignorance of the very motor of modern American life was a disaster.[64]

James compensated by ignoring the subject, or by writing about it in obfuscatory or symbolic language, as in his refusal in *The Ambassadors* to specify just what the Newsome firm manufactures, or in his treatment of Milly Theale's fairy-tale wealth in *The Wings of the Dove*. But he made one final attempt to expand his range—the unfinished novel *The Ivory Tower*. This was the account of contemporary America Wharton eagerly wanted *him* to write. She even asked Scribners to offer James a large advance (silently paying it from her own royalties) to commit him to the task. She was begging him to *Do America!* as he had once urged her to *Do New York!*[65]

The book is set in the Newport of the outsize American fortunes, in an atmosphere of greed, opportunism, and betrayal. Unlike Christopher Newman or Adam Verver, these millionaires are tainted, some unrepentant, others contrite. James says he is interested in "the black and merciless things that are behind the great possessions."[66] His plutocrats are obsessed by money. Abel Gaw and Mr. Betterman, former partners whose unsavory alliance ended acrimoniously, are both approaching death. Gaw wants to live long enough to make sure his fortune dwarfs his rival's. He sits on Betterman's verandah like a cormorant waiting for him to die. But Betterman seems to gain strength with the arrival of Gray Fielder, his nephew and heir, who has remained untouched by the forces both men embody by spending his life in Europe. Gray represents Betterman's salvation, his deathbed revulsion from his sordid commercial life. The nephew's total ignorance of money—he hasn't "done three cents' worth of business" in his life—is what makes him so appealing. He is *clean*, a business virgin, a model of probity, unlike anyone the uncle has previously encountered. In leaving Gray his estate, he hopes the endless "hustle" of his commercial life, which he has mastered "but too abominably well," will finally end.[67]

James's sketch for the rest of the novel, which he abandoned in 1914, makes it clear these hopes are delusory. Gray will be surrounded by sharks—the boyhood friend to whom he entrusts the management of his fortune, the attractive young woman who suddenly materializes, the predators who smell blood. The only escape from this world is to abandon it. Gray divorces himself from his dirty money by "resigning it to its natural associations."[68] It is the old Jamesian imperative of renunciation; his new subject changes nothing essential in his approach. The trouble is that he doesn't know the commercial world from the inside. The story of how these fortunes were accumulated remains unnarrated. James's ignorance and disapproval get in the way, and plausibility suffers. It is hardly likely that a man of Betterman's business acumen would leave a vast fortune to a commercially innocent young man without elaborate safeguards to make sure it doesn't fall into unworthy hands. He knows better. Yet his will is unconditional; his lawyer tells Gray that he has never "seen such an amount of property disposed of in terms so few and simple and clear."[69] In his notes, James admits the "enormous difficulty of pretending to show things here as with a business vision, in my total absence of business initiation."[70] It proves an insurmountable obstacle and helps to explain why the novel, like *The Sense of the Past*, is unfinishable. He is sailing into uncharted waters.

James's return to the United States, though it produces *The American Scene*, the autobiography, and a few masterful tales like "The Jolly Corner," undermines his confidence in his vision of America. It even casts doubt on the accuracy of his earlier American settings. As a result, he excludes *The Europeans, Washington Square, The Bostonians,* and most of the American tales from the ironically titled "New York Edition" of his works.[71] And he becomes increasingly English in his loyalties, as a late letter to William's widow shows. She appeals to him to come "home" at last. He replies that he "could come back to America (could be carried back on a stretcher) to *die*—but never, never to live." As he patiently explains, using the language an American would presumably understand, "You see my capital—yielding all my income, intellectual, social, associational, on the old investment of so many years—my capital is *here*, and to let it all slide would be simply to become bankrupt."[72]

The difference between the two countries crystallizes for him in the 1913 tributes for his seventieth birthday. His British friends subscribe to commission the Sargent portrait that hangs in London's National Portrait Gallery. The Americans plan to send him money, as though he were a superannuated pauper, before he puts a stop to the scheme. His English "capital" is metaphorical, his American apparently a matter of cold cash. The decisive moment is the start of the war, in which Britain's peril and America's neutrality offers James a choice. In 1915 he becomes a British subject. He asks Herbert Asquith, the prime minister, to be one of his sponsors, explaining, "I find my wish to testify at this crisis to the force of my attachment and devotion to England, and to the cause for which she is fighting, finally and completely irresistible."[73]

The decision offers a sense of closure, yet James had no time to act on it. He had been for so long an outsider—a spectator rather than a participant. Even his earliest international tales, like "Eugene Pickering" (1874), are narrated by a minor character who claims objective knowledge by seeing both sides. Objectivity is to be the spectator's reward. James has been attacked for using his spectatorial distance as a form of power and surveillance.[74] There are signs that he prides himself on his exceptional gifts of observation and is willing to pay the price. He treasures his outsider's perspective because he thinks it frees him from an absurd parochialism. Two self-congratulatory letters of the 1890s offer testimony. He writes William that "an individual so capable as I am of the uncanniest self-effacement in the active exercise of the passion of observation, always exposes himself a little to *looking* like a dupe—and he doesn't care a hang!" And he enunciates a voyeur's credo: "There is nothing I like better than that others should live *for* me, as it were—in case, of course, I can catch them *at* it."[75] Edmund Gosse, who was the librarian of the House of Lords, recalled that James liked to "stand looking down from one of the windows of the Library on the Terrace, crowded with its motley afternoon crew of Members of both Houses and their guests of both sexes. He liked that better than to mingle with the throng itself."[76] To be above, to look down, is a supposed reward of his situation.

In his last decades, however, James comes to see the connection between this taste and his perpetual sense of loneliness. Expatriation fosters the spectatorial habit. Even the most significant events in the foreign country come to seem like a performance. James's description of William Story and his friends watching from his grand apartment as the French troops invade Rome in 1849 is heavily ironic: "It was at this battle that foreign visitors 'assisted,' as in an opera-box, from anxious Pincian windows." The houses on the Pincio seem more perturbed than their American tenants. The hectic atmosphere increases the festive air: "Delightful Revolution, which, we seem to see, promoted afternoon drives and friendly parleys."[77] It is in part to avoid such unseemly detachment from carnage that James abandons his cherished cosmopolitan identity when his adopted country is fighting for her life.

But his late revulsion from his spectatorial habit has deeper roots and is only partly related to his expatriation. James exposes them in "The Beast in the Jungle" (1903). The idea of "watching" is central to this story, yet both major characters are English and their nationality irrelevant. John Marcher has become convinced, early in life, that he is reserved for an exceptional fate—"something rare and strange, possibly prodigious and terrible."[78] He has no notion what form it will take but is sure it will be extraordinary. Only one person knows of his fear, or hope—May Bartram, to whom he had once confessed it. When he meets her again, she recalls the conversation in detail and is eager to know if the prophecy has come to pass. Marcher confesses it has not, but her apparent belief in it, and in him, makes him offer her a ringside seat to "watch" with him. For reasons of her own, she accepts, and the two turn into their own audience.

It becomes a way of life, *their* life, for years. May at first finds it equally fascinating: "If I've been 'watching' with you, as we long ago agreed that I was to do, watching is always in itself an absorption." Theirs is an uninterrupted auto-voyeurism, passive, expectant, uneventful. Yet something is happening all the same, though Marcher fails to notice. Time is passing; they are growing old; May falls ill and now understands Marcher's terrible fate—a knowledge from which in her silent, unreciprocated love she protects him. Only after her death, when he visits her grave, does the long withheld revelation come. The sight of another mourner in the cemetery, a man whose shocking grief is painted in "the deep ravage of the features that he showed," in a face that is "the image of scarred passion," makes Marcher grasp the bizarre fate reserved for him—to be "the man of his time, *the* man, to whom nothing on earth was to have happened." The mourner's vivid intensity illuminates his own "arid end," "the sounded void of his life."[79] He understands for the first time what his spectatorial passivity has cost him—not only the knowledge of May's love, of which he was oblivious, and to which in any case he showed no inclination to respond, but any access whatever to his own lost pulse of feeling.

Spectatorship offers no rewards in this tale. There is no semi-attached narrator to put the story in neat ironic perspective. The observer is finally—but only finally—the most deeply affected participant, whose disaster lies precisely in his arrogant refusal to surrender his Olympian observation post and explore his human needs. James wrote the story in his sixtieth year and invested it with his increasingly desperate desire to seize his own last chances. It prefigures his experience in Mt. Auburn cemetery, when he visits the graves of those *he* has loved and suddenly understands why he has come back and "how *not* to have come would have been miserably, horribly to miss it." For this filial and fraternal act of devotion he is on time. But what does it mean, at sixty, to have your deepest feelings literally buried? Doesn't it portend that for the present and future, it is too late?

This fear dominates many of James's final works. It is hard to exaggerate the power of the phrase "too late" as his old age approaches. In 1902 he writes his friend Sarah Wister—who urges him to return before the relics of the past like Charleston, South Carolina, are destroyed—"You see I *am* 'too late'; not yet too late for Charleston, etc., but too late for myself."[80] He had wrestled with that fear in *The Ambassadors*, finished in the previous year. But James records the germ of that novel much earlier, in 1895, when he first hears the story of Howells's outburst during a visit to Paris. It was Howells who had dutifully stayed at home, constructed an impeccable literary career, become the dean of American letters, but who in his mid-fifties suddenly grasped all he had sacrificed to convention. When he meets a young friend of James's in Paris, his bitterness turns into an urgent appeal to the young man not to make his mistake: "And now I'm too old. It's too late. . . . You have time. You are young. Live!"[81]

James instantly imagines the use he can make of this scene. He incorporates it virtually intact into Strether's speech to Little Bilham in Gloriani's garden. Even in the 1895 notebook entry he sees the fictional character he will invent: "He has never really enjoyed—he has lived only for Duty and conscience—his conception of them; for pure appearances and daily tasks—lived for effort, surrender, abstention, sacrifice. . . . I don't see him as having battled with his passions . . . or as having, in the past, suspected, very much, what he was losing, what he was not doing." Only one essential aspect of Strether's character is missing at this point— his national identity: "He may be an American—he might be an Englishman."[82] In *The Ambassadors*, the character is unmistakably American, a man with a literary bent who might have chosen to live in Europe as James did but went back instead. The original uncertainty about his nationality suggests that the focus was not on the losses of expatriation but on the more general regret about a road not taken, a road now overgrown. As in his earlier fiction, the international theme becomes a cover story for more private conflicts James is reluctant to expose: "I don't see him as having battled with his passions."

Life is full of exclusionary choices, and of late regrets for those made long ago. On the surface, Strether mourns having immured himself in provincial Massachusetts rather than acting on his early attraction to Paris's rich cultural opportunities. But his deeper regret is for the loss of passion, felt from the first moment of his arrival in Europe in the unfamiliar stirring of his senses, and expressed vicariously in his unambassadorial empathy with Chad and Madame de Vionnet. Despite his conviction that the things he had once wanted "were lost for ever," that "the train had waited at the station" and left without him, the novel gives him a second chance. Though he is over fifty, he seems to be eating his first adult meal: "The Paris evening in short was, for Strether, in the very taste of the soup, in the goodness, as he was innocently pleased to think it, of the wine, in the pleasant coarse texture of the napkin and the crunch of the thick-crusted bread." Touch, taste, smell, sound are all miraculously still alive, and so are sight and desire: "Her bare shoulders and arms were white and beautiful; the materials of her dress, a mixture, as he supposed, of silk and crape, were of a silvery grey so artfully composed as to give an impression of warm splendour." This is his response to Madame de Vionnet. But he reacts similarly to a woman he meets in Europe who might be his—Maria Gostrey. When she joins him for dinner, he notices that her dress is "cut down," that she wears a red velvet band around her throat; he notes her smile, her complexion, the way she holds her head, "her lips, her teeth, her eyes, her hair."[83] His own eyes are traveling up. There is something comic in this methodical catalog of Maria's charms, but its awkwardness is like the creaking of a rusty hinge. Strether looks at her very differently from the way he sees Mrs. Newsome, with her ruff like Queen Elizabeth's.

Maria's role in *The Ambassadors* is not only to initiate Strether and the reader into morally ambiguous Paris. She is also an alternative to the life he has lived. He has long been a widower, bereft early of his wife and later of his son. The woman he expects to marry is a widow of his own generation. But Maria Gostrey is thirty-five, attractive, intelligent, delightful, and delighted with him. She in effect proposes to Strether at the end of the book, after his engagement has been broken off. They could marry; they might have children; they could live in Paris. The possibility gives Strether another chance to catch the train he has missed. Perhaps it is *not* too late. As James puts it in the preface, "*Would* there yet perhaps be time for reparation? reparation, that is, for the injury done his character . . . ?"[84]

The answer, of course, is no. His character is unalterable. His puritan training has formed him, and constructing a life based on gratification is, if not unthinkable, unrealizable. He cannot take up his opportunity because it *seems* wrong, and he needs still "to be right." Even his unexpected about-face in urging Chad to stay with Madame de Vionnet is moralistic rather than hedonistic. He tells the young man that leaving her would be "infamy," would be "base," and he threatens to "curse him" if he does. This is not the music of liberation. Despite his rediscovered sensuality he is not in harmony with his new surroundings. He must go back to the arid life that has made him what he is. His feeling early in the novel of being "launched in something of which the sense would be quite disconnected from the sense of his past and which was literally beginning there and then"[85] is a delusion. The psychic life is conservative, continuous with what came before. For Strether it is, after all, "too late."

James thus feared the worst even before he embarked on his reverse pilgrimage. But the year in America intensified both his desire and his disappointment. Before, the question of alternatives was alive, unsettling, exciting; afterwards, it was settled—"for life, as it were," to quote the ominous last words of *Washington Square*, in which James's heroine sentences herself to spinsterhood. There is a subterranean link between James's sense of all his missed opportunities and his suppressed erotic impulse and lifelong celibacy. His rejection of marriage and his inability to act on his homoerotic desire help to give these works their tone of urgency and passionate regret.[86] The nexus of feelings dominates *The Ambassadors* and "The Beast in the Jungle" as well as late tales like "Crapy Cornelia" and "The Bench of Desolation." But it is nowhere more powerfully articulated than in "The Jolly Corner" (1908).

James's tale is a direct product of his trip to America. Its basic elements are autobiographical. Spencer Brydon returns to his native New York after decades of living in Europe. His ostensible purpose is to supervise the refurbishing of his apartment house, the income from which has supported him in elegant leisure abroad. But he also wants to see what has happened to his native land, though he naively expects few surprises. He is completely unprepared for the transformation of New York and for his own response. He feels the shock of *non*recognition and a surprising attraction to the dynamic city that has risen up in his absence. He finds himself supervising the modernization of his building, vigorously reproving a recalcitrant contractor. "In a compartment of his mind never yet penetrated," he discovers an astonishing "capacity for business and a sense for construction." As his old friend Alice Staverton tells him, "he has clearly for too many years neglected a real gift. If he had but stayed at home he would have anticipated the inventor of the sky-scraper."[87]

This amiable remark engenders a powerful fantasy of an alter ego, a

Spencer Brydon who stayed rather than left and who fully participated in the aggressive expansion of the city. "What would it have made of me, what would it have made of me?" he demands. "I keep for ever wondering, all idiotically; as if I could possibly know." But his bafflement does not stop his imagination, and the figure of the alter ego suddenly materializes. In addition to the apartment building, Spencer has kept, and kept inviolate, the old family house on "the jolly corner" of his childhood. There he retreats when the day's work is done, and there he encounters, in the watches of the night, the object of his fantasy—the man he might have been. The "ghost" is a creature of commanding power, a capitalist, an entrepreneur, "something planted in the middle of the place and facing him through the dusk." The description of this apparition suggests an aggressive, battle-scarred virility: an "erect confronting presence," "hammered so hard," "made so keen," "hard and acute." His powerful hands are disfigured: Two of the fingers of one "were reduced to stumps, as if accidentally shot away." Though Spencer begins by stalking the figure through the house, he soon himself becomes the prey. And when the ghost confronts him, Spencer refuses to recognize the version of his own face he sees: "the bared identity was too hideous as *his*. . . . It was unknown, inconceivable, awful, disconnected from any possibility—!" He breaks down when confronted with this "roused passion of a life larger than his own, a rage of personality before which his own collapsed."[88] The figure bears a striking resemblance to the scarred, ravaged, passionate mourner of "The Beast in the Jungle."

When he awakes from this traumatic experience, he finds himself cradled in Alice Staverton's arms, his head pillowed on her maternal bosom, in the unchanged house on the jolly corner. His return to consciousness leaves him "so gratefully, so abysmally passive." He protests that the hideous figure couldn't possibly be a version of *himself*. Alice ventures to ask, "Isn't the whole point that you'd have been different?"[89] before offering the reassurance he craves. James's story is not an attack on the rapacious forces that have destroyed the haven of his childhood but a meditation on how continuous exposure to them might have made what seems frighteningly alien familiar. Instead of a passionate life larger than the one he has lived, Spencer settles for the past, and the passive. Like James on Ellis Island, he has "seen a ghost in his supposedly safe old house" and retreats in panic.

The alter ego is a thick cord of the strands James has had to sever to weave his particular expatriate identity: his American roots, his links to the dominating forces of his time, even his active male identity, in order to transform himself into the perfect spectator on whom nothing is lost. Like Marcher in "The Beast in the Jungle," like Strether in *The Ambassadors*, he discovers his sacrifice too late to remake himself. But one can't in any case have it both ways. "The Jolly Corner" tenders the bill for the exclusionary choices of a lifetime. It is neither a protest nor a lament, nor a confession of failure, nor a wish to have chosen the alternate path. James's lifetime has been one of achievement, after all, whether instantly recognized or not. But the choices have been very costly.

The strength of James's vision lies in his refusal to ignore the price. The impulse to sum up in these late works offers the temptation to juggle the accounts and make the record show a steady growth. But he is unable to see his career in this way. As he reflects on his own life and those of artists who have made similar choices, he becomes aware that the dream of his youth — to write about, and for, a cosmopolitan world in which the issue of his national identity is unproblematic — has not been realized. He has had to settle for less — much less. And in pursuing an Olympian aloofness he has had to sacrifice more. Like Adams, he feels uncertain about his audience, unconvinced that a supportive community can exist, either in the present or the future, for a writer who chooses the route of "detachment from his plain primary heritage," for which, as William Story had warned, "a man always pays." James had paid and paid. Yet neither he nor Adams suspected that for all their legitimate sense of loss, their investment would one day garner very rich — though posthumous — rewards. Their alienation was to become a literary fashion, as their disciples and inheritors set the standards for a modernist literary career. In the new century, a willingness to think of oneself as a being apart, to offend or baffle the general reader, was to become the ambitious writer's price of admission.

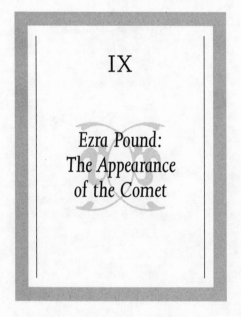

IX

Ezra Pound:
The Appearance
of the Comet

NEARLY HALF a century separates the generation of Henry Adams and Henry James from that of Ezra Pound and T. S. Eliot. Yet they were participants in what can be seen as a single, continuous cultural shift in which more was shared or jointly constructed than strictly inherited. Despite the large difference in their ages, their lives and careers overlap, with the older writers producing some of their most significant work just as the younger ones are defining themselves. The birth of Anglo-American modernism as a self-conscious movement owes a great deal to the overlap (and the shared assumptions) of these displaced Americans. They may be said to constitute a transgenerational ideological dispensation, with common assumptions about nation and culture, the role of the metropolis, the relationship between artist and audience, and between America and Europe.

This is not to deny the differences between them. When Adams and James first came to London, the culture they entered still thought of itself as crescent and peerless. By the first decade of the new century, when Pound and Eliot arrived, this confidence had significantly eroded in artistic circles. It was not only Britain's imperial power that was on the wane but the sense of the country as a cultural arbiter, setting the standard at least for the English-speaking world. For the younger writers, the ground had been cleared, the territory made safe, the natives disarmed, or nearly so. They might settle in with a sure sense that the task of establishing a place for themselves was not beyond the power of an ambitious American writer. There was precedent.

The fact of their own country's new international prominence helped them enormously, even though ironically enough they were in flight from some of the local effects of this new ascendancy. It was as if their confidence now had powerful familial backing, despite their estrangement from the family. Unlike Adams and James, Pound and Eliot no longer had to rely as much on the literal family to identify them as someone who mattered; their American roots now began to count more for them than against them. Americans, as Cooper had predicted long before, would move from being condemned or patronized, to being respected, to being feared. The day of reckoning was at hand.

Finally, Adams and James wrote prose, Pound and Eliot poetry. As a result, the younger writers began with considerably less anxiety about appealing to a large, anonymous, alien readership. By the beginning of the twentieth century poetry had become an acquired, an educated taste, even though there would still be important writers (like Kipling or Frost) with a large popular following. The despair of an Adams or a James for their lost general audience, and the possible causal link between that loss and the fraying of their national loyalties, was not something Pound or Eliot felt very deeply. And one of the reasons they did not, quite aside from the fact that they wrote in a less accessible form, was that Adams and James had willy-nilly established the pattern many modern writers would treat as inevitable: the link between high artistic achievement and small sales. For this too there was precedent—one that Pound in particular would not only accept but celebrate. He, even more than Eliot, felt a strong sense of kinship with his older compatriots.

Yet in his case the kinship was purely metaphorical. Adams and James were known quantities before they arrived on the London scene, their class and family ties assuring them instant entry to the city's cultured elite. Though Pound sometimes tried to pass himself off as a member of the same American aristocracy, his claims were dubious. He could, it was true, trace his ancestry back to America's earliest settlers and was not reluctant to announce the fact. Virtually the first mention of him in a British periodical describes him as "a young American of English descent, his forebears having been among those early settlers who went out to the New World in the seventeenth century."¹ And in an autobiographical experiment modeled on James's, Pound thanks his progenitors "for not taking passage on the 'Mayflower'; they arrived decently upon the 'Lion,' before the rush and about three years after the Aldens."² This awkward mixture of self-deprecating irony and boasting is not the tone of one to the manner born. He has reason to be uneasy: Despite its long pedigree, his is not an illustrious line, on either side. And there is a distinct downward slide. Although his paternal grandfather was a wealthy congressman, his parents are only comfortably situated middle-class unknowns. It would not be through Homer Pound, the steady, affable assistant assayer of the U.S. mint in Philadelphia, that the young Ezra could claim elite status. He would have to blast an opening for himself.

Pound's success is due entirely to his own gifts—his brilliance, ambition, and phenomenal energy. The ambition takes the form of serving himself by serving others, of making himself into the impresario of the modernist movement. He is something of an infant phenomenon. He arrives in London in 1908, at twenty-three, his luggage consisting mostly of copies of his first volume of verse, privately printed by an obscure Venetian publisher: a wise capital investment. He instinctively knows how to proceed. A copy is dispatched to William Butler Yeats at the peak of Parnassus. He stalks this giant single-mindedly for the next nine months, gains entry to his famous Monday evenings, and proves himself indispensable there as a kind of majordomo.³ Of Yeats's sponsorship he writes home, "If one gets quite near the flame ones shadow looks quite large."⁴ And to his friend William Carlos Williams he announces with pride, "I have been praised by the greatest living poet."⁵ The Yeats-Pound relationship ripens and becomes a turning point in both careers, as the master-disciple connection becomes more collaborative.⁶

Other copies of *A Lume Spento* go to the bookseller and publisher Elkin Mathews, whose shop in Vigo Street is exactly the sort of meeting place for poets Pound had dreamed of finding. Mathews agrees to stock the book and also becomes his publisher for verse: Seven volumes would appear between 1908 and 1920, the years of Pound's London residence. Mathews sponsors him in the tight circles of London literary life, introduces him to writers he is eager to meet, presents him at a Poets' Club dinner, allows him to browse the shelves of new writing, where, Pound writes his father, "I find the contemporary people seem to be making as good stuff as the theoretical giants of the past." The irreverent judgmental confidence has the true Poundian ring. He is certain any door will open to him; he has only to choose. "I am engaged in that gentler pursuit, meeting the few people I want to know," he boasts in 1909; "As for the rest, I read their books to see if I want to meet them."[7] An examination is being set here, but it is not the brash young American who needs to pass it.

Between 1908 and 1914, the path of this comet is swift and dazzling. In those years, Pound produces eight books, original poetry, translations, critical prose, and over a hundred periodical pieces. Ford Madox Ford accepts some of his finest poems for the short-lived but brilliant *English Review* and helps to make his name. As with Yeats, this master-disciple relationship deepens as its power valences change. Pound seems omnipresent, in West End drawing rooms and scruffy ateliers, with *eminences grises* like Henry James or young petitioners like D. H. Lawrence. Lawrence describes Pound with awe as "a well-known American poet . . . a good bit of a genius, and with not the least self consciousness."[8] Both men are twenty-four, but Lawrence is a provincial unknown, while Pound has acquired the metropolitan stamp. Even *Punch*, London's widely read satirical review, mockingly praises "the palpitating works of the new Montana (U. S. A.) poet, Mr. Ezekiel Ton" as "the most remarkable thing in poetry since Robert Browning." Pound was born in Idaho and left it in infancy, but no matter. By 1913 *Punch* shifts the balance of praise and mockery:

> The bays that formerly old Dante crowned
> Are worn today by Ezra Loomis Pound.[9]

It is a remarkably swift entry for an American still in his twenties, particularly since Pound later disowns most of the poems of these years. It is only in *Ripostes* (1912) and *Cathay* (1915), his sixth and seventh volumes of verse, that he produces whole books—rather than isolated poems—that contribute significantly to the modernist movement. There are earlier signs of his coming breakthrough, like the vigorous "Sestina: Altaforte." But too much of the early verse is cripplingly faithful to a moribund way of writing: a poetry of dogged spiritual ascent couched in the enervated language of the Pre-Raphaelites. In the "Sestina for Isolt," for example, his idealized lady is a creature of half-lights and muffled sounds, "most fragile," with her "long hands that lie as flowers," her "dim hair," her "deep eyes like pools," etc. Only a small fraction of the early poems will survive Pound's ruthless winnowing for the 1926 edition of *Personae*, his selection of the pre-*Cantos* work he wants to preserve. And when, much later, his daughter asks him for a preface to the early poems, he dismisses them as "a collection of stale creampuffs."[10]

It is not his youthful verse that makes Pound the essential figure in the birth of Anglo-American modernism but an inchoate vision of what ought to be, an uncanny ability to recognize it, and a formidable energy in promoting the genuine article. For all this, his American identity proves indispensable. There are advantages to being an outsider, particularly in a culture in which advancement depends upon recognizable family, class, and school ties. Americans like Pound are not easily placed. What does it mean to be the product of Hamilton College and the University of Pennsylvania? to be born in Idaho and grow up in suburban Philadelphia? to have been, however briefly, chairman of the Department of Romance Languages at Wabash College in Indiana? Such signs were unreadable, and Pound made the most of his inscrutability. Before long the Polytechnic announces "A Course of Lectures on Mediaeval Literature" by "Ezra Pound, M. A. (Sometime Fellow in the University of Pennsylvania)."[11]

He is a free agent, without long-standing debts or the need to please venerable mentors. Particularly in the brittle and etiolated literary climate of turn-of-the-century London, irreverence was exhilarating. Pound foresees, or widens, a chasm between old and new before others realize it exists. Some welcome his American activism and eagerness for change as antidotes to the insularity and "inanition" of literary London. Or so claims the young renegade British poet Richard Aldington, a fresh disciple who announces to Harriet Monroe, the editor of the Chicago-based *Poetry* magazine, that his countrymen are bored to death and that "The future is America's!"[12] Pound's brashness helps to make South Lodge, the London salon of Ford Madox Ford and Violet Hunt, a center for the disaffected young associated with the *English Review*. Despite his eye for innovation, Ford needs rescue from his gentlemanly training. In the words of an early observer, "Ezra's irreverence toward Eminent Literary Figures was a much needed corrective to Ford's excessive veneration," and his "American exuberance" enabled the required demolition job.[13] Ford was an established novelist and Pound's senior by a dozen years, but as he recalls, "In a very short time he had taken charge of me, the review and finally of London."[14]

Taking charge: Pound's modus operandi. His striking executive capacity converted hints and hunches into deeds. An unknown compatriot appears with the manuscript of a poem, "The Love Song of J. Alfred Prufrock." Pound instantly recognizes his importance, gets the poem into print, and becomes Eliot's passionate advocate and trusted adviser. His "discovery" of James Joyce is even more dramatic. The name, first dropped in his ear by Yeats, becomes the proverbial word to the wise. Joyce is living in obscurity in Trieste and has failed to find a publisher for *Dubliners*, though the book is long finished. Pound writes in 1913, offering to serve as go-between for several British and American journals. The grateful Joyce sends the first chapter of what would become *A Portrait of the Artist as a Young Man*. Thanks to Pound's vigorous marketing skills, *Portrait* eventually appears in serial form in *The Egoist* and the chapters of *Ulysses* in *The Little Review*. He also helps to secure Joyce a substantial grant from the Royal Literary Fund. His recommendation shows both his judgmental confidence and the calculated use of his American identity. He insists that the not-yet-published *Portrait* proves Joyce to be *"without exception* the best of the younger prose writers." And he hopes that "as a foreigner, viewing as a spectator the glories and shames of your country, I might say that it seems to me ridiculous that your government pensions should go for the most part to saving wrecks rather than in the fostering of letters."[15] The hectoring tone is dangerous: It can create resistance rather than compliance. But it will not go unnoticed.

Pound knows that living in the literary capital of the English-speaking world (rather than in remote Trieste) makes such influence possible. He is a great propagandist for metropolitan culture and leaves the United States in search of one. As he writes in *Patria Mia* (1912–13), the product of his brief, abortive attempt to establish himself in New York, "America, my country, is almost a continent and hardly yet a nation, for no nation can be considered historically as such until it has achieved within itself a city to which all roads lead, and from which there goes out an authority."[16] Such a formula makes no provision for regional culture. Works of art are judged by a single standard, centrally established and enforced. "All great art is born of the metropolis (or *in* the metropolis)," Pound writes Harriet Monroe, with whom he thrashes out this issue through the years of his association with *Poetry*; "The metropolis is that which accepts all gifts and all heights of excellence, usually the excellence that is *tabu* in its own village."[17] From this perspective, *all* American cities are villages, since none sets the standard. Boston, New York, Washington, Chicago—all might have claimed cultural standing around 1910; none would have delegated authority to its rivals. For Pound, this produces a clash of provincial notions and a series of unmonitored experiments in what should have been a national, or international, enterprise.

His recurrent analogy is to the traditional notion of scientific research, with its fear that those working in isolation will replicate earlier experiments rather than building on the known. For Pound, literature's local roots are accidental. Courses in, say, American literature are as absurd as "courses in 'American chemistry', neglecting all foreign discoveries."[18] This is an unexpected echo of Matthew Arnold's scorn for the very notion of an American literature and his insistence that "we are all contributors to one great literature—English literature."[19] But Pound is not arguing for the special importance of his country's English roots. He wants to make sure that American artists have kept up. They must know European culture not in order to imitate it but to avoid "making unconscious, or semi-conscious, imitations of French and English models thirty or forty or an hundred years old."[20]

This pairing of England and France is not accidental and is a sign of Pound's hoped-for cosmopolitanism. Like Adams and James, he ignores boundaries and constructs a notion of "Europe" that would have baffled most "Europeans." To his eyes, America is the "Western province" that exports its artists "to the Eastern capital," a place he calls "the double city of London and Paris."[21] He would eventually move to Paris, after he had worn out his London welcome. But in the years before World War I, he sees these cities engaged in a single collaborative project—that of assuring cultural vitality by preserving the old and fostering the new, no matter what its source. They are an international patent office for new literary ideas.

The metropolis also fosters generational continuity, where "the best minds among the older men and the ready minds of the younger enthusiasts have mingled and have taken fire one from another."[22] Pound idealizes both a male line of descent and the idea of "fire" passed in either direction. His encounter with living writers in London is like the "pleasure that a schoolboy has in hearing of the star plays of former athletes"; the generational link is a kind of "Apostolic Succession."[23] Pound comes to London not only to meet the Irishman Yeats but the one living American writer he regards with awe, Henry James. This unbroken chain of authority connects the youngest claimant to all his precursors. For such continuity a capital is indispensable; it can bring about a "great age" through "the deliberate fostering of genius, the gathering-in and grouping and encouragement of artists."[24] The authority thus conferred, the laying on of hands, licenses the new generation to remake tradition.

The cultural metropolis gathers groups of the like-minded and enables them to meet easily and often. It creates the coterie, the collectivity of rebellious spirits who eagerly seek each other out and form the first audience. As Pound writes to a young American correspondent who asks for advice on the subject, "At the start a man must work in a group; at least that seems to be the effective modus."[25] Where Adams and James finally accepted a coterie audience with bitter disappointment, Pound begins by seeing it as inevitable. One of his early poems, "In Durance," expresses his hunger for kindred spirits: "I am homesick after my own kind," the poem begins. But this is not an exile's lament for family or countrymen but a search for what he calls "mine own soul-kin." Pound imagines identifying them by a sort of radar:

> And yet my soul sings "Up!" and we are one.
> Yea thou, and Thou, and THOU, and all my kin.[26]

For such meetings, the heterogeneous population of a capital city offers the best hope. The atomistic nature of urban life—its isolation, privacy, and myriad subcultures—encourages small-group identity as a mode of survival. It offers opportunities for collaboration: Even tiny units can bond. Pound uses the terms describing selective literary institutions unapologetically: elite, coterie, clique, salon, *succès d'estime*, *gloire de cénacle*. All are French, and only some have become English expressions, often acquiring a negative charge in transmission. Coterie culture challenges egalitarian values, for which Pound has no use.

His London life is structured around the rituals of such groups. Yeats's Mondays, Ford's and Bowen's South Lodge tennis parties, the Thursday meetings of the Poets' Club, T. E. Hulme's Secession Club, later his own Tuesdays; private performances and readings; certain Soho restaurants, the literary bookshops: All offer chances to find "thou, and Thou, and THOU, and all my kin." His need for mentors, equals, and disciples is fed by the chance encounters of these overlapping circles. They offer community while preserving artistic independence. Yeats calls Pound a "solitary volcano,"[27] but Pound considers himself a member of an illustrious fraternity. "Lordly men are to earth o'ergiven / these the companions:" begins his famous obituary catalog of the modernist generation in the *Pisan Cantos*—Ford and Yeats and Joyce as well as lesser lights like Plarr, Jepson, Hewlett, and Newbolt.[28] London is the city in or from which he established contact with them all.

But it is not just spiritual kinship he craves. Such group identities have advertising value and can launch careers. Pound's organizational talent marshals the rebels for a joint assault on the Establishment. He is a master of publicity who understands what a new movement needs to attract notice: group identity, labels and slogans, manifestos, meeting places, journals, patrons. He works tirelessly, and at times cynically, to provide modernism with these essentials of survival. His national identity again proves useful. Despite his contempt for the commercialism of American culture—a running theme in his critique of his country—the huckster spirit and the careerist move are integral to his early success.

He understands what is now called networking: "this being in the gang & being known by the right people," as he writes his father[29]; or in the more sarcastic version for his mother: "A few teas, and the old ring-around with wire-pulling concealed."[30] And he informs her that he is "conducting a literary kindergarten for the aspiring etc etc" when he starts his own weekly salon.[31] The tone is disturbing, not because it uncovers unacknowledged practices but because it suggests Pound's inability to fuse his genuine literary vocation with the strategies of creating a movement. This revulsion from his own practices in trying to conquer London will finally alienate him from the scene of his early triumphs and hasten his flight.

But this is to anticipate. In the years before the war, these ways of gaining a hearing for the movement seem legitimate and necessary. Names, labels, and group organs help establish a communal identity and to challenge the impression of mere idiosyncrasy. The way he transforms his American friend Hilda Doolittle into the poet H. D. offers a telling example. She shows him the poem "Hermes of the Ways" in manuscript; he slashes what he takes to be the superfluous words and lines, scrawls the mysterious notation "H. D. Imagiste" at the bottom of the page, and sends it off to Harriet Monroe.[32] Doolittle has instantly acquired a leaner style, a new name, a group affiliation with Pound's nascent imagist movement, and a publisher. Her career is launched, but she has been conscripted. Her sponsor's genuine helpfulness is linked to his coerciveness and need to stamp his identity on the product.

Labeling is one of Pound's propagandistic tools. A couple of years later he joins the novelist and artist Percy Wyndham Lewis, the sculptor Henri Gaudier-Brzeska, and the painter Edward Wadsworth in a movement he calls vorticism, "for good reasons enough," in his cryptic words.[33] It is an age of "isms"—impressionism, postimpressionism, imagism, futurism, vorticism, surrealism, all converging on modernism itself. Such labeling is useful. It suggests that something momentous has arrived, and encourages those anxious to be in the vanguard, or not to be written off as cultural laggards, to understand it. And there are Pound's manifestos, like the group he collects in 1918 under the title "A Retrospect." His language is that of the Mosaic commandments: "Use no superfluous word, no adjective which does not reveal something"; "Go in fear of abstractions"; "Don't be 'viewy'—leave that to the writers of pretty little philosophic essays." Though Pound insists he is undogmatic, the sentences belie his claim. And his ominous warning that "No good poetry is ever written in a manner twenty years old"[34] speaks to the fear of being out of date, passed over, a fatal "ism" behind.

Pound's anxious au courantism is rooted in his doubts about his early poetry. He knows he is vulnerable to the charge of following Victorian medievalists like Morris and Rossetti instead of obeying his own injunction to "make it new." His loyalty to these nineteenth-century masters makes him less threatening to transitional figures like Yeats and Ford. But his rhetoric is unconciliatory. His coercive spirit in promulgating group identities and programs is suggested in Wyndham Lewis's later skeptical account of Pound's activities: "He was never satisfied until everything was *organized*. And it was he who made us into a youth racket—that was his method of organization." Yet Lewis acknowledges that this strategy for creating the sense of a coherent movement actually worked: "He did succeed in giving a handful of disparate and unassimilable people the appearance of a *Bewegung*."[35]

Every movement requires a house organ. Pound's invaluable work in founding, transforming, and acting as a contributor to and talent scout for the little magazines associated with the modernist movement has long been celebrated. The list includes most of the journals in England and America that first publish the work that eventually becomes the modernist canon: *The New Age, Poetry, The Egoist, Blast, The Little Review, The Dial, The English Review, The Transatlantic Review*. Pound's motives are to get the writers he respects into print, to spell out the principles of the movement, and to steer it away from the parochialism of national boundaries. He seems to ignore the Atlantic Ocean and the English Channel, as well as the gap between the present and the remote past. He has an unshakable faith in his own judgment and an urgent need to make others share it. His hundreds of periodical contributions over the years primarily call attention to the new writing. Most are never reprinted; they are instruments designed to secure a hearing. But Pound later notes with justifiable pride that "for a decade and more I was instrumental in forcing into print, and *secondarily* in commenting on, certain work now recognized as valid by all competent readers."[36]

This task requires that certain writers be linked with certain journals. He wants to concentrate their force and maximize their group impact. This is why Pound remains Harriet Monroe's London agent despite his impatience with what he considers her accommodating spirit. When he finally defects to Margaret Anderson's *Little Review*, he insists that the writers he brings along be published as a group: "It would only be a waste of energy to bring in the new set of contributors one by one. Must use fire-control. BOMM! Simultaneous arrival of new force in pages of 'Little Review'." He also proposes a motto a clever copywriter might envy: "*The L. R. The magazine that is read by those who write the others.*"[37] And he strives to retain personal control. As he explains to his American patron John Quinn, "My capital as editor is precisely . . . that I can concentrate all the current stuff of any literary merit in one place."[38] The strategic intelligence and marketing skill here show that Pound has learned a few tricks from the entrepreneurs transforming his own country, despite his frequently voiced scorn.

But of course such journals are *not* commercial ventures. Most pay their contributors only a pittance. Their circulation rarely rises above a thousand; they have a short life expectancy; and they need patrons regularly willing to disburse moderate sums. Unlike Adams and James, Pound does not have a reliable income from either capital or royalties. Publishing poetry or uncommercial fiction requires a subvention. These elementary facts of the literary life underlie Pound's theory of artistic patronage, spelled out in *Patria Mia* and essays like "The Renaissance" (1914). A cultural renaissance is the product of predictable forces, including a secure material base. "A great age is brought about only with the aid of wealth," Pound insists.[39] Even the despised American plutocrat may be useful, if he can be turned into a patron. As Pound coolly puts it, "It is his function as it is the function of any aristocrat to die and to leave gifts."[40]

Even better than posthumous patronage—which favors museums and other large, anonymous institutions—is the sponsorship of the young artist by the live patron, a relationship with immediate rewards for both. The artist is freed to work productively at the most difficult career stage by those who take a personal interest in the work and can legitimately feel that they have enabled it. Pound grasps that this arrangement may be attractive to the newly wealthy but culturally insecure Americans of his time. This is the bait he uses to lure John Quinn, the driving, intelligent New York lawyer and self-made man who becomes, largely through Pound's intervention, one of the great patrons of the modernist movement.[41] His seductive argument plays on

Quinn's vanity and insecurity by offering equal billing: "If a patron buys from an artist who needs money (needs money to buy tools, time and food) the patron then makes himself equal to the artist, he is building art into the world. He creates."[42] In the visual arts, "buying" is a matter of simple purchase. For literature, the process is less direct. The patron can sponsor a journal that pays contributors, funnel money through an intermediary, purchase manuscripts, or (best of all) guarantee a reliable income that allows a writer to work without the distraction of journalism or other paid labor. Pound's argument strikes home, and his patron signs on.

Quinn is a kindred spirit: aggressive, energetic, impatient, and in his own field absolutely sure of himself. Like Pound, he is disgusted with American provincialism and works for closer ties to Europe. At the opening of the 1913 Armory Show—the exhibition he helps to organize to introduce postimpressionism to the United States—Quinn insists that young American artists "do not dread . . . the ideas or the culture of Europe."[43] The same spirit animates his literary sponsorship of Conrad, Yeats, Joyce, Eliot, and Pound. The journals he supports— *The Egoist, The Little Review, The Transatlantic Review*—all strive for cosmopolitanism. As Pound sarcastically describes the opposing provincial spirits to his patron, "The conception of America communicating with the outside world is so new and strange to all of them, I suppose they think it a disease."[44]

Quinn offers Pound the chance to sponsor his own literary generation by arranging with the editors of *The Little Review* that Pound select (and pay for) the contributions of his own *cénacle*—Joyce, Eliot, Wyndham Lewis, and of course himself. Here for the first time group identity, an established yet adventurous journal, reliable financing, and Pound's artistic control come together. Patronage, the coterie, an uncommercial standard briefly fuse, with legendary results. No journal associated with the modernist movement has a more distinguished record. Yet for all the legitimate pride Pound can take in such work, it is striking that he is never offered a journal of his own. All his associations are collaborative, though his is not a collaborative temperament. Despite his generosity, Quinn keeps a tight control, and he never simply offers Pound the money for a magazine permanently associated with his name, nor provides a regular income that would keep him from squandering his energy on too many unrelated ventures. Joyce has his Harriet Shaw Weaver and his Edith Roosevelt McCormick, who instruct their bankers to forward a regular stipend to free their author from financial worries.[45] T. S. Eliot finds his Lady Rothermere, the original angel behind *The Criterion*, which he edits without much interference from 1922 to 1939. But Pound has to scramble. If Quinn had simply offered him an annual subsidy of five thousand dollars, a sum easily within his means, Pound might well have produced the most important literary journal of his time.

It was never to be; he was just not safe and solid enough to engender such trust. His negotiations with those in authority—editors, publishers, reviewers, academics, established writers—are too often undermined by impatience and contempt. Those at the top are guilty until proven innocent. Pound's intransigence, his inability to compromise or see the other person's point of view, may be essential to him as a writer. Though noisier, it is probably less extreme than Joyce's. But Pound and Joyce choose different paths: The Irishman is entirely devoted to his writing and allows nothing to interfere with it; the American divides his energy between fostering a movement and pursuing his own career. Ultimately these require different abilities. An editor and literary sponsor must work cooperatively and think seriously about the tastes of an audience, no matter how narrowly defined.

This problem is at the heart of Pound's quarrels with Harriet Monroe, which begin in 1912 when he becomes *Poetry*'s foreign correspondent. He objects to her chosen motto for *Poetry*—Whitman's "To have great poets there must be great audiences too."[46] In a 1914 essay published in that magazine, "The Audience," he challenges Whitman's dictum in words bound to offend the journal's readers: "The artist is not dependent upon the multitude of his listeners. Humanity is the rich effluvium, it is the waste and the manure and the soil, and from it grows the tree of the arts."[47] Though he grants that each audience includes a few choice spirits, it can scarcely have escaped his readers' notice that being called "the rich effluvium" is hardly a compliment. Increasingly, Pound cannot stop himself from voicing such gratuitous insults. The absence of suavity or circumspection and the refusal to count the cost are striking. They may be courageous or foolhardy, but they are sure to make enemies. To read the poems, essays, and letters of the London years sequentially is to become aware of Pound's increasing reliance on the language of abuse and the steady shrinking of his intended audience.

This is not how he began. He recalls that when he wrote the "Ballad of the Goodly Fere" in 1909—in which one of the disciples says proudly of Christ, "No capon priest was the Goodly Fere / But a man o' men was he"[48]—he felt "that for the first time in my life I had written something that 'everyone could understand,' and I wanted it to go to the people."[49] Much of his criticism, beginning with the 1910 study of medieval literature, *The Spirit of Romance*, was written for a more general audience. Pound was trained at Hamilton and Penn as a scholar of Continental literature, but this book is not intended for academics. Half anthology, half introductory commentary, it ranges from the ninth to the seventeenth centuries. Nor does it assume a command of the original languages: The passages from Dante, for example, appear in the standard Temple Classics prose translation. Pound helpfully offers plot summaries of *The Cid*, *The Song of Roland*, and *The Divine Comedy*.[50] Even as late as 1917 he proclaims, in spite of imagined "groans from the scholar, the aesthete, the connoisseur," that "the ultimate goal of scholarship is popularisation."[51]

Pound never entirely abandons this hope of finding a general audience. He pushes constantly to make the classics generally available. Yet from the first there are signs that he will move in the opposite direction. The letters to and from Williams carry on a vigorous transatlantic conversation about how much a poet needs to consider the audience's needs. "As for the 'eyes of too ruthless public': damn their eyes," Pound writes in 1908; "No art ever yet grew by looking into the eyes of the public, ruthless or otherwise." The opposing sides of the argument acquire national identities. Pound writes his friend, "The thing that saves your work is *opacity*, and don't you forget it. Opacity is NOT an American quality. Fizz, swish, gabble of verbiage, these are echt Amerikanisch."[52]

By these standards, Pound's poetry is never American. Even the title of "Ballad of the Goodly Fere" has to be footnoted, and the explanatory "Note Precedent to 'La Fraisne'" is almost as long as the poem while not mentioning that "La Fraisne" means the ash tree.[53] Most of the earliest poems puzzle the unprepared American reader because their titles allude to a European literary work or are in a foreign tongue: "Cino," "Na Audiart," "Fifine Answers," "Famam Librosque Cano," "Scriptor Ignotus," "Donzella Beata," "Li Bel Chasteus," and so on. Granting that an educated reader around 1910 would have been less stymied by such difficulties, and that the poems themselves are not as baffling as their titles, it is obvious that Pound is narrowing the entrance. His impulse is to select, to exclude. His decision to be a cosmopolitan rather than narrowly American poet makes him choose the opaque style. But the opacity comes and goes. Some of the pre-*Cantos* poems, especially the satiric ones, are accessible, and the poems in *Cathay* are miracles of apparent simplicity despite their unfamiliar Chinese setting. Yet the overall drift is toward the allusiveness, fragmentation, and polylingualism of *The Cantos*. Joyce imagined an "ideal reader suffering from an ideal insomnia."[54] He was not alone.

Pound's statements on the subject of audience become steadily more belligerent. In 1912 he asks despairingly, "How, then, shall the poet in this dreary day attain universality, how write what will be understood of 'the many' and lauded of 'the few'?"[55] A couple of years later he simply assumes that the audience for serious writing will number in the hundreds or low thousands. This affects his plan for a journal Quinn initially offers to sponsor. Pound writes him that he is *not* interested in thinking "BIG" with a "circulation to 70,000 fools. . . . There are only a few hundred or a very few thousands of people capable of doing anything of *any* sort, or of getting anything done." Like Adams and James in old age, he can number his readers; but he is barely thirty. Essays like "The Audience" and "The Constant Preaching to the Mob" (1916) dismiss the argument for popular appeal, and a 1917 letter to Quinn insists that "Great Art is NEVER popular to start with," that "The Greek populace was PAID to attend the great Greek tragedies, and it damn well wouldn't have gone otherwise, of if there had been a cinema," that even Elizabethan drama depended on patronage rather than the pennies of the groundlings.[56]

The apoplectic violence of such pronouncements, often couched in capital letters and peppered with exclamation points, suggests that Pound is near the end of his rope. The confidence of his early London years is displaced by a sense that he is fighting a losing battle and even relishing defeat. The turning point is his 1914–15 association with the vorticist journal *Blast*. Any accommodation to established institutions or cultural arbiters is exuberantly smashed in this venture, so characteristic of its historical moment. One of the poems Pound publishes here begins:

> Let us deride the smugness of "The Times":
> GUFFAW!
> So much for the gagged reviewers.

A typical member of this fraternity is addressed in these terms:

> You slut-bellied obstructionist,
> You sworn foe to free speech and good letters.
> You fungus, you continuous gangrene.

This is less a poem than a temper tantrum, calculated to say unforgivable things and make a break. The gesture is cathartic ("Let us dump our hatreds into one bunch and be done with them"[57]), but it has consequences. The editor of the venerable *Quarterly Review*, according to Pound's account, fastidiously declines further submissions from "any one associated with such a publication as *Blast*. It stamps a man too disadvantageously."[58] Pound is cutting his ties to Establishment journals like the *TLS*, mainstream critics like Edmund Gosse, poets with respectable credentials, whom he had earlier carefully cultivated. In this he differs strikingly both from James and (as we will see) from Eliot.

There are many reasons for this rupture; only a full-scale biography could do them justice. Briefly, Pound's estrangement from literary London between 1914 and 1920 is linked to his 1914 marriage to Dorothy Shakespear (which guarantees them a small but reliable income, frees them to travel, and ends the farce of Pound's attempt to demonstrate his steadiness to her middle-class family); to the contagious violence of the war, which kills or injures some of his closest friends; and to his growing sense that London is not much more enlightened than the American cities he left behind. His quarrel with his country had focused on its Puritan legacy and the censorious spirit it fostered, a judgment confirmed by the suppression of *The Little*

Review for publishing one of Lewis's stories and the early chapters of
Ulysses. The magazine is enjoined from bringing out more of Joyce's
novel and forced to move abroad. Pound sees this as symptomatic,
while ignoring the signs of a growing *American* modernist insurgency.

But is London any better? In 1915, Lawrence's novel *The Rainbow* is
declared obscene and the remaining copies destroyed. English printers
and publishers consequently become more cautious. To Pound's disgust, his 1916 collection of poems, *Lustra*, is brought out by Elkin
Mathews in two versions, the "castrato" edition for public consumption, another (in two hundred copies) for private circulation.[59] Quinn
has good reason to protest Pound's attacks on American law for censor-
ing Lewis and Joyce: "Don't for God's sake write to me any more about
the illiberality of the United States, or its laws. The statute [regarding
obscenity] is identical with the British act, copied from it."[60] Anglo-
American cultural differences evaporate in Pound's mind, and he finds
himself ready to move on.

His ideal audience for serious work simultaneously shrinks and
spreads. The thousands become hundreds and then dozens, and have
no fixed address. The long essay on the Provençal poet Arnaut Daniel
Pound publishes in *Instigations* (1920) is very different from the treatment of his work in the earlier *Spirit of Romance*. It consists largely of
Pound's translations, unapologetically using such archaisms as fordel,
quhitter, inkirlie, wriblis, frieks, auzels, and so on. To those seeking
additional help he writes, "The twenty-three students of Provençal and
the seven people seriously interested in the technic and aesthetic of
verse may communicate with me in person."[61]

This shrunken sense of audience is both the cause and effect of his
decision to devote himself to *The Cantos*, the unfinished project he
begins in 1915. By 1919 he writes Quinn, "I suspect my 'Cantos' are getting too too too abstruse and obscure for human consumption."[62] The
suppression of the *Ulysses* chapters and the fact that the novel could
only be published in Paris confirms Pound's judgment that neither of
the major English-speaking countries now tolerates radical artistic ventures. The taboos of the village have migrated to the metropolis. The
audience for serious literary work is a mere remnant, an international
underground, Pound concludes in 1922: "There is no organized or
coordinated civilization left, only individual scattered survivors."[63]

These dark prophecies are of course wildly inaccurate. The year 1922 is considered the annus mirabilis of modernism, with the publication of *The Waste Land* and *Ulysses*. It is more plausibly a zenith than a nadir. Pound's pessimism reflects not the end of civilization but the failure of his own attempt to become the literary dictator of London. We have seen some of the self-destructive gestures that hastened his demise. But there are deeper reasons for the exclusion—or even banishment—of Ezra Pound, American, from his adopted country.

X

Pound's
Meteoric Descent

I

UNLIKE SOME of the other passionate pilgrims from across the Atlantic, Pound had no sense of Britain as the mother country or of the primacy of Anglo-Saxon culture. It is true that he begins with the pride in his English roots his mother has instilled. He writes from London that her family's treasured coat of arms resembles that of the earls of Warwick, and so "you can pretend that you're descended from one of the 7 champions of Christendom if it'll give you any particular plea-sure."[1] Despite the irony, Pound is not indifferent to such links. He writes to his English fiancée from Dorset that he has found "several of my family names about here" and that the trip "is like getting back to the roots of things."[2] But the pride in his Anglo-Saxon heritage is finally weaker than his desire to be a world citizen. By 1921, after he has left England, he explosively asks "why the HELL shd. I deform my bloomin thought by being reminded of the existence of the ang-sax race in any or either of its branches, both of which are probably superfluous."[3]

This contempt for the Anglo-American link is evident in Pound's revisionist view of tradition, which is unlikely to flatter his British readers. In "The Tradition" (1913), he plays down the originality of English literature by tracing its models to southern Europe and concluding that from the Middle Ages to the present, *"The English cribbed their technique from over the channel."*[4] Calling his essay *"The* Tradition" is significant. The term was used more vaguely, as in "the voice of tradition." Attaching the definite article to it proclaims that literary tradition is single and unique, and that he can define it.

In his criticism Pound shifts the center of "the tradition" away from England. The misguided Anglocentric reader he addresses in *The Spirit of Romance* has to be shown that England's culture is a tributary stream, that her writers have more often been followers and redactors than inventors. He stresses the heavy debt of medieval and Renaissance poets to their Italian precursors (and not just to Boccaccio and Petrarch, who are barely mentioned); he pours scorn on those who presume to speak of Milton in the same breath as Dante; he concludes that Lope de Vega is more original and influential than his admittedly brilliant contemporary, Shakespeare.[5] And in the 1929 "How to Read" (which should be called "What to Read"), he produces a literary canon that relegates English literature to the second division. He treats the whole culture as belated: "Anything that happens to mind in England has usually happened somewhere else first." His coup de grace is the announcement that the inventors of contemporary writing are his countrymen: "All the developments in English verse since 1910 are due almost wholly to Americans. In fact, there is no longer any reason to call it English verse, and there is no present reason to think of England at all."[6]

This is a campaign in cultural politics. Pound reverses the familiar British view of Americans as provincials by calling the accusers insular. His command of foreign tongues parades his learning and shapes his poetry. His celebrated or notorious polylingualism and allusiveness turn his reader into an anxious student needing help. Only in this state can the "educated" English lover of poetry acknowledge his ignorance of Provençal, or Italian, or even the classical languages supposedly mastered at school, and surrender to the new, more cosmopolitan authority. That Pound's "tradition" is not primarily English, that after *Cathay* it is Asian as well, that by *The Cantos* it has also become American and is far from exclusively literary—all suggest that he is simply making the concept of tradition coterminous with his own vital but idiosyncratic intellectual life. It is a regal gesture: *La tradition c'est moi*. This is not the subtle, gradual reshaping of the past Eliot describes in "Tradition and the Individual Talent" but a personal canon, what one Pound critic refers to as "Talent and the Individual Tradition."[7]

Of course Pound is eager to propagate that tradition. He devotes a great deal of creative energy to poetic translation. The New Directions edition of his *Translations* runs to well over four hundred pages and does not include works more plausibly seen as imitations, adaptations, or what Hugh Kenner calls "acts of homage,"[8] like the sequence *Homage to Sextus Propertius*. He often assures his readers that mastering "the" tradition is not an impossible enterprise, especially if one accepts him as middleman. His canon is no more daunting than that famous enterprise of his time, "Dr. Eliot's Five-Foot Shelf of Books" (1910), which the president of Harvard also designed for autodidacts. But it lacks the institutional (and commercial) imprimatur and has to await the advent of a new type the modernist movement creates: the reverent academic ready to devote a lifetime to elucidating a difficult contemporary writer. What Pound and his fellow modernists need, and get, is the kind of attention—word by word, line by line—generally accorded only to Greek and Latin texts. They had to become "classics" to be read with the requisite attention.

In the meantime, Pound's English audience shrinks; the doors once readily opened close. The process he describes in *Hugh Selwyn Mauberley* (1920) as Mauberley's "final / Exclusion from the world of letters"[9] proceeds. Many come to see that the American in their midst is not only challenging the centrality of English literature but wresting control away from Europe altogether. His 1912 poem "Epilogue," a comment on his translations, addresses his countrymen in the proud voice of a returning warrior:

> I bring you the spoils, my nation,
> I, who went out in exile,
>> Am returned to thee with gifts.

> I, who have laboured long in the tombs,
>> Am come back therefrom with riches.[10]

The conqueror of Europe seeks his compatriots' gratitude for the booty of a successful campaign and for pilfering the graves of hidden treasure. James's Adam Verver might have carved the lines at the entrance to his American Museum.

The spirit that transformed America from a self-contained country into a world power around the turn of the century is mirrored in Pound's activities. Wyndham Lewis notes the echo of Teddy Roosevelt: "If we remember that the voice of the Bull Moose president resounded in his young days, it is perhaps less to be wondered at that Ezra himself should have wished to wield the 'Big Stick.'"[11] The imperialist force that carries American power into the Pacific finds a parallel in Pound's expansion of the European canon to include China and Japan. He adopts the high-minded cultural appropriation of Ernest Fenollosa, the American scholar whose notebooks, sent to him by Fenollosa's widow in 1913, become the source for Pound's Chinese translations in *Cathay*, the ideograms of *The Cantos*, and his work on the Japanese Noh plays. Fenollosa sees the center of gravity shifting from Europe to Asia and warns of the threat to American hegemony. "The Chinese problem alone is so vast that no nation can afford to ignore it," he writes; "We in America, especially, must face it across the Pacific, and master it or it will master us." He proposes cultural annexation: "We need their best ideals to supplement our own—ideals enshrined in their art, in their literature and in the tragedies of their lives."[12] If "westward the course of empire takes its way," as Bishop Berkeley foresaw, it will *not* finally stop in America but move on, and the United States should not be a mere stopover on this vast historical journey.[13] The country must take advantage of her strategic position facing Europe and Asia to seize the global primacy within her grasp.

Pound assumes the role of intermediary between decadent and crescent imperial ventures. Unlike James, he treasures his detachment from Britain's decline: "I know that I am perched on the rotten shell of a crumbling empire, but it isn't my empire," he writes in "Through Alien Eyes" (1913). Though he doesn't deny America's problems, he feels "some sort of force—call it the spirit of the country, or a belief in the future—moving to its assistance. Does anyone honestly feel the same for England?"[14] His proposed expansion of tradition enlarges America's cultural range, ending its colonial indebtedness to Europe by moving beyond what Pound airily calls "the conventional taste of four or five centuries and one continent."[15] He is sure that posterity will vindicate his faith in himself and his associates. Ford sees the "aggressively trans-Atlantic" spirit of this faith and concludes that the expatriated Pound "could give any fervent home-stayer seven lengths and a beating in the way of patriotism."[16]

Is it any wonder that this nakedly confrontational cultural program should be recognized as inimical to British interests? Pound's obvious *national* chauvinism is fueled by a force stronger than politics, an erotic economy in which the assertive foreigner sees himself as male and the culture he hopes to dominate as helplessly, hopelessly female. Pound gives the game away after his escape to Paris by comparing his English campaign to sexual conquest: "Even oneself has felt it, driving any new idea into the great passive vulva of London, a sensation analogous to the male feeling in copulation." His is the phallic drive, "charging, head-on, the female chaos."[17]

But long before he writes this notorious passage, his tactics can be seen as an aggressive bid for male control. In his early self-critical poem "Revolt: Against the Crepuscular Spirit in Modern Poetry" he rejects "the pale sick phantoms" of fin-de-siècle English verse and idealizes a virile dispensation to replace them. He praises "strong men" who "grapple chaos and beget / Some new titanic spawn to pile the hills and stir / This earth again."[18] Revitalization is rape. Many of Pound's most energetic early poems celebrate a specifically masculine form of power. In the "Ballad of the Goodly Fere," Christ is a warrior, a force of nature, a "master of men" rather than a mere "mouse of the scrolls." Bertran de Born's monologue in "Sestina: Altaforte" begins memorably with the belligerent line, "Damn it all! all this our South stinks peace." And "Piere Vidal Old" recalls the passion of his youth, when in erotic pursuit he turns into a wolf attacking the fleeing deer: "God! how the swiftest hind's blood spurted hot / Over the sharpened teeth and purpling lips!"[19]

Pound's modernism is a male rebellion against what he takes to be a feminized culture, an anxiety that echoes James's and parallels Eliot's. He even suggests to Quinn that their planned journal be called the "Male Review" and that it carry the warning "No woman shall be allowed to write for this magazine."[20] When he meets Gaudier-Brzeska, whose work he already admires, he primes the friendship by showing Gaudier his most blatantly masculinist poems. Pound recalls "it was the 'Altaforte' that convinced him that I would do to be sculpted."[21] The famous sculpture-portrait this association produces is the enormous "Hieratic Head of Ezra Pound," in which the head and neck take the unmistakable form of a phallus.

The virile dispensation he celebrates is linked to his American identity. He writes Wyndham Lewis that in his own country "men take the penis for granted" and are angry and astonished if they should find themselves impotent. "The Englishman, on the contrary, gives in with the *morne* [gloomy] and desolate air, of one who says, 'this is but what I had expected.'"[22] His vision of vorticism is a masculine fantasy: "jism bursting up white as ivory. . . . Spermatozoon, enough to repopulate the island with active and vigorous animals."[23] Like Shakespeare's Caliban, Pound imagines himself peopling the isle with his progeny. He pictures an exhausted Britain in need of sexual reawakening. In the English portraits of "Moeurs Contemporaines" (1918), women feel a "distaste for caresses," men like Mr. Hecatomb Styrex remain virgins long into adulthood, and a neuter figure referred to only as "it" still lives at home at twenty-seven, its life supervised by its parents.[24]

Such sexual condescension was the latest form of the old slanging match. Pound's cocksure confidence in his own superior generative power will not endear him to the English, who come to see the root of his explosive energy. They are not amused. Wyndham Lewis's impression that the English increasingly thought of Pound as "an unassimilable and aggressive stranger"[25] rings true. By 1917, F. S. Flint, one of Pound's original British imagist associates, who had once seen him as the "generalissimo" of their concerted attack on the literary establishment, announces in *The Egoist*, "In truth we are all tired of Mr. Pound. . . . His manners have become more and more offensive; and we wish he would go back to America." His complaint stresses Pound's male bravado, his "continual attempts to puff and swell himself and his friends into a generation of bulls."[26]

Pound knows that he offends but simply cannot stop himself. His more circumspect associates caution him, he says, to "lay aside all petulance," write more balanced sentences, and cultivate "suavity" to woo his elders.[27] But a bull terrier cannot behave like a lapdog. Pound is constitutionally incapable of modifying his behavior. The offensiveness is somatic. His English wife is sure that it is less his work than his *"energy"* that "upsets people."[28] He makes the more cautiously intelligent writers around him, trained in indirect persuasion, ironic discourse, and the self-deprecating style a sophisticated metropolitan culture encourages, feel anxious. Would the laurels go to this queue-jumper rather than to those who work and wait patiently for their reward?

The opposed forces are moving toward confrontation. The erstwhile wunderkind has become a troublesome, tiresome adult. Best to get rid of him. The welcome mat is withdrawn; the disciples abscond or turn unresponsive; once eager editors sever the connection. Pound had foreseen this turn as early as 1915 in the self-pitying "Villanelle: The Psychological Hour." It records a panic state in which he feels discarded by the young in his London circle. Two admirers fail to show up at the promised hour. He records the "middle-ageing care" with which he had prepared his rooms, the waste of time, the fear that they have bigger fish to fry. Though the poem is published when Pound is only thirty, it is full of a terminal despair: *"So few drink of my fountain,"* he laments; "my youth is gone from me."[29]

In his retrospective accounts, Pound slightly exaggerates the British rejection of his work around this time. Though the *Quarterly* and the *TLS* are no longer interested, though Macmillan turns down his proposal for an anthology of poetry, he is still published in *The New Age*, in *Future*, in the *Athenaeum* and *The Egoist*. Although he had quarreled with Elkin Mathews about the "castrato" version of *Lustra*, Mathews brings out his selected early poems. Nevertheless, Pound's sense that his opportunities are shrinking after the war is accurate. Most of his work for *The New Age* is hack journalism—pseudonymous reviews; the *Athenaeum* fires him after a short stint as drama critic; and the masterwork of this period, *Hugh Selwyn Mauberley*, is published not by Mathews but by the little known Ovid Press in only two hundred copies. The epitaph for Pound's London literary life is written by the American who displaces him. In 1920, Eliot voices his concern about Pound's growing invisibility to Quinn, their mutual patron: "The fact is that there is now no organ of any importance in which he can express himself, and he is becoming forgotten." And Eliot puts his finger on the cause: "I know that Pound's lack of tact has done him great harm."[30]

Disappointment only increases Pound's truculence. Confidence becomes undisguised arrogance; sarcasm gives way to open abuse. His English friend Richard Aldington returns from the war to be told that "the English had no brains."[31] Pound writes Quinn that resuscitating culture in postwar London is "like massaging a corpse."[32] By 1920 he throws caution to the winds and attacks any figure associated with the literary establishment. Wyndham Lewis's novel *Tarr*, he predicts, "will not receive the sanction of Dr Sir Robertson Nicoll, nor of his despicable paper *The Bookman*."[33] And in his 1920 essay on Remy de Gourmont, he contrasts the French writer with the London literati: "If only my great correspondent could have seen letters I received about this time from English alleged intellectuals!!!!!! The incredible stupidity, the ingrained refusal of thought!!!!!"[34] His typewriter is a machine gun spewing exclamation points, its target simply the legions of "the enemy."

Clearly the time has come to pack his bags. But where can he go? He decides to leave London before he knows. And he thinks seriously of returning to America. For years he has been telling his parents that "America is NOT a place to live in or go to," that "I loathe the American state of mind." Yet in 1920 he asks his father to find out from the University of Pennsylvania, whose graduate program he had left after his second year, "on what terms they wd. give me the Ph. D. 'in consideration of my published work,'" including *The Spirit of Romance*.[35] The negotiations are protracted, but the final answer is on no terms.

Pound has no use for the Germanic style of academic training American graduate programs offer, but the degree might secure him a comfortable berth in some American institution. He writes Quinn that "I wd. be perfectly willing to professize in Columbia or the College of the City of N. Y."[36] It is all a fantasy, of course, but it suggests that New York again seems a possible place to live. Quinn's seven-page, single-spaced reply is extraordinary. He plays down the academic question but offers an indictment of New York that consciously translates James's critique of his native land in *Hawthorne* and *The American Scene* into apocalyptic terms. Not only would Pound find "no art that would interest you except imported art. No first-rate man of letters. No pleasant coterie." New York "is a noise surrounded by kikes," unlike homogeneous London. He would be marooned among "a million Jews who are mere walking appetites, seven or eight hundred thousand dagos, a couple of hundred thousand Slovaks, fifty or sixty thousand Croats and seven or eight hundred thousand sweating, pissing Germans." Jews have taken over the local institutions, especially "the University of the Shitty of New York," as well as the press, the theater, the judiciary, the philanthropies; they "bid fair to own the God damned town."[37] In short, the city is no place for a white man.

Pound thanks Quinn "for your long thoughtful letter re/ my descensus averni"[38] and concludes that this path to hell is best avoided. For all his irony about his Anglo-Saxon heritage, he is not willing to surrender its benefits. The anti-Semitism that becomes a fixed idea in his later years is fueled by this warning. Before opting for France, he writes a mock-Hamletian soliloquy to Ford in which he wonders "Whether twere better in the jettison of noncombustibles to treck for Paris, and forget the natural idiom of this island, or in the face of all too damn tumultuous seas and boat-rates emigrate, and on the quayed and basket-covered banks of bleak Manhattan chase the trade of letters!!!"[39] His nightmare of return casts him in the role of new immigrant rather than returning native, a dispossessed and penniless stranger, forced to carve out a niche for himself in a Jewish New York marketplace.

The fruitless months he had spent in that city ten years earlier had alerted him to "the size and vigour of this new strange people." In *Patria Mia* he ruefully notes that the new immigrants "are not Anglo-Saxon; their gods are not the gods whom one was reared to reverence." Although he admires their vitality and ambition, he concludes that for the present they have no interest in the cultural continuity that concerns him: "One knows that they are the dominant people and that they are against all delicate things." This will eventually change. Europe was once "mongrel" too, the climate and passage of time gradually making its diverse races more homogeneous.[40] But one alien type remains unassimilable. In a sentence Pound cuts from the original version of *Patria Mia* when preparing it for book publication, he writes: "The Jew alone can retain his detestable qualities, despite climatic conditions."[41]

In Pound's later works, his obsession with Jews will overwhelm any semblance of circumspection. For a time, however, he contains it in the relatively private forms of the letter and the coterie journal. The anti-Semitic lines from "Salutation the Third" published in *Blast* ("Let us be done with Jews and Jobbery, / Let us SPIT upon those who fawn on the JEWS for their money") are toned down for the 1926 *Personae:* "Let us be done with pandars and jobbery, / Let us spit upon those who pat the big-bellies for profit."[42] And the attack in a 1917 *Little Review* essay—"Unfortunately the turmoil of yidds, letts, finns, esthonians, cravats, niberians, nubians, algerians, sweeping along Eighth Avenue in the splendour of their vigorous unwashed animality will not help us. They are the America of tomorrow"—is softened in the later book version by capitalizing the names of the intruders while eliminating the "yidds" entirely.[43] But the violence is not far from the surface.

The Jews are merely the most visible foreign presence in the new New York. They seem to Pound (as to Adams and James) part of the cohort of aliens who are depriving him and his kind of their birthright. This sense of being *displaced* from a position of privilege by outsiders who will eventually take over the land is graphically recorded in Pound's only attempt at autobiography, his Jamesian *Indiscretions: or, Une Revue de Deux Mondes,* published in *The New Age* in 1920. The theme of this lightly disguised genealogical history of his father's and mother's ancestors is the decay of class privilege. The once prominent families have been reduced from gentry to commerce, from commerce to minor officialdom, from plantation to suburbia. He charts this decline in the prototypical Bohun family. In the more discreet version of *Indiscretions* published later in book form, "Old Man Bohun was not only a gentleman but the fine old type. And his son is a stockbroker, roaring himself hoarse every day in the Wheat Pit, and using the word gentlemen (which his father did seldom or never) very freely in the necessary committee work at the golf club." But the original periodical account of this decline continues: "and *his* son will look like a Jew, and his grandson, old Bohun's great-grandson, will talk Yiddish."[44]

This is the new American power structure, in which Pound can see no place for himself. The rage behind the sarcasm is pure *ressentiment,* differing mainly in tone from the reproof of an Adams or a James. Pound's anger is heightened by his ambiguous class identity. Despite his pride in his colonial roots, he is not descended from a landed or political or intellectual aristocracy. And his family is hanging on to its middle-class status by its fingernails.[45] He imagines returning in 1920 to "a country where the Anglo-Saxon stock is now said to be in a minority," where the fact that all his known progenitors "arrived in that country between 1630 and 1650" will earn him no points, where he will feel "racially alien to the mass of the population." He calls himself one of the "Landlose" (bereft of country) and decides that there is no home to welcome him. He can be alien anywhere. He has had a good deal of practice.[46] This mixture of patriotism and the sense of betrayal never evaporates. Three years after settling in Europe, he demands of an American correspondent, "When are you going to make the place safe for *natives*?"[47] Quinn's vitriolic attack on the degeneration of New York must have confirmed his own worst nightmares.

There is a time warp in Pound's vision of his country. His image was formed in the decades when European immigration was entirely unregulated, before the 1920 restriction law, with its dramatic changes, went into effect. As we have seen, he was not the only "native" American to feel that the deluge would drown him. But the emerging national consensus on this subject meant that the pattern would change, *did* change. Pound's absence from America for the whole period between the wars meant that he could never make his peace with the new America nor even think realistically about the transformation that was taking place, as most of his countrymen would learn to do. The whole process of response to change—resistance, conciliation, tolerance, accommodation, assimilation—was entirely unknown to him. He was not only living in the past but extrapolating from it in a way that made no allowance for the gradual absorption of the "alien" taking place in his absence. He could not grow with the country because he had left it behind. And he could not understand what was happening because he could not imagine a noncatastrophic version of his nation's fate.

What begins as an expatriate experiment with the possibility of return turns into a life sentence. Pound's bitter quarrel with America finally focuses on its resurgent puritanism. The organizations and individuals working to restrict freedom of expression—"Chautauqas, Mrs. Eddys, Dr. Dowries, Comstocks, societies for the prevention of all human activities"[48]—are the rapidly expanding conspiracy all those plurals suggest. When in 1915 Dreiser's *The "Genius"* is attacked by Anthony Comstock's Society for the Suppression of Vice and withdrawn by the publisher, Pound mockingly commands his father to wipe out the responsible bodies: "Strangle Ellis and Sunday and the Comstock family, and abolish the Christian superstition or do something to cleanse the country you live in."⁴⁹ It is now his father's country, apparently—no longer his own. By 1918, the advent of Prohibition produces, in a letter to H. L. Mencken, a paranoid fantasy of American males slated for extinction: "I have indeed little doubt that within the decade, semen will be carefully put up in thermos flasks, distributed by a committee, wholly regimented and impartial, for the continuance of the American race, and the elimination of all indelicate relations between the American sexes, a consummation devoutly to be desired."⁵⁰

Liberal-minded, uncensorious Paris becomes the plausible alternative to New York and London. In "The Island of Paris: A Letter," a series Pound publishes in *The Dial* in 1920, he describes that "paradise of artists" as "a poetic serum to save English letters from postmature and American telegraphics from premature suicide and decomposition." It is the city of Proust, of Gide, of Cocteau, of Louis Aragon and André Breton, where the ghosts of Remy de Gourmont and Guillaume Apollinaire cast a spell, of salons where "conversation still exists" and young writers might avoid the seductions of Mammon and the curse of respectability. It is "more pan-continental than London," its artists "more serious in experiment and more thorough than other people."⁵¹ After 1920 it is also, through Pound's intervention, the city to which Joyce moves to finish *Ulysses*, and in which he can manage to get it published. More than anything else, Pound's success in convincing the Irish writer to come to Paris confirms his irrevocable break with London. By the spring of 1921 he is settled in Montparnasse, and the London years are over.

II

In RETROSPECT, the stretch between the beginning of the war and Pound's departure seems a protracted farewell. If the Continent had been accessible after 1914, he would certainly have left earlier. As Ford writes in a later account, "The war put an end to his remarkable activities in London of the '13s and '14s. Without that, London might well today be the literary, plastic and musical centre of at least Anglo-Saxondom."⁵² Ford's is a nostalgic fantasy, not merely of Anglo-Saxon primacy but of a single cultural metropolis. The legacy of modernism is carried on in the following decades not only in London, Paris, New York, Berlin, Dublin, or Prague but in implausible places like Rapallo, Italy—to which Pound retreats after a mere four years in Paris—or Oxford, Mississippi, or Taos, New Mexico, or Rutherford, New Jersey. In Yeats's resonant, prophetic words, published in the year of Pound's decampment: "Things fall apart; the centre cannot hold."

Yeats also famously concluded that rhetoric is what we make of our quarrel with others, while poetry is the record of our quarrel with ourselves. As we will see, this insight illuminates the difference in tone between Pound's finest poetry and his more prosaic though impassioned propaganda. As though to measure the centrifugal force driving him away, Pound writes a sequence of poems he later calls "so distinctly a farewell to London"—*Hugh Selwyn Mauberley*.[53] It is his most ambitious original work aside from *The Cantos*, and it offers a retrospective analysis of his whole London expatriate career. Unlike the heated prose and poetry of 1908–20, *Mauberley* suggests detachment from the cultural battles Pound has fought and a verdict of "irreconcilable differences" to explain the divorce. It is an expressive vehicle for his disappointment, but it does not simply accuse a conspiratorial "them" without also assessing the weaknesses of "me" in the breakdown of communication. And like many expatriate works, its judgmental authority is undermined by a crippling spectatorial distance.

Mauberley is not a lyric poem. It transforms its author into the obscure poet E. P., the subject of a coolly dismissive career summary by the age itself in the first poem of the series. In this confident case for the prosecution, E. P. is seen as hopelessly out of touch and out of date, striving "to resuscitate the dead art / Of poetry; to maintain 'the sublime' / In the old sense. Wrong from the start—." His mistakes are attributed, in the usual patronizing British fashion, to the fact that "he had been born / In a half savage country." This is the only reference in the whole sequence to transnational misunderstanding, as though the differences between English and American culture were by now barely worth noticing. Yet the other poems in Part I allow E. P. to become the observer rather than the observed. What he sees eradicates Pound's early sense of London as the blessed alternative to American provincialism.

Under scrutiny here is the whole English literary scene in which Pound had immersed himself for the past dozen years—its recent history and present assumptions, its current luminaries and hangers-on. The tone is varied and complex, at different times critical, ironic, tragic, nostalgic, or merely bemused. But the salient fact about Pound's picture of modern English culture is that it is insular. Nothing exists beyond London and its suburbs, or at the furthest remove a country cottage with a leaky roof where a disaffected "stylist has taken shelter." The literary history offered in poems VI–XII (1860 to the present) includes *no* forces from beyond the scepter'd isle. It is a purely local tradition. The poems express Pound's disappointment in failing to push Britain toward a more cosmopolitan culture while now seeing the task as hopeless—wrong from the start.

This picture of literary London mocks Pound's early vision of "a city to which all roads lead, and from which there goes out an authority," a place where the generations "have mingled and have taken fire one from another," in which tradition is constantly renewed. The portraits of contemporary writers and patrons—M. Verog, Brennbaum, Mr. Nixon, the unnamed stylist, the suburban matron who fancies herself a cultural "conservatrix," The Lady Valentine entertaining poets as "a means of blending / With other strata"—all suggest isolation rather than community. Each portrait is framed within its own poem. Verog is "out of step with the decade"; Nixon cynically advises E. P. to "'Butter reviewers . . . / 'And give up verse, my boy, / 'There's nothing in it'"; the stylist is "unpaid, uncelebrated"; and the patrons are anxious not about the survival of culture but about their own place in it. These people do not form a community; they are atoms unable to bond, with no connection to any literary movement.

And tradition? The war, in its obsession with "the march of events," has undermined any market for that item. Pound's elegy for the betrayed defenders of a moribund culture treats their deaths as a senseless sacrifice:

> There died a myriad,
> And of the best, among them,
> For an old bitch gone in the teeth,
> For a botched civilization . . .
> For two gross of unbroken statues,
> For a few thousand battered books.

The survivors have only the merchant's measure to assess the culture that was supposedly saved, now seen as feminine and geriatric ("an old bitch gone in the teeth"), an antique shop full of junk. But this commercial vision only mirrors modern urban life. The player piano, the cinema, mass-produced objects and newspapers have replaced the older, slower, one-of-a-kind cultural artifacts. The beautiful is "decreed in the market place" and "The sale of half-hose has / Long since superseded the cultivation / Of Pierian roses." London is no Pieria: The Muses are departed, have left no addresses.

One can read this as an indictment of mass culture by a disgruntled adherent of The Tradition. But surprisingly, Pound's critique cuts both ways. In the second part of the poem, the figure of E. P. gives way to a surrogate, the failed artist Hugh Selwyn Mauberley. Like Eliot's Prufrock, to whom he is obviously related, Mauberley is defeated because he cannot muster the strength to resist his society. Both characters are hopelessly ineffectual males. In Part II, Mauberley is not a great artist unappreciated by his culture but a miniaturist and escapist, unobservant, anesthetized, incoherent. His porcelain portraits are elegant and bright but too neatly contained in their "suave bounding-line." He lacks inventive or confrontational force, fullness, reach. Unfit for the tasks "the age demanded," he retreats into a hedonistic pursuit of fleeting visions, adrift in the real or imagined Spice Islands. Pound stresses his "exclusion" and "isolation," hopes for a "more tolerant, perhaps, examination" of his case, but makes no larger claim. Mauberley is a pitiful failure, "Incapable of the least utterance or composition, / Emendation, conservation of the 'better tradition,' / Refinement of medium, elimination of superfluities, / August attraction or concentration."

The sound that echoes in these lines is "shun": to evade, avoid. Mauberley is a most unexpected stand-in for Pound's pugnacious temperament. What makes the fiery propagandist of modernism, the insolent accuser of the London literati, imagine himself in this guise? Perhaps he is taking a hard look at the cost of his alienation. Pound is excluded from a culture that doesn't value what he offers. Mauberley too is written off by his judges: "Non-esteem of self-styled 'his betters' / Leading, as he well knew, / To his final / Exclusion from the world of letters." The two figures fuse in these lines; Mauberley the visual artist

is banished from a literary culture. Like Pound's, his is "a consciousness disjunct," separated from rather than integral to a larger community. And the description of Mauberley's *work*—the obsessive perfec-
tionism that allows his quest to be summarized in the lines the age
uses to dismiss E. P. ("His true Penelope / Was Flaubert")—also links
their careers. The "curious heads in medallion," the engravings that
are "but an art / In profile" lacking richness and color, are minor
work.

At his most self-critical, Pound too is painfully aware of the gap
between his lofty ambitions and his actual poems. The "crepuscular
spirit in modern poetry" has too often crept into his early verse, which
is why the five volumes published before *Ripostes* are reduced to a
mere fifty pages of text in the 1926 *Personae*. His divorce from American culture, no matter how unformed it seems to him, is an escape
into a rarefied atmosphere that will mean little to the audience he
leaves behind. And the absence of response increases his willingness to
write in a language that expects none, fostering an aesthetic solipsism
that widens the gap. The result, Pound knows in his darkest moments,
is a fatal alienation from everything and everyone, like Mauberley's
"Olympian *apathein*," the suicidal indifference that comes from sever-
ing his roots. In Mauberley it produces a clinical detachment in which
he feels no connection to anyone.

"Have I a country at all . . . ?" Pound wonders in a 1920 letter to
Williams.[54] His anxiety about his place in American culture is often
expressed in his relationship with this lifelong friend. And no wonder.
Williams's is the rejected path, his career offering proof that expatriation is not necessary for an ambitious American poet. In his letters
Pound badgers Williams to move to London, tells him he is "out of
touch" and that his first book "would not attract even passing attention
here."[55] Williams takes his revenge by accusing Pound of being "the
best enemy United States verse has" and mocking him for presenting
his "parodies of the middle ages, Dante and Langue D'Oc . . . as the
best in United States poetry."[56] Pound vigorously defends his role in
getting many American poets noticed or into print: Frost, Eliot, H. D.,
Marianne Moore, Williams himself.

Behind the rhetoric of attack and defense lies a serious uneasiness.
Pound knows that Williams's best work cannot be dismissed. His 1912

review of *The Tempers* takes back his recent judgment in *Patria Mia* that "no man now living in America writes anything that is of interest to the serious artist."[57] Williams is a kindred spirit with similar aims, even though he shows no desire to leave. How to account for it? Pound insists on the inevitability of an "exiled" perspective for the serious artist by imagining "Carlos" Williams, with his Puerto Rican mother and English father, as a new immigrant gaping at the Statue of Liberty: "He claims American birth, but I strongly suspect that he emerged on shipboard just off Bedloe's Island and that his dark and serious eyes gazed up in their first sober contemplation at the Statue and its brazen and monstrous nightshirt." It is only because Williams's family is not U.S. born that he can look at America with the eyes of an "observant foreigner," allowing him to "inspect it, analyse it, and treat it as subject,"[58] Pound's formula for the rewards of exile.

Pound refuses to acknowledge that Williams's decision to stay has made his relation to America less troubled than his own can ever be. And yet he is forced to admit that his friend's alternative path has produced a body of work as interesting as his own yet more readily accessible to an American audience. In Pound's foreword to the 1965 edition of his early poems, his dismissal of them as "stale creampuffs" is linked to his pained sense that they were written "at a time when Bill W. was perceiving the 'Coroner's Children.'"[59] He refers to Williams's "Hic Jacet," which begins:

> The coroner's merry little children
>   Have such twinkling brown eyes,
> Their father is not of gay men
>   And their mother jocular in no wise,
> Yet the coroner's merry little children
>   Laugh so easily.[60]

There is no sign of alienation in such verse: detached, observant, ironic, but not superior to its subject nor excluding the American reader. As Pound puts it, Williams conveys "the absolute conviction of a man with his feet on the soil, on a soil personally and peculiarly his own. He is rooted."[61] It is worth comparing Williams's poem to one of Pound's contemporaneous works, "Prelude: Over the Ognisanti":

High-dwelling 'bove the people here,
Being alone with beauty most the while,
Lonely?
    How can I be,
Having mine own great thoughts for paladins
Against all gloom and woe and every bitterness?[62]

Where Williams is looking straight at those around him, Pound looks down. These Italians are literally and figuratively beneath him, barely worth noticing by someone whose exalted thoughts are compared to Charlemagne's peers. The condition of "exile"—alone in a foreign city with no connection to "the people here"—creates such sight lines and makes community impossible. The view from above recalls James's expatriate spectators in *William Wetmore Story and His Friends* watching the French invade Rome from their balconies "as in an opera-box" and his summary judgment in that book: "A man always pays, in one way or another, for expatriation, for detachment from his plain primary heritage."

This sense of loss is only gradually acknowledged. It is far from Pound's first reaction to leaving. He talked exuberantly then not of exile but of escape. Like James's "Passionate Pilgrim," many of his early poems record the delight of connecting with an older tradition. In "Redivivus," the spirits of Michelangelo and Dante preside over his resurrection from a condition in which "my soul lay slain / Or else in torpor." They offer the depleted poet a blood transfusion, restoring his sight and pulse, restoring the hope that his own reviving flame can add to their brilliant light.[63] Though the poems in *A Quinzaine for This Yule* (1908) unpeople present-day Venice, they turn that city into a luminous, timeless aesthetic object.

In the early poems, Pound's expatriate solitude is a welcome alternative to the world he leaves behind, as in the self-congratulatory "Anima Sola": "I flee on the wings of a note ye know not, / My music disowns your law, / Ye can not tread the road I wed." And Europe readily makes a place for him. Venice and London vie for the privilege of sponsoring him in "Fortunatus," the most confident of these early accounts of his arrival:

> though I seek all exile, yet my heart
> Doth find new friends and all strange lands
> Love me and grow my kin, and bid me speed.

There are no apparent losses attached to "exile" here. And the benefits will accrue to those left behind. In "Purveyors General," the wandering poets are seen as hunter-gatherers collecting exotic tales amid alien folk so "That new mysteries and increase / Of sunlight should be amongst you, / you, the home-stayers."[64] It is this anticipation of being useful to an American audience that will gradually evaporate, as the image of exile grows grimmer.

The rootless traveler appears constantly in the early poems, most often in the troubadours and wandering minstrels whose Provençal or Italian verse Pound translates or imitates. Their vagabondage is usually seen as freedom. Poems like "Cino," "In Epitaphium Eius," and "Fifine Answers" are odes to the joy of traveling light, of loving and leaving 'em: "Eyes, dreams, lips, and the night goes. / Being upon the roads once more, / They are not."[65] Rootlessness is a liberating improvidence here, as against the deathly prudence of staying put. Of course such figures would have seemed attractive to a young American in his early twenties suddenly freed from the discipline of graduate school, from alienated labor at a puritanical midwestern college, and from close parental supervision.

This careless freedom will not last. In her earliest letters, his mother sends him articles from *Life* with relevant passages underlined — "certain commendations of matrimony," "a disparaging paragraph on expatriates," as Pound describes them.[66] His irony suggests that the propaganda can be ignored across an ocean. How can this lucky escape be called "exile"? It is an odd word to choose, yet Pound regularly uses it for his transplanted state rather than the more accurate "expatriation." Exile is forced expulsion or banishment, not an optional departure. Yet Pound feels he *has* no option and regularly uses the stronger word. It alerts us to the darker side of his newfound freedom. His departure is a professional necessity, both for his career and for the home culture that supposedly awaits the fruits of his return. Like a soldier serving his country's needs or a commercial traveler working a territory, he sees what he does as necessary.

Pound's account of this condition in *Patria Mia* imagines the cost of a permanent alienation: "If a man's work require him to live in exile, let him suffer, or enjoy, his exile gladly. But it would be about as easy for an American to become a Chinaman or a Hindoo as for him to acquire an Englishness, or a Frenchness, or a European-ness that is more than half a skin deep."[67] Unlike James and later, Eliot, Pound cannot imagine a transfer of loyalties. He remains inalienably American despite his increasing estrangement. From his early delight in his freedom, the emphasis gradually shifts to suffering. In "The Rest" (1916), Pound addresses the hapless American artists who stay at home: "You of the finer sense, . . . / Hated, shut in, mistrusted." But leaving is equally painful. It means wearing yourself out, steeling yourself "into reiteration" to achieve a Pyrrhic victory in which you can only claim, "I have weathered the storm, / I have beaten out my exile."[68]

The pain of his exile is seldom described so directly (or so melodramatically); yet it recurs. Pound is seldom at his best as a lyric poet but needs the disguises of dramatic monologues and translations, in which he can express himself through someone in similar circumstances. The 1909 *Personae* is full of such poems. In "At the Heart of Me," "From Syria," and "From the Saddle," Pound imagines himself as an Anglo-Saxon sailor on the seas, a crusader far from his lady, a soldier in battle, each anxious to maintain the link to home but uncertain it will hold. And in his translation of the Anglo-Saxon poem "The Seafarer," the lines expressing the speaker's solitude must have echoed powerfully:

> Nathless there knocketh now
> The heart's thought that I on high streams
> The salt-wavy tumult traverse alone.
> Moaneth alway my mind's lust
> That I fare forth, that I afar hence
> Seek out a foreign fastness.[69]

"The Seafarer" was first published in book form in *Ripostes* (1912) and then reprinted three years later—bizarrely—in the middle of *Cathay*. It is the only poem not taken from Chinese sources in the later volume. A powerful link is the common subject matter of exile. It has long been thought that Pound's narrow selection of Chinese poems—only about a tenth of those in Fenollosa's notebooks—reflects his intense preoccupation, in 1914–15, with that historical moment. In Hugh Kenner's words, "The *Cathay* poems paraphrase an elegiac war poetry nobody wrote. . . . [T]hey are among the most durable of all poetic responses to World War I."[70] But there is another occluded elegiac subject the poems allow Pound to explore indirectly: the condition of being far from home, which is not necessarily linked to war.

The sadness of separation is the dominant emotion of *Cathay*, which is why the otherwise unrelated "Seafarer" seems to belong here. It can take the form of the river-merchant's wife lamenting his long absence, the bitterness of soldiers stuck in no-man's-land, the parting of intimate friends whose commitments take them in opposite directions. The sense of losing touch across thousands of miles of empty space resonates in Pound's psyche. The vastness of China—suggested in "Taking Leave of a Friend" in the lines "Here we must make separation / And go out through a thousand miles of dead grass," or in "Exile's Letter" in the rueful thought that "There is no end of things in the heart" which must remain unspoken as the writer sends his letter "a thousand miles"—suggests the breadth of the Atlantic rather than the width of the Channel.[71] The poems Pound selects deal obsessively with departure, long separation, solitude, loss. Their expressive power suggests his investment in the subject, discreetly hidden behind the masks of his Chinese speakers. The book also reveals Pound's increasing isolation in London. The first edition contains an extraordinary note voicing his fear that his critics are waiting to pounce, their hostility fueled by "the personal hatred in which I am held by many, and the *invidia* which is directed against me because I have dared openly to declare my belief in certain young artists."[72] Adams read James's *William Wetmore Story and His Friends* as a crypto-autobiography. *Cathay* is another.

This link to Adams and James is not incidental. Pound pairs the two writers in a later essay by contrasting "the temper, thickness, richness of the mental life of Henry Adams, and Henry James" with the prevailing cultural banality of turn-of-the-century America.[73] But the price *they* pay for their alienation or expatriation is not as heavy as his. They begin with a stronger sense of local roots and family tradition: "Henry James is as New England as Henry Adams because of the same racial origins and mixed by education with the same other chemical," Pound writes in 1938. And he contrasts their achievement with his own felt incoherence by lamenting his lack of a solid American identity: "There is I think little doubt that I should have more quickly attained a unity of expression had I been also New England without disorderly trek of four or five generations across the whole teeming continent."[74]

Pound's sense of exile is exacerbated by his lack of an identifiable home. He cannot, like James, "put America on the map" because his roots are shallowly planted and easily pulled up. He is nostalgic for an American life he never lived and longs for a link that exists only in fantasy. So he imagines a kinship with James that is purely fabricated. In his reverent 1918 essay on the novelist, he imagines that "H. J. might have stayed at the same hotel on the same day as one's grandfather" and confesses to "a purely selfish, personal, unliterary sense of intimacy" with him. James's is his model for a transatlantic career. He sees his achievement as triumphant, calling him "the greatest writer of our time and of our own particular language."[75]

Yet Pound knows that his own "approach to the Metropolis" can never match that of his great precursor, given "the vast unbridgeable difference of settling-in and escape."[76] The "settling-in," as we have seen, began auspiciously enough but was never smooth and ended badly. The upper-class links to the London establishment that held fast for Adams and James long after each withdrew from that world did not exist for Pound. He begins as a petitioner and demands the rights of a Solon. The acute sense of discomfort Pound both feels and generates during his London years is in part the product of his ambiguous place in the pecking order. And what he calls his "escape," presumably from the America that gave him birth, is never final. He remains quintessentially American in his manners, restlessness, and ambition; he hangs on to American speech patterns by inventing a cracker-barrel colloquial style for his letters; and he never surrenders the myth that he is serving as an American intelligence agent. Yet he insults his American readers and editors as he has insulted his British ones. His general unruliness is linked to his imaginative vitality, and he is unwilling to give them up. But Harriet Monroe warns him from America—as Eliot warns him in London—that his truculence will deny him a hearing: "Something in you fails to recognize that a little rudimentary tact is not compromise; that anyone who carries a bludgeon for friend and foe finds himself before long, butting the empty air."[77]

Her words were prophetic. Pound leaves London in 1920 with a very uncertain sense of destination and purpose. The departure from London, the four years in Paris, the longer stay in Rapallo, the Rome broadcasts for the fascist cause, the incarceration at Pisa, the treason trial, the confinement at St. Elizabeths, the return to Italy were not predictable; but they do reveal a nomadic pattern, chosen or forced, in which national identity counts for little. They suggest the trail of what would come to be called a Displaced Person. The rootlessness of such a life does not exclude the possibility of extraordinary achievement. The years in question produced *The Cantos*, after all. But if the accomplishment is literary, it is likely to be idiosyncratic, written in solitude for an imaginary audience, and long denied recognition. In his 1938 *Guide to Kulchur*, Pound calls *The Cantos* "the tale of the tribe" and predicts that they will become "steadily more intelligible to the general reader."[78] But the deluded words only reveal his desperate need for an audience he will never have and a role he will not be offered.

Gradually, inexorably, he burns his bridges to the Anglo-American literary centers. As he takes stock of his new solitude, he notes a newly emergent figure engaged in a very different enterprise—a young American described by his professor, Bertrand Russell, as "very well-dressed & polished, with manners of the finest Etonian type."[79] Pound agrees that the manners are impeccable and notes with acerbity that his compatriot "wd. adorn any yacht club."[80] He is of course T. S. Eliot, a man whose un-Poundian patience, suavity, prudence, and tactical shrewdness would earn him the public role his early mentor had pursued, held within his grasp, and forfeited.

XI

T. S. Eliot's
Career Strategy

I

IT IS EASY to treat T. S. Eliot's rise to cultural prominence in London as an uninterrupted triumphal progress. In the half century between his arrival in 1915 and his death, every conceivable honor of such a career came his way. He was treated as *the* English-language poet and critic of his generation. "The Love Song of J. Alfred Prufrock" and *The Waste Land* were committed to memory by two generations of the young. His controversial critical opinions achieved the status of fact. In editing *The Criterion* in the years between the wars, he created an instrument to advance his cultural agenda; and in making the Faber imprint the guarantee of high quality in verse, he promoted his own candidates for Parnassus and established a powerful legacy. In 1948, at sixty, he received both the Order of Merit, Britain's highest honor, and the Nobel Prize. James had secured the first but been passed over for the second. After his death, his ashes were taken to East Coker, the Somerset village from which Andrew Eliot, his first American-bound ancestor, had set out for the New World three centuries earlier; and a memorial tablet in Westminster Abbey's Poets' Corner joined his name with those of Chaucer, Spenser, Shakespeare, Milton, Dryden, Wordsworth, Browning, Tennyson—and Longfellow, the only other American poet in that majestic assembly.

This is not an accidental tale of success. The failures and frustrations that had dogged his American precursors become warning signals to their successor. Adams, James, and Pound have paved the way, but Eliot is determined not to repeat their mistakes. He consciously carries on their tradition, and feels a deep kinship with Adams and James. He and Adams are in fact distantly related: "I am writing now about a cousin of ours, who has written a very interesting book which you would like to read: *The Education of Henry Adams*," Eliot writes his mother when he reviews the first edition.[1] His paternal grandmother, born Abigail Adams Cranch and proud of her connection to that family, survived until he was twenty; and the *first* American Henry Adams (c. 1583–1646) had like Andrew Eliot set out for Massachusetts from Somerset.[2] In commenting on Pound's "Adams Cantos," Eliot refers to America's second president with pride and mockery as Uncle John.[3] The Adams of the *Education*, he feels, is "a type that I *ought* to know better than any other."[4]

In calling Adams a type Eliot acknowledges more than literal kinship. His review of the *Education* is like a medical diagnosis: Adams suffers from latter-day puritan anxiety, a disorder in which an exigent conscience demands self-improvement, a religious imperative diluted by Unitarianism survives into a skeptical age, and a daunting family tradition of public service dogs the hapless inheritor. That inheritor, Eliot writes of Adams, "was much more refined than the equivalent Englishman, and had less vitality, though a remarkably restless curiosity, eager but unsensuous."[5] Although Eliot was not descended from two presidents, he could trace his distinguished family to America's first settlers. Like Adams, he feels belated and betrayed. America before 1830, he says, would have felt like "a family extension." His biographer Lyndall Gordon notes that the date coincides with the moment when "the civilized élite of the Eastern seaboard lost its power in the bitter election of 1828, when John Quincy Adams fell before the rude, uncultivated Andrew Jackson."[6] What worries him is not the loss of power but of vitality. In Eliot's review, Adams emerges as a sophisticated but desiccated writer whose work is undermined by a constitutional failure of energy, hope, bodily awareness. Eliot might have recoiled but would not have been surprised when an American reviewer in 1926 called his work "a spiritual epilogue to 'The Education of Henry Adams.'"[7] Clearly, the inventor of J. Alfred Prufrock knows the type, and fears the fate.

Henry James is the more attractive precursor. Eliot compares the linked careers of these friends and contrasts two descriptions of landing on British soil from their work. Adams is matter of fact, general, generic-tourist; James is alive to "appearances, aspects, images, every protrusive item" impinging on him, from the gusty weather to the buttered muffins arriving under their domed cover. "It is the sensuous contributor to the intelligence that makes the difference," Eliot concludes.[8] For a young writer eager to be a poet, "the sensuous contributor" is indispensable, though the clumsiness of his phrase suggests that the words will not come easily.

Despite Eliot's choice of poetry, he emulates James's achievement. An intriguing entry in Virginia Woolf's diary records his confessing that "a personal upheaval of some kind came after Prufrock & turned him aside from his inclination—to develop in the manner of Henry James."[9] One can only guess what this means; but there are signs in Eliot's 1917 collection, *Prufrock and Other Observations*, that he can use his satiric gift to skewer the worthy citizens of Boston in a series of sharply etched portraits—"The *Boston Evening Transcript*," "Aunt Helen," "Cousin Nancy," "Mr. Apollinax," and the consciously Jamesian "Portrait of a Lady."

In exploiting this typecasting talent Eliot uses his spectatorial detachment from his native land, as James had done. He praises the novelist's critical observation, especially of the American scene. Eliot often alludes to James's book of that name. He empathizes with the baffled expatriate returning late in life to a transformed America, "asking his way of an Italian mill-hand in the streets of Salem."[10] But the James he recommends to a cousin asking for guidance is the youthful social satirist: "I have a great admiration for him. Not so much the later stuff, but read *The Europeans* and *The American*, and *Washington Square*, and *Daisy Miller*. The first especially is a wonderful criticism of New England. . . . As a critic of America he is certainly unique."[11]

This is not Eliot's final judgment. The twists and turns of his own career reveal parallel after parallel, some reassuring, some alarming. Both writers think of themselves not as English or American but as European. Eliot's appraisal of James's success is calculatedly outrageous in its chauvinism: "It is the final perfection, the consummation of an American to become, not an Englishman but a European— something which no born European, no person of any European nationality, can become."[12] The passage is from an obituary essay published only in the *Egoist* and the *Little Review*. Eliot must have known that it would offend the English audience he was courting. He never reprints "In Memory of Henry James." Not until Edmund Wilson publishes this important essay much later in *The Shock of Recognition* do Eliot's brash words appear between hard covers—and then only in a book intended for the American market.

By that time Eliot understands what James's triumph had cost: the response of a sympathetic audience. His transnational detachment had alienated both his English and American audience, as we have seen. Eliot recognizes the dangers of such an ambition: James "is an author who is difficult for English readers, because he is an American; and who is difficult for Americans, because he is a European; and I do not know whether he is possible to other readers at all."[13] The claim to a European, supranational identity offends every natural constituency. Although Eliot—like Pound and many modernists—seems to write for an unlocatable cultured elite, his ambitions are reluctantly contained by that dispensation. And though he is a poet, he hopes to have a much larger impact. He will not settle for James's bitter withdrawal to the coterie.

As with Adams, spiritual kinship can spell danger. Eliot realizes that his deepest link is not to James the confident social satirist but to the anatomist of the deformed survivors of New England puritanism—the protagonists of late works like *The Ambassadors*, "The Beast in the Jungle," and "The Jolly Corner," with their passivity, blocked sexuality, and crippling ambivalence. These become "The Hollow Men" of Eliot's 1925 poem—"Paralysed force, gesture without motion."[14] His choice of James over Adams was based on a false distinction. What Edmund Wilson labels, in one of the foundational insights of Eliot commentary, the "theme of emotional starvation" runs through the line that passes from Hawthorne to Adams, James, and Wharton to

Eliot—"the desolation, the aesthetic and spiritual drouth, of Anglo-Saxon middle-class society."[15] A warning about the cost of James's expatriation also comes from on high. As Eliot ponders cutting his ties to America, he receives a letter from an aged but by no means dismissable voice—that of his distant cousin Charles W. Eliot, Harvard's president during his undergraduate years. The letter warns him not to "live much longer in the English atmosphere" but to recover his national heritage. And it recounts a meeting during James's final American visit in which the novelist hinted that his expatriation had "contributed neither to the happy development of his art nor to his personal happiness."[16] James's powerful example is more than a difficult act to follow, then. It is a chilling prospect.

What Eliot needs—and finds—is an American of his generation who has infiltrated London literary life without losing his vitality or his national birthright. The historic meeting with Pound in September 1914, during Eliot's Oxford year, transforms their careers. Although both are still in their twenties, Pound has lived in London for six years and become *the* person for young writers to meet. Eliot duly turns up with a sheaf of poems, including "The Love Song of J. Alfred Prufrock." He is pursuing a Harvard doctorate in philosophy and has no confidence in himself as a writer. Pound's instant recognition and energetic sponsorship reinvents the hesitant young man as a poetic genius. "My meeting with Ezra Pound changed my life," Eliot was to recall. "He was enthusiastic about my poems, and gave me such praise and encouragement as I had long since ceased to hope for."[17]

Pound announces his new discovery to Harriet Monroe and insists (over her protest) that *Poetry* publish what is sure to become a classic. Eliot, he tells her, "is the only American I know of who has made what I call adequate preparation for writing. He has actually trained himself *and* modernized himself *on his own*."[18] He urges Eliot to escape the doom of his academic career, settle in the metropolitan center of the English-speaking world, and pursue his poetic vocation—Pound's own exact course. He writes an outrageous testimonial about the indispensability of London for an aspiring American writer to Eliot's recalcitrant father in St. Louis: "As to his coming to London, anything else is a waste of time and energy. No one in London cares a hang what is written in America." And he asks the elderly gentleman to "bear in mind that London imposes her acceptance of a man's work on all the English speaking world and that she accepts no other standard than her own."[19]

One can imagine the impact of this missile on Eliot's anxious parents, who have just heard that he has hastily married an Englishwoman they have never met and is thinking of scuttling his promising academic career without even bothering to finish his dissertation. Eliot's radical decision to expatriate goes against every principle he was taught from birth. Given his reluctance to offend his family and his often crippling self-doubt, he desperately needs a surrogate rebel. Pound is that irresistible force. His is also a precocious career worth emulating. In the anonymous pamphlet Eliot writes to introduce Pound's first publication in America, he informs their compatriots that Pound has triumphed in "the siege of London" despite being "a complete stranger, without either literary patronage or financial means."[20] Eliot's use of James's title silently recalls the group history of American assault. Behind this heroic tale is the expectation that the latest intruder will also enter the citadel.

But Eliot values not only Pound's energetic sponsorship. He shares many of his cultural values and tastes. Both disdain what they take to be America's populist standards as well as the safe but arid academic retreat. Both flee what they consider American provincialism and idealize a cosmopolitan code enforced in a European metropolis. Both fear the specter of woman as "Kulturträgerin," dominating the magazines by enforcing conservative taste. The confident women around Prufrock "talking of Michelangelo" discourage that compromised rebel from speaking out—silencing his attempts to communicate with a dismissive impatience: "That is not what I meant at all. / That is not it, at all."[21] In the poem the gender quarrel never erupts. But in his letters Eliot's vitriolic attacks on women with cultural power easily match Pound's. He commiserates with his friend Scofield Thayer, the editor of the *Dial*, for having to report to a woman: "Of course your superior officer is a Lady. They always are. Be PATIENT, I say PATIENT. Be Sly, INSIDIOUS, even UNSCRUPULOUS, Suffering Many Things, Slow to WRATH, concealing the Paw of the Lion, the Fang of the Serpent, the Tail of the Scorpion, beneath the Pelt of the ASS. . . . I WILL REPAY, saith the LORD."[22] Such private rage reveals a violence similar to Pound's beneath Eliot's public urbanity.

His respect for Pound's judgment is evident in his submission of poems for revision. This produces not only the famous collaborative labor on *The Waste Land* (1922) but many earlier interventions, in which Pound wields his scalpel on poems published between 1917 and 1920. The manuscript of "Whispers of Immortality" includes a note from Eliot asking Pound if it is even worth revising. Many drafts survive, with Pound's detailed suggestions.[23] And even after *The Waste Land* makes him famous, Eliot still submits poems for Pound's editing. With "The Hollow Men" comes an anxious letter asking what might be done to salvage this flawed draft.[24]

Their most important cooperative product is *The Waste Land*, as we have known since the long-lost manuscript with Pound's corrections and deletions turned up.[25] The original draft Pound reads in 1921 is not a poem but a loose collection of verses, written over several years, and over twice as long as the final version. He hacks huge chunks from the original, cutting sections that sound dated or resemble pastiche or echo Eliot's earlier poems, deleting long realistic narratives like the first eighty-three (out of ninety-three) lines of what is now the brief, enigmatic "Death by Water." He discourages Eliot from including five additional poems only marginally related to the work he envisages. He turns a miscellany into a unified and memorable poem—coherent but extremely difficult, since so many accessible parts have been cut. Pound's version enciphers the poem, forcing the reader to decode it unaided, yet also makes it short enough to be grasped *as* a unit. He writes Eliot that at nineteen pages he has written "the longest poem in the English langwidge."[26] He knows that the canon includes book-length poems but follows Poe's precept in "The Poetic Principle" (1850) that a long poem is a contradiction in terms, that real poetry sustains its intensity unrelentingly, and that the limit is half an hour of reading time. This is the *kind* of work Pound makes of Eliot's manuscript. Implicitly, it challenges the reader: Make sense of this; the sense is there.

Eliot would have been afraid to impose such a burden, and he remains in Pound's debt for enabling the radical demolition and creation. In sending the manuscript to their patron John Quinn, he writes that it is worth preserving "solely for the reason that it is the only evidence of the difference which his criticism has made to this poem."[27] There is a public acknowledgment in the dedication "For Ezra Pound, *il miglior fabbro.*" But though Pound is, like Dante's Arnaut Daniel, "the better craftsman," and Eliot addresses him as "Cher maître," the power relations are subtly shifting. Pound sums it up to Quinn: "About enough, Eliot's poem, to make the rest of us shut up shop."[28] His letter to Eliot with the final revisions recognizes that the poem is, after all, not his, and that it is better than anything he has written: "Complimenti, you bitch. I am wracked by the seven jealousies, and cogitating an excuse for always exuding my deformative secretions in my own stuff, and never getting an outline."[29] Yet Pound does not offer his "secretions" to Eliot's shaping hand. It is the younger poet's willingness to submit to authority, to listen to suggestion, that makes him the superior survivor in the literary marketplace, if not the better craftsman.

This temperamental difference is evident in Eliot's earliest work. The posthumously published collections of his juvenilia reveal a boy and young man writing in two antithetical voices—one private and obsessive, the other public and official. Poems like "Circe's Palace," "The Death of St. Narcissus," or "The Love Song of St. Sebastian" are raw erotic daydreams, recording sadomasochistic fantasies of martyrdom, rape, and masturbation:

> Then he knew that he had been a fish
> With slippery white belly held tight in his own fingers,
> Writhing in his own clutch.[30]

Eliot prudently withdraws this poem before it appears in *Poetry*.[31] But an entirely different impulse is also evident in these works: the licensed bard producing the required product. At seventeen he writes the class poem for his Smith Academy graduation; five years later he is the Harvard Odist, urging his classmates never to forget

> What we owe for the future, the present, and past,
> Fair Harvard, to thine and to thee.[32]

This is the work of a laureate in training, reverent, metrically conventional—a style Pound would have scorned even in adolescence.

That Eliot can command both voices serves his career. At bottom, he is as rebellious as Pound; but he is capable of assuming conventional disguises. Everyone who knows them sees the difference. Quinn advises him that he can find a more mainstream publisher for his poetry than Pound, since "after all, your work is not quite as revolutionary and as explosive as E. P.'s."[33] Pound himself predicts an easier passage for his tactful protegé. He tells Eliot's father that success is determined both by the quality of a writer's work and his conciliatory talents: "It depends on the number of feuds he takes on for the sake of his aesthetic beliefs. T. S. E. does not seem to be as pugnacious as I am and his course should be the smoother and swifter."[34] These words prove prophetic.

Eliot's diplomacy is instinctive. He is not a leaky vessel: He knows what he can and cannot say, and to whom. Though he is as hard to please as Pound—perhaps harder—he censors his judgments or relegates them to obscure publications. He decides *not* to review contemporary poetry and stay "out of the intrigues and personal hatreds of journalism," as he tells his mother. By being judicious, seemingly above the fray, he "can influence London opinion and English literature in a better way." He consciously assumes the role of arbiter: "All sorts of literary affairs seem to claim at least my counsel, and there are often jarring interests to be reconciled by diplomacy."[35] His career is strategically managed from the first.

The same tactical shrewdness is evident in Eliot's decisions about where to publish what. The London Letters he writes for the American-based *Dial* are not available in England, and are never reprinted. For that audience, then, he can blast British cultural complacency and insularity with devastating force. In one such piece, he describes the atmosphere of literary London as one of "moral cowardice . . . ; lack of ambition, laziness, and refusal to recognize foreign competition; a tolerance which is no better than torpid indifference."[36] This is distinguishable from Poundian rant only in its elegance of phrasing. But it is a sentence Eliot's English audience will not read in his lifetime.

To censor or contain his abusiveness is an instinct confirmed by watching his mentor self-destruct. He arrives in London in the waning years of Pound's influence and observes the ugly last stages with fascination and dismay. Eliot's first wife has left a vivid account of his response to the heightened literary infighting brought by the changing of the guard: "He hates and loathes all sordid quarreling and gossiping and intrigue and jealousy, *so much*, that I have seen him go white and *be ill* at any manifestation of it." She cites Pound as one of the casualties: "Pound was ruined by it. See what he has become. A laughing stock."[37] Despite the frenzied tone, Vivien Eliot's judgment is accurate enough. Eliot offers a more measured assessment in a kind of obituary letter to Quinn. He notes that most English journals are now hostile to Pound, that not even Eliot's newfound influence can get him a hearing, that he is being forgotten. His analysis is tactical: "Here in London a man's first work may always attract attention, because while he is unknown he has no enemies, but later it is essential that he should establish solid connections with at least one important paper." He blames Pound's tactlessness, expresses concern over his future, and asks Quinn for advice in an avuncular tone that would have enraged Pound: "I should at some point—when you have time, if you ever have any time—like very much to know your candid and confidential opinion about Pound and his future, if you have enough confidence in my discretion to express it."[38]

His presumption is breathtaking. It was Pound who initiated the fruitful relationship between Quinn and Eliot, which led to the publication of Eliot's work in America on advantageous terms. That he has become the subject of confidential letters between them, the worrisome unruly child monitored by two concerned adults, suggests how much ground he has lost. But Quinn refuses to play Eliot's game, predicting that "if a man is a great poet or a great writer, he will win finally, whether the reviews are for him or against him."[39] Yet the crisis in Pound's career is real enough; in 1920 he abandons London forever, leaving Eliot in control of the movement. This moment also changes the tone of modernist discourse in England, from passionate advocacy of the new and contempt for the old to a more managerial, diplomatic control—in short, to its institutionalization.[40]

From his perch on the Continent, Pound ridicules Eliot's increasing respectability: "The Dean of English criticism, Mr. T. S. Eliot, pronounces that 'the greatest poets have been concerned with moral values'; this red-herring is justifiable on the grounds of extreme mental or physical exhaustion."[41] He greets Eliot's appointment as editor of *The Criterion* with mingled envy and derision. Here is a chance the unreliable Pound is never offered—his own journal. But he foresees the compromises Eliot will make to keep his patron, Lady Rothermere, happy and is not surprised when she dislikes the journal's calculated respectability: "Of course if she says it looks like a corpse, she's right, mon POSSUM, do you expect her to see what is scarce discernable to the naked eye, that it is *supposed* to be PLAYIN' POSSUM."[42] Eliot's compromises and inhibitions have earned him the nickname he himself will use; he often addresses Pound as Rabbit and signs himself Possum. He can also mock *The Criterion* by calling it "The Mortuary." Pound, in turn, is sarcastic about Eliot's pandering to the "Brutish pooplik."[43] Yet the correspondence is virtually unbroken; as Pound's publisher at Faber Eliot makes sure his work appears regularly no matter how offensive it has become. They remain allies. But they go their separate ways; or rather, Pound goes and Eliot stays.

Unlike Pound, Eliot never even thinks of going back to America. He sees the United States *dis*uniting through "the existence of large undigested lumps of foreign races."[44] These new minorities threaten the authority of his own culture as they did for all these writers. In a 1919 review, Eliot scorns the American vogue for "the aborigines of every complexion and climate, who have arrived, each tribe pressing upon us its own claims to distinction in art and literature."[45] The loss of Anglo-Saxon primacy disturbs him deeply because he so clearly identifies with that tradition. At the same time, the legacy is threatened from within by a wasting disease that Pound calls "a blood poison." Eliot, he writes William Carlos Williams, "has it perhaps worse than I have—poor devil." The more vital new inheritors of the land can thrive because they "had not the thin milk of New York and New England from the pap."[46]

Eliot's resentment at being displaced by the Irish, the Jews, and the eastern Europeans is evident in his correspondence and his poetry. Quinn again plays resident informant, warning Eliot about grasping, unreliable Jewish publishers and reviewers like Horace Liveright and Louis Untermeyer. He describes what he takes to be Liveright's reneging on a promise to publish Eliot's poetry in America as "a dirty piece of Jew impertinence." He fantasizes taking part in "a pogrom here," with "a couple of additional pogroms in the outlying districts, one in the Bronx and one in Brooklyn." When Liveright later publishes *The Waste Land*, Eliot explodes because his royalty check is late and asks Quinn to find him a Christian sustitute.[47]

Aside from the threat of the new immigrants, Eliot has a more pressing racial anxiety. Because his branch of the family had moved from New England to St. Louis in his grandfather's day, his eastern roots have become tangled in the local underbrush. He plans an essay from the point of view of an American of the old stock who "was born in the South and went to school in New England as a small boy with a nigger drawl."[48] He sees himself as "a New Englander in the South West and a Southwesterner in New England."[49] This hybrid creature has to deny the less desirable parts of himself. Eliot's uneasy mockery of non-Anglo-Saxons is a way of distancing himself from them. So he projects a melodrama about a white hero pursued by various passionate "ethnic" women—PAPRIKA! the Mexican dancer, EARLY BIRD the Indian maiden, PEGOON the colleen whose mother runs the hash house. In another, he casts himself as "the REV. HAMMOND AIGS comic negro minstrel, of the 'come breddern' type."[50] There are also the obscene, privately circulated but still partially unpublished King Bolo–Christopher Columbus poems, in which Eliot's repressed sexuality finds release in fantasies of insatiable Spaniards and Caribbean blacks with gargantuan genitals, satisfying their desires in any available orifice.[51] Clearly, this is not the voice of a confident Anglo-Saxon male basking in his inherited authority.

This race and class anxiety, often linked to sexual envy, finds its way into Eliot's published work, and has become notorious. The Prufrock volume published in England in 1917 reveals relatively little. But the first collection to appear in America, the 1920 *Poems*, relegates the earlier work to the back pages and highlights more recent verse in which the barbarians at the gate—Jews, Irish, eastern Europeans—are everywhere pressing forward. In "Gerontion," "the jew squats on the window sill," like a cormorant waiting for Eliot's old man to die. A character named Bleistein—"Chicago Semite Viennese"—can barely lift himself above the mud to see a painting: "A lustreless protrusive eye / Stares from the protozoic slime / At a perspective of Canaletto." Jews are swimming below the rats in fetid canals; a subhuman "Rachel *née* Rabinowitch / Tears at the grapes with murderous paws"; the rapacious Grishkin distils a rank "feline smell" stronger than the Brazilian jaguar's. And Sweeney, Eliot's Irish sexual athlete, is also subhuman, with "gesture of orang-outang," pendulous arms, "The zebra stripes along his jaw / Swelling to maculate giraffe."[52] It is easy to compile such an anthology of outrageous passages, harder to explain Eliot's emotional investment in them. They suggest revulsion from and attraction to a vigorous animal life, the disgust and envy of a paralyzed spectator forced to watch what he cannot perform. Eliot's Anglo-Saxon protest at the pollution of the land reveals both morbid fear about a contest that threatens to obliterate his kind and a longing to abandon his lonely tower and descend to the gutter. The impulses are at war; he needs an escape from the confusion they provoke. London offers an apparent retreat and the chance to become what Wyndham Lewis later dubbed him: "the premier poet of Anglo-Saxony."[53]

II

BEFORE ELIOT CAN devote himself to this goal, however, he must decide that poetry is his calling; and this is no foregone conclusion. The decision to expatriate is linked to the difficult decision to abandon the academic career for which he has been carefully groomed. He is in the final stages of his Harvard doctoral work in philosophy and finds himself in Europe on a traveling fellowship. The outbreak of war cuts his German stay short and propels him across the Channel. The 1914 meeting with Pound is really a historical accident. Despite the boost Pound's enthusiasm gives to making Eliot a poet rather than a professor, the decision is tortured.

There are powerful antagonists to contend with—his enthusiastic Harvard sponsors, coaxing him to return to the academy; his anxious parents and the Adams-like familial tradition of institutional service; his inner voices preaching caution. But his resistance is stronger. He declines positions at Harvard and Wellesley but does not burn his bridges.[54] Unlike Pound, who alienates his mentors, abandons his thesis, and comes close only in fantasy to holding a university job, Eliot's path to academia is strewn with flowers. His parents, who support him through graduate school and expect a return on their investment (as well as their son's return to his native country), exact a promise that he will finish his thesis on the philosopher F. H. Bradley. As his mother writes Bertrand Russell, "I have absolute faith in his Philosophy but not in the vers libre."[55] James's family sponsorship was unconditional; Eliot's is not.

That he is financially dependent despite his resistance makes the break harder. Even after he is married, juggling schoolteaching and reviewing to stay afloat in London, he remains gallingly dependent on his disapproving father, who sends him money to pay the rent—and for new underwear! He is twenty-nine years old.[56] His letters home are full of apologies, boasts, promises—but no regrets. The decision to abandon his academic career is final. When the thesis he finished and forgot is unearthed and published decades later, Eliot claims a useful memory lapse: "I find myself unable to think in the terminology of this essay. Indeed, I do not pretend to understand it."[57]

Eliot's aborted academic career and the "blood poison" Pound diagnosed in the offspring of the first settlers are linked. The academy—Harvard especially—fosters the disease. The absence of sensuous vitality Eliot finds in Adams's *Education* is associated with that hothouse, as Adams felt when he resigned from Harvard to settle in Washington. For years, Eliot writes, "I had a gnawing doubt, which I could not altogether conceal from myself, about my choice of a profession. . . . My heart was not in the study."[58] It is not philosophy but the academic atmosphere that repels him. Nor is it Harvard per se. The same fear haunts him at Oxford in the 1914–15 academic year. He takes every chance to go to London because he hates the university's effect on him. "In Oxford I have the feeling that I am not quite alive—that my body is walking about with a bit of my brain inside it, and nothing else," he writes his friend Conrad Aiken.[59]

He stresses the irreconcilability of his academic and literary options. Nietzsche, whose work fuses philosophy and literature, only provokes Eliot's scorn. He is "one of those writers whose philosophy evaporates when detached from its literary qualities" and who appeals primarily to amateurs "who enjoy the luxury of confounding, and avoid the task of combining, different interests."[60] This perceived antithesis helps to explain Eliot's peculiar assessment of James, whose genius is manifest in his "mastery over, his baffling escape from, Ideas." He praises James for having "a mind so fine that no idea could violate it."[61] Only someone running from the supposedly arid world of "Ideas" would consider this a tribute.

Two close associates confirm Eliot's need to think of the routes as divergent—Pound, and the woman he marries. The kinship with Pound is strengthened by their shared contempt for American academic life. As Eliot describes Pound's response, he is also voicing his own opinion: "Mr. Pound has spoken out his mind from time to time on the subject of scholarship in American universities, its deadness, its isolation from genuine appreciation, and the active creative life of literature."[62] Pound finds an ally in Vivien Haigh-Wood, the young English-woman Eliot meets in 1915. Their hasty courtship and disastrous marriage is inextricable from Eliot's desire to become a poet and to expatriate. He writes retrospectively, "I came to persuade myself that I was in love with her simply because I wanted to burn my boats and commit myself to staying in England. And she persuaded herself (also under the influence of Pound) that she would save the poet by keeping him in England."[63] Her unwavering belief in his poetic gift is of the essence. She writes to Eliot's father with characteristic vehemence, "I look upon Tom's poetry as real genius—I *do* think he is made to be a great writer—*a* poet. His prose is very good—but I think it will never be *so* good as his poetry."[64] For the anxious and confused Eliot, her certainty, and Pound's, supply the needed willpower.

The belief that analytic thinking and poetry cannot be reconciled is only a temporary fiction, however. Once released from the life sentence of an academic career, Eliot finds a way of combining them. There is a fertile middle ground: literary criticism. It will allow him to become not only a major innovative poet but give him a cultural authority no American has *ever* had in Britain. His philosophical training will make him the most influential critic in the English-speaking world. Unlike Pound, who writes criticism promiscuously, to push the movement and his friends' careers, Eliot learns to ration his words and make them count. His early critical books, *The Sacred Wood* (1920), *Homage to John Dryden* (1924), and *For Lancelot Andrewes* (1928), are carefully shaped works rather than miscellanies. The making of *The Sacred Wood* is deliberate and strategic: "I thought that instead of reprinting essays (a form of book making to which I am averse) I would boil down the lecture and the essays together into a small but constructed book ... in order to make it a single distinct blow."[65] Eliot's pugilism is a disciplined art.

His models are not the literary pundits of the day but the most influential analytic minds of the tradition—Aristotle, Dr. Johnson, Coleridge, Arnold. As he puts it in a review, "In our time, the most vigorous critical minds are philosophical minds."[66] He lays out the territory in his important essay, "The Function of Criticism" (1923), which alludes to Arnold's "The Function of Criticism at the Present Time" (1865) but goes it one better: Eliot's title suggests timelessness. He attacks self-indulgent critics whose individual taste is law. A serious critic will look for "common principles," not "the inner voice."[67] He scorns "creative" critics like John Middleton Murry and claims an impersonal authority based in tradition, deference toward great writers, and the rejection of criticism as a self-sufficient province. There is a boastful humility in such pronouncements that recalls the tone of Henry Adams. Behind it a confident mind is laying down the law. *The Sacred Wood* starts with an essay called "The Perfect Critic." The ideal critic does not legislate but inquires and is notable for "the disinterested exercise of intelligence." Yet Eliot adds another requirement that is hardly unbiased: "The critic and the creative artist should frequently be the same person."[68]

The theory commends Eliot's own credentials: a poet trained in "disinterested" analytic thinking; an outsider who knows more than the local tradition; a critic who is also a practitioner. Eliot's boldest move is to attack the Romantic dispensation and restore the taste for a style of writing remarkably like his own. He revises literary history by positing a post-Renaissance break for which he coins a memorable phrase—"a dissociation of sensibility" that separated ideas from sensations and impoverished all subsequent English poetry to the present day.[69] The term itself becomes canonical and shapes the standards of several generations. But its usefulness for Eliot is to create a taste for verse in which intellectual urgency is not off-limits and intense mental activity coexists with deep feeling. The recovery of this tradition, Eliot concludes, means that the modern poet "must be *difficult* . . . more comprehensive, more allusive, more indirect, in order to force, to dislocate if necessary, language into his meaning."[70] There is an obvious ulterior motive behind this once revisionist theory: to honor the work of philosophical minds who use poetry as an expressive vehicle. There is no doubt whose interests are being served. Eliot's "objective" critical essays are covert manifestos silently advancing his own poetic program. By contrast, Pound is nakedly direct.

The difference is stylistic. Eliot's prose is remarkable for its compression and tone of authority. He attacks the English cult of the amateur critic. A *TLS* writer questioning "professionalism in art" is taken to task for "slackness." "Surely professionalism in art is hard work on style with singleness of purpose," Eliot writes. "We must learn to take literature *seriously*."[71] The real enemy is the casual reader who must be cajoled and prevented from turning the page. The journalist-critic never "quite dares to treat a book austerely by criteria of art and of art alone."[72] This is a battle James had fought in producing the craftsman's prefaces to his own novels.

Eliot writes in shorthand for the informed reader. He also perfects a style of impersonal address, a sort of fatalistic prose that claims to see things as they are. Controversial opinions are presented as ex cathedra pronouncements, a style more familiar in Continental than in English criticism. Two examples from the essay on *Hamlet* give the flavor: "So far from being Shakespeare's masterpiece, the play is most certainly an artistic failure." "The only way of expressing emotion in the form of art is by finding 'an objective correlative.'"[73] Such statements brook no argument: "most certainly," "the only way." Though they may inspire opposition, they are memorable. Eliot masters the lapidary phrase, the formulaic sentence, the paradoxical judgment, as in this example from the essay on Massinger: "Immature poets imitate; mature poets steal."[74] The compression and judgmental confidence mimic Aristotle in defining the subject's quintessential nature. That the generalization defends literary allusion is not presented as bearing on Eliot's poetic practice, since the tone is so impersonal. The rules laid down are meant to have the status of scientific truth, like Pound's model of poetic experiment or Adams's historical "laws."

In professionalizing criticism, Eliot is also negotiating a truce with the academy. Although he gives up the role of Philosopher, he assumes that of Literary Critic. Between the journalists addressing the general reader and the academics writing monographs for specialists, he stakes out a middle ground. His essays translate the often arcane and ponderous language of research into trenchant and sweeping generalizations. Yet he honors the scholarly editor and biographer, the period specialist, and dismisses the amateur. The Massinger essay proclaims that "To understand Elizabethan drama it is necessary to study a dozen playwrights at once, to dissect with all care the complex growth, to ponder collaboration to the utmost line."[75] Such work coincides with university training. But this does not allow professors to move beyond their assigned domain. By setting such bounds, Eliot can police those who overstep them. Gilbert Murray, the hapless victim of his "Euripides and Professor Murray," may be "the most popular Hellenist of his time," but this does not make him a poet. The tired Swinburnian cadences of his Greek translations are lifeless. Real poets like Pound or H. D., Eliot says, can do this work, even if they sometimes translate inaccurately. But the Professor Murrays of the world have "simply interposed between Euripides and ourselves a barrier more impenetrable than the Greek language."[76]

This does not mean that there is to be a gulf between the academy and contemporary writing. Eliot's truce offers academics a role they will embrace. They are to be the middlemen between the difficult poetry of the present and the new reader it requires. Modernist literature is demanding; some help is needed. Scholars trained to elucidate classic texts can use these methods to analyze modernism. The hard work he asks of the audience creates such an opportunity for intervention. In his essay on Pound, for example, readers are put on the defensive. Those who dismiss the *Cantos* have failed: "We will leave it as a test: when anyone has studied Mr. Pound's poems in *chronological* order, and has mastered *Lustra* and *Cathay*, he is prepared for the *Cantos*—but not till then. If such a reader still does not like them, he has probably omitted some step in his progress, and had better go back and retrace the journey."[77] The aggressiveness is startling. But more remarkable than the tone is the fact that the strategy works. Eliot and his fellow modernists shift the burden of communication from sender to receiver. Readers' difficulties produce a new opening for academics. Here is the impetus for the New Criticism, the discipline of close reading. The university as a readerly training ground is redefined on terms much more favorable to the contemporary writer. In accepting those terms, the twentieth-century university critic institutes the new training and decisively reshapes modern interpretation. Reading is work. The reader is a student; the scholar serves as a go-between; the text is a mystery.[78]

This arrangement is welcomed by a new generation of literary commentators. Professional analysis of Eliot begins at once. Three major books dealing with his work appear while he is in his forties: Edmund

Wilson's *Axel's Castle* (1931), F. R. Leavis's *New Bearings in English Poetry* (1932), and F. O. Matthiessen's *The Achievement of T. S. Eliot* (1935). The attitude is quasi-reverent. Wilson, the least academic of the three, is nevertheless in awe of Eliot's critical influence. His compact essays "have not only had the effect of discrediting the academic clichés of the text-books, but are even by way of establishing in the minds of the generation now in college a new set of literary clichés."[79] Eliot's theory and practice create a dispensation no young poet can ignore. Leavis sees the *Prufrock* volume as "a complete break with the nineteenth-century tradition, and a new start." As a result, the new practitioners "are now using words very differently from the poets of the last age."[80] And Matthiessen, in his book-length study, treats Eliot's works as instant classics and becomes his systematizer and facilitator.

Critics are the poet's acolytes. Their task is not evaluation but patient analysis. This could not have come easily to these independent-minded young men, each destined to become highly influential, writing about a poet only about a decade older. But Eliot's career helps to advance theirs. Criticism of the new literature can be rescued from the journalist-reviewers and be professionalized. The relationship is symbiotic. Eliot's early break with the university is temporary, and the bridge is mended. This helps to make him the first modernist to achieve academic respectability. Pound, Woolf, Stevens, Joyce, Williams, Faulkner, Lawrence, Stein would all have to wait longer.

How could an outsider to the London literary world command such cultural authority so swiftly? Why does Eliot's radical reordering provoke so little successful opposition? Why is he gathered into the fold while Pound is ejected? The most comprehensive answer may be that for all his provocative ideas and methods he is not seen as a threat. He has a bedrock loyalty to what he calls Tradition, a less idiosyncratic concept than Pound's "The Tradition." It is spelled out in Eliot's most influential essay, "Tradition and the Individual Talent." This remarkably compressed statement of the relation between past and present is the document of record setting the terms of his pact with the academy with magisterial diplomacy.

Tradition, it turns out, is enabling, not crushing for the new artist. It is malleable, not rigidly in place; yet its authority is not challenged. The new writer imbued with tradition writes "not merely with his own

generation in his bones, but with a feeling that the whole of the literature of Europe from Homer and within it the whole of the literature of
his own country has a simultaneous existence and composes a simultaneous order."[81] There is no generational break. Past and present are
nested like Russian matrioshka dolls, with the European tradition
enfolding the national one, the national one sponsoring the work of
the present, new individual talents held by their generation.

Yet this comforting maternal embrace can also be stifling, and Eliot
allows for the creative disruption and reordering that any new birth
brings. In his carefully weighed, well-known formula, revolution
becomes evolution:

> The existing order is complete before the new work arrives; for order
> to persist after the supervention of novelty, the *whole* existing order
> must be, if ever so slightly, altered; and so the relations, proportions,
> values of each work of art toward the whole are readjusted; and this
> is conformity between the old and the new.[82]

This sentence offers a reassuring set of checks and balances. What one
phrase takes away, the next restores. In this accommodation, rival
claims surrender to ultimate concord; the shock of the new reconfig-
ures the landscape without making it unrecognizable. Vitality and stability coexist, within a process stressing order, conformity, and continuity rather than a paradigm shift.

The formula allows the "individual talent" an extraordinary power
to reshape tradition. But it also expects the inheritor to carry on the
line, which placates custodians outraged by the disruptive tone of less
accommodating spirits like Pound's. Equally encouraging is Eliot's use
of "we": "In English writing we seldom speak of tradition, though we
occasionally apply its name in deploring its absence."[83] So the brash
American is "one of us"! He makes no claims for his own culture and
has not come to bury ours. In such quiet rhetorical ways, Eliot convinces his audience that the modernist break is only a hairline fracture
and will heal. Nowhere in his criticism is this more subtly suggested
than in "Reflections on *Vers Libre*" (1917). Free verse alarmed conventional lovers of poetry because it threatened order, form, measure.
Eliot mocks both the radical young proclaiming liberation, and those

manning the dikes, by finding parallels between old and new. He juxtaposes unidentified passages from Hulme, Pound, and H. D. with ones from Arnold and Renaissance drama, showing continuities and concluding that "the division between Conservative Verse and *vers libre* does not exist, for there is only good verse, bad verse, and chaos."[84]

In this comforting formula, disruption is continuity; the foreign interlopers carry on English tradition; freedom is bounded. Eliot envisions a culture where good new work grows out of "the good Old, without the need for polemic and theory . . . a society with a living tradition."[85] By working for such a society, Eliot establishes a reputation as a trustworthy cultural arbiter. His defense of the new stresses tradition and containment. Even Joyce in *Ulysses*, that most disruptive of modernist texts, works for order and continuity. His use of the *Odyssey*, Eliot writes, is "simply a way of controlling, of ordering, of giving a shape and a significance to the immense panorama of futility and anarchy which is contemporary history."[86] These are words the survivors of the Great War, the anxious observers of the Russian Revolution, need to hear. Eliot's Tradition reassures perturbed spirits eager to believe that things do *not* fall apart, that the center *can* hold.

He chooses allies with care. Eliot's London ascent is carefully orchestrated and involves others' intervention and cooperation. They are strategically selected—English and American, younger and older, men and women, rebels and established voices. Although he arrives a virtual unknown, he has powerful connections and soon acquires others. Pound is indispensable, but so are those beyond Pound's reach. Bertrand Russell—Eliot's professor when he visited Harvard, and now his indefatigable sponsor in England—helps him find employment, lends him his flat, writes his parents, introduces him in exclusive circles where the titled and intellectual aristocracies meet. Lady Ottoline Morrell's London and Garsington salon, the Woolfs' Bloomsbury milieu, the Edith-Osbert-Sacheverell Sitwell triumvirate all welcome him. These doors were not open to Pound, who would in any case have scorned them.

Eliot's patrician background makes such alliances possible, as they were for Adams and James. As he puts it in a letter home two years after settling in London, his family is one "who represent to me absolutely the best that America can produce; and by right of whom I feel that I can claim equality with anybody." He contrasts his experience with Maxwell Bodenheim's, a young writer who finds that his (modest) American reputation cuts no ice in London. Eliot explains the difficulties to him and, he writes his mother, leaves him "to consider whether an American Jew, of only a common school education and no university degree, with no money, no connections, and no social polish or experience, could make a living in London. Of course I did not say all this; but I made him see that getting recognised in English letters is like breaking open a safe—for an American, and that only about three had ever done it."[87] Whoever these three were, Eliot is poised to join them.

His upper-class credentials secure an entry, then, but the opening must be patiently worked. It can be exhausting labor, and victory is not assured. His account of London social rituals makes them sound like engagements in a long campaign. Despite his confident use of "we" in his essays, in private letters the English are usually "they." "They are always intriguing and caballing," he writes his brother; "one must be very alert. . . . London is something one has to fight very hard in, in order to survive." In such an arena, "A dinner party demands more skill and exercises one's psychological gifts more than the best fencing match or duel."[88] His words suggest relish for a contest he may not win.

Eliot has the requisite gifts, but his large-scale ambition demands an unremitting vigilance. Literary London is a tight network of writers, editors, publishers, reviewers, and patrons. There are sets, factions, conflicts, alliances, opportunities, and tests. Crossing this minefield requires a mix of deference and assertiveness, since no mere sycophant will interest a world that asks to be astonished as well as mollified. Eliot learns to walk this tightrope confidently, and there are virtually no spills. But the effortlessness is only a theatrical illusion.

Making one's way is almost a full-time occupation. As the war ends, the literary world offers great opportunity, especially with so many bright young men gone. Eliot seizes his chance. He writes his mother after the armistice, predicting the birth of many periodicals and assuring her that "with my extended connections, and becoming more and more well known in London I could keep myself busy with contracts the whole time."[89] Eliot has learned the importance of conciliation and is unlikely to repeat Pound's mistakes. When Aiken returns to London after the war, he finds his old friend "so rootedly established, both socially and in the 'politics' (as it were) of literature, not to mention personally, as to have achieved what Emily Dickinson had called 'overtakelessness'."[90] In 1914 Aiken had introduced Eliot to Pound.[91] By 1920 Eliot is ready to dispense with him, writing Pound in Paris that "Conrad Aiken is here; stupider than I remember him; in fact, stupid."[92]

Not all his literary contacts could be discarded so brutally. The best example is his fruitful, long-term collaborative friendship with Leonard and Virginia Woolf. They will become intimate, and there is much more here than opportunism. Nevertheless, Eliot sees them first as possible publishers of his work; their Hogarth Press brings out the 1919 *Poems*, the English edition of *The Waste Land*, and his second critical book. There is logrolling on both sides. In October 1920, with his father-in-law in critical condition after surgery and his wife on the edge of collapse, he takes the time to remind Leonard of his promise to review *The Sacred Wood* in the *Athenaeum* and writes the editor to make sure the copy is sent. Leonard's notice duly appears and compares Eliot to Aristotle. Eliot later writes that he is forwarding one of Leonard's stories to Scofield Thayer at *The Dial*. This is the sort of thing Pound regularly did. But Pound probably would *not* have included a cover note calling the story disappointing and facilitating its rejection.[93]

The relationship with Virginia Woolf is more complex but no less tactically astute. Eliot admires her work and sponsors it vigorously. He praises *Jacob's Room*, her breakthrough novel, and publishes some of her most important essays in *The Criterion*.[94] Their increasingly intimate correspondence is a literary courtship, with the obligatory professions of admiration, self-deprecating airs, and wit. Yet it is also tactical because each knows that the other is intellectually powerful enough to make or break reputations: Woolf's inclusion of his name in her short list of important new writers in "Mr. Bennett and Mrs. Brown" does him no harm. As time passes, it becomes inevitable that one will be asked to write the other's obituary. In the event, it turns out to be Eliot's duty—and opportunity. He uses the occasion to demystify Bloomsbury and praise Woolf as "the centre not merely of an esoteric group, but of the literary life of London."[95] He must have realized as he wrote the words in 1941 that he was the natural heir to that office and that it had now passed to him. As he surveyed his triumph, only he could have known exactly how much it had cost him.

XII

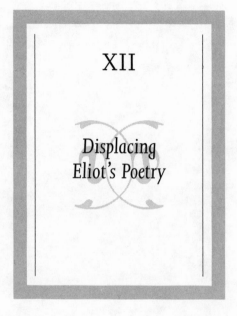

Displacing
Eliot's Poetry

And, now that life had so much human promise in it, they resolved to go back to their own land; because the years, after all, have a kind of emptiness, when we spend too many of them on a foreign shore. . . . Thus, between two countries, we have none at all, or only that little space of either, in which we finally lay down our discontented bones. It is wise, therefore, to come back betimes — or never.

Hawthorne, *The Marble Faun*

I

THE SOURCE of Eliot's authority lies in his poetry, of course. The right contacts, the commanding critical voice, the control of a major journal prove invaluable; but they are no substitute for poetic power. The remarkable fact about Eliot's early poetry is the immediacy of its impact. Only five years, 1917–1922, separate *Prufrock and Other Observations* from *The Waste Land*; yet it is enough. His fame is secured by his influence on the young and on his fellow poets. In 1922 Ottoline Morrell's sixteen-year-old daughter recites "Prufrock through by heart"; Virginia Woolf, a witness, asks Ottoline to testify to this feat, since Eliot refuses to believe her.[1] It is unlikely that she was coached. We have seen how the poem galvanized Pound at first sight. Louis Untermeyer, reviewing the 1920 *Poems*, notes that Eliot "threatened at the age of thirty-one to take on the proportions of a myth." He quotes passages of Eliot pastiche embarrassing in their naked indebtedness from the work of even younger poets.[2]

How does such a superficially unpretentious work have such an impact? The original *Prufrock* volume is an insignificant-looking bombshell. Its twelve poems, spread out over thirty-two pages, capitalize on Eliot's gift for making every word count. The selection, ordering, and grouping achieve a remarkable development and coherence. We move from the masterly portrait of Prufrock to the closely linked "Portrait of a Lady," to a group of squalid cityscapes that in effect puts to rest the geriatric tradition of late-Romantic pastoral, to four portrait-poems that satirize Boston/Cambridge—the particular city Eliot abandons, to three quasi-confessional poems that reveal the observer behind the observations.

It is the grimy urban scene that paradoxically looks so fresh in a genre that has for generations celebrated the vitality of the natural world. In *Prufrock and Other Observations*, "Nature" no longer deserves its capital letter. It is displaced by the city—not the humming, vital metropolis but a gutter scene of miasma and decay (familiar from Dickens's prose, but not considered elevated enough for English-language poetry). Yet elevation is fraud; we see at street level. A yellow fog lingers over "pools that stand in drains"; soot "falls from chimneys." The poems entitled "Preludes" might better be called "Postludes," with their "grimy scraps," "withered leaves," "broken blinds," "sawdust-trampled street," their "ancient women / Gathering fuel in vacant lots." This polluted world, an enormous urban graveyard, is peopled by face-less automatons: "all the hands / That are raising dingy shades / In a thousand furnished rooms."[3]

About the time Eliot writes these lines, Robert Bridges is appointed poet laureate. His 1912 collected edition is full of elevated poems that sound like this:

> There is a hill beside the silver Thames
> Shady with birch and beech and odorous pine:
> And brilliant underfoot with thousand gems
> Steeply the thickets to his flood decline.
> Straight trees in every place
> Their thick tops interlace,
> And pendant branches trail their foliage fine
> Upon his watery face.[4]

And so on for eight more decorative, decorous stanzas. No wonder that an audience of the young is ready for an entirely different vision of the Thames, and of the world around them. In *The Waste Land* the same river becomes a sour canal; the interlacing branches are stripped; "the river's tent is broken." Eliot has shrunken the Romantic plenum. His grimly unlovely picture of the cities in which people actually live opens their senses and makes them ask, How have we ignored *this*? And *why* isn't it a fit poetic subject?

The erasure of identifiable setting in many of Eliot's poems makes them recognizable to any urban audience. He deliberately eliminates specific locales in revision. Early drafts and suppressed poems are often geographically precise: "First Caprice in North Cambridge," "Fourth Caprice in Montparnasse," "Interlude in London." The published "Preludes" I and II were originally called "Prelude in Dorchester" and "Prelude in Roxbury."[5] But Eliot is trying to represent any industrial or commercial city. He has both a uniform vision of the metropolis and a melancholy temperament that finds desolation everywhere. Eliot's rootlessness makes this vision portable; that it is not simply the product of his temperament is shown by how well it travels.

The people in these poems are similarly unplaceable. With the significant exception of the Boston/Cambridge portraits, most of his characters remain anonymous. "The Portrait of a Lady" is generic, though its subject has been identified by Eliot's biographers. No detail of "The Love Song of J. Alfred Prufrock" locates its particular milieu. Despite his unforgettable name, Prufrock accurately sees himself as a type, "Deferential, glad to be of use, / Politic, cautious, and meticulous."[6] After Eliot moves to London, the characters turn into specimens: A Prufrock becomes "Gerontion," or Little Old Man; individuals melt into the anonymous "I" or "we" of "The Hollow Men." Names seem picked from some international registry: Mr. Silvero, Hakagawa, Madame de Tornquist, Fräulein von Kulp, De Bailhache, Fresca, Mrs. Cammel in "Gerontion"; Marie, Madame Sosostris, Mrs. Equitone, Mr. Eugenides, Phlebas, Albert, and Lil in *The Waste Land*.

Pound congratulates Eliot for achieving this "ubiquity of application" and sees it as a cosmopolitan sign: His "men in shirt-sleeves, and his society ladies, are not a local manifestation; they are the stuff of our modern world, and true of more countries than one."[7] Pound favorably contrasts this technique of simply "setting his 'personae' in modern life" with Robert Frost's "provincial studies, local, a bit dull."[8] From the expatriates' perspective, Frost's New England regionalism—despite his precise observation—is inferior to their own global reach. Stripping his characters and settings of local roots establishes Eliot as a transatlantic and European voice. His style offers a passe-partout to careful readers anywhere. It helps to make him a world figure.

But Eliot has another reason to expunge the identifiable elements of his early poems. Their buried subjects are often intensely personal, and like James he needs disguises to conceal this fact. Many of these poems offer unguarded sadomasochistic sexual fantasies and signs of an incurable emotional impotence. They are either left in manuscript or revised to become less confessional. Eliot turns "Prufrock" into a public poem both by making his protagonist middle-aged when he himself is young, and by cutting passages that pointedly identify the sexual hunger behind Prufrock's slumming.[9] He expunges the autobiographical from his poetry and distances himself from it. As he writes Aiken, "The thing is to be able to look at one's life as if it were somebody's else."[10] Reading poetry biographically seems to him futile in any case, since poets cover their tracks. He argues that it is impossible to lay bare the real story behind Shakespeare's sonnets, for instance: "This autobiography is written by a foreign man in a foreign tongue, which can never be translated."[11] Eliot's metaphor suggests how his expatriation serves to disguise his unguarded lyric impulse. It allows him to travel incognito.

The most striking example of turning local into universal and lyric into dramatic is *The Waste Land*. Its cacophony of voices and languages, its rapidly shifting settings and epochs destabilize the poem and mask its speaker. Eliot originally thought of calling it "He Do the Police in Different Voices."[12] But there is no easily identifiable "he" behind the voices. Eliot's misleading note, declaring that the briefly present Tiresias is "the most important personage in the poem, uniting all the rest,"[13] invents a central character where none exists. The grand claim of the chosen title encourages readers to treat it thematically, as an impersonal poem generally "about" sexual aridity, or an unnamed spiritual quest, or an exhausted postwar world. Its disruptive structure, in conflict with the readerly need to find order in apparent chaos, encourages us to superimpose the broadest interpretive schemes.

The strategy succeeds almost too well. Decades later Eliot complains that critics have turned his poem into a faceless public document, a "criticism of the contemporary world," which he insists was far from his intention: "To me it was only the relief of a personal and wholly insignificant grouse against life; it is just a piece of rhythmical grumbling."[14] This throwaway deflationary gesture is as unconvincing as the inflated rhetoric of the poem's windiest interpreters. The more we learn about Eliot's life, the clearer it becomes that *The Waste Land* is elegiac, rooted in the death of his friend Jean Verdenal in the war, the failure of his marriage, the spiritual hunger that had not yet found a belief, and the pain of uprooted solitude. There is evidence for each of these sources, despite Eliot's efforts to keep his private life private.[15]

Yet his determination to obscure the poem's autobiographical roots is not simply evasive. It also recognizes that the "insignificant grouse against life" is potentially significant and shared. The anxiety and despair so powerfully conveyed in *The Waste Land* are not his alone; nor is grief or a failed marriage or religious emptiness or loss of community an idiosyncratic experience. That so many readers over the century have grasped the poem's emotional core though they could not follow it line by line justifies Eliot's decision to abandon more stable methods and keep the poem anonymous, many-voiced, vagrant.

To achieve this effect he turns a potential liability—his uprootedness—into an opportunity. Having no fixed address lets him wander the globe in spirit and write for readers with a comparable sense of displacement. From the first moment, the poem asks for a multilingual, cosmopolitan audience. Its epigraph from Petronius, in both Latin and Greek, is followed by a tribute to Pound in Italian. Part I ("The Burial of the Dead") begins not with the locatable Boston narrative of the original draft, which Pound cuts, but with the very general "April is the cruellest month," followed by passages in German and French. It moves from Munich to an unidentified desert to some city where Madame Sosostris, "the wisest woman in Europe," plies her trade, to modern London, to ancient Mylae. The notes cite Jessie Weston and *The Golden Bough*, the Old Testament, *Tristan and Isolde*, Dante, Webster and Baudelaire, the cards in the tarot pack. All this demands a gypsy reader, ready to move at a moment's notice. The whole section stresses rootlessness: Marie leads a driftwood existence; Madame

Sosostris's vision of "crowds of people, walking round in a ring" blends with the anonymous crowd in the "Unreal City" section, combining modern London, Baudelaire's Paris, and Dante's Hell. It is a world of restless, homeless people. The apparently disconnected sections demand an alert audience willing to follow without reliable maps or the iron rails of narrative continuity. For such work the traveled reader is more prepared, the provincial one likely to feel lost.

The Waste Land might be seen as a poetic version of "Tradition and the Individual Talent" but is a far more bumpy departure from precedent than that reassuring essay offers. Its instability challenges the image of continuity Eliot's criticism proposes. The idea of Tradition suggests the handing down of a recognizable body of texts and customs from one generation to the next. It will respond to demands for change, but only gradually. Eliot's practice in The Waste Land is more disruptive. His sense of traditional materials is in many ways idiosyncratic, though less so than Pound's. For every allusion to the classic canon (the Bible or Antony and Cleopatra or The Divine Comedy, say), there is a reference to a text unfamiliar to most Western readers at the time: the Buddha's Fire Sermon, the Upanishads, Verlaine, Gerard de Nerval, obscure Renaissance plays, Australian ballads, works of contemporary history, ragtime pieces, and bits of local lore. An air of the jumble sale hangs over this heterodox mix. Rather than letting readers ease themselves into each of these worlds sequentially, Eliot jumps around, shifting registers, juxtaposing disparate traditions.

This is probably what the American poet John Crowe Ransom meant when, in his highly critical original review, he called The Waste Land "one of the most insubordinate poems in the language."[16] He is surely right. A poet of Eliot's generation should have subordinated "foreign" works to the native tradition, recent writing to the canon, popular to high culture. But he denies primacy to any of these dispensations. The vitality of the poem owes much to his refusal to honor the expected hierarchy. Crosscutting increases the instability, for example in the leap from Shakespeare's Tempest to a popular song:

> I remember
> Those are pearls that were his eyes.
> "Are you alive, or not? Is there nothing in your head?"

                                                                    But
O O O O that Shakespeherian Rag—
It's so elegant
So intelligent

Or the jump in the opposite direction, from the drunken farewells of
the characters in the pub scene, to Ophelia's last words:

Goonight Bill. Goonight Lou. Goonight May. Goonight.
Ta ta. Goonight. Goonight.
Good night, ladies, good night, sweet ladies, good night,
    good night.[17]

For Eliot the past is present and can be appropriated by an irreverent writer with the confidence to use whatever suits his purposes. *The
Waste Land* is an atemporal poem that sees the figures of tradition not
in a pantheon but as alive now, mingling with the urban crowd. The
juxtapositions of past and present, Western and Eastern, low and high
are fostered by Eliot's American insider/outsider mentality, which
encourages the poem's impurity. Each allusion is an ingredient in a
complex dish, and the recipe is his own. Such poetic insubordination
is much bolder than the guarded and respectful stance of his criticism.

His raid on the European storehouse is an antidote to what he calls
"the fatal American introspectiveness." The phrase comes from an
assessment of Aiken's work, which he sees as "oversensitive and wor-
ried"—the product of genteel isolation; as a cure he recommends
"contact with European civilisation."[18] The model is Pound's practice.
As Eliot describes it, "Mr. Pound proceeds by acquiring the entire past;
and when the entire past is acquired, the constituents fall into place
and the present is revealed."[19] The metaphor of acquisition is significant. Eliot frequently refers to his poems as assets and uses the language of investment.[20] Such methods recall James's connoisseurs bid-
ding at an international bazaar, like Adam Verver in *The Golden Bowl*
collecting masterpieces for his eclectic museum. Eclecticism is freedom: The lone accumulator not accountable to a venerable institution
can please himself. Although Eliot is writing a poem in the English
tradition, he feels free to interlard allusions to Greek, Latin, Hebrew,

French, Italian, German, and Indian texts. He continues the line but bends it to his will.

His appropriation of the anthropological and mythological syncretism of James Frazer and Jessie Weston proves useful. Each stresses echoes in seemingly unrelated cultures, and this encourages Eliot to practice a cosmopolitanism of the library.[21] In effect, global myths are trumps in the game he is playing. As Matthiessen saw, Eliot appropriates the anthropologists' conclusion "that surface differences between the customs and beliefs of mankind tend to mask profound resemblances."[22] The English, say, would not have considered distinctions between their culture and Italy's "surface differences." But to the confident American inheritor, the cultural capital of each country is simply currency to be used, exchanged, accumulated. And the capital in another sense is also fluid. London, the city in which Eliot settles, is very much present in the poem: The river is recognizably the Thames, streets and churches have London names, the pub is unmistakably British, the "Unreal City" is at first easily identified. But gradually the local gives way to the international, and by the last section London is merely the latest doomed metropolis:

> What is the city over the mountains
> Cracks and reforms and bursts in the violet air
> Falling towers
> Jerusalem Athens Alexandria
> Vienna London
> Unreal.[23]

The perspective is Olympian and synoptic—a god's-eye view.

There is a connection between the superior position such lines suggest and the changed political relations between Europe and America, a change Eliot capitalizes on. In his first year in England, he participates in a student debate on the resolution "that this society abhors the threatened Americanisation of Oxford." He teasingly supports the negative, argues that a depleted Britain needs American vitality, and is delighted when his side surprisingly wins.[24] He reports on President Wilson's postarmistice visit to England—the first by a sitting American president—and the excitement it produces in a nation grateful that the

United States finally joined the Allies. Wilson stays at Buckingham Palace; and *The Times* grandly concludes that his visit is "one of the greatest events in our own and in American history."[25] Eliot later publishes (and writes a preface for) Edgar Ansel Mowrer's *This American World*, a version of the Anglo-American reconciliation fantasy in which leadership passes to the United States. By associating themselves with America's Manifest Destiny, Mowrer promises, Britons "can prolong their period of empire by at least a century." He predicts that in this form "Euro-American civilization will conquer the earth."[26]

The conquest can also be literary. In London Eliot sees signs of an American cultural takeover. He meets H. D., "who like most, or a good half of the world of art and letters in London, is an American."[27] He celebrates this changing of the guard because it frees English poets from terminal Romanticism. He attributes Marianne Moore's mental independence to her American identity, which has "perhaps aided her to avoid the diet of nineteenth-century English poetry."[28] But he publishes these remarks under a pseudonym. We have seen that his most chauvinistic comments on this subject remained unpublished in his adopted country. He plays possum. But he is not reluctant to use the opportunities "the American century" opens up.

The Waste Land's global reach is an expression of that ambition, a literary manifestation of America's new imperial power. Its reception on both sides of the Atlantic records this cultural shift. F. R. Leavis in England praises Eliot for the renovation of poetic speech his entry into the insular scene allows. Leavis's *New Bearings in English Poetry*, despite its title, begins with an almost abject appeal to Americans: "There may, of course, especially in America, be important poets of whom I am ignorant: I hope that American readers will be placated by observing that two out of my three main subjects [Eliot and Pound] are American by birth."[29] This tone is new: Since when did English writers on such a subject need to placate Americans?

In the United States, Eliot wins the prestigious two-thousand-dollar *Dial* award for *The Waste Land*. The terms of the editors' praise link his achievement to the end of U.S. cultural provincialism: "He is one of the small number of Americans who can be judged by the standards of the past—including therein the body of Occidental literature.... There is nowhere in his work that 'localism' which at once takes so much of American writing out of the field of comparison with European letters."[30] Eight years before an American writer wins the Nobel Prize, Eliot had matched the international competition. This becomes the basis of his recognition in the United States, despite his defection. In 1945, as the war that decisively establishes America's primacy over Europe ends, Delmore Schwartz writes a celebratory essay in the *Partisan Review*. He treats Eliot as an international hero—a Jamesian "heir of all the ages," a conquistador of the Old World: "The reader of T. S. Eliot by turning the dials of his radio can hear the capitals of the world, London, Vienna, Athens, Alexandria, Jerusalem." In this reference to the poem's capsule history of falling cities, all cultures have become American satellites. In Schwartz's chauvinistic view, "Only an American with a mind and sensibility which is cosmopolitan and expatriated could have seen Europe as it is seen in *The Waste Land*. . . . We have become an international people, and hence an international hero is possible."[31] Even Theodore Roosevelt might have forgiven an expatriated American embarked on such a grand mission.

There is, however, a hidden cost to Eliot's triumph. His own country's culture is not incorporated into this poem. Ironically, *The Waste Land* erases the United States from the map. With the single exception of the Ziegfeld Follies' "Shakespeherian Rag," itself of course an allusion to an English writer, no American text, author, place name, historical character, or event is included in this feast of languages. In a poem as wide-ranging as *The Waste Land*, this is a conspicuous absence. Although two long passages in the original draft are about Americans—the Boston "boys' night out" that opens the poem and the long narrative that precedes what is now the brief "Death by Water"—both are scrapped. A version of English that originally included popular American speech— "Tease, Squeeze lovin & wooin / Say Kid what're y' doin'"[32]—is now written in a vocabulary more familiar to English than American readers: *demobbed, bring it off, gammon, city directors, solicitor.*

Apparently the way for an American to appropriate the European legacy is to pull up his roots. Eliot goes to great pains to *pass*. Williams had called him a "subtle conformist" before *The Waste Land* even appeared,[33] and much later he pronounced the poem's publication a disaster for himself and for American culture: "It wiped out our world as if an atom bomb had been dropped upon it." He claims the poem set his career back twenty years because it made any art "rooted in the locality which should give it fruit" seem less legitimate and because it abandoned "the western dialect" for the King's English.[34] But for Eliot it is precisely the American locale and idiom that don't travel. Not only does he eliminate virtually all American allusions in his poetry between 1917 and the mid-1930s (though Emerson appears briefly in "Sweeney Erect"); his choices as editor of the *Criterion* and at Faber minimize American contributions to modernism. The language is the first casualty. Unlike Pound, he self-consciously distances himself from American idioms, even in conversation and in his correspondence. So a letter to Scofield Thayer proclaims, "I shall receive you with great pleasure in the autumn, or as you say, in the fall!"[35] And he advises Joyce, who in *Ulysses* is trying to mimic an American revivalist preacher, about the national provenance of "ring up" and "call up," "trunk line" and "long distance."[36]

There is a moment in Eliot's career, as in James's, when he considers settling in Paris and writing in French; and some of the French poems appear in his collections. But he quickly understands that he cannot write in two languages. His later reflections on this experiment also illuminate his choice of *English* English over what H. L. Mencken called the American language: "I don't think that one can be a bilingual poet. . . . I think that one language must be the one you express yourself in in poetry, and you've got to give up the other for that purpose."[37] There is no doubt which English he chooses. He argues against Mencken's celebration of American linguistic independence and insists (more than twenty years after James had pushed this argument in "The Question of Our Speech") that "America is not likely to develop a new language until its civilization becomes much more complicated and more refined than that of Britain; and there are no indications that this will ever happen." In the meantime, appealing American neologisms "can be usefully digested by the parent language."[38] Like James, he calms British anxieties, disregards the erosion of Anglo-Saxon primacy in America, ignores the fact that linguistic invention has little to do with refinement and that children eventually displace parents.

Simultaneously, Eliot masters idiomatic English for his own work. His marriage to Vivien Haigh-Wood not only assures his expatriation but provides a linguistic cicerone. She translates some of his clumsiest attempts at English demotic speech in *The Waste Land* into vigorous vernacular: her "'It's them pills I took, to bring it off'" replaces Eliot's stilted "'It's that medicine I took, in order to bring it off'"; his lame "'You want to keep him at home, I suppose'" becomes Vivien's "What you get married for if you dont want to have children."[39] Though Eliot's Anglophile roots make the upper-class idiom easy, he is out of touch with the common tongue. But once he picks it up he uses it, even if it excludes Americans. The reference to Guy Fawkes Day in "The Hollow Men"—"*A penny for the Old Guy*"—is clear to every man, woman, and child in Britain but requires explanation for Americans. And in the American edition of his early poems, he footnotes a reference to the A. B. C. in "A Cooking Egg": "*i. e.*, an endemic teashop, found in all parts of London. The initials signify: Aerated Bread Company, Limited."[40]

No comparable explanations of American references are offered for British readers because so few appear in his work. By the late 1920s, his new poems are published only in English editions.[41] Nor does he try to stretch the limits of their knowledge. As his firm publishes Pound's Adams Cantos, he warns his fellow poet that British readers will not understand his American allusions; they barely know who Jefferson was and can't be expected to tell one President Adams from another. As for Charles Francis Adams, Lincoln's ambassador to Britain and Henry's father, not one British reader in ten thousand will know of his existence.[42] Eliot lets even this illustrious American family, though it is linked to his own, remain unknown.

He has crossed over and makes every effort to blend in. Lyndall Gordon's description of his manner and appearance summarizes the bemused impressions of many Britons who encountered him in the interwar years: "As Eliot shed his American youth, he cultivated the front of an English gentleman. . . . He surrounded himself with the props of respectability: the correct City uniform, the dark suit and spats, the rolled umbrella, the deferential attentiveness, the voice so measured as to sound almost dead-pan."[43] Virginia Woolf announces that he is coming to lunch in his four-piece suit. This is camouflage. By assuming the disguise of an English gentleman, he can conceal the American takeover actually occurring.

He uses *The Criterion* in the same way. Since Eliot is its sole editor from first to last, soliciting and selecting all contributions, his disappearing act is clearly calculated. In the first four years, he is nowhere even identified as the editor. The early issues contain *no* manifesto or statement of editorial policy beyond a blandly uncombative three-paragraph note, "The Function of a Literary Review," signed T. S. E.⁴⁴ The contrast with the heated controversies surrounding contemporaneous artistic movements like surrealism, futurism, and others is striking. Eliot is playing a deep game. Behind the cover of anonymity and propriety (the lead essay in the first issue, "Dullness," is by the venerable English critic George Saintsbury, born 1845), behind the serious, judicious tone, Eliot challenges English parochialism. The first issues include *The Waste Land*, a groundbreaking study of *Ulysses*, essays on contemporary German poetry and Spanish literature, on Flaubert, Mallarmé, Balzac, Freud, as well as works by Yeats, Pound, Woolf, Forster, and May Sinclair. This becomes the pattern: respectable English criticism, cultural reports from European capitals, new writing by "les jeunes" surreptitiously folded in. Eliot uses *The Criterion* to publish important work by his fellow expatriates and British contemporaries, and to introduce major voices from the Continent—Hesse, Valéry, Pirandello, Hofmannsthal, Hauptmann, Cavafy, Proust, Croce, Cocteau, Bunin, Maritain, Capek, Mann.

The record of American writers remains close to blank, as in *The Waste Land*. A few of the non-Europeanized ones (Hart Crane, Marianne Moore) find a minor place, a "New York Chronicle" occasionally appears, and works like *The Great Gatsby* are favorably reviewed. But *The Criterion* is never an Anglo-American journal, and it ignores most of Eliot's contemporaries working in the United States—Cather, Faulkner, Frost, Stevens, Williams, and other luminaries. Apparently Americans can become Europeans only if they sever their ties to *any* nation. Although Eliot becomes a British subject in 1927, he does not use *The Criterion* to advance the cause of English letters either. Its carefully chosen title (like Pound's "The Tradition") suggests a universal standard of judgment. When he is awarded the Nobel Prize, his acceptance speech makes no mention of the land of his birth, unlike Sinclair Lewis, the first American laureate, who proudly announces that the United States is producing "a literature worthy of her vastness," or Eugene O'Neill, who sees the award as "the recognition by

Europe of the coming-of-age of the American theatre." Nor does Eliot speak as a Briton. He concludes that when a poet wins the Nobel Prize, it is "primarily an assertion of the supra-national value of poetry."[45] This dubious claim is advanced by insisting that a poet's country doesn't matter.

II

Is SUCH cosmopolitanism a viable identity? Are national loyalties archaic? Eliot certainly thinks so at first. One of his (and James's) earliest models is Turgenev, born in Russia, settled in Paris, committed to pan-Europeanism. Eliot praises him as "a perfect example of the benefits of transplantation; there was nothing lost by it; he understood at once how to take Paris, how to make use of it." Turgenev adopts the role of professional foreigner, which allows him to reach a Russian or European audience because he is free of the standards of either. No environment produces him; he is self-defined: "He has a position which he literally made for himself, and indeed almost may be said to have invented."[46] In Turgenev, Eliot sees the kind of writer he wants to become, one who will "take" London as Turgenev takes and uses Paris.

The increasing internationalism of his poems bypasses national standards. Their identifying labels disappear. The named or unnamed cities in the early poems give way to symbolic landscapes not found on any map. And historical time disappears. The references to the war in *The Waste Land*, the trams and cigarette ends and taxis and soda water, reminders of the present, are gone. The mysterious dream kingdoms, deserts, and valleys of "The Hollow Men" are the products of an unmoored imagination. Unlike the poet in *A Midsummer Night's Dream*, who "gives to airy nothing / A local habitation and a name," Eliot does not specify. The creator of *Ash-Wednesday* dismisses the importance of actual time and place:

> Because I know that time is always time
> And place is always and only place
> And what is actual is actual only for one time
> And only for one place.[47]

The speakers of these poems, unlike the earlier named characters, are unidentifiable. The features of the face, shape of the body, patterns of speech, accent, or gesture are erased. Only the "universal" remains.

If this is what cosmopolitanism costs, the price may be too high. There are signs that Eliot needs to belong to a more local supportive community. As early as 1921 he contemplates becoming a British subject.[48] And his urgent religious search moves him from his inherited Unitarianism to the Church of England. This allows him to root a general Christian faith in a particular national institution. He adopts (or is adopted by) his new nation and church at the end of 1927. The notorious announcement of his changed loyalties, in the Preface to *For Lancelot Andrewes* (1928), seems designed to alienate American readers. He describes himself as "classicist in literature, royalist in politics, and anglo-catholic in religion," an act of self-labeling deliberately designed "to refute any accusation of playing 'possum."[49]

The provocative words redefine his expatriation and root him in British soil. For an American to call himself "royalist in politics" writes off the Declaration of Independence. And the term "anglo-catholic" is not reassuring to Protestant ears. Eliot transplants himself, and his countrymen are predictably angry. *Time* magazine sarcastically informs its readers that "a certain superciliousness in his attitude toward U. S. letters caused him to feel more at home in England, where neo-literary figures abound profuse as the autumn leaves."[50] When Eliot returns for a visit, he even needs to assure a *Boston Evening Transcript* reporter "that his royalism was not designed to overthrow the Constitution of the United States."[51]

The uneasiness about where he belongs has a tragicomic air. Changing his citizenship is not decisive. As his countrymen express dismay over his defection, the English remain mistrustful. Eliot predicted when he first arrived, "I don't think that I should ever feel at home in England." The elaborate makeover, from the English idioms to the spats and rolled umbrella, fails to convince the natives. Eliot's cultural displacement is painfully articulated in a letter to his brother: "It is damned hard work to live with a foreign nation and work with them—one is always coming up with differences of feeling that make one feel humiliated and lonely. . . . It is like being always on dress parade—one can never relax."[52] No matter how intimate he becomes with British writers, they think of him simply as "the American." Louis

MacNeice patronizes both Eliot and Pound as "first and foremost American tourists."[53] On this issue Virginia Woolf finds herself agreeing with H. G. Wells, for whom she otherwise has little use. She records that they discuss James and Eliot, note "how formal they are & overdone with manner," and conclude "it was American. They were alien to our civilisation."[54] As late as 1934, Faber letterhead has the notation "(U. S. A. origin)" after Eliot's name, though he is a director of the firm.[55] He cannot escape the tag.

Eliot has a different label for himself. He writes to an English friend, "Remember that I am a *metic*—a foreigner."[56] Metics were a special group of permanent residents in Greek city-states, not granted the full rights and responsibilities of citizenship, accorded certain privileges but also circumscribed in what they could do, respected yet segregated—in short, inalienable aliens. By seeing himself in such terms, Eliot acknowledges a permanent estrangement from any country while accepting the terms of the bargain. He is in it but not of it, not after all "one of us."

This feeling lingers long after he becomes British. Despite his conquest of literary London, his marriage to an Englishwoman, his naturalization, his embrace of the state religion, his estrangement persists. It cannot have surprised him; remarkably, he anticipates the effects of a chosen exile in a poem written before he was seventeen for his Smith Academy commencement. He already foresees his fate:

> As colonists embarking from the strand
> To seek their fortunes on some foreign shore
> Well know they lose what time shall not restore,
> And when they leave they fully understand
> That though again they see their fatherland
> They there shall be as citizens no more.[57]

Giving up his American identity proves to be much harder than anticipated. Not only will his hosts not let him forget it but it is deeply embedded. From his earliest years, his family instilled pride in its American heritage. His most vivid memories are of summers in their Cape Ann house, which makes him feel he is a New England poet. His connections to the region and its colonial legacy are primary, even though his branch has moved to St. Louis. As a founding member, and later president, of the Missouri chapter of the Colonial Dames, his mother sends Eliot copies of her writings for that organization.[58] As we have seen, such bodies were founded in the 1890s to honor the country's earliest settlers.

The paternal legacy is even more powerful. His prominent grandfather, the Unitarian minister William Greenleaf Eliot, arrived in St. Louis in 1834 and soon became a force in many endeavors, a founder (and later chancellor) of Washington University. Throughout his life he represented what his grandson calls the "law of Public Service."[59] Eliot's family tradition, like Adams's, stresses social usefulness and civic loyalty. Its members run institutions—cultural bodies, government agencies, schools, churches, welfare organizations. Eliot's break with Harvard and his country, his marriage to a complete outsider, his choice of an unreliable (and self-indulgent) profession are betrayals of this legacy. His father refuses to visit him and writes his daughter-in-law out of his will, should she survive Eliot.[60] The two are never reconciled, but this does not mean the paternal values can be extirpated. The young rebel does, after all, become "The Dean of English criticism," and his associations with a major bank, a prestigious publisher, and an authoritative journal are versions of family tradition.

Despite his troubled relationship with his parents, Eliot is proud of his heritage and makes certain the memorabilia are preserved after his father's death. He asks for "a copy, illuminated, of the Eliot arms." Its motto—"*tacuit et fecit*"—appears on the dedication page of *The Sacred Wood* and throws light on Eliot's verbal parsimony. When his mother asks what he wants saved, he lists "documents of New England civilization," the sermons of Andrew Eliot, family antiquities and genealogies, links to Emerson and his circle. Despite his alienation, he foresees a later phase: "I have an idea that such of these things as you could save would be of use to me eventually."[61] In editing Pound's essays, he corrects a mistaken notion that the Salem witches were burned: "We didn't burn them. We hanged them."[62] "We," says this descendant of one of the judges.

His return is a long way off, but it finally comes. Eliot does not visit the United States between his brief trip in 1915 and 1932. In the decades of his absence he firmly establishes himself in London, and his central place in British culture is assured. But the *source* is drying up. He writes little poetry in the decade after *The Waste Land*. "The

Hollow Men," *Ash-Wednesday*, and the Ariel Poems take up less than twenty pages of his *Complete Poems and Plays*. The second flowering that produces *Murder in the Cathedral*, *The Family Reunion*, and the *Four Quartets* follows the year he spends in his native land, renewing contact with what James in his return had called "*les miens.*"

That his American roots are not so easily pulled up is evident in his frantic appeal to his mother to visit him after his father's death. He has not seen his family in five years; his marriage is foundering; his demanding position at Lloyds Bank gives him only a few weeks off. But his mother is free, solvent, and in good health. If she comes to London, they can see each other for months. She finally arrives, with two of her other children. The Eliots turn their flat over to the family for the summer of 1921. His desperate need to see them again is suggested in a letter to his mother before the visit: "I only repeat that if you cannot come, if I can never again see you for more than ten days or two weeks, that I shall never be happy."[63]

This is an extraordinary threat for a married man in his thirties to deliver to his mother. But the troubled marriage is a major part of the problem. That it has not given Eliot a home is evident from letters that follow the visit. He writes his mother that their flat "seems to belong to you now and is very strange and desolate without you in it." As she comments to her other son, "I am surprised at Tom saying that when we were in the flat it had a cosiness which it misses now. I think the poor boy misses the affection that makes no demands from him, but longs to help him." The home as a haven, the family as unconditional sponsor become essential when the surrounding world seems unwelcoming. Eliot misses not only his family but a known and supportive community—the feeling of *belonging*. His improvised London life, and the stranger he marries "simply because I wanted to burn my boats and commit myself to staying in England,"[64] cannot answer the need.

His 1932–33 return to America coincides with his decision to leave Vivien for good. We do not yet have the materials to reconstruct this phase of his life. The letters of the period remain unpublished, and the most important—the thousand or so to Emily Hale, the intimate American friend with whom he renews contact—are sealed until the year 2019.[65] Yet there is no doubt that Eliot increasingly acknowledges the formative quality of his American experience. Even before his visit he tells an American journalist, "I find that as one gets on in middle life the strength of early associations and the intensity of early impressions becomes more evident; and many little things, long forgotten, recur."[66]

Those memories are associated with water—the sea off Cape Ann, the Mississippi at St. Louis. "I feel that there is something in having passed one's childhood beside the big river," Eliot writes, "which is incommunicable to those who have not."[67] Some of his most charged poetic passages, written shortly before and long after his return, are steeped in these recollections, recognizable even if not named. At the climax of *Ash-Wednesday*, there is a flash through "the wide window towards the granite shore" of white sails flying seaward, at which "the lost heart stiffens and rejoices." The speaker of "Marina" remembers a sailboat built long ago, now decaying, calling to him: "The garboard strake leaks, the seams need caulking." After his return, he publishes a series of vivid American landscape poems: "New Hampshire," "Virginia," "Cape Ann." Finally, in "The Dry Salvages" (1941), the third of the *Quartets*, he fuses the revisited river and seascapes with a Proustian recall of his childhood home in verse of great lyric power:

> His rhythm was present in the nursery bedroom,
> In the rank ailanthus of the April dooryard,
> In the smell of grapes on the autumn table,
> And the evening circle in the winter gaslight.

> The river is within us, the sea is all about us.[68]

These recaptured memories take Eliot back to his earliest years, when the landscape was not external but part of himself. The recuperation is associated with loss, like James late in life homesick for New England summers, wide verandahs, peaches and cream, "white frocks and Atlantic airs." The recall is teasing, elusive, momentary, surrounded by long arid stretches; but that only heightens its power. In the words of "Burnt Norton," "Ridiculous the waste sad time / Stretching before and after."[69] Such links between local memory and lyric force ask Eliot to reconsider his cosmopolitanism and reclaim his American identity.

In critical essays and interviews of the 1950s, he associates himself with an American literary tradition he had ignored. He writes an introduction to *Huckleberry Finn* in which he abashedly confesses to just discovering Twain's classic. That preface, full of lavish praise, is also personal. He bears witness to the accuracy of Twain's vision of the ungovernable Mississippi: "In my own childhood, it was not unusual for the spring freshet to interrupt railway travel. . . . The river is never wholly chartable; it changes its pace, it shifts its channel, unaccountably." He claims a place for Twain among the greatest writers—Joyce, Goethe, Cervantes, Shakespeare—and pronounces the book's colloquial style "an innovation, a new discovery in the English language." Twain's is a bolder linguistic experiment than the more contained use of dialect by Dickens, Scott, and Thackeray.[70] The American writer here is the forerunner, his language not subject to an English imprimatur.

Eliot links himself with an American literature different from the enervated New England line. "American Literature and the American Language," the revisionist lecture he delivers in 1953 at Washington University, argues that there *are* after all "two literatures in the same language," and that the American tradition contains three landmarks "not found in New England": Poe, Whitman, and Twain. Like the much younger Pound proposing a reconciliation with Whitman in "A Pact" ("We have one sap and one root— / Let there be commerce between us."), Eliot belatedly claims kinship. He also concedes that the American language *is* a separate tongue and that "at present the current of language flows from west to east." And finally, he grants that "the pioneers of twentieth-century poetry were more conspicuously the Americans than the English, both in number and in quality." He mentions Pound, Williams, Stevens, Moore, Cummings, Crane, Ransom, Tate; and of course he tacitly adds his own name. Though he does not define the differences, he insists that the lineages are separate.[71]

In a late 1950s interview, Eliot pushes the argument further, claiming that "my poetry has obviously more in common with my distinguished contemporaries in America than with anything in my generation in England." He concedes that his expatriation has allowed him to draw on both traditions but concludes that "in its sources, in its emotional springs, it comes from America."[72] It is not clear how to interpret these remarks: as a genuine if belated self-recognition? as an opportunistic way to placate the audience to whom cultural power has now passed? as a simplification of tangled loyalties that have become insupportable? Much recent criticism sees Eliot as essentially—and willy-nilly—an American writer.[73] But that is not how he originally defined himself. Eliot's late attempt to rejoin the American family departs from his early cosmopolitan ideal. He gradually concludes that the cost-free transplantation he claimed for Turgenev is a myth. Writers (particularly poets) *cannot* give up their native country, with its links to childhood, familial bonds, the discovery of language and the world, without enfeebling the current of their art.

Despite Eliot's estrangement from America and eagerness to leave, he finds no adequate substitute in the improvised life he constructs abroad. Its incoherent, makeshift quality is anatomized in some of his early expatriate poems. "Gerontion"'s setting is one of national displacement and fragmentation, a world of neurotics who pace the room at night, substitute aesthetic for human experience, "stiffen in a rented house." Solitary, adrift, without a common culture, these isolates are "whirled / Beyond the circuit of the shuddering Bear / In fractured atoms."[74] Such poems do not present Eliot as the confident heir of the tradition. The lightly disguised confessions of the French poems— "Lune de miel," "Dans le restaurant," and especially "Mélange adultère de tout"—reveal a figure whose cosmopolitanism is a ragbag of unstable identities: professor, journalist, banker, philosopher, brain for hire, drifting from America to England to the Continent, from Damascus to Omaha to Mozambique. That the poems are in French exposes Eliot's inability to voice his feelings in his own tongue.

What he surrenders in the early expatriate poems is the lyric "I." Eliot's ideal of impersonality, his major contribution to modernist literary theory, has unacknowledged personal roots. He turns his need to eradicate himself, to become unlocatable, into a general ideal of objectivity, most powerfully articulated in "Tradition and the Individual Talent" and the essay on *Hamlet*. The passages have achieved such authority that they can hardly be read as the completely unsupported dogma they are, like responses in a catechism: "The progress of an artist is a continual self-sacrifice, a continual extinction of personality." "The more perfect the artist, the more completely separate in him will be the man who suffers and the mind which creates." "Poetry is not a turning loose of emotion, but an escape from emotion; it is not an expression of personality, but an escape from personality."[75] These pronouncements claim universal authority but are by no means self-evident. Counterexamples are ignored, though many easily come to mind. But of course someone who writes off *Hamlet* and Shakespeare's sonnets as failures is likely to be speaking out of private need. And Eliot even suggests this by noting that "only those who have personality and emotions know what it means to want to escape from these things."[76]

Impersonality becomes the standard by which he evaluates all literary work. The more subjective Romantic poets are expunged from the canon. His self-revealing early poems are suppressed. The title *Prufrock and Other Observations* stresses clinical detachment. Eliot says about his taste, "I like to feel that a writer is perfectly cool and detached, regarding other people's feelings or his own, like a God who has got beyond them."[77] There is something willed in this aesthetic, as though he needs to deny a literary standard that might disempower him. He cannot afford to give himself away.

The fear of confession also troubles his dramatized characters. Prufrock's love song is not voiced, is addressed to an unidentified "you," and encounters only indifference. The poem's Italian epigraph is spoken by a character in *The Inferno* who reveals himself to Dante only because he is sure no one ever returns from hell to expose its secrets. The male character in "Portrait of a Lady" remains pointedly silent while the Lady does all the talking. And the pervasive use of myth and allusion, of dramatized characters and dramatic monologue, all disguise the lyric impulse.

This fear of subjectivity has links to Eliot's abandoned dissertation, *Knowledge and Experience in the Philosophy of F. H. Bradley*. It is not only that philosophy and poetry are divergent career paths but that Bradley denies the possibility of knowing anything objectively. Eliot's account of Bradley on this topic suggests how disturbing he finds the absence of common knowledge: "The world, as we have seen, exists only as it is found in the experiences of finite centres, experiences so mad and strange that they will be boiled away before you boil them down to one homogeneous mass." And this leads to Bradley's troubling conclusion that "All significant truths are private truths. As they become public they cease to become truths."[78]

Here is an epistemological barrier Eliot finds difficult to accept and will not celebrate, unlike many of his fellow modernists. It echoes disturbingly the solitude his expatriation has thrust upon him. He does not want to be told that his vision is idiosyncratic. He needs to feel a sense of shared purpose and perception. If every spectator sees differently, inhabiting a parish of one, what hope is there for the central authority Eliot (and Pound) seek in the metropolis? He has to find a way around the perspectival limitations of his limited experience and local identity. And so he invents a theory of poetry as an escape from personality and transforms himself for a time into what Hugh Kenner has called "The Invisible Poet."

Invisibility makes it possible to see without being seen. It purchases spectatorial power at the cost of self-erasure. That Eliot is not finally willing to pay the price is suggested by his recovery of the lyric "I" in the *Four Quartets* (1935–42). The speaker of these poems is not a figure in a dramatic monologue or a generic character. He is closely linked to the poet himself, humbled by age and the sense of lost chances, dismayed by failing to find the right words:

> So here I am, in the middle way, having had twenty years—
> Twenty years largely wasted, the years of *l'entre deux guerres*—
> Trying to learn to use words, and every attempt
> Is a wholly new start, and a different kind of failure.[79]

Nor is he unplaceable. Each Quartet is named after a locale in England or America that has personal meaning for Eliot—"Burnt Norton" where he and Emily Hale are reunited in England, "East Coker" from which Andrew Eliot set out for the New World, the rocks off Cape Ann called "the Dry Salvages" round which he used to sail, the spiritual retreat at "Little Gidding" he has come to long for. And the poems themselves, though often abstract, also describe particular times and places—the London underground, the Mississippi, the New England seashore, the air raids over Britain. These regional, personal, and temporal elements are not subjective limitations but open out to generic human concerns. "Home is where one starts from," Eliot now acknowledges.[80]

This partial recovery of the transplanted American individual behind the featureless mask of the cosmopolite echoes the late journeys back in time of the other improvised Europeans whose careers we have traced: Adams's saturated recall of his earliest years in the *Educa-*

tion, James's massive reconstruction of his childhood and youth in his autobiography, Pound's chaotic jumble of memories stretching from Coney Island through London and Paris and Rome to the cage where he writes "The Pisan Cantos," "As a lone ant from a broken ant-hill / from the wreckage of Europe, ego scriptor."[81]

Such journeys back suggest breaks rather than continuities. They echo the fate of most pioneers: the loss of home and community, the absence of models, the need to reinvent oneself. The strains show in all these careers: in Adams's inability to sit still, the estrangement that makes him write about himself as "he"; in James's lost audience, his sense of isolation and missed opportunities; in Pound's expulsion from London and his blind, unwitting treason; in Eliot's long self-betrayal as the perfect Englishman, a figure even he finds absurd:

> How unpleasant to meet Mr. Eliot!
> With his features of clerical cut,
> And his brow so grim
> And his mouth so prim
> And his conversation, so nicely
> Restricted to What Precisely
> And If and Perhaps and But.[82]

This kind of pitiless self-inspection is the product of a lifetime spent preparing "a face to meet the faces that you meet." The triumphs come. The massive *oeuvre* stands as a monument to a dedication to the highest artistic standards. The final acclaim is not merely local. But the "international hero" who has accomplished all this stands outside the circle of his reputation and tries to recall what it has to do with himself or the smaller world that fostered him. To become the cosmopolitan writers they aspired to be, all these "improvised Europeans" had for a time to forget their origins. Their prolonged amnesia is all the more striking when one remembers from what powerful families Adams, James, and Eliot come, and how quintessentially American Pound, for all his multilingual virtuosity, actually is. Their late recovery of the distant past becomes a necessary act of self-possession.

But it is not only the expatriated writers who require reparation. So does the world they left behind, and some of the late works they write are communal as well as personal gestures. James's *The American Scene* is a major document of social history. Eliot's attempt to reground himself as an American writer is an apology for his earlier dismissiveness. As Williams angrily sums up the effect of Eliot's desertion, "By his walking out on us we were stopped, for the moment, cold. . . . If he had not turned away from the direct attack here, in the western dialect, we might have gone ahead much faster."[83] His defection left a vital cultural task to lesser talents.

Eliot understands early—as do all the writers in this cohort—that such a charge might be leveled against him. He is willing to take the consequences. At the age of twenty, he writes a precocious review in the Harvard *Advocate* of Van Wyck Brooks's *The Wine of the Puritans*. Brooks speaks for a whole class of Americans—the disaffected group who remain in the country out of need or duty but who long to escape because "their hearts are always in Europe," Eliot says. "To these, double-dealers with themselves, people of divided allegiance except in times of emotional crisis, Mr. Brooks' treatise will come as a definition of their discontent." Even this early, Eliot understands the source of his uneasiness, and that of his kind. Altho*ugh duty does not keep him at home, he will not escape the sense of double-dealing. His largest ambitions are realized; he proves that an American poet can achieve international recognition. But in his review he also pointedly quotes a passage from Brooks's book that outlines a different task to which Eliot will contribute little. "I think a day will come," Brooks writes, "when the names of Denver and Sioux City will have a traditional and antique dignity like Damascus and Perugia— and when it will not seem grotesque to us that it is so."[84]

That moment is not yet here. But that some American cities embody the dignity of tradition and others are as vital as any place on earth no longer seems grotesque. The changed perspective owes a great deal to writers who were willing to think locally—Wharton, who accepted James's passionate command to *"Do New York!"*; Faulkner, who created a cosmos out of an imaginary rural county with a barely pronounceable name; Frost, who came home to New England after making a name for himself in London; Williams, who chose Paterson, New Jersey, as the site for an epic poem; and many others. In all these cases, the focus on region was no barrier to a larger vision. It is fortunate for America's cultural independence that not all the talented writers of the turn of the century severed their local ties, and that still others paid close attention to initially alien groups who threatened the Anglo-Saxons' authority, the "undigested lumps of foreign races," the "aborigines of every complexion and climate," as Eliot had once contemptuously described them.

These choices characterized a moment in the country's history when antithetical opportunities opened up. A weakened Europe was ripe for American cultural conquest. A rapidly changing but not yet imaginatively realized United States called out for local bards and fresh observers. The country had become a world power before it was fully formed: It showed all the confusion and uncontrolled growth of the awkward age. The times encouraged the rival parties to lengthen the space between them. Some left for good; others arrived; still others burrowed in. The decisions seemed final, the breaks irreparable. Yet the options only expressed the opportunities of the moment; each route has finally proven essential to making American literature of interest within and beyond its borders. It was like a war that had to be fought simultaneously on several fronts. Sidney Smith's dismissive words of 1820 — "In the four quarters of the globe, who reads an American book?" — still rankled a century after they were written. A generation later, they had finally lost their sting. That American literature has achieved international as well as national prominence owes more than a little to those who left as well as those who arrived or returned or stayed. For all their confused lives, mixed motives, and double-dealing, the improvised Europeans extended the reach of American literature in ways essential to achieving the nation's long-delayed cultural authority.

Acknowledgments

R esearch and writing can be lonely work; but my labor on this book has been shared and shaped by others, and I am happy to acknowledge their generosity.

My most important debts are institutional. Much of the book was drafted in two remarkable settings that provide a splendidly supportive environment for such work—the Woodrow Wilson International Center for Scholars in Washington, and the National Humanities Center in North Carolina. Each offered an ideal combination of elements: colleagues in a variety of fields to talk to, argue with, and learn from; a superbly efficient and helpful staff; and—most precious because most rare—an abundance of silence and slow time. I am deeply grateful to both institutions for financial and less tangible support. Thanks are also due to the National Endowment for the Humanities and to the University of California for fellowships that enabled me to concentrate on research and writing. In addition, a number of archives and special collections provided access to rare materials that proved indispensable—the Library of Congress, the Beinecke Library of Yale University, and the Berg Collection and Manuscripts Division of the New York Public Library. Any work done in such settings is in part collaborative and sustains one's sometimes flagging faith in the very existence of a scholarly community. Long may they flourish.

The personal debts are less anonymous and therefore easier to record. I am grateful to colleagues and close associates who read portions of this book in draft and offered invaluable advice and support: Michael André Bernstein, Mitchell Breitwieser, Frederick Crews, Florence Elon, Marianne Hirsch, Barbara Herrnstein Smith, and the members of the Autobiography and Subjectivity seminar at the National Humanities Center, especially Temma Kaplan and Leo Spitzer. Portions of this book have appeared in the journals *Ideas* and *The Wilson*

Quarterly. I want to thank Jean Anne Leuchtenburg and Jeffrey Paine for requesting and seeing them into print. Several editors at Basic Books—Steve Fraser, Linda Kahn, John Donatich, and Don Fehr—offered advice and counsel through more years than I care to count and helped to bring the manuscript to its final form. Sandra Dijkstra, my indefatigable agent, provided welcome injections of optimism when the going got rough. Robert Wicks proved energetic and resourceful in tracking down fugitive pieces. For the timely arrival of camera-ready copy of the illustrations I am grateful to Martyn Evans. Donna Kaiser's patient work in checking quotations, decoding and responding to the copyeditor's arcane symbols, securing permissions, and preparing the index with characteristic intelligence and attention to detail helped to make this a better book. To each of these collaborative spirits, my deepest gratitude.

Notes

I. The Transatlantic Slanging Match

1. Theodore Roosevelt, *African and European Addresses* (New York and London: G. P. Putnam's Sons, 1910), pp. 161, 167, 169, 171.

2. *Parliamentary Debates*. House of Commons, 1910 Session, vol. 17, no. 52, columns 1112, 1147, 1129, 1370, 1372–73.

3. Useful studies of this transatlantic dialogue include H. C. Allen, *The Anglo-American Relationship since 1783* (London: Adams and Charles Black, 1959); Cushing Strout, *The American Image of the Old World* (New York: Harper and Row, 1963); Richard L. Rapson, *Britons View America: Travel Commentary, 1865–1930* (Seattle and London: University of Washington Press, 1971); Stephen Spender, *Love-Hate Relations: English and American Sensibilities* (1974; New York: Vintage, 1975); Marc Pachter and Frances Wein, eds., *Abroad in America: Visitors to the New Nation 1776–1914* (Reading, Mass.: Addison-Wesley, 1976); Richard Kenin, *Return to Albion: Americans in England 1760–1940* (New York: Holt, Rinehart and Winston, 1979); Peter Conrad, *Imagining America* (New York: Oxford University Press, 1980); Benjamin Lease, *Anglo-American Encounters: England and the Rise of American Literature* (Cambridge: Cambridge University Press, 1981); Robert Weisbuch, *Atlantic Double-Cross: American Literature and British Influence in the Age of Emerson* (Chicago and London: University of Chicago Press, 1986); Christopher Mulvey, *Transatlantic Manners: Social Patterns in Nineteenth-Century Anglo-American Travel Literature* (New York: Cambridge University Press, 1990); Christopher Hitchens, *Blood, Class, and Nostalgia: Anglo-American Ironies* (New York: Farrar, Straus & Giroux, 1990); James Buzard, *The Beaten Track: European Tourism, Literature, and the Ways to "Culture," 1880–1918* (Oxford: Oxford University Press, 1993); William W. Stowe, *Going Abroad: European*

Travel in Nineteenth-Century American Culture (Princeton: Princeton University Press, 1994). Rapson's annotated bibliography, pp. 213–65, is particularly valuable.

4. [Sydney Smith], review of *Statistical Annals of the United States of America* by Adam Seybert, *Edinburgh Review* 33 (1820): 79. It is interesting that more than a century after Smith's words were published, the wound still festered: See Robert E. Spiller, "The Verdict of Sydney Smith," *American Literature* 1 (1929–30): 3–13. Spiller's was the lead essay in the inaugural issue of what became the premier journal in the field, yet he confesses that "It is hard, even at this distance of time, to view Sydney Smith's criticism of America dispassionately" (p. 13).

5. Anthony Trollope, *North America*, vol. 1 (London: Chapman and Hall, 1862), p. 3. There was no doubt about the original aggrieved response: The American reviews of Frances Trollope's book were so violent that they spawned an ancillary volume (*American Criticisms on Mrs. Trollope's "Domestic Manners of the Americans"* [London: O. Rich, 1833]) designed to show English readers the American side of the case.

6. Frances Trollope, *Domestic Manners of the Americans*, ed. Richard Mullen (1832; Oxford: Oxford University Press, 1984), pp. 111, 226, 133.

7. Frederick Marryat, *A Diary in America, with Remarks on Its Institutions*, ed. Sydney Jackman (1839; New York: Alfred A. Knopf, 1962), pp. 347, 370, 449–50.

8. Harriet Martineau, *How to Observe. Morals and Manners* (London: Charles Knight, 1838), pp. 5, 23.

9. Harriet Martineau, *Society in America*, vol. 3 (London: Saunders and Otley, 1837), pp. 228, 70, 30, 24.

10. Charles Dickens, Preface to the Cheap Edition of *American Notes*, 1850, in *Dickens on America and the Americans*, ed. Michael Slater (Austin: University of Texas Press, 1978), p. 216.

11. *The Letters of Charles Dickens*, ed. Madeline House et al., vol. 3. The Pilgrim Edition (Oxford: Clarendon, 1974), p. 156.

12. Charles Dickens, *American Notes for General Circulation*, ed. John S. Whitley and Arnold Goldman (Harmondsworth: Penguin, 1972), p. 287.

13. Charles Dickens, *The Life and Adventures of Martin Chuzzlewit*. The Oxford Illustrated Dickens (London: Oxford University Press, 1968), p. 273.

14. Ibid., p. 370.
15. Dickens, *American Notes*, p. 164.
16. Letters to John Forster, 22 December 1867, and to Georgina Hogarth, 4 January 1868, in *Dickens on America and Americans*, pp. 227, 229.
17. Dickens, "Postscript," *Martin Chuzzlewit*, p. 839.
18. For representative quotations, see Weisbuch, *Atlantic Double-Cross*, pp. 12, 130–31.
19. Quoted in Lease, *Anglo-American Encounters*, p. 61. See [John Neal], "United States," *Westminster Review* 5 (1826): 173–201. The essay as a whole is sanguine about the future of American writing, and Neal even suggests that English tradition is a poor guide, since "the literature of an aristocratic and corrupt country may not be beneficial to the citizens of a new and free democratic state" (p. 194).
20. Matthew Arnold, *Discourses in America* (London: Macmillan, 1885), p. 70.
21. Matthew Arnold, *Civilization in the United States: First and Last Impressions of America*, 4th ed. (Boston: Cupples and Heard, 1888), pp. 61–62.
22. Ibid., pp. 183, 176, 181.
23. Howard G. Baetzhold, *Mark Twain and John Bull: The British Connection* (Bloomington and London: Indiana University Press, 1970), pp. 119–20.
24. Mark Twain, *The American Claimant and Other Stories, The Writings of Mark Twain*, vol. 21 (London: Chatto and Windus, 1900), p. 80.
25. *The Letters of Henry Adams*, vol. 2, ed. J. C. Levenson et al. (Cambridge: Harvard University Press, 1982), p. 527.
26. Marc Pachter, Introduction to *Abroad in America: Visitors to the New Nation 1776–1914*, ed. Marc Pachter and Frances Wein (Reading, Mass.: Addison-Wesley, 1976), p. xv.
27. James Fenimore Cooper, *Gleanings in Europe: England*, ed. Robert E. Spiller (1837; New York: Oxford University Press, 1930), pp. 363, 228, xxii–xxiii, 297.
28. [James Fenimore Cooper], *Notions of the Americans: Picked Up by a Travelling Bachelor*, vol. 2 (London: Henry Colburn, 1828), pp. 168, 453–54.
29. Ralph Waldo Emerson, *English Traits*, ed. Howard Mumford Jones (1856; Cambridge: Harvard University Press, 1966), pp. 23, 178–79.
30. Nathaniel Hawthorne, *Our Old Home: A Series of English Sketches*.

Centenary Edition (1863; Columbus: Ohio State University Press, 1970), p. 64.

31. [John L. O'Sullivan], "Annexation," *The United States Magazine, and Democratic Review*, n.s. 17 (July and August, 1845): 9.

32. Andrew Carnegie et al., "Do Americans Hate England?" *North American Review* 150 (1890): 754.

33. James Russell Lowell, *My Study Windows*, 2d ed. (London: Sampson Low, Son, and Marston, 1871), pp. 57, 62–63.

34. Quoted in George W. Smalley, *London Letters and Some Others*, vol. 1 (London: Macmillan, 1890), p. 253.

35. Henry James, *Letters*, vol. 2, ed. Leon Edel (Cambridge: Harvard University Press, 1975), p. 213.

36. William Dean Howells, "Henry James, Jr.," in *Discovery of a Genius: William Dean Howells and Henry James*, ed. Albert Mordell (New York: Twayne, 1961), p. 121.

37. Quoted in the Introduction to *John Hay–Howells Letters: The Correspondence of John Milton Hay and William Dean Howells 1861–1905*, ed. George Monteiro and Brenda Murphy (Boston: Twayne, 1980), p. xxii.

38. Lawrence Levine has argued persuasively that in the mid- and later nineteenth century, an indigenous American culture was *increasingly* judged by European norms and standards. See the section on "The Sacralization of Culture" in his *Highbrow/Lowbrow: The Emergence of Cultural Hierarchy in America* (Cambridge and London: Harvard University Press, 1988), pp. 85–168.

39. Marcus Cunliffe, *The Literature of the United States*, 4th ed. (New York: Penguin, 1986), p. 76.

40. Goldwin Smith, "The Hatred of England," *North American Review* 150 (1890): 555.

41. *Transatlantic Dialogue: Selected American Correspondence of Edmund Gosse*, ed. Paul F. Mattheisen and Michael Millgate (Austin and London: University of Texas Press, 1965), pp. 191–92.

42. Martin Wiener offers a detailed analysis of the underlying reasons for this change in his *English Culture and the Decline of the Industrial Spirit, 1850–1980* (Cambridge: Cambridge University Press, 1981). Some of the British anti-industrial forces Wiener analyzes had their equivalent in the United States, though they were felt later. See T. J. Jackson-Lears, *No Place of Grace: Antimodernism and the*

Transformation of American Culture 1880–1920 (New York: Pantheon, 1981).

43. The economist D. J. Coppock's calculations, as summarized in Aaron L. Friedberg, *The Weary Titan: Britain and the Experience of Relative Decline, 1895–1905* (Princeton: Princeton University Press, 1988), p. 25.

44. F. A. McKenzie, *The American Invaders* (London: Grant Richards, 1902), p. 1.

45. William T. Stead, *The Americanization of the World or The Trend of the Twentieth Century* (1902; New York: Garland, 1972), p. 5.

46. Letter to Henry Cabot Lodge, quoted in Howard K. Beale, *Theodore Roosevelt and the Rise of America to World Power* (Baltimore: Johns Hopkins University Press, 1956), p. 257.

47. John Hay, "William McKinley," *Addresses of John Hay* (New York: Century, 1906), p. 165. For the difficulty of dating this significant change precisely, see Richard H. Heindel, *The American Impact on Great Britain 1898–1914* (Philadelphia: University of Pennsylvania Press, 1940), p. 180.

48. Friedberg, p. 152; for the later stages of this decline, culminating in the humiliating terms Britain is forced to accept at the 1921–22 Washington Naval Conference, see Hitchens, *Blood, Class, and Nostalgia*, p. 198. The twentieth-century consequences of this shift in power are analyzed in D. Cameron Watt's *Succeeding John Bull: America in Britain's Place 1900–1975* (Cambridge: Cambridge University Press, 1984).

49. A. E. Campbell, *Great Britain and the United States 1895–1903* (1960; Westport, Conn.: Greenwood, 1974), pp. 192–93.

50. Price Collier, *England and the English from an American Point of View* (London: Duckworth, 1909), p. 271.

II. The Reconciliation Fantasy

1. Bradford Perkins, *The Great Rapprochement: England and the United States, 1895–1914* (London: Victor Gollancz, 1969), p. 116.

2. Charles S. Campbell, Jr., *Anglo-American Understanding, 1898–1903* (Baltimore: Johns Hopkins University Press, 1957), p. 235.

3. George W. Smalley, *Anglo-American Memories*. Second Series (London: Duckworth, 1912), p. 187.

4. Quoted in Allan Nevins, *Grover Cleveland: A Study in Courage* (New York: Dodd, Mead, 1932), p. 640. Emphasis added.

5. Henry Adams, *The Education of Henry Adams*, ed. Ernest Samuels (Boston: Houghton Mifflin, 1973), p. 172.

6. Stuart Anderson, *Race and Rapprochement: Anglo-Saxonism and Anglo-American Relations, 1895–1904* (Rutherford, N.J.: Fairleigh Dickinson University Press, 1981), p. 73. Anderson notes that "The detailed study that this group merits has never been written" (p. 191); however, a more recent book, Christopher Hitchens's *Blood, Class, and Nostalgia: Anglo-American Ironies* (New York: Farrar, Straus & Giroux, 1990), devotes considerable attention to their close connections and cooperative labor.

7. *The Letters and Friendships of Sir Cecil Spring Rice: A Record*, vol. 1, ed. Stephen Gwynn (1929; Westport, Conn.: Greenwood, 1971), p. 66.

8. Ibid., vol. 1, p. 119.

9. Quoted in Aaron L. Friedberg, *The Weary Titan: Britain and the Experience of Relative Decline, 1895–1905* (Princeton: Princeton University Press, 1988), p. 197.

10. Quoted in Richard H. Heindel, *The American Impact on Great Britain, 1898–1914* (Philadelphia: University of Pennsylvania Press, 1940), pp. 50, 15.

11. *Letters and Friendships of Sir Cecil Spring Rice*, vol. 1, p. 248.

12. *Letters of John Hay and Extracts from Diary*, vol. 3 (Washington: privately printed, 1908), pp. 119, 120–21.

13. Quoted in J. L. Garvin, *The Life of Joseph Chamberlain*, vol. 3 (London: Macmillan, 1934), pp. 301, 302.

14. Anderson, *Race and Rapprochement*, p. 119.

15. Henry Cabot Lodge, *One Hundred Years of Peace* (New York: Macmillan, 1913), p. 130.

16. *The Letters of Theodore Roosevelt*, vol. 2, ed. Elting E. Morison et al. (Cambridge: Harvard University Press, 1951–54), pp. 1175–76.

17. Hitchens, *Blood, Class and Nostalgia*, pp. 63–64, 66.

18. Rudyard Kipling, "The White Man's Burden," *The Complete Verse*, ed. M. M. Kaye (London: Kyle Cathie, 1990), pp. 261–62. "Great-Heart," Kipling's valedictory poem for Roosevelt, with whom he had carried on a long correspondence, sees his loss as equally devastating for "both peoples," who lament: "'Our realm is diminished / With Great-Heart away'" (pp. 473–74).

19. Rudyard Kipling to Theodore Roosevelt, 23 September 1898, Theodore Roosevelt Papers, Library of Congress, reel 2.

20. John Fiske, *American Political Ideas Viewed from the Standpoint of Universal History* (New York: Harper and Bros., 1885), p. 143.

21. See Reginald Horsman's *Race and Manifest Destiny: The Origins of American Anglo-Saxonism* (Cambridge: Harvard University Press, 1981) for the roots of Anglo-Saxon racial theory.

22. *Letters and Friendships of Sir Cecil Spring Rice*, vol. 1, p. 270.

23. *Addresses of John Hay* (New York: Century, 1906), pp. 78–79.

24. A. E. Campbell, *Great Britain and the United States 1895–1903* (1960; Westport, Conn.: Greenwood, 1974), p. 210.

25. Quoted in Basil Williams, *Cecil Rhodes* (1921; New York: Greenwood, 1968), p. 51.

26. Hitchens, *Blood, Class and Nostalgia*, p. 300.

27. John Roy [pseud., Henry Mortimer Durand], *Helen Treveryan or The Ruling Race* (New York: Macmillan, 1892), p. 483.

28. Arthur Conan Doyle, "The Adventure of the Noble Bachelor," *The Complete Sherlock Holmes*, ed. Christopher Morley (Garden City, N.Y.: Doubleday, n.d.), pp. 299–300.

29. William T. Stead, *The Americanization of the World or The Trend of the Twentieth Century* (1902; New York: Garland, 1972), pp. 5, 152.

30. John R. Dos Passos, *The Anglo-Saxon Century and the Unification of the English-Speaking People* (New York and London: G. P. Putnam's Sons, 1903), pp. 157, 68, 216–35.

31. Anderson, *Race and Rapprochement*, pp. 90–91.

32. Bernard Shaw, *The Apple Cart: A Political Extravaganza*, in *The Collected Works of Bernard Shaw*, vol. 17. Ayot St. Lawrence Edition (New York: William H. Wise, 1930), pp. 260–61.

33. George W. Smalley, *London Letters and Some Others*, vol. 2 (London: Macmillan, 1890), p. 346.

34. Nathaniel Hawthorne, *The American Claimant Manuscripts: The Ancestral Footstep, Etheredge, Grimshawe*, ed. Edward H. Davidson et al. (Columbus: Ohio State University Press, 1977), pp. 147–48, 168, 259–60.

35. Mark Twain, *The American Claimant and Other Stories and Sketches* (London: Chatto and Windus, 1900), p. 198.

36. William McHaig, as quoted in Ann Thwaite, *Waiting for the Party: The Life of Frances Hodgson Burnett 1849–1924* (London: Secker

and Warburg, 1974), p. 93. Burnett was born in England, came to the United States at the age of sixteen, married an American, and felt equally at home in both countries.

37. Ibid., pp. 107–8.

38. Frances Hodgson Burnett, *Little Lord Fauntleroy* (1886; New York and London: Garland, 1976), p. 19.

39. Nathaniel Hawthorne, *Our Old Home: A Series of English Sketches*. Centenary Edition (Columbus: Ohio State University Press, 1970), pp. 155–56.

40. Andrew Carnegie, "Do Americans Hate England?" *North American Review* 150 (1890): 758.

41. Brooks Adams, *America's Economic Supremacy* (New York: Macmillan, 1900), p. 10.

42. Thomas F. Gossett, *Race: The History of an Idea in America* (1963; New York: Schocken, 1973), p. 118.

43. For Darwin's complex discussion of this issue, see chapter 7 of *The Descent of Man*. He emphasizes "the numerous points of mental similarity between the most distinct races of man" despite the striking physical differences between them; yet he consistently points to the evolutionary differences between "civilized" races and "barbarians." (Charles Darwin, *The Descent of Man and Selection in Relation to Sex*, 2d ed. [1874; Akron: Werner, n.d.], pp. 182, 633–34.)

44. For examples of the appropriation of Darwin's ideas about race by proponents of Anglo-Saxon racial superiority, see Anderson, *Race and Rapprochement*, pp. 28–36.

45. L[ouis] A[gassiz], "The Diversity of Origin of the Human Races," *Christian Examiner* 49 (July 1850): 142, 144. Darwin knew and admired Agassiz's essay, though he did not agree with the general conclusions of the "polygenist school." See his *Descent of Man*, p. 172.

46. Adams, *The Education of Henry Adams*, p. 60. Although he would come to reject Agassiz's ideas, several references to his early mentor in the *Education* suggest that in his adulthood, Adams came to know him well and continued to admire him. In his 1868 review of Sir Charles Lyell's *Principles of Geology* (10th ed.), Adams refers with respect to Agassiz's argument that the different races belong to different species and refuses to choose between the rival theories of fixed and evolving species (*North American Review* 107 [1868]: 485).

47. For a detailed account of the influence of the Teutonic origins

school in late-nineteenth-century England and America, see Gossett, *Race*, pp. 88–122.

48. Henry Adams, "The Anglo-Saxon Courts of Law," *Essays in Anglo-Saxon Law* (Boston: Little, Brown and London: Macmillan, 1876), p. 1.

49. For the use of these phrases by English and American public figures, see Anderson, *Race and Rapprochement*, pp. 107, 110.

50. *Letters of Theodore Roosevelt*, vol. 7, p. 710.

51. Ibid., vol. 1, p. 304.

52. Ibid., vol. 4, p. 1102.

53. *Letters of John Hay*, vol. 3, p. 239.

54. *Letters of Theodore Roosevelt*, vol. 6, pp. 1497, 1490.

55. Theodore Roosevelt, "Expansion and Peace" (1899) in his *The Strenuous Life: Essays and Addresses* (Philadelphia: Gebbie, 1903), pp. 36–37.

56. *Letters of Theodore Roosevelt*, vol. 2, pp. 1176–77.

57. Theodore Roosevelt, "Biological Analogies in History," *Works*, vol. 12. National Edition (New York: Charles Scribner's Sons, 1926), p. 41.

58. Roosevelt, "Nationalism in Literature and Art" (1916), *Works*, vol. 12, p. 330. It is worth noting that Roosevelt allowed the British writer Israel Zangwill to dedicate his play *The Melting Pot* (1909), which popularized that term, to him. (*Letters of Theodore Roosevelt*, vol. 7, p. 1288.)

59. Roosevelt, "Biological Analogies in History," *Works*, vol. 12, pp. 29, 49, 50, 51, 59, 52.

60. Ibid., p. 54.

III. Anglo-Saxon Panic

1. Preface to the 1855 edition of *Leaves of Grass*, in Walt Whitman, *The Complete Poems*, ed. Francis Murphy (Harmondsworth: Penguin, 1977), pp. 741, 762.

2. John R. Commons, *Races and Immigrants in America* (1907; New York: Macmillan, 1930), p. 81; John Higham, *Strangers in the Land: Patterns of American Nativism 1860–1925*, 2d ed. (New Brunswick and London: Rutgers University Press, 1988), p. 110.

3. Henry James, *The American Scene* (1907; New York: Horizon, 1967), p. 196.

4. William Z. Ripley, *The Races of Europe: A Sociological Study* (New York: D. Appleton, 1899), pp. 103, 527.

5. See Madison Grant, *The Passing of the Great Race, or the Racial Basis of European History* (New York: Charles Scribner's Sons, 1916), pp. 17–18 and passim; and Lothrop Stoddart, *The Rising Tide of Color Against White World-Supremacy* (New York: Charles Scribner's Sons, 1920), pp. 261, 263.

6. A selection from the bibliography in Philip Davis, ed., *Immigration and Americanization: Selected Readings* (Boston: Ginn, 1920), pp. 749–65. Many other titles suggest a more neutral or positive attitude toward the new immigrants, but this list, which could easily be extended, illustrates the extreme negative response.

7. Goldwin Smith, "The Hatred of England," *North American Review* 150 (1890): 548.

8. Stoddart, *Rising Tide of Color*, pp. 263, 266.

9. Thomas Bailey Aldrich, *Unguarded Gates and Other Poems* (Boston and New York: Houghton Mifflin, 1895), pp. 16–17. For Lodge's March 16, 1896 speech, see *Congressional Record*, 54th Congress, 1st Session, pp. 2817–20. Lodge acknowledges his debt to Aldrich in the subsequently published version: Henry Cabot Lodge, *Speeches and Addresses 1884–1909* (Boston and New York: Houghton Mifflin, 1909), p. 266.

10. Lodge, March 16, 1896, speech, p. 2820.

11. Grant, *Passing of the Great Race*, pp. 15–16.

12. Edward A. Ross, "The Causes of Race Superiority," *Annals of the American Academy of Political and Social Science*, 18 (1901): 88.

13. Edward A. Ross, *The Old World in the New: The Significance of Past and Present Immigration to the American People* (New York: Century, 1914), pp. 285, 304. That Ross became president of the American Sociological Society in this year suggests the academic respectability of his work.

14. *The Letters of Theodore Roosevelt*, ed. Elting E. Morison et al. (Cambridge: Harvard University Press, 1951–54), vol. 3, p. 86; vol. 5, pp. 637, 638. He reiterated the warning in his popular autobiography: Theodore Roosevelt, *An Autobiography* (1913; New York: Charles Scribner's Sons, 1920), p. 162.

15. Commons, *Races and Immigrants in America*, p. 200.

16. Grant, *Passing of the Great Race*, pp. 43, 45, 46.

17. Ibid., p. 200.

18. Stoddart, *Rising Tide of Color*, pp. 196, 183.

19. Ibid., p. 253.

20. For the early history of Anglo-Saxonism and nativism in America,

see Reginald Horsman, *Race and Manifest Destiny: The Origins of American Racial Anglo-Saxonism* (Cambridge: Harvard University Press, 1981).

21. *Journals of Ralph Waldo Emerson*, vol. 7, ed. Edward Waldo Emerson and Waldo Emerson Forbes (Boston and New York: Houghton Mifflin, 1912), p. 116.

22. Herman Melville, *Redburn: His First Voyage*, ed. Harrison Hayford et al. (Evanston and Chicago: Northwestern University Press and the Newberry Library, 1969), p. 169.

23. John Higham, *Strangers in the Land: Patterns of American Nativism 1860–1925*, 2d ed. (New Brunswick and London: Rutgers University Press, 1988). The phrase is the title of Higham's second chapter.

24. Theodore Roosevelt, "Annual Message to Congress, 1905," *Works*, vol. 17. Memorial Edition (New York: Charles Scribner's Sons, 1925), p. 374.

25. *Letters of Theodore Roosevelt*, vol. 8, p. 867.

26. Theodore Roosevelt, "Americanism" (1915), in Davis, ed., *Immigration and Americanization*, pp. 654, 648–49, 659.

27. Brooks Adams, *America's Economic Supremacy* (New York: Macmillan, 1900), p. 212.

28. Henry Cabot Lodge, "The Restriction of Immigration," *North American Review* 152 (1891): 30, 32, 36.

29. Henry Cabot Lodge, "The Distribution of Ability in the United States," in his *Historical and Political Essays* (Boston and New York: Houghton Mifflin, 1892), pp. 159, 147.

30. Lodge, March 16, 1896 speech, pp. 2819–20.

31. On James and Eliot, see Barbara Miller Solomon, *Ancestors and Immigrants: A Changing New England Tradition* (Cambridge: Harvard University Press, 1956), pp. 181, 184, 187; on the Immigration Restriction League, see pp. 102ff. Her whole discussion of the subject is invaluable.

32. Higham, *Strangers in the Land*, pp. 102–3.

33. Prescott F. Hall, *Immigration and Its Effect on the United States*, 2d ed. (New York: Henry Holt, 1908), pp. 99, 101.

34. The information in these paragraphs is taken primarily from William S. Bernard's "Immigration: History of U. S. Policy," in the *Harvard Encyclopedia of American Ethnic Groups*, ed. Stephan Thernstrom (Cambridge and London: Harvard University Press, 1980), pp. 486–95.

35. H. C. Allen, *Conflict and Concord: The Anglo-American Relationship since 1783* (New York: St. Martin's Press, 1959), p. 106.

36. Whitman, "Song of the Exposition," *Complete Poems*, p. 232.

37. Henry Adams, *The Education of Henry Adams*, ed. Ernest Samuels (Boston: Houghton Mifflin, 1973), p. 238.

38. *Letters of John Hay and Extracts from Diary*, vol. 1 (Washington: privately printed, 1908), p. 327.

39. *The Letters of Henry Adams*, vol. 4, ed. J. C. Levenson et al. (Cambridge and London: Harvard University Press, 1988), p. 405.

40. Quoted in Thomas F. Gossett, *Race: The History of an Idea in America* (1963; New York: Schocken, 1973), p. 282.

41. E. Digby Baltzell, *The Protestant Establishment: Aristocracy and Caste in America* (New Haven and London: Yale University Press, 1964), pp. 114–15.

42. See particularly his "Introduction: Inventing Traditions" and "Mass-Producing Traditions: Europe, 1870–1914," in *The Invention of Tradition*, ed. Eric Hobsbawm and Terence Ranger (Cambridge: Cambridge University Press, 1983), pp. 1–14, 263–307. On the vogue of genealogy, see Gossett, *Race*, pp. 158–59.

43. George Santayana, *The Genteel Tradition: Nine Essays*, ed. Douglas L. Wilson (Cambridge: Harvard University Press, 1967), p. 78. The passage was originally published in his *Character and Opinion in the United States* (1920), a work intended for an English audience.

44. Brooks Adams, *The Law of Civilization and Decay: An Essay on History* (1896; Freeport, N.Y.: Books for Libraries Press, 1971), pp. 58–59, 61.

45. Barrett Wendell, "The American Intellect," in *The Cambridge Modern History: The United States*, vol. 7, ed. A. W. Ward et al. (New York: Macmillan, 1906), p. 747. Fred Lewis Pattee's proposed title for Wendell's book is quoted in Gossett, *Race*, p. 134.

46. *Letters of Henry Adams*, vol. 6, p. 355.

47. H. G. Wells, *The Future in America: A Search after Realities* (London: Chapman and Hall, 1906), p. 320.

48. *Letters of Henry Adams*, vol. 2, p. 228.

49. Henry James, *Letters*, vol. 1, ed. Leon Edel (Cambridge: Harvard University Press, 1974), p. 484.

50. William Dean Howells, "American Literature in Exile," in his *Literature and Life* (New York: Harper and Bros., 1902), p. 203.

51. Oliver Wendell Holmes, *Our Hundred Days in Europe* (1887; New York: Arno Press and New York Times, 1971), p. 313.

52. James, *American Scene*, p. 231.

53. James, *Letters*, vol. 3, p. 244.
54. See *Report of the Royal Commission on Alien Immigration*, vol. 1 (London: His Majesty's Stationery Office, 1903), pp. 40–42, for the proposed restrictions and Paul Foot, *Immigration and Race in British Politics* (Baltimore: Penguin, 1965), pp. 93–100, for the bill's enactment and implementation. For a more detailed account of the Aliens Act and its effects—including its deflection of prospective immigrants from England to America—see Bernard Gainer, *The Alien Invasion: The Origin of the Aliens Act of 1905* (London: Heinemann, 1972), pp. 166–215.
55. W. Evans-Gordon, *The Alien Immigrant* (London: William Heinemann, 1903), pp. 7–8, 12, 5.
56. Allen, *Conflict and Concord*, pp. 96–97.
57. Price Collier, *England and the English from an American Point of View* (London: Duckworth, 1909), p. 331. Henry Adams had read the book with interest when it was published serially in *Scribner's*. See his comments in *Letters of Henry Adams*, vol. 6, p. 216.
58. James, *Letters*, vol. 3, p. 244.
59. On the claim to "cultural authority" by the dispossessed patriciate and its belief that "it still owned and could defend civilization," see Marcus Klein, *Foreigners: The Making of American Literature 1900–1940* (Chicago and London: University of Chicago Press, 1981), p. 18. Klein's discussion of their role in his first chapter (pp. 5–38) analyzes their revulsion from the new American culture taking shape.

IV. Henry Adams's Baffled Patriotism

1. *The Letters of Henry Adams*, vol. 6, ed. J. C. Levenson et al. (Cambridge and London: Harvard University Press, 1988), p. 406.
2. Ibid., vol. 5, p. 524.
3. Henry James, *Letters*, vol. 4, ed. Leon Edel (Cambridge: Harvard University Press, 1984), p. 289.
4. *Letters of Henry Adams*, vol. 6, p. 724.
5. James, *Letters*, vol. 2, p. 246.
6. Quoted in Otto Friedrich, *Clover* (New York: Simon and Shuster, 1979), p. 220.
7. Henry James, "Pandora," *Complete Tales*, vol. 5, ed. Leon Edel (London: Rupert Hart-Davis, 1963), p. 382.

8. *Letters of Henry Adams*, vol. 2, p. 448.
9. Henry Adams, *The Education of Henry Adams*, ed. Ernest Samuels (Boston: Houghton Mifflin, 1973), p. 33.
10. James, *Letters*, vol. 2, p. 246.
11. *Letters of Henry Adams*, vol. 2, p. 367.
12. Ibid., vol. 4, p. 111.
13. Ibid., vol. 2, p. 135.
14. Quoted in Paul Nagel, *Descent from Glory: Four Generations of the John Adams Family* (New York: Oxford University Press, 1983), p. 53. Nagel's book illustrates both the enabling and the disastrous effects of such training.
15. Quoted in ibid., p. 185.
16. Adams, *Education*, pp. 70, 211.
17. *Letters of Henry Adams*, vol. 1, p. 419.
18. Ibid., pp. 127–28.
19. Ibid., p. 291.
20. Adams, *Education*, p. 52.
21. Ibid., pp. 128, 163, 157.
22. *Letters of Henry Adams*, vol. 1, p. 248.
23. Ibid., p. 458.
24. These dispatches have never been reprinted, though they are described at length by Ernest Samuels in *The Young Henry Adams* (Cambridge: Harvard University Press, 1948), pp. 104–17. They are listed in Samuels' bibliography, pp. 315–16.
25. [Henry Adams], "Important from England," *New York Times*, June 7, 1861.
26. [Henry Adams], "From London," *New York Times*, August 24, 1861.
27. [Henry Adams], "The War Panic in England," *New York Times*, December 25, 1861.
28. *Letters of Henry Adams*, vol. 4, p. 377.
29. Samuels, *Young Henry Adams*, p. 124.
30. Samuels describes Adams's social and intellectual set in ibid., pp. 122–27.
31. *Letters of Henry Adams*, vol. 1, p. 399.
32. Ibid., p. 402.
33. Adams, *Education*, p. 203.
34. Ibid., p. 236.
35. *Letters of Henry Adams*, vol. 2, p. 326.

36. Adams, *Education*, pp. 170, 180.

37. *Letters of Henry Adams*, vol. 2, pp. 67, 69.

38. Adams, *Education*, p. 286.

39. *Letters of Henry Adams*, vol. 2, p. 138.

40. Quoted in Friedrich, *Clover*, p. 219.

41. James, *Letters*, vol. 2, p. 366.

42. Quoted in Eugenia Kaledin, *The Education of Mrs. Henry Adams* (Philadelphia: Temple University Press, 1981), p. 164.

43. Henry Adams, "The Session," in *The Great Secession Winter of 1860–61 and Other Essays*, ed. George E. Hochfield (New York: A. S. Barnes, 1963), p. 93.

44. Adams, *Education*, p. 114.

45. *Letters of Henry Adams*, vol. 5, p. 163.

46. Ibid., vol. 6, p. 757.

47. Van Wyck Brooks, *New England: Indian Summer* (1940; New York: E. P. Dutton, 1950), p. 207.

48. *Letters of Henry Adams*, vol. 1, p. 106.

49. Ibid., pp. 315–16.

50. Ibid., p. 23.

51. Samuel Taylor Coleridge, *On the Constitution of the Church and State According to the Idea of Each*, ed. John Barrell (1830; London: J. M. Dent, 1972), pp. 39–40.

52. *Letters of Henry Adams*, vol. 1, p. 350.

53. Ibid., p. 555.

54. Samuels, *Young Henry Adams*, p. 206.

55. *Letters of Henry Adams*, vol. 2, pp. 31–32.

56. Adams, *Education*, p. 259.

57. Adams, *Great Secession Winter*, p. 191.

58. Adams, "The Session" (1869), ibid., p. 70.

59. Adams, "The Session. 1869–1870," ibid., p. 219. For a searching critique of the narrowness of Adams's reformism, see William H. Jordy, *Henry Adams: Scientific Historian* (New Haven: Yale University Press, 1952), pp. 270–71.

60. Adams, "The Session" (1869), *Great Secession Winter*, p. 74.

61. Adams, "Civil Service Reform," ibid., p. 127.

62. Adams, "The Session. 1869–1870," ibid., p. 222.

63. Adams, "Civil Service Reform," ibid., p. 128.

64. Adams, *Education*, p. 282.

65. *Letters of Henry Adams*, vol. 6, p. 480.

66. For an account of Adams's continuation of his reformist project during these years, see Samuels, *Young Henry Adams*, pp. 275–89.

67. *Letters of Henry Adams*, vol. 2, p. 326.

68. Ibid., pp. 249–52.

69. Ibid., p. 279.

70. Charles and Henry Adams, "The 'Independents' in the Canvass," *Great Secession Winter*, p. 298.

71. *Letters of Henry Adams*, vol. 1, p. 91.

72. Ibid., vol. 2, p. 418.

73. Ibid., p. 448.

74. Ibid., p. 33.

75. Adams, *Education*, pp. 248, 418.

76. *Letters of Henry Adams*, vol. 1, p. 557.

77. Dennis Wrong, *Power: Its Forms, Bases, and Uses* (Chicago: University of Chicago Press, 1988), p. 2 (emphasis in original).

78. *Letters of Henry Adams*, vol. 2, p. 371.

79. Ibid., vol. 1, p. 149.

80. Ibid., vol. 2, p. 139.

81. On Adams's British and American models in the province of history, see William Dusinberre, *Henry Adams: The Myth of Failure* (Charlottesville: University of Virginia Press, 1980), p. 107.

82. *Letters of Henry Adams*, vol. 1, p. 204.

83. J. C. Levenson, *The Mind and Art of Henry Adams* (Stanford: Stanford University Press, 1957), p. 83.

84. Henry Adams, review of J. R. Green's *A Short History of the English People*, in *Sketches for the* North American Review, ed. Edward Chalfant (Hamden, Conn.: Archon, 1986), p. 82.

85. Dorothy Ross, "The American Exceptionalist Vision," in her *The Origins of American Social Science* (Cambridge: Cambridge University Press, 1991), pp. 29, 23, 26. For an overview of the debate on the subject, see Ian Tyrrell, "American Exceptionalism in an Age of International History," *American Historical Review* 96 (1991): 1031–55.

86. Henry Adams, *History of the United States of America During the Administrations of Thomas Jefferson*, ed. Earl N. Harbert (New York: Library of America, 1986), pp. 52, 53.

87. Ibid., p. 1126.

88. Ibid., pp. 110, 123.

89. Ibid., p. 389.

90. Adams, *History of the United States of America During the Adminis-trations of James Madison*, ed. Earl N. Harbert (New York: Library of America, 1986), pp. 216, 457.

91. Adams, *History . . . Jefferson*, p. 364.

92. Ibid., pp. 124, 125.

93. Adams, *History . . . Madison*, p. 1332.

94. Ibid., p. 1345. One only has to compare the ringing patriotic conclu-sion of Bancroft's *History of the United States*, the final version of which was also published in 1891, to get some sense of the difference in tone between the older history and the new. Of the American people in 1789 Bancroft writes, "In the happy morning of their exis-tence as one of the powers of the world, they had chosen justice for their guide; and while they proceeded on their way with well-founded confidence and joy, all the friends of mankind invoked suc-cess on the unexampled endeavor to govern states and territories of imperial extent as one federated republic." (George Bancroft, *His-tory of the United States of America, from the Discovery of the Conti-nent*, vol. 6 [New York: D. Appleton, 1891], p. 474.)

95. *Letters of Henry Adams*, vol. 3, p. 408.

96. Ernest Samuels, *Henry Adams: The Middle Years* (Cambridge: Har-vard University Press, 1958), p. 386; Levenson, *Mind and Art of Henry Adams*, p. 183; Barbara Miller Solomon, *Ancestors and Immi-grants: A Changing New England Tradition* (Cambridge: Harvard University Press, 1956), pp. 35, 36; George Hochfield, *Henry Adams: An Introduction and Interpretation* (New York: Barnes and Noble, 1962), p. 62.

97. As one of Adams's most searching interpreters puts it, "Although the stylistic constraints that govern all nine volumes of the *History* tend to disguise the historian's change of heart in the course of its ten-year composition, at the end the tone differs markedly from that with which Adams had opened his inquiry into national character." (William Merrill Decker, *The Literary Vocation of Henry Adams* [Chapel Hill and London: University of North Carolina Press, 1990], pp. 185–86.)

98. *Letters of Henry Adams*, vol. 2, p. 535.

99. Ibid., p. 421. The reference is to the hostile reception of James's book

on Hawthorne (1880), which included a critique of American provincialism that outraged many of his compatriots.

100. Samuels, *Henry Adams: The Middle Years*, p. 339.

101. Henry Adams, "A Letter to American Teachers of History," in *The Degradation of the Democratic Dogma*, ed. Brooks Adams (1919; New York: Peter Smith, 1949), p. 230.

102. The fullest account is Patricia O'Toole, *The Five of Hearts: An Intimate Portrait of Henry Adams and His Friends 1880–1918* (New York: Clarkson Potter, 1990).

103. *Letters of Henry Adams*, vol. 2, p. 473.

104. Ibid., p. 466.

105. Ibid., vol. 3, p. 34.

106. Ibid., vol. 5, p. 414.

107. Henry Adams, *Democracy* (New York: New American Library, 1961), p. 176.

108. Ibid., p. 155.

109. Ibid., p. 48.

110. Ibid., p. 18.

111. Ibid., pp. 55, 181, 50, 31, 50.

112. Ibid., p. 67.

113. It is difficult to agree with Ernest Samuels's judgment that "The Spirit in which the novel was conceived was kin to the fierce idealism that had moved him ten years earlier to write the 'Session' articles. . . . Violent as the satire was, it reflected a mind eager to amend democracy. To the philosophic reader the tone was by no means hopeless" (Samuels, *Henry Adams: The Middle Years*, p. 84).

114. Adams, *Democracy*, p. 189.

115. O'Toole, *Five of Hearts*, p. 75.

116. *Letters of Henry Adams*, vol. 2, p. 467.

117. *Letters of Henry Adams*, ibid., p. 495n.

118. Samuels, *Henry Adams: The Middle Years*, p. 102.

119. *Letters of Henry Adams*, vol. 4, p. 451.

120. Ibid., vol. 3, pp. 138, 160.

121. Ibid., p. 108.

122. Quoted in Samuels, *Henry Adams: The Middle Years*, p. 88.

123. *Letters of Henry Adams*, vol. 3, pp. 246–47.

V. Adams Adrift, 1890–1918

1. *The Letters of Henry Adams*, vol. 3, ed. J. C. Levenson et al. (Cambridge: Harvard University Press, 1982), p. 49.

2. For a detailed itinerary of his travels, see Ernest Samuels, *Henry Adams: The Major Phase* (Cambridge: Harvard University Press, 1964), pp. 587–90.

3. *Letters of Henry Adams*, vol. 1, p. 291.

4. Ibid., vol. 3, pp. 106, 429; vol. 4, p. 701.

5. Ibid., p. 423.

6. Ibid., vol. 4, p. 327; vol. 5, p. 225.

7. [Henry Adams], "American Finance, 1865–69," *Edinburgh Review* 129 (1869): 521, 524, 533.

8. Henry Adams, "The New York Gold Conspiracy," in *The Great Secession Winter of 1860–61 and Other Essays*, ed. George E. Hochfield (New York: A. S. Barnes, 1963), pp. 164, 161, 162, 164. The essay, originally published in the *Westminster Review* after it had been turned down by two other British journals, perhaps out of fear of a libel suit, was reprinted in Adams's *Chapters of Erie* (1871) and *Historical Essays* (1891).

9. Ibid., p. 188.

10. Ernest Samuels, *Henry Adams: The Middle Years* (Cambridge: Harvard University Press, 1958), pp. 312–13, and *Henry Adams: The Major Phase*, pp. 125–26.

11. Henry Adams, *Letters to a Niece and Prayer to the Virgin of Chartres*, ed. Mabel La Farge (Boston and New York: Houghton Mifflin, 1920), p. 131.

12. *Letters of Henry Adams*, vol. 5, pp. 189, 250; vol. 6, pp. 44, 355.

13. For an account of Charles's speculative investments and the family's response, see Paul C. Nagel, *Descent from Glory: Four Generations of the John Adams Family* (New York: Oxford University Press, 1983), pp. 303–6.

14. *Letters of Henry Adams*, vol. 5, pp. 529, 115; vol. 4, pp. 156–57, 419.

15. Brooks Adams, *The Law of Civilization and Decay: An Essay on History* (1896; Freeport, N.Y.: Books for Libraries, 1971), pp. 58–59.

16. *Letters of Henry Adams*, vol. 5, p. 222; vol. 6, p. 780. Bernard Baruch was the self-made stock-market millionaire appointed by President Wilson in 1918 to chair the War Industries Board.

17. Quoted in Barbara Miller Solomon, *Ancestors and Immigrants: A Changing New England Tradition* (Cambridge: Harvard University Press, 1956), p. 29.

18. Ibid., p. 27.

19. *Letters of Henry Adams*, vol. 6, p. 301.

20. Henry Adams, *The Education of Henry Adams*, ed. Ernest Samuels (Boston: Houghton Mifflin, 1973), pp. 419, 238.

21. Adams, *Great Secession Winter*, p. 163.

22. *Letters of Henry Adams*, vol. 2, p. 381.

23. Ibid., vol. 4, pp. 128, 157; vol. 6, pp. 566, 635.

24. Theodore Roosevelt, *An Autobiography* (1913; New York: Charles Scribner's Sons, 1920), pp. 2, 55, 56.

25. *Letters of Henry Adams*, vol. 3, p. 175; vol. 5, pp. 295, 291; vol. 4, p. 142.

26. T. S. E[liot], "A Sceptical Patrician," *The Athenaeum* 4647, May 23, 1919, p. 361.

27. Adams, *Education*, p. 317; *Letters of Henry Adams*, vol. 4, p. 52; vol. 5, pp. 539, 315.

28. Adams, *Education*, pp. 169, 417.

29. *Letters of Henry Adams*, vol. 5, p. 485.

30. Ibid., vol. 4, pp. 594–95.

31. Adams, *Education*, pp. 418, 248.

32. *Letters of Henry Adams*, vol. 5, p. 88.

33. Ibid., vol. 4, p. 184.

34. Quoted in Leon Edel, *Henry James: The Middle Years 1884–1894* (London: Rupert Hart-Davis, 1963), p. 69.

35. *Letters of Henry Adams*, vol. 3, pp. 298, 446, 337.

36. Robert E. Spiller, Introduction to Henry Adams, *Tahiti: Memoirs of Arii Taimai e Marama of Eimeo, Teriirere of Tooarai, Terrinui of Tahiti, Tauraatua i Amo* (New York: Scholars' Facsimiles and Reprints, 1947), p. v.

37. Adams, *Tahiti*, p. 126.

38. Ibid., p. 136.

39. Matthew Arnold, "The Scholar-Gypsy," *The Poems of Matthew Arnold*, ed. Kenneth Allott (London: Longmans, 1965), p. 344.

40. *Letters of Henry Adams*, vol. 4, p. 174.

41. Ibid., vol. 3, pp. 8, 572; vol. 4, p. 8.

42. Ibid., vol. 5, pp. 300, 464, 399, 480.

43. Ibid., vol. 3, pp. 557, 588, 593, 596.

44. Henry Adams, *History of the United States During the Administra-*

tions of Thomas Jefferson, ed. Earl N. Harbert (New York: Library of America, 1986), pp. 100–101.

45. Adams, *Education*, p. 360.

46. *Letters of Henry Adams*, vol. 5, pp. 4, 511; vol. 4, p. 495; vol. 6, p. 394.

47. R. P. Blackmur, *Henry Adams*, ed. Veronica A. Makowsky (New York: Harcourt Brace Jovanovich, 1980), p. 310.

48. *Letters of Henry Adams*, vol. 6, p. 263.

49. Ibid., vol. 4, p. 327.

50. Ibid., vol. 6, p. 224.

51. Ibid., vol. 4, pp. 331, 321.

52. Adams, *Letters to a Niece*, p. 127.

53. Henry Adams, *Mont-Saint-Michel and Chartres* (1913; Boston and New York: Houghton Mifflin, 1936), pp. 2, 20.

54. Ibid., pp. 96–97, 110, 180.

55. Ibid., p. 375.

56. For a general study of this antimodernist spirit, see T. J. Jackson Lears, *No Place of Grace: Antimodernism and the Transformation of American Culture 1880–1920* (New York: Pantheon, 1981).

57. Adams, *Mont-Saint-Michel and Chartres*, p. 195.

58. Ibid., p. xiv.

59. *Letters of Henry Adams*, vol. 5, pp. 624, 628.

60. Ralph Adams Cram, Introduction to Adams, *Mont-Saint-Michel and Chartres*, p. vi.

61. William Dusinberre sees this event as the breaking point for Adams's original ambition: "In contrast to Henry James, he had gambled before 1890 that an artistic career could be pursued in his native land, and he had affirmed that earlier American writers were unjust to complain of an indifferent public. But after 1890, with the lack of public recognition of his *History*, Adams felt his race for acclaim a failure." (William Dusinberre, *Henry Adams: The Myth of Failure* [Charlottesville: University of Virginia Press, 1980], p. 31.)

62. Adams, *Mont-Saint-Michel and Chartres*, p. 31.

63. For Pound's appropriation of this concept from Mallarmé and Rudyard Kipling, see Michael André Bernstein, *The Tale of the Tribe: Ezra Pound and the Modern Verse Epic* (Princeton: Princeton University Press, 1980), pp. 6–10.

64. Adams, *Education*, p. 259.

65. *Letters of Henry Adams*, vol. 5, pp. 669, 668; vol. 6, p. 357.

66. Ibid., vol. 6, pp. 177, 237.

67. On the dual traditions of public and private writing in the Adams family, see Earl N. Harbert, *The Force So Much Closer to Home: Henry Adams and the Adams Family* (New York: New York University Press, 1977), p. 12. On the letter addressed to "his perfect audience of a single person," see Newton Arvin, Introduction to his edition of *The Selected Letters of Henry Adams* (New York: Farrar, Straus and Young, 1951), p. xiv.

68. Gertrude Stein, *Selected Writings*, ed. Carl Van Vechten (New York: Vintage, 1990), p. 262.

69. Henry Adams, *The Life of George Cabot Lodge* (1911; Delmar, N.Y.: Scholars' Facsimiles and Reprints, 1978), pp. 16, 138.

70. George Santayana, "The Moral Background," in *The Genteel Tradition: Nine Essays*, ed. Douglas L. Wilson (Cambridge: Harvard University Press, 1967), pp. 78–79.

71. Santayana, "The Genteel Tradition in American Philosophy," ibid., p. 54.

72. *Letters of Henry Adams*, vol. 5, p. 524.

73. Samuels, *Henry Adams: The Major Phase*, p. 334. For a detailed analysis of Adams's chosen first readers and their response, see William Merrill Decker, *The Literary Vocation of Henry Adams* (Chapel Hill and London: University of North Carolina Press, 1990), pp. 44–47.

74. For an account of the publishing arrangements, see Samuels, *Henry Adams: The Major Phase*, pp. 559–60.

75. Adams, *Education*, p. xxviii.

76. Ibid., p. xxx.

77. Quoted in Samuels, *Henry Adams: The Middle Years*, p. 96.

78. *Letters of Henry Adams*, vol. 2, p. 463.

79. Adams, *Education*, pp. 53, 238, 280, 345.

80. Ibid., p. 3.

81. Ibid., pp. 271–72, 282.

82. Ibid., p. 403.

83. Ibid., pp. 380, 406.

84. Both essays are included in the collection of his late works that Brooks Adams edited and entitled *The Degradation of the Democratic Dogma* (1919).

85. Adams, *Education*, p. 501.

86. Blackmur, *Henry Adams*, p. 243.
87. Adams, *Education*, p. xxx.
88. Samuels, *Henry Adams: The Major Phase*, p. 540.
89. J. C. Levenson, *The Mind and Art of Henry Adams* (Stanford: Stanford University Press, 1957), p. 2.
90. *Letters of Henry Adams*, vol. 6, p. 480; vol. 1, p. 315.

VI. Henry James's Cosmopolitan Opportunity

1. Henry James, *Letters*, vol. 3, ed. Leon Edel (Cambridge: Harvard University Press, 1974–84), 244.
2. *The Letters of Henry Adams*, vol. 2: 1868–1885, ed. J. C. Levenson et al. (Cambridge and London: Harvard University Press, 1982), 326.
3. James, *Letters*, vol. 1, pp. 247, 240; vol. 2, p. 110.
4. R. W. B. Lewis, *The Jameses: A Family Narrative* (New York: Farrar, Straus & Giroux, 1991), p. 31.
5. *The Death and Letters of Alice James*, ed. Ruth Bernard Yeazell (Berkeley, Los Angeles, and London: University of California Press, 1981), p. 148.
6. James, *Letters*, vol. 1, p. 77.
7. Ibid., pp. 252, 484.
8. Leon Edel, *Henry James: The Conquest of London 1870–1883* (London: Rupert Hart-Davis, 1962), p. 200. For James's interest in power and its links to American imperialism, see Leo Bersani, "The Subject of Power," *Diacritics* 7, no. 3 (1977): 2–21, and Mark Seltzer, *Henry James and the Art of Power* (Ithaca: Cornell University Press, 1984).
9. Henry James, "Americans Abroad," *The Nation* 27 (1878): 209.
10. Henry James, *The American*, in *Novels 1871–1880*, ed. William T. Stafford (Library of America, 1983), p. 574; *The Golden Bowl* (Harmondsworth: Penguin, 1966), p. 40.
11. Henry James, *Parisian Sketches: Letters to the* New York Tribune *1875–1876*, ed. Leon Edel and Ilse Dusoir Lind (New York: New York University Press, 1957), pp. 34–35.
12. Henry James, *Transatlantic Sketches* (Boston: James R. Osgood, 1875), p. 276.
13. Henry James, *The Portrait of a Lady*, in *Novels 1881–1886*, ed. William T. Stafford (Library of America, 1985), p. 194.
14. T. S. Eliot, "On Henry James," in *The Question of Henry James: A*

Collection of Critical Essays, ed. F. W. Dupee (London: Allan Wingate, 1947), pp. 123–24.

15. James, *Transatlantic Sketches*, p. 359.

16. Quoted in Lewis, *The Jameses*, p. 430.

17. James, *Letters*, vol. 2, pp. 135, 258.

18. Henry James, *The Europeans*, in *Novels 1871–1880*, p. 956.

19. Leon Edel, *Henry James: The Untried Years 1843–1870* (London: Rupert Hart-Davis, 1953), p. 197.

20. Thomas Wentworth Higginson, quoted in Edmund Gosse, "Henry James," *Aspects and Impressions* (London: Cassell, 1922), p. 28.

21. James, *Letters*, vol. 1, p. 246.

22. Ibid., pp. 422, 449, 470, 297.

23. Ibid., pp. 160, 241, 331.

24. Henry James, *Complete Tales*, vol. 3, ed. Leon Edel (London: Rupert Hart-Davis, 1962), pp. 14–15.

25. Henry James, *Roderick Hudson*, in *Novels 1871–1880*, p. 432.

26. James, *Letters*, vol. 2, pp. 51, 23, 20–21.

27. Henry James, *French Poets and Novelists* (London: Macmillan, 1878), p. 253.

28. James, *Letters*, vol. 2, p. 58.

29. *The Complete Notebooks of Henry James*, ed. Leon Edel and Lyall H. Powers (New York and Oxford: Oxford University Press, 1987), pp. 216–17.

30. James, *The American*, pp. 542, 546.

31. Ibid., p. 555.

32. Henry James, *The Art of the Novel: Critical Prefaces*, ed. R. P. Blackmur (New York: Charles Scribner's Sons, 1934), p. 22.

33. James, *Letters*, vol. 2, p. 86.

34. *Complete Notebooks of Henry James*, p. 217.

35. N. G. Annan, "The Intellectual Aristocracy," in *Studies in Social History: A Tribute to G. M. Trevelyan*, ed. J. H. Plumb (London: Longmans, Green, 1955).

36. James, *The Portrait of a Lady*, p. 248. For his strenuous denial that he *had* a place in English society, see Edel, *Henry James: The Conquest of London*, p. 324.

37. See particularly Books 6 and 7 of Edel, *Henry James: The Conquest of London*, pp. 271–383.

38. Ibid., p. 325.

39. James, *French Poets and Novelists*, pp. 56, 59, 223, 374.
40. James, *Letters*, vol. 2, pp. 197, 145. For a brief account of the historical events to which James is responding, see the section on "Britain Overseas, 1870–1886," in R. K. Webb's *Modern England: From the Eighteenth Century to the Present* (New York and Toronto: Dodd, Mead, 1975), pp. 345–66. See also his anxious 1882 letter to Lord Rosebery about the Arabi revolt in Egypt: James, *Letters*, vol. 2, p. 380.
41. Henry James, "London" (1888), in *English Hours*, ed. Leon Edel (New York: Oxford University Press, 1981), pp. 22, 8, 21; "London at Midsummer" (1877), ibid., pp. 98, 95.
42. Henry James, "A Passionate Pilgrim," *Complete Tales*, vol. 2, pp. 227, 286.
43. Ibid., p. 285.
44. James, *The Portrait of a Lady*, p. 259.
45. For Edward's interest in Americans, see Giles St. Aubyn, *Edward VII Prince and King* (London: Collins, 1979), pp. 126–29, and Philip Magnus, *King Edward the Seventh* (New York: E. P. Dutton, 1964), p. 244.
46. Henry James, *Literary Criticism: Essays on Literature, American Writers, English Writers*, ed. Leon Edel (The Library of America, 1984), p. 670.
47. *The Reminiscences of Lady Randolph Churchill* (New York: Century, 1909), p. 60.
48. Anthony Trollope, *North America*, vol. 1 (London: Chapman & Hall, 1862), p. 185.
49. James, *Letters*, vol. 2, p. 215.
50. *Henry James: The Critical Heritage*, ed. Roger Gard (London: Routledge & Kegan Paul, 1968), pp. 71–72, 115, 407, 222–23.
51. James, *The Art of the Novel*, p. 202.
52. James, *The American*, pp. 515–16.
53. Ibid., pp. 551, 664, 589.
54. James, *Letters*, vol. 1, p. 357.
55. Henry James, "Daisy Miller," in *Complete Tales*, vol. 4, pp. 182, 191, 180.
56. James, *The Europeans*, p. 905.
57. Ibid., pp. 903, 907, 1026.
58. Ibid., p. 929.
59. Henry James, "The Pension Beaurepas," in *Complete Tales*, vol. 4, p. 330.

60. Henry James, "The Point of View," ibid., pp. 508, 516.

61. Henry James, *Washington Square*, in *Novels 1881–1886*, pp. 41, 75, 46, 186.

62. James, *The Portrait of a Lady*, pp. 201, 227, 228, 251.

63. Ibid., p. 371.

64. Ibid., pp. 425, 447, 459.

65. James, *The Art of the Novel*, pp. 48, 56.

66. James, *The Portrait of a Lady*, pp. 221, 314, 597.

67. Ibid., pp. 725, 726, 630, 632, 633.

68. Such an interpretation takes issue with Peter Brooks's influential reading of James's mature work as transmuting a basically melodramatic vision. See his *The Melodramatic Imagination: Balzac, Henry James, Melodrama, and the Mode of Excess* (New Haven: Yale University Press, 1976), pp. 153–97.

69. James, *The Portrait of a Lady*, pp. 694, 671, 785–86.

VII. James's Patriotic Readers
and the Perils of Transatlantic Union

1. Henry James, *Letters*, vol. 2, ed. Leon Edel (Cambridge: Harvard University Press, 1974–84), p. 132.

2. Anne T. Margolis, in her shrewd assessment of James's negotiating strategy with his Anglo-American readers, aptly calls *The Europeans* "a piece of consummate literary diplomacy" in her *Henry James and the Problem of Audience: An International Act* (Ann Arbor: UMI Research Press, 1985), p. 39.

3. Henry James, *The Portrait of a Lady*, in *Novels 1881–1886*, ed. William T. Stafford (The Library of America, 1985), pp. 295, 296.

4. James, *Letters*, vol. 2, pp. 361, 367.

5. Leon Edel, *Henry James: The Conquest of London 1870–1883* (London: Rupert Hart-Davis, 1962), p. 463; James, *Letters*, vol. 2, p. 371.

6. Leon Edel and Dan H. Laurence, *A Bibliography of Henry James*, 3rd ed. (Oxford: Clarendon, 1982), p. 59.

7. Henry James, "An International Episode," *Complete Tales*, vol. 4, ed. Leon Edel (London: Rupert Hart-Davis, 1962), p. 312.

8. James, *Letters*, vol. 2, pp. 209, 213.

9. [Anon.], "Recent Novels," *Blackwood's Magazine* 131 (1882): 374, 375.

10. [Anon.], "A Sentimental Traveller," *The Spectator* 57 (1884): 160.

11. [Anon.], "American Novels," *Quarterly Review* 155 (1883): 204, 224.

12. Ibid., pp. 212, 220.

13. Quoted in *Henry James: The Critical Heritage*, ed. Roger Gard (London: Routledge and Kegan Paul, 1968), p. 139.

14. James, *Letters*, vol. 2, p. 104.

15. Ibid., pp. 189, 72.

16. James, *The Portrait of a Lady*, p. 800. Robert Weisbuch's analysis of the novel illustrates more fully what he calls the "carefully hedged but wonderfully detailed pact that James negotiates between England and America, involving author, work, and reader" (*Atlantic Double-Cross: American Literature and British Influence in the Age of Emerson* [Chicago and London: University of Chicago Press, 1986], p. 285).

17. Henry James, *Hawthorne*, in *Literary Criticism: Essays on Literature; American Writers; English Writers*, ed. Leon Edel (The Library of America, 1984), pp. 351–52.

18. James, *Letters*, vol. 2, p. 263.

19. James, *Hawthorne*, p. 403.

20. James, *Letters*, vol. 2, p. 274; Edel, *Henry James: The Conquest of London*, p. 394.

21. *The Complete Notebooks of Henry James*, ed. Leon Edel and Lyall H. Powers (New York and Oxford: Oxford University Press, 1987), p. 218.

22. James, *Letters*, vol. 1, p. 454.

23. Ibid., vol. 2, pp. 300, 324.

24. Herman Melville, "The Paradise of Bachelors and the Tartarus of Maids," in *Billy Budd and Other Prose Pieces*, vol. 13, ed. Raymond W. Weaver, *The Works of Herman Melville* (London: Constable, 1922–24), p. 228.

25. James, *Letters*, vol. 2, p. 363; vol. 1, p. 385; vol. 2, pp. 43–47, 53.

26. Ibid., vol. 2, pp. 101, 102.

27. Ibid., p. 175.

28. Ibid., p. 174.

29. Henry James, "The Story of a Masterpiece," *Complete Tales*, vol. 1, pp. 278, 294.

30. Henry James, *The Art of the Novel: Critical Prefaces*, ed. R. P. Blackmur (New York: Charles Scribner's Sons, 1934), p. 4.

31. James, *Letters*, vol. 2, p. 167.

32. Henry James, *Watch and Ward* (New York: Grove Press, 1959), pp. 189, 190–91.

33. Ibid., pp. 81, 236.

34. Morton Fullerton, "The Art of Henry James," *Quarterly Review* 212 (1910): 398.

35. Arthur Conan Doyle, "The Adventure of the Noble Bachelor," *The Complete Sherlock Holmes* (Garden City, NY: Doubleday, n.d.) p. 289.

36. Ralph G. Martin, *Jennie: The Life of Lady Randolph Churchill: The Romantic Years 1854–1895* (Englewood Cliffs, NJ: Prentice-Hall, 1969), p. 339n.

37. Nigel Nicolson, *Mary Curzon* (London: Weidenfeld and Nicolson, 1977), p. 108.

38. William T. Stead, *The Americanization of the World or the Trend of the Twentieth Century* (1902; New York: Garland, 1972), p. 124.

39. Ruth Brandon, *The Dollar Princesses: Sagas of Upward Mobility, 1870–1914* (New York: Alfred A. Knopf, 1980), p. 1.

40. Edith Wharton, *The Buccaneers* (New York and London: D. Appleton-Century, 1938), p. 356.

41. For examples, see James, *Letters*, vol. 2, pp. 27, 102, 148, 167, 324n.

42. Anthony Trollope, *The Duke's Children* (Oxford and New York: Oxford University Press, 1983), pp. 219, 488–89, 380.

43. For a discussion of the complicated issue of possible influence, see John Halperin, *Trollope and Politics: A Study of the Pallisers and Others* (London: Macmillan, 1977), pp. 247–54.

44. James, *The Portrait of a Lady*, p. 296.

45. Henry James, "Madame de Mauves," *Complete Tales*, vol. 3, p. 162.

46. Henry James, *The American*, in *Novels 1871–1880*, ed. William T. Stafford (The Library of America, 1983), pp. 784, 785, 789.

47. Henry James, "The Siege of London," *Complete Tales*, vol. 5, pp. 47, 31, 91, 75.

48. Henry James, "Lady Barberina," ibid., pp. 258, 274, 230.

49. James, *The Art of the Novel*, pp. 201, 207.

50. *Complete Notebooks of Henry James*, p. 21.

51. James, "Lady Barberina," pp. 223, 216, 239.

52. Ibid., p. 301.

53. Quoted in Maureen E. Montgomery, *'Gilded Prostitution': Status, Money, and Transatlantic Marriages, 1870–1914* (London & New York: Routledge, 1989), pp. 97, 154.

54. Consuelo Vanderbilt Balsan, *The Glitter and the Gold* (New York: Harper & Brothers, 1952), pp. 242, 45.

55. Nicolson, *Mary Curzon*, pp. 30, 59, 79.

56. Gertrude Atherton, *American Wives and English Husbands* (New York: Dodd, Mead, 1898), pp. 217, 185. Atherton's American bride in *His Fortunate Grace* voices similar sentiments (New York: D. Appleton, 1897), pp. 175–76. See also the comments on Atherton's belief in Nordic superiority and on the ideal union of English men and American women in Emily Wortis Leider, *California's Daughter: Gertrude Atherton and Her Times* (Stanford: Stanford University Press, 1991), pp. 5, 172, 181–82.

57. James, *Letters*, vol. 3, p. 244.

58. Henry James, *Confidence*, in *Novels 1871–1880*, p. 1153.

59. Henry James, *The Europeans*, in *Novels 1871–80*, p. 910.

60. Ibid., p. 943.

61. Ibid., pp. 982, 983, 1035, 1038.

62. James, *Letters*, vol. 2, p. 105.

63. Richard Poirier, *The Comic Style of Henry James: A Study of the Early Novels* (London: Chatto & Windus, 1960), p. 107.

VIII. Henry James: The Return of the Native

1. Henry James, *Letters*, vol. 3, ed. Leon Edel (Cambridge: Harvard University Press, 1974), pp. 209, 511.

2. Ibid., p. 244.

3. Ibid., p. 106.

4. Quoted in Michael Anesko, *"Friction with the Market": Henry James and the Profession of Authorship* (New York: Oxford University Press, 1986), p. 99.

5. James, *Letters*, vol. 4, p. 778.

6. Ibid., vol. 3, p. 284.

7. Anon., review of *The Princess Casamassima*, *Blackwood's Magazine*, 140 (1886): 792.

8. For James's rejection of the optimistic formulas for resolving social conflicts in the popular fiction of his day, see Marcia Jacobson, *Henry James and the Mass Market* (University, AL: University of Alabama Press, 1983).

9. Henry James, *A Small Boy and Others*, in *Autobiography*, ed. F. W. Dupee (New York: Criterion, 1956), p. 92.

10. For James's sales, see Appendix 2 in Roger Gard, *Henry James: The*

Critical Heritage (London and New York: Routledge & Kegan Paul, 1968), pp. 545–57.

11. James, *Letters*, vol. 3, pp. 508, 515.

12. Ibid., pp. 367, 47.

13. Henry James, *The American*, in *Complete Plays*, ed. Leon Edel (New York and Oxford: Oxford University Press, 1990), p. 238. In an 1892 revision the last act not only reconciles the lovers but resurrects Claire's brother Valentin and turns the calculating adventuress Noémie de Nioche into the agent of resolution. (Ibid., pp. 243–52.)

14. That his motives for this move were in part financial is suggested by his account of Lamb House, his new residence, in an 1897 letter: "The merit of it is that it's such a place as I may, when pressed by the pinch of need, retire to with a certain shrunken decency." (James, *Letters*, vol. 4, pp. 58–59.)

15. Henry James, "Broken Wings," *Complete Tales*, vol. 11, ed. Leon Edel (London: Rupert Hart-Davis, 1964), p. 235.

16. James, *Letters*, vol. 4, pp. 43, 507, 520.

17. Ibid., p. 48.

18. Ibid., pp. 132, 271.

19. Ibid., pp. 184, 271.

20. Quoted in Leon Edel, *Henry James: The Master: 1901–1916* (Philadelphia and New York: J. B. Lippincott, 1972), p. 227.

21. There had been minor excursions into this realm in previous years: shallow stories like "A London Life" or the potboiling novel *The Reverberator* (1888); the more disturbing long tale of Americans abroad, "The Pupil" (1891), which the *Atlantic* rejected, much to James's dismay; the play he wrote for Ellen Terry's American tour, *Summersoft* (1895). None showed the ambition of the last novels.

22. W. M. Payne, in Gard, *Henry James: The Critical Heritage*, p. 153.

23. So Leon Edel writes, "In setting his 'ambassador' in Paris he was rewriting his old story of *The American*, who had gone to Paris and sought the high world, the feudal magnificence of Europe." (Edel, *Henry James: The Master*, p. 28.)

24. Oliver Elton, "The Novels of Mr Henry James," *Quarterly Review* 198 (1903): 369.

25. Henry James, "Miss Gunton of Poughkeepsie," *Complete Tales*, vol. 11, p. 89.

26. Henry James, *The Wings of the Dove* (Harmondsworth: Penguin,

1986), p. 507; *The Golden Bowl* (Harmondsworth: Penguin, 1973), pp. 545, 547.

27. Richard H. Collin, *Theodore Roosevelt, Culture, Diplomacy, and Expansion: A New View of American Imperialism* (Baton Rouge & London: Louisiana State University Press, 1985), p. 156.

28. Henry James, *The Ambassadors* (New York: Viking Penguin, 1986), pp. 96, 98.

29. Ibid., pp. 90, 94, 323, 317, 415, 422, 341.

30. Ibid., pp. 153, 170, 155, 168.

31. Ibid., pp. 504–5, 508.

32. Ibid., pp. 483, 485, 475, 512.

33. James, *Letters*, vol. 4, pp. 338, 355, 356–57. James's response to Chicago is echoed in Adams's *Education*, in which the city's 1893 Columbian Exposition, with its focus on industry and electrical energy, is seen as "the whole mechanical consolidation of force." (*The Education of Henry Adams*, ed. Ernest Samuels [Boston: Houghton Mifflin, 1973], p. 345.)

34. Henry James, *The American Scene* (New York: Horizon, 1967), p. 366.

35. James, *A Small Boy and Others*, pp. 42, 116.

36. *The Complete Notebooks of Henry James*, ed. Leon Edel and Lyall H. Powers (New York & Oxford: Oxford University Press, 1987), p. 240.

37. James, *The American Scene*, pp. 53, 112.

38. Ibid., pp. 180, 221–22.

39. Ibid., pp. 8, 192, 64.

40. John Higham, *Strangers in the Land: Patterns of American Nativism 1860–1925*, 2d ed. (New Brunswick and London: Rutgers University Press, 1988), p. 110.

41. James, *The American Scene*, p. 85.

42. Ibid., pp. 125, 86, 119, 265.

43. Ibid., p. 139.

44. Ibid., p. 232.

45. Henry James, *The Question of Our Speech; The Lesson of Balzac: Two Lectures* (Boston and New York: Houghton, Mifflin, 1905), pp. 6, 45, 43.

46. Irving Howe, "Introduction," to James, *The American Scene*, p. xii.

47. James, *The American Scene*, pp. 120, 124, 86.

48. James, *Notes of a Son and Brother*, in *Autobiography*, p. 425.

49. James, *The American Scene*, pp. 2, 51–52.

50. *The Education of Henry Adams*, pp. 11, 53.

51. Henry James, "Crapy Cornelia," *Complete Tales*, vol. 12, pp. 348, 353, 354, 357.

52. Henry James, *The Sense of the Past* (New York: Charles Scribner's Sons, 1917), pp. 32, 327, 335. The last two quotations are taken from James's detailed scenario for the unfinished portions of the novel.

53. Henry James, *William Wetmore Story and His Friends*, vol. 1 (New York: Grove Press, 1957), p. 333.

54. *The Letters of Henry Adams*, vol. 5, ed. J. C. Levenson et al. (Cambridge and London: Harvard University Press, 1988), p. 524.

55. James, *William Wetmore Story and His Friends*, vol. 2, pp. 68, 81, 77, 222–23, 224. See also James's fictional version of such an artistic beguilement, "The Tree of Knowledge" (1900), in his *Complete Tales*, vol. 11, pp. 93–110.

56. James, *Letters*, vol. 4, pp. 170, 171, 235–36 (emphasis in original).

57. Quoted in Edel, *Henry James: The Master*, p. 312. Edel argues that these words do not support the conclusion that James considered his expatriation a mistake. Rather, he insists, "James always felt that he was a consistent cosmopolitan."

58. James, *Letters*, vol. 4, p. 100.

59. Henry James, Preface to "Lady Barberina," in *The Art of the Novel: Critical Prefaces*, ed. R. P. Blackmur (New York: Charles Scribner's Sons, 1934), p. 209.

60. Henry James, "The Question of the Opportunities," in *Literary Criticism: Essays on Literature, American Writers, English Writers*, ed. Leon Edel (The Library of America, 1984), p. 655.

61. For a critique of James's unrealistic depiction of Adam Verver, see Peter Conn, *The Divided Mind: Ideology and Imagination in America, 1898–1917* (Cambridge: Cambridge University Press, 1983), pp. 27–30.

62. James, *The American Scene*, p. 80.

63. James, *A Small Boy and Others*, p. 35.

64. James, "The Lesson of Balzac," in *The Question of Our Speech; The Lesson of Balzac*, pp. 67, 77.

65. Edel, *Henry James: The Master*, pp. 476–77.

66. Henry James, "Notes for *The Ivory Tower* (Summer 1914)," *Complete Notebooks of Henry James*, p. 476.

67. Henry James, *The Ivory Tower* (New York: Charles Scribner's Sons, 1917), pp. 112, 113, 114.

68. James, "Notes for *The Ivory Tower*," p. 477.

69. James, *The Ivory Tower*, pp. 194–95.

70. James, "Notes for *The Ivory Tower*," p. 475.

71. Edel, *Henry James: The Master*, p. 325. There is some question about whose decision it was to exclude *The Bostonians*, James's or his publisher's. See Anesko, *"Friction with the Market,"* p. 152.

72. James, *Letters*, vol. 4, p. 657–58.

73. Ibid., pp. 652–54, 764. See the propagandistic pieces James writes for the Allied cause, collected in his *Within the Rim and Other Essays 1914–15* (London: W. Collins Sons, 1919). The book did not appear in the United States.

74. See Mark Seltzer, *Henry James and the Art of Power* (Ithaca: Cornell University Press, 1984), especially his chapters on *The Princess Casamassima* and *The American Scene*. The argument is rooted in Michel Foucault's account of surveillance in *Discipline and Punish*.

75. James, *Letters*, vol. 3, p. 450; vol. 4, p. 58.

76. Edmund Gosse, *Aspects and Impressions* (London: Cassell, 1922), p. 46. The image recalls Madeleine Lee's insistence in Adams's *Democracy* on observing the White House reception from above rather than joining the receiving line to shake the President's hand.

77. James, *William Wetmore Story and His Friends*, vol. 1, pp. 108, 119. This is a variant of what Mary Louise Pratt has called the archetypal "monarch-of-all-I-survey" scene in Western travel writing. See her illuminating *Imperial Eyes: Travel Writing and Transculturation* (New York: Routledge, 1992).

78. Henry James, "The Beast in the Jungle," *Complete Tales*, vol. 11, p. 259.

79. Ibid., pp. 370, 400, 401.

80. James, *Letters*, vol. 4, p. 259.

81. *Complete Notebooks of Henry James*, p. 141.

82. Ibid.

83. James, *The Ambassadors*, pp. 215, 130, 156, 90.

84. James, Preface to *The Ambassadors*, in *Art of the Novel*, p. 308.

85. James, *The Ambassadors*, pp. 512, 510–11, 59.

86. Eve Kosofsky Sedgwick's analysis of "The Beast in the Jungle" as an occluded expression of James's homosexual desire shows how powerfully such unacknowledged energy shapes these works. See her *Epistemology of the Closet* (Berkeley and Los Angeles: University of California Press, 1990), pp. 195–212.

87. Henry James, "The Jolly Corner," *Complete Tales*, vol. 12, pp. 195, 197.

88. Ibid., pp. 203, 198, 204, 225, 226.

89. Ibid., pp. 227, 231.

IX. Ezra Pound: The Appearance of the Comet

1. Quoted from *The Bookman* in "An American Discovered in England," *Literary Digest* (1909). Reprinted in *Ezra Pound's Poetry and Prose Contributions to Periodicals*, vol. 1, ed. Lea Baechler, A. Walton Litz, and James Longenbach (New York & London: Garland, 1991), p. 28. Hereafter cited as *Poetry and Prose Contributions*.

2. Ezra Pound, "Indiscretions," in *Pavannes and Divagations* (Norfolk, CT: New Directions, 1958), p. 25.

3. Douglas Goldring, *South Lodge: Reminiscences of Violet Hunt, Ford Madox Ford, and the English Review Circle* (London: Constable, 1943), pp. 48–49.

4. Ezra Pound to Mary Moore, undated letter #63 (1909?), Special Collections, Van Pelt Library, University of Pennsylvania.

5. *The Letters of Ezra Pound*, ed. D. D. Paige (New York: Harcourt, Brace, 1950), pp. 7–8.

6. For the most detailed study of the Yeats-Pound connection, see James Longenbach, *Stone Cottage: Pound, Yeats, and Modernism* (New York and Oxford: Oxford University Press, 1988).

7. Ezra Pound to Homer L. Pound, 11 February and 17 March 1909, Paige carbons, Beinecke Library, Yale University.

8. *The Letters of D. H. Lawrence*, vol. 1, ed. James T. Boulton (Cambridge: Cambridge University Press, 1979), p. 145.

9. Quoted in J. J. Wilhelm, *Ezra Pound in London and Paris 1908–1925* (University Park and London: Pennsylvania State University Press, 1990), pp. 29, 107.

10. Ezra Pound, *Collected Early Poems*, ed. Michael John King (New York: New Directions, 1976), pp. 114, 314. Hereafter *CEP*.

11. *Ezra Pound and Dorothy Shakespear, Their Letters: 1909–1914*, ed. Omar Pound and A. Walton Litz (New York: New Directions, 1984), p. 21. Hereafter *Pound/Shakespear*.

12. Quoted in Robert M. Crunden, *American Salons: Encounters with European Modernism, 1885–1917* (New York and Oxford: Oxford University Press, 1993), p. 227.

13. Goldring, *South Lodge*, p. 47. At the time, Ford was still known as Ford Madox Hueffer; but I use the later name throughout to avoid confusion.

14. Quoted from Ford's *Return to Yesterday* in Wilhelm, *Ezra Pound in London and Paris*, p. 25.

15. *Pound/Joyce: The Letters of Ezra Pound to James Joyce, with Pound's Essays on Joyce*, ed. Forrest Read (New York: New Directions, 1967), pp. 38–39.

16. Ezra Pound, *Selected Prose 1909–1965*, ed. William Cookson (New York: New Directions, 1973), p. 101.

17. *Letters of Ezra Pound*, p. 25.

18. "The Renaissance," in *Literary Essays of Ezra Pound*, ed. T. S. Eliot (Norfolk, CT: New Directions, 1954), p. 218.

19. Matthew Arnold, *Civilization in the United States: First and Last Impressions of America*, 4th ed. (Boston: Cupples and Heard, 1888), pp. 61–62.

20. Pound, "The Renaissance," *Literary Essays*, p. 214.

21. Pound, *Patria Mia*, in *Selected Prose*, p. 114.

22. Ezra Pound, "America: Chances and Remedies" Part V, originally published in *New Age* 13 (1913). Reprinted in *Poetry and Prose Contributions*, vol. 1, p. 143. This passage was not included in the book version of these essays, *Patria Mia*.

23. Ezra Pound, "How I Began," *T. P.'s Weekly* 21 (1913): 707.

24. Pound, "The Renaissance," *Literary Essays*, p. 221.

25. *Letters of Ezra Pound*, p. 199.

26. *CEP*, pp. 86–87.

27. Ezra Pound to Homer L. Pound, undated (spring 1910), Paige carbons, Yale.

28. Ezra Pound, *The Cantos* (New York: New Directions, 1970), pp. 446–47. The passage is from Canto LXXIV.

29. Quoted in Humphrey Carpenter, *A Serious Character: The Life of Ezra Pound* (London: Faber and Faber, 1988), p. 107.

30. Ezra Pound to Isabel W. Pound, 29 November 1912, Paige carbons, Yale.

31. Quoted in Carpenter, *Serious Character*, p. 185.

32. H. D., *End to Torment: A Memoir of Ezra Pound, with the Poems from "Hilda's Book" by Ezra Pound*, ed. Norman Holmes Pearson and Michael King (New York: New Directions, 1979), p. 18.

33. Ezra Pound, *Gaudier-Brzeska: A Memoir* (New York: New Directions, 1974), p. 18.

34. Pound, *Literary Essays*, pp. 4–6, 11.

35. Wyndham Lewis, *Blasting & Bombardiering* (London: Eyre & Spottiswoode, 1937), p. 254.

36. Pound, "Date Line" (1934), *Literary Essays*, p. 80.

37. *Pound/The Little Review: The Letters of Ezra Pound to Margaret Anderson: The Little Review Correspondence,* ed. Thomas L. Scott, Melvin J. Friedman, with the assistance of Jackson R. Bryer (New York: New Directions, 1988), pp. 15, 119 (Pound's emphasis).

38. *The Selected Letters of Ezra Pound to John Quinn 1915–1924,* ed. Timothy Materer (Durham and London: Duke University Press, 1991), p. 162. Hereafter *Pound/Quinn.*

39. Pound, "The Renaissance," *Literary Essays*, p. 221.

40. Pound, *Patria Mia,* in *Selected Prose*, p. 126.

41. For an account of Quinn's career, see B. L. Reid, *The Man from New York: John Quinn and His Friends* (New York: Oxford University Press, 1968).

42. *Pound/Quinn*, p. 23.

43. Quoted in *Pound/Quinn*, p. 8.

44. Ibid., p. 37.

45. Richard Ellmann, *James Joyce* (New York: Oxford University Press, 1959), pp. 426–27, 435.

46. Harriet Monroe, *A Poet's Life: Seventy Years in a Changing World* (New York: Macmillan, 1938), p. 257.

47. Reprinted in *Poetry and Prose Contributions*, vol. 1, p. 286.

48. *Personae: The Collected Poems of Ezra Pound* (New York: New Directions, 1926), p. 33.

49. Pound, "How I Began," p. 707.

50. Ezra Pound, *The Spirit of Romance* (New York: New Directions, 1968), pp. 67–79, 127–54.

51. Pound, "Provincialism the Enemy," *Selected Prose*, p. 198.

52. *Letters of Ezra Pound*, pp. 4, 124.

53. *CEP*, p. 8.

54. James Joyce, *Finnegans Wake* (New York: Viking, 1955), p. 120.

55. Pound, "I Gather the Limbs of Osiris," *Selected Prose*, p. 32.

56. *Pound/Quinn*, pp. 46–47, 93–94.

57. *Personae*, pp. 145–46.

58. Pound, "Remy de Gourmont," *Literary Essays*, p. 358.
59. *Pound/Lewis: The Letters of Ezra Pound and Wyndham Lewis*, ed. Timothy Materer (New York: New Directions, 1985), p. 39. For a full bibliographical description of the differences, see Donald Gallup, *Ezra Pound: A Bibliography* (Charlottesville: University Press of Virginia, 1983), pp. 20–21.
60. Quoted in Reid, *Man from New York*, p. 447.
61. Pound, "Arnaut Daniel," *Literary Essays*, p. 115.
62. *Pound/Quinn*, p. 181.
63. *Letters of Ezra Pound*, p. 172.

X. Pound's Meteoric Descent

1. Ezra Pound to Isabel W. Pound, undated 1911 letter, Paige carbons, Beinecke Library, Yale University.
2. *Ezra Pound and Dorothy Shakespear, Their Letters: 1909–1914*, ed. Omar Pound and A. Walton Litz (New York: New Directions, 1984), p. 55. On Pound's later sense of the formative effect of this familial pride, see Humphrey Carpenter, *A Serious Character: The Life of Ezra Pound* (London: Faber and Faber, 1988), p. 29.
3. *Pound/The Little Review: The Letters of Ezra Pound to Margaret Anderson: The Little Review Correspondence*, ed. Thomas L. Scott, Melvin J. Friedman, with the assistance of Jackson R. Bryer (New York: New Directions, 1988), p. 267.
4. *Literary Essays of Ezra Pound*, ed. T. S. Eliot (Norfolk, CT: New Directions, 1954), p. 92 (Pound's emphasis).
5. Ezra Pound, *The Spirit of Romance* (New York: New Directions, 1968), pp. 112, 156–57, 201.
6. Pound, *Literary Essays*, pp. 32–33, 30, 34.
7. Michael André Bernstein, "Robert Duncan: Talent and the Individual Tradition," *Sagetrieb* 4, nos. 2–3 (1985): 177–90. Bernstein's essay focuses on Duncan and distinguishes his form of syncretism from those of his precursors. But his general point that a sign of the "imaginative strength" of the modern writer was "the skill with which he could weld together a personal choice of master-texts" (182) seems to me to apply equally well to Pound.
8. Hugh Kenner, "Introduction" to Ezra Pound, *Translations* (New York: New Directions, 1963), p. 10.

9. *Personae: The Collected Poems of Ezra Pound* (New York: New Directions, 1926), p. 202.

10. Ezra Pound, *Collected Early Poems*, ed. Michael John King (New York: New Directions, 1976), p. 209. Hereafter *CEP*.

11. Quoted in *Pound/Lewis: The Letters of Ezra Pound and Wyndham Lewis*, ed. Timothy Materer (New York: New Directions, 1985), p. xii.

12. Ernest Fenollosa, "The Chinese Written Character as a Medium for Poetry," in Ezra Pound, *Instigations* (New York: Boni and Liveright, 1920), p. 358.

13. For Pound's early consciousness of such a historical destiny, see his poem "From Chebar," in which the speaker is the expansionist spirit that moves westward from Mesopotamia, through Europe, to America, but that finds no rest there: "I did not begin with you, / I do not end with you, America" (*CEP*, p. 269). Donald Gallup dates the posthumously published poem between 1912 and 1915 (*Ezra Pound: A Bibliography* [Charlottesville: University Press of Virginia, 1983], p. 361).

14. *Ezra Pound's Poetry and Prose Contributions to Periodicals*, vol. 1, ed. Lea Baechler, A. Walton Litz, and James Longenbach (New York & London: Garland, 1991), p. 114. Hereafter cited as *Poetry and Prose Contributions*.

15. Ezra Pound, *Gaudier-Brzeska: A Memoir* (New York: New Directions, 1974), p. 90.

16. *Pound/Ford: The Story of a Literary Friendship: The Correspondence Between Ezra Pound and Ford Madox Ford and Their Writings about Each Other*, ed. Brita Lindberg-Seyersted (New York: New Directions, 1982), p. 83.

17. Ezra Pound, "Postscript to *The Natural Philosophy of Love* by Rémy de Gourmont," *Pavannes and Divagations* (Norfolk, CT: New Directions, 1958), p. 204. The essay appeared in 1922.

18. *CEP*, pp. 96–97.

19. *Personae*, pp. 33, 28, 30.

20. *The Selected Letters of Ezra Pound to John Quinn 1915–1924*, ed. Timothy Materer (Durham and London: Duke University Press, 1991), pp. 71, 53. Hereafter *Pound/Quinn*. Sandra Gilbert and Susan Gubar connect Pound's fear of a feminized culture with that of other male modernists in their *No Man's Land: The Place of the Woman Writer in the Twentieth Century*, vol. 1 (New Haven: Yale University Press, 1988), pp. 125–62.

21. Pound, *Gaudier-Brzeska*, p. 45.

22. *Pound/Lewis*, p. 114.

23. *Pound/Quinn*, p. 66.

24. *Personae*, pp. 178–79.

25. Quoted in *Pound/Lewis*, p. 4.

26. Quoted in Robert M. Crunden, *American Salons: Encounters with European Modernism, 1885–1917* (New York and Oxford: Oxford University Press, 1993), pp. 213, 271.

27. Ezra Pound, "Ferrex on Petulance," *Egoist* (1914), reprinted in *Poetry and Prose Contributions*, vol. 1, p. 212.

28. *Pound/Quinn*, p. 176 (Pound's emphasis).

29. *Personae*, p. 158 (Pound's emphasis).

30. *The Letters of T. S. Eliot*, vol. 1, ed. Valerie Eliot (New York: Harcourt Brace Jovanovich, 1988), p. 358.

31. Richard Aldington, *Life for Life's Sake: A Book of Reminiscences* (New York: Viking, 1941), p. 216.

32. *Pound/Quinn*, p. 203.

33. Pound, "Wyndham Lewis," *Literary Essays*, p. 429.

34. Pound, "Remy de Gourmont: A Distinction," *Literary Essays*, p. 357.

35. Ezra Pound to Isabel W. Pound, 31 October and 15 November 1916; to Homer L. Pound, 1 February 1920; Paige carbons, Yale. On Pound's disastrous second year at Penn, see J. J. Wilhelm, *The American Roots of Ezra Pound* (New York & London: Garland, 1985), p. 152.

36. *Pound/Quinn*, p. 193. On Pound's contempt for the pseudo-objective ideals of academic scholarship and the professionalization of literary study, see Sanford Schwartz, *The Matrix of Modernism: Pound, Eliot, and Early Twentieth-Century Thought* (Princeton: Princeton University Press, 1985), pp. 142–46.

37. John Quinn to Ezra Pound, 21 October 1920, John Quinn Collection, New York Public Library. Quinn's anti-Semitism is an obsession. Three years later, in a letter to Lady Gregory, he puts the number of Jews in New York at 2.7 million and attacks the Emperor Titus for destroying the Temple and bringing about the diaspora, rather than allowing the Jews to remain in Palestine where they would conveniently have "eaten and fed on each other." (Quoted in B. L. Reid, *The Man from New York: John Quinn and His Friends* [New York: Oxford University Press, 1968], p. 597.)

38. *Pound/Quinn*, p. 204.

39. *Pound/Ford*, p. 49.

40. *Patria Mia*, in Ezra Pound, *Selected Prose 1909–1965*, ed. William Cookson (New York: New Directions, 1973), pp. 104, 103.

41. Pound, "Patria Mia" Part II, *New Age* (1912), reprinted in *Poetry and Prose Contributions*, vol. 1, p. 78.

42. *Poetry and Prose Contributions*, vol. 1, p. 254; *Personae*, p. 145.

43. Ezra Pound, "Imaginary Letters: IV," *Little Review* (1917), reprinted in *Poetry and Prose Contributions*, vol. 2, p. 268; *Pavannes and Divagations*, p. 56. The most systematic denunciation of Pound's anti-Semitism is Robert Casillo's *The Genealogy of Demons: Anti-Semitism, Fascism, and the Myths of Ezra Pound* (Evanston: Northwestern University Press, 1988). Casillo sees it as pervasive, though he tends to survey the whole career from the vantage point of Pound's World War II Rome broadcasts. See also James Breslin, "Ezra Pound and the Jews," *San Jose Studies* 12, no.3 (Fall 1986): 37–45. Breslin makes the point that Pound's anti-Semitism, so often linked to American populism, "can be more accurately related to that of Henry Adams, Henry James, and T. S. Eliot" (p. 39).

44. Pound, *Pavannes and Divagations*, p. 46; *Poetry and Prose Contributions*, vol. 4, p. 79.

45. For a detailed account of Pound's genealogy, see Wilhelm, *American Roots of Ezra Pound*, pp. 4–65.

46. Ezra Pound, "The Revolt of Intelligence: V," *New Age* (1920), reprinted in *Poetry and Prose Contributions*, vol. 4, p. 6.

47. *The Letters of Ezra Pound*, ed. D. D. Paige (New York: Harcourt, Brace, 1950), p. 322.

48. Pound, "Irony, Laforgue, and Some Satire," *Literary Essays*, p. 283.

49. Ezra Pound to Homer L. Pound, 27 September 1915, Paige carbons, Yale.

50. Ezra Pound to H. L. Mencken, 12 March 1918, Paige carbons, Yale. This passage was cut in Paige's edition: *Letters of Ezra Pound*, p. 132.

51. Reprinted in *Poetry and Prose Contributions*, vol. 4, pp. 102, 121, 124.

52. *Pound/Ford*, p. 131.

53. *Personae*, p. 185. Subsequent quotations from the poem are from this edition, pp. 185–204.

54. *Letters of Ezra Pound*, p. 159.

55. Ibid., p. 8.

56. William Carlos Williams, "Prologue," *Kora in Hell: Improvisations* (Boston: Four Seas, 1920), p. 28.

57. Pound, introductory note to "A Selection from *The Tempers*," *Poetry Review* (1912), reprinted in *Poetry and Prose Contributions*, vol. 1, p. 82.

58. Pound, "Dr Williams' Position," *Literary Essays*, pp. 390–92.

59. *CEP*, p. 314.

60. William Carlos Williams, *Collected Earlier Poetry* (New York: New Directions, 1951), p. 30.

61. Pound, "In the Vortex," *Instigations*, p. 241.

62. *CEP*, p. 59.

63. Ibid., p. 44.

64. Ibid., pp. 21, 69, 62.

65. Ibid., p. 11.

66. Ezra Pound to Homer L. Pound, 13 September 1909, Paige carbons, Yale.

67. Pound, *Patria Mia*, in *Selected Prose*, p. 124.

68. *Personae*, pp. 92–93.

69. Ibid., pp. 64–65.

70. Hugh Kenner, *The Pound Era* (Berkeley and Los Angeles: University of California Press, 1971), p. 202.

71. *Personae*, pp. 137, 136.

72. Ezra Pound, *Cathay* (London: Elkin Mathews, 1915), [p. 32].

73. Pound, "The Jefferson-Adams Letters as a Shrine and a Monument," *Selected Prose*, p. 147.

74. Pound, "National Culture: A Manifesto 1938," *Selected Prose*, p. 164.

75. Pound, "Henry James," *Literary Essays*, pp. 332, 331.

76. Ibid., p. 332.

77. Quoted in Ellen Williams, *Harriet Monroe and the Poetry Renaissance: The First Ten Years of* Poetry, *1912–22* (Urbana Chicago London: University of Illinois Press, 1977), p. 210.

78. Ezra Pound, *Guide to Kulchur* (New York: New Directions, 1970), p. 194.

79. Quoted in Crunden, *American Salons*, p. 252.

80. *Pound/Quinn*, p. 206.

XI. T. S. Eliot's Career Strategy

1. *The Letters of T. S. Eliot*, ed. Valerie Eliot (San Diego, New York, London: Harcourt Brace Jovanovich, 1988), p. 290. Hereafter cited as *Letters*.

2. See the Adams family tree, *The Letters of Henry Adams*, vol. 1, ed. J. C. Levenson et al. (Cambridge and London: Harvard University Press, 1982), p. xlvii. For the Adams–Eliot connection, see the genealogy in Eric Sigg, "Eliot as a Product of America," in *The Cambridge Companion to T. S. Eliot*, ed. A. David Moody (Cambridge: Cambridge University Press, 1994), pp. 16–17.

3. Lyndall Gordon, *Eliot's New Life* (New York: Farrar, Straus & Giroux, 1988), p. 272n.

4. *Letters*, p. 313.

5. T. S. E[liot]., "A Sceptical Patrician," *Athenaeum* 4647 (1919): 361.

6. Eliot quotation from Lyndall Gordon, *Eliot's Early Years* (Oxford London New York: Oxford University Press, 1977), p. 14. Gordon, *Eliot's New Life*, p. 272. Eliot himself confirms the link in a 1935 letter to Stephen Spender, in which he writes of his family, "*our* America came to an end in 1829, when Andrew Jackson was elected president." (Quoted in Spender's "Remembering Eliot," *T. S. Eliot: The Man and His Work*, ed. Allen Tate [New York: Delacorte, 1966], p. 56.)

7. Allen Tate, in *T. S. Eliot: The Critical Heritage*, ed. Michael Grant (London: Routledge & Kegan Paul, 1982), 1: 242.

8. Eliot, "A Sceptical Patrician," 362.

9. *The Diary of Virginia Woolf*, vol. 2, ed. Anne Olivier Bell (London: Hogarth, 1977–84), p. 68. On Eliot's sense of kinship with Adams and James, see Eric Sigg, *The American T. S. Eliot: A Study of the Early Writings* (Cambridge: Cambridge University Press, 1989), pp. 124–44.

10. T. S. E[liot]., "Reflections on Contemporary Poetry," *Egoist* 4 (1917): 151.

11. *Letters*, pp. 217, 227.

12. T. S. Eliot, "In Memory," *Little Review* 5 (1918): 44. For a stinging attack on the arrogance of Eliot's claim, see James Buzard, "Eliot, Pound, and Expatriate Authority," *Raritan* 13, no. 3 (1994): 106–22.

13. T. S. Eliot, "A Prediction in Regard to Three English Authors," *Vanity Fair* 21 (1924): 29.

14. T. S. Eliot, *The Complete Poems and Plays 1909–1950* (San Diego, New York, London: Harcourt Brace Jovanovich, 1952), p. 56. Hereafter abbreviated *CPP*.

15. Edmund Wilson, *Axel's Castle: A Study of the Imaginative Literature of 1870–1930* (1931; New York: Charles Scribner's Sons, 1959), pp. 102, 104, 105. F. O. Matthiessen's seminal studies of Eliot in both *The Achievement of T. S. Eliot* (1935) and the chapter "From Hawthorne

to James to Eliot" in *American Renaissance* (1941) stress the lineage, which has been most fully explored in Richard Brodhead's *The School of Hawthorne* (1990).

16. *Letters*, p. 323.

17. Quoted in Valerie Eliot's "Introduction," *Letters*, p. xvii.

18. *The Letters of Ezra Pound*, ed. D. D. Paige (New York: Harcourt, Brace, 1950), p. 40.

19. Published in Eliot's *Letters*, p. 102.

20. T. S. Eliot, "Ezra Pound: His Metric and His Poetry," in *To Criticize the Critic and Other Writings* (New York: Farrar, Straus & Giroux, 1965), p. 164.

21. *CPP*, p. 6. In Eliot's manuscript of the poem, the subtitle or alternate title "Prufrock among the women" appears in parentheses below the title. See T. S. Eliot, *Inventions of the March Hare: Poems 1909–1917*, ed. Christopher Ricks (London: Faber and Faber, 1996), p. 39.

22. *Letters*, p. 236.

23. See T. S. Eliot, "Holograph, typescript, and typescript (carbon), incomplete, with the author's ms. corrections, unsigned and undated," Berg Collection, New York Public Library.

24. T. S. Eliot to Ezra Pound, 13 October 1925, YCAL MSS 43, box 13, folder 504, Beinecke Library, Yale University.

25. T. S. Eliot, *The Waste Land: A Facsimile and Transcript of the Original Drafts Including the Annotations of Ezra Pound*, ed. Valerie Eliot (New York: Harcourt Brace Jovanovich, 1971). Hereafter *Waste Land Facsimile*.

26. *Letters*, p. 497.

27. Quoted in Valerie Eliot's "Introduction" to *Waste Land Facsimile*, p. xxiv.

28. Ibid., p. xxii.

29. *Letters of Ezra Pound*, p. 169.

30. T. S. Eliot, "The Death of St. Narcissus," *Poems Written in Early Youth* (New York: Farrar, Straus & Giroux, 1967), p. 29. Hereafter *PWEY*. For "The Love Song of St. Sebastian," see Eliot, *Inventions of the March Hare*, pp. 78–79.

31. Gordon, *Eliot's Early Years*, p. 94.

32. "Ode," *PWEY*, p. 27.

33. John Quinn to T. S. Eliot, 3 December 1918, reel 10, John Quinn Memorial Collection, New York Public Library.

34. Published in Eliot's *Letters*, pp. 103–4.

35. *Letters*, pp. 280, 290.

36. T. S. Eliot, "London Letter," *Dial* 72 (1922): 510.

37. Published in *Letters*, pp. 288–89.

38. *Letters*, p. 358.

39. John Quinn to T. S. Eliot, 6 March 1920, reel 10, Quinn Collection.

40. This shift is seen by Michael Levenson as the turning point in the consolidation of the modernist movement: "Eliot wilfully merging into his surroundings, no longer easily distinguishable from the established literary order, and modernism thus having won a place within that order." (A *Genealogy of Modernism: A Study of English Literary Doctrine 1908–1922* [Cambridge: Cambridge University Press, 1984], p. 220.)

41. Ezra Pound, "Historical Survey," *Little Review* 8 (1921): 39.

42. Published in *Letters*, p. 589.

43. T. S. Eliot to Ezra Pound, 19 July 1934; Ezra Pound to T. S. Eliot, 4 February [1935?], YCAL MSS 43, box 13, folders 508, 509, Beinecke Library, Yale University.

44. T. S. Eliot, "President Wilson," *New Statesman* 9 (1917): 140.

45. T. S. Eliot, "War-paint and Feathers," *Athenaeum* 4668 (1919): 1036.

46. *Letters of Ezra Pound*, p. 158.

47. John Quinn to T. S. Eliot, 30 June 1919; T. S. Eliot to John Quinn, 12 March 1923, reel 10, Quinn Collection.

48. T. S. Eliot to Herbert Read, 1928, quoted in Sigg, *The American T. S. Eliot*, pp. 110–11.

49. T. S. Eliot, "Preface" to Edgar Ansel Mowrer, *This American World* (London: Faber & Gwyer, 1928), p. xiii.

50. *Letters*, pp. 76–77.

51. A selection of these, sent at various times to Pound, is in YCAL MSS 43, box 132, folder 5400, Beinecke Library, Yale University. The largest group is published as an appendix to Eliot, *Inventions of the March Hare*, pp. 305–21.

52. *CPP*, pp. 21, 24, 35, 33, 25, 35. The question of Eliot's anti-Semitism and other racial and religious prejudices remains hotly contested, with critical responses ranging from the exculpatory to the prosecutorial. Two books that treat the subject in less predictable ways are Christopher Ricks's *T. S. Eliot and Prejudice* (Berkeley and Los Angeles: University of California Press, 1988), and Anthony Julius's

T. S. Eliot, Anti-Semitism, and Literary Form (Cambridge: Cambridge University Press, 1995). Both analyze the notorious passages at length and consider the possible link between offensive attitudes and aesthetic vitality, though their tactics and tone differ markedly. As Ricks notes, "no one can write seriously and at length about anti-Semitism without giving offence" (p. 76).

53. Wyndham Lewis, *Blasting & Bombardiering* (London: Eyre & Spottiswoode, 1937), p. 272.

54. *Letters*, pp. 108–9, 114.

55. Published in *Letters*, p. 139.

56. *Letters*, pp. 160, 161–62, 209.

57. T. S. Eliot, "Preface" to *Knowledge and Experience in the Philosophy of F. H. Bradley* (1964; New York: Columbia University Press, 1989), p. 10.

58. Quoted in Valerie Eliot's "Introduction," *Letters*, p. xvii.

59. *Letters*, p. 74.

60. T. S. Eliot, review of A. Wolf's *The Philosophy of Nietzsche*, *International Journal of Ethics* 26 (1916): 426.

61. Eliot, "In Memory," 46. For a detailed and illuminating account of Eliot's gradual withdrawal from the enterprise of philosophy, see Jeffrey M. Perl, *Skepticism and Modern Enmity: Before and After Eliot* (Baltimore and London: Johns Hopkins University Press, 1989), esp. pp. 43–85.

62. Eliot, "Ezra Pound: His Metric and His Poetry," p. 166.

63. Quoted in Valerie Eliot's "Introduction," *Letters*, p. xvii.

64. Published in *Letters*, p. 156.

65. *Letters*, p. 355.

66. T. S. Eliot, "Mr. Read and M. Fernandez," *Criterion* 4 (1926): 751.

67. T. S. Eliot, "The Function of Criticism," *Selected Essays 1917–1932* (New York: Harcourt, Brace, 1932), p. 17. Hereafter *SE*.

68. T. S. Eliot, "The Perfect Critic," *The Sacred Wood* (London: Methuen, 1920), pp. 11, 14.

69. The phrase is first used in his 1921 essay, "The Metaphysical Poets," *SE*, p. 247.

70. Ibid., p. 248.

71. T. S. Eliot, "Professional, or . . . ," *Egoist* 5 (1918): 61.

72. T. S. Eliot, "Criticism in England," *Athenaeum* 4650 (1919): 456.

73. T. S. Eliot, "Hamlet," *SE*, pp. 123, 124.

74. T. S. Eliot, "Philip Massinger," *SE*, p. 182.

75. Ibid.

76. T. S. Eliot, "Euripides and Professor Murray," *SE*, pp. 48, 49.

77. Eliot, "Ezra Pound: His Metric and His Poetry," p. 182.

78. As Lionel Trilling characterized this process in his "On the Teaching of Modern Literature" (1961), "with the works of art of our own present age, university study tends to accelerate the process by which the radical and subversive work becomes the classic work." (*Beyond Culture: Essays on Literature and Learning* [New York: Viking, 1965], p. 11.) For a much fuller analysis of the modernist professionalization of literary study and its attachment to the academy, see Louis Menand, *Discovering Modernism: T. S. Eliot and His Context* (New York: Oxford University Press, 1987), pp. 97–132, and Gail McDonald, *Learning to Be Modern: Pound, Eliot, and the American University* (Oxford: Clarendon, 1993).

79. Wilson, *Axel's Castle*, p. 116.

80. F. R. Leavis, *New Bearings in English Poetry: A Study in the Contemporary Situation* (1932; Ann Arbor: University of Michigan Press, 1960), pp. 75, 76.

81. T. S. Eliot, "Tradition and the Individual Talent," *SE*, p. 4.

82. Ibid., p. 5.

83. Ibid., p. 3.

84. T. S. Eliot, "Reflections on *Vers Libre*," reprinted in *Selected Prose of T. S. Eliot*, ed. Frank Kermode (New York: Harcourt Brace Jovanovich, 1975), p. 36. Hereafter *SP*.

85. Ibid., p. 32.

86. T. S. Eliot, "*Ulysses*, Order, and Myth" (1923), *SP*, p. 177. Such formulas are linked to Eliot's career-long program of imposing a conservative ideology on British cultural judgments. For an account of his pursuit of this objective, see Kenneth Asher, *T. S. Eliot and Ideology* (Cambridge: Cambridge University Press, 1995), esp. pp. 35–59.

87. *Letters*, pp. 207, 392.

88. *Letters*, pp. 310–11, 305.

89. *Letters*, p. 259.

90. Conrad Aiken, *Ushant: An Essay* (New York: Duell, Sloan and Pearce, 1952), p. 215. Dickinson uses the word to describe the "majestic" spirits "who have accomplished Death." Aiken may be maliciously suggesting that Eliot's success is bought at the price of

life itself. See *The Complete Poems of Emily Dickinson*, ed. Thomas H. Johnson (Boston: Little, Brown, 1960), p. 690.

91. Humphrey Carpenter, *A Serious Character: The Life of Ezra Pound* (London: Faber and Faber, 1988), p. 257.

92. *Letters*, p. 384.

93. T. S. Eliot to Leonard Woolf, 18 January 1921, Berg Collection, New York Public Library; *Letters*, p. 434.

94. *Letters*, pp. 606–7. "Character in Fiction," later reprinted as "Mr. Bennett and Mrs. Brown," and "On Being Ill," in the July 1924 and January 1926 issues.

95. T. S. Eliot, 1941 memoir of Woolf reprinted in *Recollections of Virginia Woolf*, ed. Joan Russell Noble (London: Peter Owen, 1972), p. 122.

XII. Displacing Eliot's Poetry

1. *The Letters of Virginia Woolf*, vol. 2, ed. Nigel Nicolson, with Joanne Trautmann (London: Hogarth, 1975–80), p. 540.

2. Louis Untermeyer, in *T. S. Eliot: The Critical Heritage*, ed. Michael Grant (London: Routledge & Kegan Paul, 1982), 1: 126–27.

3. T. S. Eliot, *The Complete Poems and Plays 1909–1950* (San Diego, New York, London: Harcourt Brace Jovanovich, 1952), pp. 4, 12–13. Hereafter abbreviated *CPP*.

4. *Poetical Works of Robert Bridges* (London: Oxford University Press, 1953), p. 248. Although Bridges was born in 1844, nearly half a century before Eliot, he could not simply be seen as the dead hand of the past. His ambitious and enormously successful volume, *The Testament of Beauty*, only appeared in 1929.

5. T. S. Eliot, *Inventions of the March Hare: Poems 1909–1917*, ed. Christopher Ricks (London: Faber and Faber, 1996), pp. 13, 14, 16, 334.

6. *CPP*, p. 7.

7. From Ezra Pound's review of *Prufrock and Other Observations* in *Poetry*, reprinted in *T. S. Eliot: The Critical Heritage*, 1: 77–78.

8. Published in *The Letters of T. S. Eliot*, ed. Valerie Eliot (San Diego, New York, London: Harcourt Brace Jovanovich, 1988), p. 101. Hereafter cited as *Letters*.

9. See the section called "Prufrock's Pervigilium" in Eliot, *Inventions of the March Hare*, pp. 43–44.

10. *Letters*, p. 58.

11. T. S. Eliot, "The Problems of the Shakespeare Sonnets," *Nation & Athenaeum* 40 (1927): 666.

12. T. S. Eliot, *The Waste Land: A Facsimile and Transcript of the Original Drafts Including the Annotations of Ezra Pound*, ed. Valerie Eliot (New York: Harcourt Brace Jovanovich, 1971), p. 5. Hereafter *Waste Land Facsimile*.

13. *CPP*, p. 52.

14. Quoted in Valerie Eliot, "Introduction" to *Waste Land Facsimile*, p. 1.

15. See, for example, Lyndall Gordon's chapter on the confessional aspects of the poem in her *Eliot's Early Years* (Oxford: Oxford University Press, 1977), pp. 86–119; James E. Miller, Jr., *T. S. Eliot's Personal Waste Land: Exorcism of the Demons* (University Park and London: Pennsylvania State University Press, 1977); Wayne Koestenbaum, "*The Waste Land*: T. S. Eliot's and Ezra Pound's Collaboration on Hysteria," in his *Double Talk: The Erotics of Male Literary Collaboration* (New York & London: Routledge, 1989), pp. 112–39. Eliot's solicitors forced a withdrawal of the first attempt to describe the poem's putative autobiographical roots, John Peter's "A New Interpretation of *The Waste Land*," *Essays in Criticism* 2 (1952): 242–66. Peter sees the poem as a homoerotic elegy and valediction.

16. John Crowe Ransom, 1923 review reprinted in *T. S. Eliot: The Critical Heritage*, 1: 179.

17. *CPP*, pp. 41, 42.

18. T. S. Eliot, "Reflections on Contemporary Poetry," *Egoist* 6 (1919): 40.

19. T. S. Eliot, "The Method of Mr. Pound," *Athenaeum* 4669 (1919): 1065.

20. *Letters*, pp. 105, 362, 383.

21. For Eliot's indebtedness to anthropological writing, see Robert Crawford's *The Savage and the City in the Work of T. S. Eliot* (Oxford: Clarendon, 1987).

22. F. O. Matthiessen, *The Achievement of T. S. Eliot: An Essay on the Nature of Poetry*, 3d ed. (New York and London: Oxford University Press, 1958), p. 37.

23. *CPP*, p. 48.

24. *Letters*, p. 70.

25. Quoted in *Letters*, p. 265n.

26. Edgar Ansel Mowrer, *This American World* (London: Faber & Gwyer, 1928), pp. 202, 213.

27. *Letters*, p. 181.

28. T. S. Apteryx [pseud., Eliot], "Observations," *Egoist* 5 (1918): 70.

29. F. R. Leavis, *New Bearings in English Poetry: A Study in the Contemporary Situation* (1932; Ann Arbor: University of Michigan Press, 1960), p. 2.

30. Reprinted from the *Dial* editorial announcing the award in *T. S. Eliot: The Critical Heritage*, 1: 137.

31. Delmore Schwartz, "T. S. Eliot as the International Hero," *Partisan Review* 12 (1945): 199, 200, 201.

32. *Waste Land Facsimile*, p. 5.

33. In his 1919 essay in *The Little Review*, reprinted in *T. S. Eliot: The Critical Heritage*, 1: 94.

34. William Carlos Williams, *Autobiography* (New York: Random House, 1951), pp. 174–75.

35. *Letters*, p. 454. The *OED* notes that in the United States fall is "the ordinary name for autumn; in England now rare in literary use, though found in some dialects."

36. *Letters*, p. 455.

37. "T. S. Eliot," in *Writers at Work: The Paris Review Interviews, Second Series*, ed. George Plimpton (New York: Viking, 1963), p. 99.

38. [T. S. Eliot], "American Prose," *TLS* 1283 (1926): 577.

39. *Waste Land Facsimile*, pp. 13, 15.

40. T. S. Eliot, *Poems* (New York: Alfred A. Knopf, 1920), p. 23.

41. The Ariel poems ("Journey of the Magi," "A Song for Simeon," "Animula," and "Marina") are not separately printed in America except in a limited edition of the first to secure copyright. See Donald Gallup, *T. S. Eliot: A Bibliography* (New York: Harcourt, Brace & World, 1973).

42. T. S. Eliot to Ezra Pound, 9 December 1929, YCAL MSS 43, box 13, folder 505, Beinecke Library, Yale University.

43. Lyndall Gordon, *Eliot's New Life* (New York: Farrar, Straus & Giroux, 1988), p. 5.

44. *The Criterion* 1 (1923): 421.

45. *Nobel Lectures: Literature 1901–1967*, ed. Horst Frenz (Amsterdam, London, New York: Elsevier, 1969), pp. 289, 337, 436.

46. T. S. Eliot, "Turgenev," *Egoist* 4 (1917): 167. Henry James's admiration for and friendship with Turgenev is based on a similar conception of him as "a cosmopolitan, a dweller in many cities and a fre-

quenter of many societies." (Henry James, "Ivan Turgenev," *Literary Criticism: French Writers* . . . , ed. Leon Edel [The Library of America, 1984], p. 992.)

47. *CPP*, p. 60.

48. *Letters*, p. 479.

49. T. S. Eliot, *For Lancelot Andrewes: Essays on Style and Order* (1928; London: Faber and Faber, 1970), p. 7.

50. "Foreign News," *Time*, 28 November 1927, 14.

51. Quoted in Dixon Wecter, "The Harvard Exiles," *Virginia Quarterly Review* 10 (1934): 251.

52. *Letters*, pp. 61, 310.

53. Louis MacNeice, *Modern Poetry: A Personal Essay* (1938; Oxford: Clarendon, 1968), p. 84.

54. *The Diary of Virginia Woolf*, vol. 3, ed. Anne Olivier Bell (London: Hogarth, 1977–84), p. 95. See also the entry for 7 January 1936, vol. 5, p. 5.

55. T. S. Eliot to Leonard Woolf, 26 April 1934, Berg Collection, New York Public Library.

56. *Letters*, p. 318.

57. T. S. Eliot, "At Graduation 1905," *Poems Written in Early Youth* (New York: Farrar, Straus & Giroux, 1967), p. 11.

58. *Letters*, p. 187.

59. Details about the Eliot family are taken from the anonymous essay, "The Eliot Family and St. Louis," published by Washington University to commemorate his 1953 visit. See T. S. Eliot, *American Literature and the American Language* (St. Louis: Washington University, 1955), pp. 27–46.

60. T. S. Eliot to John Quinn, 26 April 1923, John Quinn Memorial Collection, New York Public Library.

61. *Letters*, pp. 443, 274.

62. *Literary Essays of Ezra Pound*, ed. T. S. Eliot (Norfolk, Conn.: New Directions, 1954), p. 391n.

63. *Letters*, p. 366.

64. *Letters*, pp. 464, xvii.

65. Gordon, *Eliot's New Life*, p. 341. Gordon sees the revived relation with Emily Hale as one of the turning points of Eliot's life, though her argument must remain speculative until the evidence is available.

66. T. S. Eliot to M. W. Childs, quoted in "From a Distinguished Former St. Louisan," *St. Louis Post-Dispatch*, 15 October 1930.

67. Ibid.

68. *CPP*, pp. 66, 72, 130.

69. *CPP*, p. 122.

70. T. S. Eliot, "Introduction" to Samuel L. Clemens (Mark Twain), *The Adventures of Huckleberry Finn* (London: Cresset, 1950), pp. xiii, ix, x.

71. T. S. Eliot, "American Literature and the American Language," in *To Criticize the Critic and Other Writings* (New York: Farrar, Straus & Giroux, 1965), pp. 51, 52–53, 51, 59.

72. "T. S. Eliot," *Writers at Work*, p. 110.

73. Most prominently, Gordon's *Eliot's New Life* and Eric Sigg's *The American T. S. Eliot: A Study of the Early Writings* (Cambridge: Cambridge University Press, 1989). See also the pioneering study of Eliot's American roots, Herbert Howarth's *Notes on Some Figures Behind T. S. Eliot* (London: Chatto & Windus, 1965).

74. *CPP*, pp. 22–23. Michael North sees such cultural fragmentation as characterizing the work of modernist writers who use discord as a structural principle: "Individuals are related in such works not by similarity but by their lack of similarity, by the suffering they endure in the absence of genuine community" (*The Political Aesthetic of Yeats, Eliot, and Pound* [Cambridge: Cambridge University Press, 1991], p. 19).

75. T. S. Eliot, "Tradition and the Individual Talent," *Selected Essays 1917–1932* (New York: Harcourt, Brace, 1932), pp. 7–8, 10. Hereafter, *SE*. Eliot's first interpreters treat such statements reverently. F. R. Leavis, for example, announces in 1932 that "*Gerontion* has the impersonality of great poetry" and praises both it and *The Waste Land* over "Prufrock" because they offer "a completer transcendence of the individual self." (Leavis, *New Bearings in English Poetry*, p. 93.)

76. "Tradition and the Individual Talent," *SE*, pp. 10–11.

77. *Letters*, p. 197. The echo of Stephen Dedalus's image of the godlike artist in Joyce's *Portrait* as "within or behind or beyond or above his creation, invisible, refined out of existence, indifferent, paring his fingernails" can hardly be accidental. The novel was published in the previous year.

78. T. S. Eliot, *Knowledge and Experience in the Philosophy of F. H. Bradley* (New York: Columbia University Press, 1989), pp. 168, 165.

79. "East Coker," *CPP*, p. 128.
80. Ibid., p. 129.
81. Ezra Pound, *The Cantos* (New York: New Directions, 1970), p. 472.
82. "Five-Finger Exercises," Part V, *CPP*, p. 93.
83. Williams, *Autobiography*, pp. 174–75.
84. T. S. E[liot]., review of Van Wyck Brooks's *The Wine of the Puritans*, *Harvard Advocate* 87 (1909): 80.

Index

Academia: and Adams, 75, 78, 79, 81, 112; and Eliot, 269, 270, 277–78, 279, 281, 283, 312; and James, 130; and modernism, 241, 280–83, 284; and Pound, 221, 231, 246, 257, 277, 279; and racial theories, 33–34

Adams, Brooks (brother), 23, 32, 73, 88, 107, 112–13, 116; and Adams circle, 36; *America's Economic Supremacy*, 17; on decline of New England patriciate, 58; on east European immigrants, 52; on *Mont-Saint-Michel and Chartres*, 116

Adams, Charles (brother), 67–68, 70, 71, 74, 76, 78, 80, 82, 100, 107, 112–13, 122; on author of *Democracy*, 91; in Civil War, 69; and *Chapters of Erie*, 75; "'Independents' in the Canvass," 79; on Irish immigrants in Quincy, 102; and Union Pacific Railroad, 101

Adams, Charles Francis (father), 66, 67, 80, 302; as Minister to Court of St. James, 68–69, 71, 72–73

Adams, Clover, 64, 65, 72, 97, 109; James on, 128

Adams, Henry, 22, 23, 138, 177, 202, 217, 218–19; academic career of, 75, 78, 79, 81, 112; and Alexis de Tocqueville, 76; alienation from America, 92, 99, 107, 112, 117, 121; on American destiny, 87; and Anglo-American accord, 68, 69, 72; anglophilia of, 70, 71–72, 73, 110; and Anglo-Saxonism, 113; and anti-British feelings, 68, 69–70, 71, 109, 110; and anti-Semitism, 56, 103, 104; as armchair politician, 79–80, 82–83, 88–89, 91, 105, 106, 107; and audience, 76, 86, 87, 88, 92, 108, 114–16, 117, 118, 119, 122, 181, 218, 338n67; on Britain and the Civil War, 23, 70; and detached spectatorship, 80, 81, 90, 119, 121; disappointment of, 78–79; discontinuous career of, 73–74; displacement of, 55–56, 58, 99–104, 101, 102, 105, 108, 120; and dynamo, 107, 120, 121; early optimism of, 74, 77, 78, 79,

100–101; and Eliot, 106, 114, 266–67, 268–69, 278, 280, 281, 285, 313–14; expatriation of, 92–93; and finances, 188; and Five of Hearts, 87;on French writers, 110; and Grant administration, 77, 89, 119, 120; and history, 81–86, 88; and immigrants, 99–100; on Irish, 102–3; and James, 63–65, 109, 110, 118, 123, 127, 128, 196, 197, 200, 214; and Jews, 55–56, 102–3; and journalism, 69, 75, 76, 77, 78, 79, 100, 105; and London, 66, 67–68, 69–72, 109, 111; and Louis Agassiz, 324n46; on Massachusetts, 58; on Matthew Arnold, 12; and medievalism, 112–14, 115; metropolitanism of, 79; and "national school," 74–76, 78, 81, 86, 92, 122, 123; and *North American Review*, 78; patriotism of, 68–70, 71, 78, 81, 83, 85, 86–87, 89, 93, 109; pessimism of, 74; and plutocrats, 99–100, 100–102, 103; and political disillusionment, 79, 85–86, 87, 88, 92, 98; and political reform, 76–79, 80, 120; and Pound, 114, 116, 259; and power, 80–81, 82, 100, 101, 105, 106–7, 121; Puritan heritage of, 67, 71; self-denigration of, 64, 117, 118–19, 120, 121, 314; in South Seas, 92–93, 97, 98, 107–8; and "Teutonic origins" school, 34; and Theodore Roosevelt, 35–36, 105; trip to Japan, 97–98; use of anonymity, 88, 91, 119; use of essay form, 75, 76, 81; version of Nordic myth, 113; vocation to public service, 73, 74–75; and Washington, 35–36, 71, 72, 79–80, 87, 92, 98, 99, 278; and William Wetmore Story, 202–3

Adams, Henry, works: "American Finance, 1865–69," 100; *Chapters of Erie*, 75, 76; *Democracy: An American Novel*, 88–91, 92, 161, 334n133; *The Education of Henry Adams*, 55–56, 76, 102–3, 106, 118, 119, 122, 196, 200–201, 266–69, 278, 313–14; *Essays in Anglo-Saxon Law*, 34, 75, 112; *Esther*, 88; *Historical Essays*, 88; *The History of*

Index

Index